WHAT THE #METOO MOVEMENT HIGHLIGHTS AND HIDES ABOUT WORKPLACE SEXUAL HARASSMENT

What the #MeToo Movement Highlights and Hides about Workplace Sexual Harassment seeks to examine both the spotlights (Part I) and the shadows (Part II) of the #MeToo movement, setting a research agenda to examine both more carefully in management research.

Sexual harassment (SH) is not a new phenomenon in organizations; it has been the topic of scholarly inquiry since the 1970s and has existed as a form of dysfunctional organizational behavior and abuse of power for much longer. Even so, the #MeToo movement thrust this organizational issue into the spotlight, raising new awareness and concern about an age-old problem, including digital forms of SH, bystander behavior, and organizational and societal ideas around masculinity and gender-based violence. At the same time, #MeToo kept other aspects of SH in the dark. Shadows addressed include the more mundane and common forms of low-severity micro-SH, how to help targets heal from trauma, the complex intersectional experiences of women of color, the experiences of male targets and those in low socioeconomic status jobs, and the implications of #MeToo on legal theory.

Insights from #MeToo highlight the power of social movements to frame the public's understanding of the issue of SH and to spark counter-movements that challenge that frame. This volume will be of interest to researchers, scholars, students, practitioners, and policymakers.

Anne M. O'Leary-Kelly, now an Emeritus Professor, held the William R. and Cacilia Howard Chair in Management at the Sam M. Walton College of Business, University of Arkansas, USA.

Shannon L. Rawski is Assistant Professor of Organizational Behaviour at Ivey Business School, University of Western Ontario, Canada.

Series in Applied Psychology

Jeanette N. Cleveland, *Colorado State University*
Donald Truxillo, *University of Limerick*
Edwin A. Fleishman, *Founding Series Editor (1987–2010)*
Kevin R. Murphy, *Emeritus Series Editor (2010–2018)*

Bridging both academic and applied interests, the Applied Psychology Series offers publications that emphasize state-of-the-art research and its application to important issues of human behavior in a variety of societal settings. To date, more than 50 books in various fields of applied psychology have been published in this series.

Patterns of Life History
The Ecology of Human Individuality
Michael D. Mumford, Garnett Stokes, and William A. Owens

Work Motivation
*Uwe E. Kleinbeck, Hans-Henning Quast, Henk Thierry,
and Hartmut Häcker*

Teamwork and the Bottom Line
Groups Make a Difference
Ned Rosen

Aging and Work in the 21st Century
Edited by Kenneth S. Schultz and Gary A. Adams

**What the #MeToo Movement Highlights and Hides about
Workplace Sexual Harassment**
Spotlights and Shadows
Edited by Anne M. O'Leary-Kelly and Shannon L. Rawski

For more information about this series, please visit: www.routledge.com/Applied-Psychology-Series/book-series/SAP

WHAT THE #METOO MOVEMENT HIGHLIGHTS AND HIDES ABOUT WORKPLACE SEXUAL HARASSMENT

Spotlights and Shadows

Edited by Anne M. O'Leary-Kelly
and Shannon L. Rawski

Routledge
Taylor & Francis Group

NEW YORK AND LONDON

Designed cover image: Getty Images © Dmitry Kovalchuk

First published 2025
by Routledge
605 Third Avenue, New York, NY 10158

and by Routledge
4 Park Square, Milton Park, Abingdon, Oxon, OX14 4RN

Routledge is an imprint of the Taylor & Francis Group, an informa business

ISBN: 978-1-032-29304-2 (hbk)
ISBN: 978-1-032-29301-1 (pbk)
ISBN: 978-1-003-30095-3 (ebk)

DOI: 10.4324/9781003300953

Typeset in Sabon
by Apex CoVantage, LLC

CONTENTS

SERIES FOREWORD

The goal of the Applied Psychology series is to create books that exemplify the use of scientific research, theory, and findings to help solve real problems in organizations and society. Anne M. O'Leary-Kelly and Shannon L. Rawski's edited book, *What the #MeToo Movement Highlights and Hides about Workplace Sexual Harassment: Spotlights and Shadows*, exemplifies this approach. We believe that the book will quickly become a key reference for research on sexual harassment (SH) awareness in organizations as well as virtual workplaces. Within this exciting book, chapter authors draw upon multiple facets of classic research on SH and link it with the emergence of the tech-driven #MeToo movement. Importantly, each chapter provides a roadmap from past research to future research on SH integrating the emerging permeability of work with non-work via technology.

The book includes 11 chapters reflecting three general themes: historical evolution and context of the #MeToo movement (Chapters 1 and 2), context factors that shape and influence the occurrence and interpretation of SH associated with #MeToo (Chapters 3–6), and understudied but critical areas (Chapters 7–11) for future research.

The first two chapters provide a historical context for the recognition of SH in our society as well as for understanding the #MeToo movement. In Chapter 1, Keshtiban describes how successive women's movements helped women gain access to political participation, paid employment, and ultimately control over one's lives/choices, independence and voice. In Chapter 2, Lundquist and Mendes provide a more focused discussion of the historical factors leading up to the emergence of the #MeToo movement. Changes in the work domain, including those that go beyond the physical boundaries of the workplace and the boom of the internet, have changed the nature and dynamics of SH. For example, the internet provides a public venue to both identify perpetrators' abuse and contribute to the difficulties of targets. It also can provide broader and more public venues for target abuse with fewer consequences or accountability for harassers.

To ensure the development of productive, healthy workplaces, organizational leaders must consider how a range of critical micro-level to macro-level factors influence SH; several of these are identified in Chapters 3 to 7. Classic SH research is presented on bystander behavior, organizational culture, the role of social culture and institutions, and the escalation of ambiguous socio-sexual, non-harassing behavior into harassing behaviors. Importantly, each of these chapters highlights novel ways of linking research on SH with the unique features and challenges associated with the MeToo movement. For example, Bowes-Sperry, Cheung, and Griffith (Chapter 3) present a 2 × 2 framework describing bystander behaviors associated with the discouragement and perpetuation of SH at work, while Workman-Stark (Chapter 4) describes a case study that identifies key organizational culture issues (e.g., toxic masculinity) that need to be (re)examined using research on sensemaking in organizations.

In Chapter 5, Raver and Kim draw upon the gender-based violence literature to understand the social-cultural influences of gender ideology, traditional views on masculinity, and the societal and cultural institutions within which organizations operate. These institutions include the legal system (e.g., laws and policies on gender-based violence), public health (e.g., domestic violence, sexual and reproductive rights, health disparities), and the media (e.g., news, movies, television), all of which significantly contribute to maintenance and perpetuation of harassment at work.

In Chapter 6, Hart and Vranjes suggest that some SH behaviors are initially ambiguous and later escalate at work over time. The work setting can provide cues on the extent to which an ambiguous behavior can be defined as reflecting a genuine concern, an "innocent" flirtation, or an increasingly uncomfortable or harmful episode of SH.

Using a trauma lens to understand SH as a form of sexual violence, Bloom and Rawski (Chapter 7) link the lasting effects of trauma on the target, bystanders, other organizational members, and the culture of organizations. They show how responses to harassment can vary depending upon such factors as the frequency and severity of harassment, as well as the way these factors combine and operate together. For example, they discuss how both infrequent but severe harassment episodes and more frequent but less severe episodes can result in similar levels of chronic trauma.

All of the chapters in this section spotlight the critical factors that shape and define the contexts within which SH occurs. One thread that runs through each of these chapters is the importance of context in shaping both the perceptions of harassment and the ways targets, bystanders, organizations, and the broader society may react to and address such behaviors. The process of interpreting and labeling such behaviors is further complicated because the same behaviors may be interpreted differently across levels of context both within the organization (e.g., target, bystanders, organizational culture/extant organizational members) and external to organizations (e.g., legal institutions, public health, the media).

The next three chapters (Chapters 8–10) turn the spotlight on revealing critical shadows or gaps in SH research. In Chapter 8, Bhattacharyya and De Souza return to the origins of the #MeToo movement, applying an interactional approach to understand the harassment of marginalized women. They highlight the greater need for research, specifically on women of color, non-straight or queer, and poor women to spotlight gaps in knowledge and research on SH.

Men also are targets of SH, especially by other men in highly traditional masculine environments. Alonso, Cheung, Washington, and Stockdale (Chapter 9) discuss how the SH of men can both challenge the current assumptions about SH and provide insights into the harassment of all individuals.

In Chapter 10, Hayman, Kish-Gephart, and Moergen describe the unique organizational context and individual factors that heighten the vulnerability of a severely neglected population in organizational research—that is, women in the lower socio-economic classes. The contextual factors they cite contribute to unique adverse consequences for lower socio-economic status women and restrict the range of coping strategies available to them.

In the final chapter of this volume (Chapter 11), Jensen and Sims offer an alternative path to addressing and reducing the harmful consequences of SH on targets, bystanders, and the organization, via restorative justice. Historically, the legal route has dominated this space, followed by practices such as changing organizational culture/climate and organizational training. The authors describe some unintended consequences of these institutional and sociological approaches and their limitations. They offer an alternative through a restorative justice process that focuses on repairing broken relationships and promoting trust among organizational members.

The chapters in this volume cover a broad range of important, current, and emerging workplace issues. They are thought-provoking and break new ground. *What the #MeToo Movement Highlights and Hides about Workplace Sexual Harassment: Spotlights and Shadows* is likely to become an essential resource for both researchers and practitioners that will have impact on both future research questions and the application of science-based practice.

We are thrilled to add this volume to the Applied Psychology Series. This book accomplishes the goals that exemplify the challenge of balancing the science and practice goals of this Series, bringing together the best scholarship to identify ideas to address the issues that have emerged from the *#MeToo* movement.

Jeanette N. Cleveland
Colorado State University, Professor Emeritus
Donald Truxillo
University of Limerick, Professor

CONTRIBUTORS

Natalya M. Alonso is an assistant professor at Simon Fraser University in the Beedie School of Business. Her research explores gender-based bias at work and how to address it.

Sandra L. Bloom, MD, is an associate professor at the Dornsife School of Public Health, Drexel University, Philadelphia, Pennsylvania. As a psychiatrist, writer, and teacher, her work has focused on the impact of trauma on individuals, families, organizations, and societies, as well as on how healing occurs.

Lynn Bowes-Sperry serves as Associate Dean in the College of Business and Economics at California State University–East Bay. Her research addresses ethical decision-making in the workplace, with a particular focus on issues related to diversity, equity, and inclusion (e.g., bystander intervention in response to harassment and discrimination and other forms of voicing one's values effectively), and provides consultation and training for organizations on these topics.

Ho Kwan Cheung, PhD, is an assistant professor of psychology at the University of Calgary in Canada. Her research focuses broadly on the manifestation, consequences, and organizational remediation for workplace discrimination, with a special interest in gender and family-related issues. She has published over 20 journal articles on these topics in leading journals of the field, and her work has also been funded by the Social Science and Humanities Research Council of Canada.

Nicky Cheung, a PhD candidate at the time of writing, studies organizational behavior at York University's Schulich School of Business in Toronto, Ontario. His research interests encompass a wide range of DEI issues, particularly stereotyping and prejudice, primarily towards those who may fit multiple categories (e.g., mixed-race identities).

Jennifer A. Griffith is an Associate Professor of Organizational Behavior and Morrison Faculty Fellow in the Peter T. Paul College of Business & Economics at the University of New Hampshire. Her research explores how to address organizational and interpersonal barriers to thriving resultant from inaccurate measurement, poor talent cultivation strategies, & unsupportive work environments.

Marilla G. Hayman, PhD, is an assistant professor of management, leadership, and human resource management at Le Moyne College in Syracuse, NY. Her research examines workplace well-being and how various identities—including gender, race, religion, and social class—shape employees' experiences, opportunities, and outcomes.

Jaclyn M. Jensen is a Professor of Management, Associate Dean for Student Success, and Driehaus Fellow in the Driehaus College of Business at DePaul University. Her research interests focus on the impact of harassment and incivility on employee performance, engagement, and well-being.

Amir Keshtiban is the Associate Dean of Business and Health at York St John University, London Campus. As a critical organisation studies scholar, his research focuses on alternative forms of organisation, critical leadership studies, social movement studies, and Equity, Diversity, and Inclusion. His work has been published in international, peer-reviewed journals such as the *Journal of Management Learning* and *Human Resource Development Quarterly.*

Jennifer Kish-Gephart is an Associate Professor of Organization Studies in the Isenberg School of Management at the University of Massachusetts. She received her Ph.D. in organizational behavior from the Pennsylvania State University. Her research focuses on the topics of behavioral ethics, social class, and inequality.

Jennifer H. Lundquist is Professor of Sociology and Senior Associate Dean of Research and Faculty Development at the University of Massachusetts Amherst. Her research examines the social demography of race and gender in institutions and our everyday technologies.

Kaitlynn Mendes is a Full Professor of Sociology and holds the Canada Research Chair in Inequality and Gender at Western University, Canada. She is an expert on rape culture and the ways digital technologies both fuel and are used to combat sexual violence. She is author or editor of five books including the award winning *SlutWalk: Feminism, activism, and media* (2015) and *Digital Feminist Activism: Girls and Women Fight Back Against Rape Culture* (2019).

Kristie J.N. Moergen is an assistant professor in the Ivy College of Business (Department of Management & Entrepreneurship) at Iowa State University. Her main research focuses on promoting more equitable workplaces by examining how inequality is maintained or disrupted, specifically focusing on social class in and around organizations. She is especially interested in the interpersonal interactions and organizational processes that facilitate mobility.

Shannon L. Rawski is an assistant professor of organizational behavior at Western University's Ivey Business School in London, Ontario. Her research addresses sexual harassment (e.g., the social sensemaking process used to interpret ambiguous social sexual behaviors and trauma-informed perspectives) and sexual harassment training effectiveness (e.g., identity threat reactions to training, use of VR training technology, gamification, and other training design features).

Carra S. Sims is a Senior Behavioral and Social Scientist at the RAND Corporation and professor of policy analysis at the Pardee RAND Graduate School. Her research includes investigating the effects of workplace stressors (including military deployment, discrimination, and sexual harassment) on job attitudes and performance; exploring issues of organizational culture and climate; assessing quality of life issues faced by military families and wounded warriors; and evaluating military physical fitness tests and selection systems.

Ivana Vranjes is an assistant professor in the Department of Social Psychology at Tilburg University. Her research focuses on understanding how workplace dynamics affect employee well-being, particularly through the lens of mistreatment and technological change. She examines behaviors such as bullying, incivility, sexual harassment, and the role of bystanders in workplace aggression while also exploring how evolving technologies introduce new challenges, like technostress, that shape work experiences.

Darius M. Washington, a PhD candidate at Indiana University, Indianapolis, focuses his research on racialized sex-based harassment and its impact on minoritized groups. His work examines how sociohistorical stereotypes, power dynamics, and racial-gender hierarchies shape harassment experiences. His broader research explores workplace bias, particularly how DEI accountability can mitigate backlash against Black women in leadership. Through this work, he aims to advance organizational policies and processes that foster equity, challenge systemic biases, and create safer, more inclusive workplaces.

Angela Workman-Stark is an Associate Professor and Canada Research Chair in Rights-Based Organizational Development at Athabasca University in Alberta, Canada. Her research focuses on workplace misconduct, including sexual harassment, the factors that contribute to misconduct and how they might be addressed. As a former senior police officer, she is primarily interested in investigating these themes within policing and other male-dominated, paramilitary occupations.

INTRODUCTION

Sexual harassment (SH) is not a new phenomenon in work organizations, but the recognition that SH is problematic and illegal behavior is relatively recent and can be traced to Catherine MacKinnon's pathbreaking book, published in 1976 and titled *Sexual harassment of working women*. Subsequent to this book, SH research emerged in the organizational sciences at an increasingly steady pace, with strong and sustained attention occurring from the late 1980s and into the early 2000s. However, as with many workplace topics that initially garner public attention and energize communities of research scholars, the zenith of research appeared to be fading . . . until the #MeToo Movement of 2017. By any account, the #MeToo Movement was a profound disruption to the SH status quo; this was true in countries and workplaces around the world, and it also is true of SH research, which is now rebounding and re-energized.

Because we sit at this inflection point, we were enthusiastic when approached by Jeanette Cleveland and Donald Truxillo, editors of the Taylor Francis Routledge Book Series on Applied Psychology. These Series Editors invited us to create an edited volume that could nurture the new research energy generated by the #MeToo movement and, importantly, could shape this research in a way that brings alignment to the program of scholarly work that evolves. We were honored to be entrusted with this important task and gladly accepted, recognizing that there are many, many incredible SH scholars who could have undertaken this challenge.

As organizational scholars, the two of us are aligned in our determination to conduct research in ways that challenge the status quo and that uncover new ideas and approaches to preventing SH. We believe that the best path for doing this is to create a community of scholars who can challenge each other, provide critique and, most importantly, collaborate on meaningful research questions. For that reason, we developed two goals for the book project. First, we decided to take a *spotlights* and *shadows* approach—that is, we wanted to encourage future research on aspects of SH that were spotlighted in the #MeToo movement but that, upon illumination, looked different than scholars had conceptualized them previously; and we also wanted to identify and name aspects of SH that were obscured by the #MeToo movement, those that were pushed into the shadows and could easily be overlooked as research proceeds. Our second goal was to use the book project as a launchpad to identify, connect, and engage a community of scholars who were well positioned to speak to these spotlight and shadow issues. In this opening essay, we would like to introduce the authors and chapters that compose the book.

Part I: Sexual Harassment Issues in the Spotlight

Chapter 1: #MeToo as Social Movement

The book begins with a chapter, authored by Amir Keshtiban, that spotlights #MeToo phenomena as illustrative of a *social movement*, one that can be put in historical context of other movements oriented toward resistance to patriarchy and domination of women in society; these include the Suffragette movement in the United Kingdom, the women's liberation movement in western countries (in Europe and America), and the Greenham Common Women's Peace Camp in the United Kingdom. The author provides insight into diverse ways that social movements can be structured, with a focus on the formality of leadership, the degree of centralization, the type of activities utilized, and communication practices.

A key insight is the importance of social movements as vehicles for shaping the *public sphere*, a concept that rarely appears in management narratives or research. As described by the scholar Jürgen Habermas, the public sphere exists when citizens have a guarantee of assembly and association, and they engage in private conversations that shape public opinion around issues of public interest. The historical context described in the Keshtiban chapter emphasizes that women have not had equal access to the public sphere and that women's rights movements are themselves efforts to provide remedy. The chapter illustrates different ways that social movements influence the public sphere, including large-scale and highly public efforts—such as political protest, creation of media channels, and violence—as well as more individual-focused efforts—such as dialogue, networking, consciousness raising, and sharing of personal experiences.

The #Me Too Movement as an effort to influence the public sphere is then described and depicted as unique in several ways. First, it was a highly decentralized movement, possible because of the digital platforms that fueled it. The author argues that the movement also is distinct in triggering multiple similarly decentralized counter movements, which allowed for strong backlash that reshaped its narrative and momentum. As discussed more fully in Chapter 2, the digital nature of the #MeToo movement spotlights new social dynamics that were not as present in previous social movements.

The author also posits suggestions for pertinent research moving forward. In particular, we are struck by the impact that algorithmic control and manual censorship may have on the direction, emotional tone, and speed of future social movements. Although all of the movements described in this chapter address efforts to bring women's stories and experiences into the public sphere, we learn that the way this happens has changed dramatically across movements and time.

Chapter 2: Ambiguous Spaces: #MeToo in the Digital Realm

The second chapter, contributed by Jennifer Lundquist and Kaitlynn Mendes, provides in-depth exploration of a second spotlight issue—the use of digital technology. The #MeToo movement occurred because women were able to add their voices (e.g., "It happened to *Me Too*") to those documenting SH on social media and other digital platforms. In line with Chapter 1, this demonstrates how social movements are facilitated by the power and reach that technology provides. However, this second chapter argues that the same power and reach that made #MeToo possible also creates "ambiguous spaces" in which misogyny proliferates unabated. Ironically, digital platforms provide greater opportunity to uncover misogynistic conduct while also delivering novel arenas in which SH can flourish.

Specifically, this chapter takes a deep dive into online spaces such as comment sections in news media, online dating apps, social media, and the gaming world. These are represented as *ambiguous* spaces because they can be perceived by users as less real, creating the potential for behavior that would be discouraged or legally actionable elsewhere. The authors argue that user perceptions of such spaces as "not real" means they come with less defined cultural norms for appropriate conduct and few standards of accountability for bad behavior. A convincing case is made that such spaces lead to women hiding, withdrawing, silencing, or living with ongoing trauma. For example, women who face death and rape threats in the gaming environment may hide their sex or gender while participating or may decide not to engage with online gaming at all. Similarly, women who face online abuse for sharing posts in news outlets may subsequently silence their opinions. Likewise, women indicate that enduring trauma from SH is a price of admission for participation in the online dating environment. It is noteworthy that these ambiguous spaces are not separate from the concept of work space; for example, women writers and journalists must be free to share opinions in the news media, women who work in the gaming industry must have access to the online gaming environment, and social media SH, which currently is ubiquitous, poisons the online presence and profile of all workers regardless of occupation.

It is noteworthy how these realities connect back to the public sphere concept mentioned in Chapter 1. In its current unregulated state, the digital world is one wherein women are less welcome, less included, and less able to participate in the public sphere. It is not a stretch to describe these ambiguous spaces as akin to the environments faced by women before they had equal access to voting, to speaking publicly, to working, to making intimate choices free of coercion and aggression, or to legal statutes that provide protection for such rights. As argued by these authors, there is a significant need for research on experiences, conduct, and outcomes in these ambiguous spaces. We note that the pathways taken by early SH researchers to explain SH in physical workspaces may provide an appropriate initial roadmap.

Chapter 3: Bystanders in the #MeToo Movement

A third area on which the #MeToo movement has shone a spotlight is bystander intervention (BI), where the attention illuminated two important issues related to bystanders. First, it became clear how many people can become aware of SH in the digital age; second, the sheer number of people who got involved online made evident that a broader definition of bystanders and their actions is required. The authors of Chapter 3, Lynn Bowes-Sperry, Ho Kwan Cheung, and Jennifer Griffith, use these new realities to argue that conceptualizations of bystanders must be entirely reworked to capture the true scope and complexity of bystander phenomena. To address this need, the authors grapple with expanded depictions of who a bystander is, what actions they might take, when they might take these actions, and where the actions might occur. The result of this assessment is their presentation of a relevant and practical taxonomy of BI that we believe can shape important future research.

First, it introduces readers to unique types of bystanders, based on their motives. Second, it makes evident that bystanders should not be defined only as individuals who take action, because some bystanders know about

SH but are too *apathetic* or *avoidant* to take action. The taxonomy also provides an important reminder that some bystanders actually work against and not for the SH target (they are *adversarial*). The taxonomy also highlights the importance of where and when the action takes place. Each of these insights provides fodder for meaningful additional research.

Chapter 3 also addresses an issue raised in the last chapter about digital spaces being outside a regulatory or accountability environment. BI has become more normative in traditional work settings, largely because of legal requirements and employer-provided training. In digital spaces where there are limited norms and accountability, how and when does BI operate? Research questions like these will be highly informative to efforts to bring equal access to digital spaces.

Chapter 4: Exposing Organizational Culture Through the Process of Sensemaking

Another issue spotlighted by the #MeToo movement was the power of organizational culture to tolerate and even encourage SH. In this fourth chapter, we learn about the toxic culture in the Royal Canadian Mounted Police (RCMP). The author, Angela Workman-Stark, describes her experiences as Chief Superintendent of the RCMP during a period in which SH was being widely reported and uncovered, with the result being a class action lawsuit filed by 3,000 women. Her leadership position provided a rare vantage point for assessment of the dynamics by which the RCMP culture created and protected a sexually harassing work environment.

The toxic work environment is defined using the concept of Masculinity Contest Cultures, wherein appropriate employee behavior was aligned with norms of masculinity. To succeed, employees behaved in accordance with these unwritten but powerful normative influences, and those who did this most successfully were elevated to leadership roles, allowing them to further enforce the norms. Through these dynamics, the RCMP culture both constrained behavior and trapped employees into enacting masculine contesting behaviors. The chapter provides narratives from a qualitative study, allowing us to understand these social dynamics operating within the environment through the words of RCMP employees themselves.

The author also describes how SH concerns were received by leadership and by other employees, using a sensemaking framework for explaining subsequent efforts to defend masculine cultural norms. This description fits well with ideas raised in the previous chapter on bystander intervention. Although many RCMP employees were aware of the abusive behavior that some women reported, sensemaking to defend the culture aligned with the

Apathetic, Avoidant, and Adversarial bystander conduct described in the expanded taxonomy presented in Chapter 3.

Finally, the author discusses the organization's resolution of the SH claims. Despite the heroic efforts of many employees to name and reset the organization's culture, there was limited alteration in the dynamics or culture at the RCMP. Specifically, the author argues that culture essentially "won out" in that the SH was attributed to a few bad apples rather than to the toxic environment that shaped the organization and its employees.

Chapter 5: Societal Culture and Gender-Based Violence

The fifth chapter also addresses culture but utilizes a lens that is broader, in two ways: (1) Chapter 5 examines *societal* culture, the beliefs, norms, and structures that are reified throughout a society and (2) the chapter presents research related to the broader category of gender-based violence (GBV), which includes not only SH but other forms of gendered aggression. The authors describe how societal beliefs and values are communicated to individual actors through societal institutions (such as laws and policy, public health, and the media) that enact and enforce those values within their respective realms. More specifically, the chapter reviews research that demonstrates how societal masculinity beliefs and values can be translated into GBV via the influence of key societal institutions.

There is significant research evidence of a connection between a society's gendered beliefs and values and the occurrence of gendered violence, with masculinity ideologies appearing to normalize violent conduct against women. The authors introduce various masculinity ideologies (e.g., status, toughness, contesting), but the chapter's primary focus is hegemonic masculinity in which men are believed to be dominant and women are expected to acquiesce to male power. The key purpose of the research review is to demonstrate to SH scholars the importance and potential predictive power of research focused at the level of societal culture, something they believe has been missing from SH research to date.

Numerous insights emerge from this broader lens. First, organizational scholars often ignore influences beyond the organization, yet because an organization's culture is embedded within societal culture, there likely is a ceiling on its ability to change societally supported employee conduct. The #MeToo movement is a good illustration of this important point. Because the movement was a societal-level disruption, it prompted changes within organizations (e.g., firings of influential men, open discussion and acknowledgment of women's concerns, prohibition of nondisclosure agreements to settle workplace claims) that were unlikely prior to this societal phenomenon.

Second, the review, with its broader focus, reminds SH scholars to examine research insights around other forms of gendered aggression, given that the root causes may be similarly situated in problematic societal masculinity ideologies. Another important insight comes from cross-community work that demonstrates how societal-level gender ideologies still can have variation based on local culture. This research demonstrates that when there is inattention to the local version of a societal ideology, interventions not only do not work but can actually cause harm. This is an important cautionary note for organizational interventions; to do no harm, scholars and practitioners must understand which masculine ideologies define the local culture (e.g., contesting, status, hegemony) before interventions are undertaken.

Ideas raised in this chapter provide insight into the inability to change the culture of the Royal Canadian Mounted Police (described in the previous chapter). It is probable that efforts to alter the toxic RCMP culture were unsuccessful because the organizational culture was itself aligned with a societal culture endorsing masculinity ideology. Further, Chapter 5 underscores that efforts to change a toxic culture could misfire even if toxic societal norms are themselves being challenged (e.g., through a societal movement like #MeToo); this happens if there is a mismatch between the societal and local concepts of masculinity. For example, efforts to change masculinity norms that privilege men around status and opportunity may have little trickle-down effect on a policing organization whose local masculinity ideology is focused on toughness and contesting.

We also note that consideration of societal-level gender ideology is likely to be important to research on all of the issues covered in this book. For example, considering the ambiguous spaces described in Chapter 2, as online spaces develop with no established local norms, there is little option but for societal ideologies to be dominant, and if these spaces are largely unregulated, then this may grant permission for even extreme versions of these ideologies to emerge. It raises the question of whether organizational regulation (i.e., policies) might prevent more extreme forms of compliance with toxic societal ideologies. For example, and related to Chapter 3 and bystander intervention, if an organization has a requirement that employees who "see something, say something" can this negate societal ideologies that encourage Avoidant or Apathetic or Adversarial responses to witnessing SH? We agree with authors Raver and Kim that consideration of societal-level values and beliefs around gender ideology can provide similarly meaningful insights into many organization- and individual-level work phenomena and research questions.

Part II: Sexual Harassment Issues in the Shadows

Chapter 6: Ambiguously Sexual Interactions

In this chapter, Chloe Hart and Ivana Vranjes assert that the #MeToo movement spotlighted primarily prototypical forms of SH but left in the shadows ambiguous conduct that also can represent SH. The authors point to a recent empirical study which demonstrates that blatant (i.e., prototypical) forms of SH have decreased following the strong attention received during the #MeToo movement, while more subtle SH conduct has actually increased. Given this, the authors turn their attention to these ambiguous sexual interactions, arguing that they frequently occur before blatant SH, making them important to our understanding of how harassment evolves. This chapter describes a valuable new construct (*trajectory guarding*) and a model that explicates the construct and how it operates.

Trajectory guarding is undertaken by targets who are uncertain about an actor's intentions or conduct; it is conceptualized as vigilance in monitoring and responding to social interactions so that SH can be deterred or deflected. In the model, trajectory guarding is positioned as a coping response that occurs when there is a perceived threat of sexually harassing conduct. Three distinct forms of this coping mechanism are described, including avoidance, distancing through behavioral signaling, and protective shielding. The model recognizes the various and broad range of costs that accrue from trajectory guarding, categorizing these into personal, relational, professional, and societal costs. In regard to societal costs, Hart and Vranjes make the important point that when SH is deterred because of trajectory guarding, this does nothing to prompt systemic change. This is reminiscent of the argument made by Workman-Stark in Chapter 4 about how leaders in the RCMP left intact the toxic masculine culture that permitted SH, instead focusing their prevention and change efforts on individual actors and interactions.

The model presented here is an excellent outline for future research that examines trajectory guarding, its value as a coping mechanism, and the costs that it creates for individuals, the organization, and for society.

Chapter 7: A Trauma-Informed Perspective on Sexual Harassment

The #MeToo movement brought into the light the types of egregious conduct that many women have endured at work. Recognition of the severity of SH and stories from women about the harm it causes made evident that researchers have not paid enough attention to SH as a trauma-inducing event. In this seventh chapter, authors Sandra Bloom and Shannon L. Rawski make the case that the experience of SH *is* trauma and that extending the insights from the scientific literature on trauma to SH is a way to bring the true traumatic nature of SH out of the shadows.

The authors begin by framing SH as a form of traumatic stress, one that triggers predictable biological, psychological, and behavioral responses in individuals who are targeted. They share insights from existing research about the importance of considering when trauma occurs, whether it is acute or chronic, and the scope of the trauma; they then apply these insights to SH research. For example, in considering scope it is clear that traumatic events have effects well beyond the individual targeted, suggesting the importance of greater attention to the harm caused to SH bystanders (see Chapter 3). Similarly, trauma research establishes the cultural aspects of trauma, suggesting that an environment like a Masculinity Contest Culture (described in Chapter 4) does not just perpetuate gender inequality but also has the potential to bring about trauma responses. Trauma can also be infused into the history of organizations or cultures, creating scenarios where even ambiguous SH conduct (as described in Chapter 6) triggers trauma responses in those who have had previous experiences.

A fascinating aspect of this chapter examines typical responses to traumatic stressors and how these are evident but under-recognized as explanations for SH target responses. Employers that want targets to "just say no" or "just report it" appear to expect Fight-Flight responses. Indeed, employers tend to expect SH targets to be able to ask harassers to stand down and to calmly share the information with the organization. However, trauma research makes such expectations appear not only naïve but also unreasonable. Other trauma responses, like Freeze-Fawn reactions, are very common and these involve actions like dissociation, reenactment of trauma responses, and acquiescence to the demands of the aggressor. Organizational practice could be informed by research that better describes the range of responses that occur when there is a workplace trauma like SH.

Another important aspect of this chapter is that it returns to the strong role of organizational culture. Employees whose work spaces support collective, cultural, and historical trauma (as when there is pervasive SH) are exposed daily to traumatogenic triggers. The authors describe alternatives to these toxic cultures and share resources for learning more about efforts to develop them in practice.

Chapter 8: The Urgency of Adopting an Intersectional Lens to Sexual Harassment Research and Practice

This is the first of three chapters that document the very narrow focus of the #MeToo movement in regard to whose stories mattered and were spotlighted, and whose experiences and narratives were ignored and shadowed. The authors of this chapter, Barnini Bhattacharyya and Lucy DeSouza, begin by calling out the *intersectional invisibility* around racial identity that was characteristic of the movement. They further argue that SH scholarship adopts research questions, theories, measures, and methodologies that privilege White women's experiences and marginalize the experiences of women of color. Intersectionality Theory is proposed as a necessary foundation for broader, better, and more inclusive scholarship moving forward.

The authors share an excellent description of Intersectionality Theory and its focus on examination of identity within the systems of power in which people are embedded. This explanation makes evident that White women were positioned as prototypical to the social group of "woman" in the #MeToo movement and that they have been similarly situated in current workplace SH research. This bias toward the experiences of White women makes marginalized women unseen and even undetectable. What is lost is the opportunity to understand the SH experiences of *most* women (including Black, Asian, Indigenous, Latina, Undocumented, and others). Without this understanding, SH research delivers a highly inadequate perspective on how SH occurs, who it happens to, what it looks like, and how SH can be mitigated. The authors make a powerful case that we should expect SH experiences to differ across women who have varied social identities (racial, cultural) because these identities are entrenched in societal power systems. Plainly put, without an intersectional lens, our research on SH will highlight the minority and disregard the majority.

An excellent component of this chapter is its subsequent focus on *how* to do better research moving forward. These insights are meaningful and informative to scholars, regardless of the SH topic they choose to examine. Specifically, the authors recommend a critical inquiry perspective within an intersectionality framework, and they discuss how this approach might be used in both qualitative and quantitative research. More specifically, they provide this guidance within the context of research strategy choices that researchers must make, including the development of research questions, the choice of sample and context, and the selection of methodologies and measures. A strength of this chapter is that it calls out a fundamental challenge to the structure of SH research (its narrow focus on one category of women), while also presenting possible solutions for future research.

Chapter 9: Masculinity and the Cycle of Sexual Harassment Against Men

This chapter brings out of the shadows another social group that was ignored in the #MeToo movement—men who are targeted for SH. It is interesting to consider arguments made in Chapter 9 in light of those made in the previous chapter about women who were overlooked in #MeToo. Adopting the intersectionality perspective used in the previous chapter, if we are to understand male-targeted SH, we must examine how male identity intersects with societal power and gender structures. The authors of Chapter 9 (Natalya Alonso, Nicky Cheung, Darius Washington, and Margaret Stockdale) do just this, although they do not as overtly adopt intersectionality theory to frame their discussion. Specifically, they argue that societal norms around masculinity are at the heart of the question *How is SH different for men?*

The importance of masculinity has been salient in many of the ideas raised in this book, but to this point, primarily has focused on how masculinity prompts *perpetration* of SH against *women*. In the current chapter, the authors take a broader view and explain in detail what current research has uncovered about when men will perpetrate *SH against other men*, as well as explaining research insights about when *men will be targeted*. Consistent with the intersectionality perspective, conformity to predominant masculinity norms (which reflect societal gender and power structures) is at the heart of this explanation. Indeed, the influence of masculinity norms even appear to prompt men who have been sexually harassed by other men (because they are "not man enough") to then sexually harass women as a way of regaining masculinity. Across the contributions in this book, the intertwined nature of male masculinity norms, power, and SH phenomena is unmistakable.

The authors also do an excellent job of reviewing current research on how bystander effects might operate differently for men. Specifically, this research uncovers how SH involving male targets is perceived and responded to differently compared to scenarios involving women. The authors interpret the underlying themes that are emerging in these studies, and again masculinity norms appear to be a key underlying force that explains differences.

This chapter also explicates future research opportunities that would be impactful and that build upon the current research described here. We believe the authors do a noteworthy job of providing a clear roadmap for scholarship moving forward. In addition, they explore the practical implications, for work organizations, of recognizing men as targets of SH.

Chapter 10: The Hidden Experience of Women in the Lower Social Classes

The third chapter that examines a social group unseen in the #MeToo movement focuses on women in the lower social class. As in the previous two chapters, the authors of this chapter (Marilla Hayman, Jennifer Kish-Gephart, and Kristie Moergen) argue that the movement promoted a universal woman perspective in which the experiences of upper class, White women not only predominated but also obscured. The #MeToo movement is regarded as a cultural phenomenon that brought greater recognition and understanding to the problem of workplace SH, but the voices of the most vulnerable women—those in low paying jobs, those with limited work rights or job security, and those who have precarious relationships with their employers—are entirely absent. This chapter on social class brings attention to these critical employee groups so that future research does not further disregard their experiences.

The approach taken in Chapter 10 is helpful to introducing the challenges faced by women in lower social classes, recognizing how these differ across employment situations, describing existing knowledge about the experiences of lower social class women, and prompting beneficial ideas for future research. Assuming that there may often be a disconnect between the social class experiences of many management scholars and those of the lower social class women they hope to study, this chapter is a necessary tool for understanding how to conduct research on this critically important topic.

The chapter examines two key issues facing lower social class women. The first describes the ways that their societal status heightens vulnerability to SH experiences. For example, women working in lower social class occupations have greater economic dependence on their employers and they often work in isolation of others, both factors that increase their vulnerability to mistreatment. The second issue described by the authors is the limited response options available to lower social class women. The authors describe the reasons for these limitations, factors that are centered in both the type of work they do and the limited power they have relative to their employers and in society. The authors also describe the unique repercussions faced by lower social class women when trying to prevent, evade, and/or escape workplace SH.

The authors also include a review of research that will be beneficial to scholars interested in the role of social class in SH perpetration and punishment. This research suggests that perceptions of responsibility for SH are more often attributed to lower social class men than to men with higher social status. Not surprisingly, the future research section of this chapter emphasizes power and stereotypes as central issues to be examined in research moving forward.

Chapter 11: Unanswered Questions of #NowWhat

The final chapter focuses on resolution of workplace SH. We wanted to include a chapter on resolution because we believe the #MeToo movement was effective in raising awareness about the pervasiveness and harm of SH, but that it did little to help people, organizations, or societies understand how to resolve the harm and to heal. Successful identification and punishment of harassers is important, but resolution should extend beyond this; it should help a SH target heal from trauma, indicate to an abuser how to make amends, and show an organization how to change its culture. Ultimately, it is the resolution of SH that is the goal, and remarkably little is known about how to undertake or achieve this goal. In Chapter 11, authors Jaclyn Jensen and Carra Sims tackle this complicated question.

They begin where previous chapters left off—with a focus on societal cultures, norms, and stereotypes that devalue women and the feminine— arguing that such forces work against change in gender and power structures. Perhaps the most obvious and people-facing societal structure is the legal system, which, in most countries, did not even have words for SH until the late twentieth century. The authors review the history of legal theory and case law in the United States, describing how these provided the first real resolution for SH complaints. They then describe how other levels of analysis—at the individual, interactional, and organizational levels— have contributed to mitigation of SH. For example, they discuss organizational efforts to set policy, to change culture, to conduct training, and to engage bystanders as efforts toward resolution.

However, the authors argue that new frameworks will be needed to reach the type of resolution that will help people heal following SH. They propose and discuss the implications of a Restorative Justice model, one that focuses on repairing harm and restoring broken relationships. This model frames resolution as involving the perpetrator making amends, the target considering forgiveness, and the possibility of reintegration of perpetrators into the social system (depending on the nature of the conduct and the level of harm). The authors' discussion emphasizes the importance of scholarship around workplace SH within context of the Restorative Justice Model. They pose numerous research questions that must be answered if we are to live into the promise offered by restorative justice initiatives.

Closing Remarks

When Catherine MacKinnon wrote her pathbreaking book that outlined a legal framework for addressing SH, she recognized the fundamentally interconnected nature of legal theory and women's experiences:

> *I envision a two-way process of interaction between the relevant legal concepts and women's experience. The strictures of the concept of sex discrimination will ultimately constrain those aspects of women's oppression that will be legally recognized as discriminatory. At the same time, women's experiences, expressed in their own way, can push to expand that concept. Such an approach not only enriches the law. It begins to shape it so that what really happens to women . . . is at the core of the legal prohibition.*

In this quote, MacKinnon (1979, p. 26) recognizes the reality that current legal theory will always constrain which aspects of women's experiences are legally actionable as SH and which are not. She also recognizes that legal theory can expand and provide more protection only through a greater understanding of women's experiences. Simply put, there is a dance between the law and women's stories such that the law cannot provide protection when the problem is not given voice by the people who experience it. We see a similar interconnection between organizational science research and women's (and men's) experiences with SH. Our role as SH scholars is to uncover and listen to the stories of people abused by workplace SH and to use this as input to theories and scientific findings that make management practice more effective in battling SH. The #MeToo movement spotlighted many stories and shadowed others, but our challenge is to listen to and conduct research on both. We hope you find insights and inspiration for doing this in the ideas and words of our extraordinary authors.

Reference

MacKinnon, C. A. (1979). *Sexual harassment of working women.* Yale University Press.

PART I

Sexual Harassment Issues in the Spotlight

1

#METOO AS SOCIAL MOVEMENT

Amir Keshtiban

The Revolution Will Not Be Televised, It Will Be Tweeted!

Social Movements

Social movements are characterized as networks of informal relationships involving a diverse range of individuals, groups, and organizations engaged in political or cultural issues, united by a common collective identity (Diani, 1992). The emergence of a social movement is driven by the belief among its followers that change is necessary. The scale of the change sought by a social movement can vary, ranging from fundamental shifts in governance to smaller-scale changes, such as the closure of an oil and gas plant in a neighborhood. What unites all social movements, regardless of scale, is their ability to impact the public sphere in pursuit of desired change.

Understanding the nature of social movements requires considering key characteristics. First, they are unpredictable and not limited to societies with higher poverty rates or political inequality. Environmental movements, for instance, may emerge in societies with less severe environmental issues, and women's movements do not solely arise in societies where women face the most significant disadvantages, although there are exceptions, as demonstrated by the recent women's movement in Iran, where women bravely chanted slogans of "Woman, Life, Freedom" while facing violence in the streets.

Second, social movements vary in their degree of organization. Some possess formally organized Social Movement Organizations (SMOs) with centralized and hierarchical structures, governed by rules and regulations, such as the Greenpeace Movement. In contrast, others adopt decentralized,

DOI: 10.4324/9781003300953-2

horizontal, and egalitarian approaches, promoting participatory democracy, as seen in the Women's Liberation Movement (Goodwin & Jasper, 2015; Freeman, 1972).

Third, social movements can vary in terms of funding and participation. They defy conventional logic by being driven not by self-interest or monetary gain, but by a collective sense of purpose. Some movements require significant funding from member donations or philanthropic foundations to sustain themselves, while others heavily rely on the time and energy contributed by their members. In certain movements, such as revolutionary or guerrilla armies, participation becomes a full-time commitment, whereas in others, it may involve only a few hours on a Saturday afternoon each month (Goodwin & Jasper, 2015). Whether formal or informal, Social Movement Organizations (SMOs) play a crucial role in collecting and strategically distributing resources, establishing institutional structures, providing strategic leadership, organizing protest events, securing media coverage, and fostering collective identity (Goodwin & Jasper, 2015). They also serve as influential sources of identity for the movement's supporters, opponents, and the general public (Della Porta & Diani, 2009, p. 137).

Calhoun (1993) categorizes twentieth-century social movements as old and new. Old social movements were primarily concerned with labor and advocated Marxist and socialist values, focusing on class as the central issue in politics and believing that a single political-economic transformation would resolve various social problems (ibid.). In contrast, new social movements that emerged from the 1960s onward operate outside formal institutional channels, emphasizing concerns related to lifestyle, ethics, and identity rather than narrowly defined economic goals (ibid.). Examples of new social movements include the student and youth, the peace movement, women's liberation movement (WLM), animal rights, LGBT, and environmental movements (see, for instance, Hetland & Goodwin, 2013; Melucci, 1980). New social movements address issues that were previously considered outside the realm of political action (Scott, 1990). Eckersley (1989) links the rise of new social movements to the rapid expansion of further and higher education in the post-war era. The increased access to higher education not only enabled individuals to acquire information but also enhanced their capacity for independent and critical thinking (Eckersley, 1989; Offe, 1985). As Eyerman and Jamison (1991, p. 55) argue, these movements create a new social space, a cognitive territory, through dynamic interactions among various groups and organizations. New social movements aim to identify problems and bring them to the forefront of public attention (Salter, 2013). The #MeToo movement falls within this categorization, actively working to introduce and discuss issues related to sexual harassment (SH) in the public sphere. As argued by Habermas, the new social movements of the post-1960s era constitute the raw material of the public sphere (Habermas, 1981). Edwards (2004) further suggests that the shift from "old" to "new" politics enhances the potential of new social movements to generate a genuine public sphere due to the fact that disputes situated at the boundary between the system and lifeworld, as articulated by Habermas, provoke the emergence of social movements in the public sphere. These conflicts are distinct from capital-labor conflicts and can be categorized as new (ibid.). Therefore, understanding the concept of the public sphere and its implications is crucial for comprehending a social movement. In the next section, I will provide a concise definition of the public sphere and discuss its development in light of the emergence of the internet and online platforms.

Public Sphere

Habermas (1974) provides a definition of the public sphere as "a realm of our social life in which something approaching public opinion can be formed. Access is guaranteed to all citizens. A portion of the public sphere comes into being in every conversation in which private individuals assemble to form a public body" (p. 49).

He argues that citizens become a public body when they freely convene, assured of the right to assemble and associate, and with the opportunity to express and publish their opinions on matters of public interest. Such communication involves specific means of disseminating information and influencing individuals within a large public body. Today, newspapers, magazines, radio, and television serve as examples of media within the public sphere.

Habermas's argument, however, has faced criticism for portraying the public sphere as dominated by elites, hence referred to as the bourgeois public sphere. His thesis has been challenged on various grounds, including the neglect of issues of participation and exclusion in relation to modes of communication and public debate of ideas. Critics have highlighted "the bourgeois public sphere as an ideal type" (Garnham, 2007, p. 207), its class and elitist bias (Kluge & Negt, 1972), and its lack of inclusivity in terms of race and gender (Jacobs, 1999; Fraser, 1996). As Garnham (2007) argues, the debates surrounding the public sphere have primarily focused on critiquing Habermas's use of the bourgeois public sphere as an ideal type. Although Habermas himself acknowledged that the emphasis on the bourgeois public realm was intended to analyze the impacts of modernity, showcasing how modernity led to the development of new institutions like representative governments and influenced public opinion through media outlets such as the press (see Chapter 2 on Social Media). As Piccato (2010) suggests, when discussing the concept of the public sphere from a historical perspective, it is essential to recognize that universal access and equality within this sphere were compromised by exclusions, particularly based on gender and social class.

Habermas (1974) provides a detailed historical and sociological analysis in which he argues that mass communication and mass participation have led to the degradation of the public sphere, transforming it into a tool for advertising and public relations. This shift has resulted in the domination of commercialization over political activity within the bourgeois public sphere (DiCenzo et al., 2010). However, in response to this trend, several social movements have attempted to challenge mainstream mass communication by developing their own alternative media. Their goal is to create a counter public sphere that considers the needs of society in everyday practice. As Castells states, "[T]he public sphere is an essential component of socio-political organization because it is the space where people come together as citizens and articulate their autonomous views to influence the political institutions of society" (2008, p. 78). This chapter will explore some examples of such movements.

It is important to note the role of technological advancements in shaping the public sphere. As technology progresses, so does the way in which the public sphere operates. The emergence of the Internet and social media platforms has drawn more citizens into ongoing debates, allowing for active participation rather than passive consumption of information. The existence of a meaningful public sphere now depends not only on physical spaces but also on accessible communication technologies and institutions that facilitate discourse beyond face-to-face interactions (Tierney, 2013).

Digital media offers a wide range of capabilities, including immediate access to information, global connectivity, active involvement and interaction, content creation, community building, customization, real-time communication, and integration of multiple media formats. According to Bode et al. (2014), social media platforms currently have over half a billion active users worldwide, with a significant majority being young people. Their study examines the factors that encourage political expression on these online platforms and the effects such expression has on traditional political participation. The results indicate that political social media use strongly influenced levels of growth in traditional political participation during the 2008 USA election.

Therefore, the use of political social media by ordinary individuals can serve as a new means of socialization, encouraging their participation in political life and fostering long-term habits of engagement and involvement that can have lasting effects. It is important to recognize that social media has had an impact on society, acting as a trigger rather than a complete replacement for the traditional public sphere. Events such as the Arab Spring, Occupy Movements, the #MeToo campaign, and the attack on the US Capitol in January 2021 all originated from online platforms but gained momentum through mainstream media coverage and their connection to the events, irrespective of the media's political biases. Scholars argue that while social media appears to present a new and/or broader public sphere, there may be limitations to its influence. For example, studies by Kruse et al. (2018) suggest that individuals, particularly Millennials and Generation Xers, avoid political discourse online due to concerns of harassment and workplace surveillance and tend to engage only with like-minded individuals in a more positive environment. Johannessen et al. (2016) similarly argue that the involvement of different stakeholders in social media varies based on their level of influence, with more salient stakeholders being less likely to participate. This was evident in the #MeToo movement, where the movement gained traction when a famous person, Alyssa Milano, tweeted about her own SH case in 2017, rather than when the term was used by its founder, Tarana Burke, in 2006. The movement gained momentum as it received attention and coverage from the mainstream media, leading to the initiation of open discussions on previously taboo topics and engaging the public in the conversation, primarily facilitated through online platforms, particularly X.

To provide a comprehensive understanding of how the public sphere is constructed, it is necessary to consider both offline and online public spheres, as well as the interactions within these spheres. In the next section, I will explore the evolution of public space through the suffragette movement, women's liberation movement, Greenham Common Women's Peace Camp, and the #MeToo movement. In the following section, I will briefly discuss these movements and their impact on the public sphere in their respective time periods, including the role of expanding press and print media as a significant political opportunity, as well as the emergence of platforms like X that have created a decentralized public sphere allowing audiences to express their thoughts and engage in current debates.

Suffragette Movement

The industrial revolution in Britain solidified the division between men and women, separating their lives into public and private spheres. Catherine Hall (1990) argues that the industrial revolution led to men occupying the newly defined public world of business, commerce, and politics, while women were confined to the private sphere of home and family (p. 52). This gender-based division limited women's participation in public affairs, positioning them as sacred figures responsible for domestic duties, while men had the freedom to engage in political and community matters. Any woman who sought a public role was often stigmatized as a prostitute (Caine, 1997, p. 7).

In 1832, the enactment of the Representation of the People Act marked the first official recognition of the long-standing practice of excluding women from the British electorate. The initial non-militant women's suffrage group was established in Manchester, a hub of political activity in northern England, in 1866. Within two years, similar organizations emerged in London and other major cities. Over the subsequent 40 years, these groups spearheaded a coordinated lobbying campaign aimed at securing voting rights for women in Parliamentary elections. Despite their vigorous advocacy, no legislation to break this barrier was successfully passed. As the twentieth century began, the British women's suffrage movement was all but dormant (Lance, 1979). In response to the stalemate, the Women's Social and Political Union (WSPU) was established to challenge this perception by presenting the movement as a new religious order distinct from the existing one (Hartman, 2003). The Pankhurst family, particularly Emmeline Pankhurst, played a significant role in the militant suffrage campaign. In 1903, Emmeline Pankhurst and other activists founded the WSPU with the motto "Deeds not words," driven by frustration with the slow progress on women's rights. Emmeline Pankhurst, who had been involved in the suffrage movement since 1880, became a founding member of the WSPU and led it until its dissolution in 1918. The WSPU, open only to female members, employed highly organized tactics that included civil disobedience and disruption. When peaceful methods proved ineffective, they resorted to more radical and occasionally violent actions, resulting in imprisonment and hunger strikes. During Emmeline Pankhurst's imprisonment, Emmeline Pethick Lawrence, co-editor of the Votes for Women newspaper, compared the situation to the crucifixion of Christ. As Hartman (2003) points out, suffragettes likened themselves not only to Christ but also to novices taking orders, pilgrims embarking on a pilgrimage, or warriors donning armor for a holy crusade (p. 36). These militant actions attracted significant attention to the cause of women's suffrage. Meanwhile, moderate organizations like the National Union of Women's Suffrage Societies (NUWSS), led by Millicent Fawcett, pursued women's enfranchisement through legal and constitutional means, although their efforts often took a backseat to the WSPU's activities in terms of progress as discussed earlier. The WSPU's adoption of militant tactics led to their breakaway from the non-militant suffragists of the National Union of Women's Suffrage Societies (NUWSS), as the WSPU sought to incorporate more confrontational approaches into their protest methods (Edwards, 2013).

Suffragettes carried out significant window-breaking attacks in London's West End retail districts in March 1912. These raids involved the participation of hundreds of women who supported the militant struggle for the right to vote, and the majority of them were subsequently imprisoned. By engaging in this extreme and provocative form of protest, which contradicted the accepted norms of womanhood at the time, the suffragettes managed to capture public attention in a dramatic and unprecedented manner within a matter of days (Parkins, 1997). This was crucial for the suffragette movement, as it sought to employ communication methods that would attract public attention and be covered by mainstream newspapers, even if the media coverage was not always favorable to their cause.

In addition to their militant tactics, suffragettes utilized their own media channels to communicate their message. "Votes for Women" serves as the prime example of such media, running on a monthly basis between 1907 and 1908 and then transitioning to a weekly publication until 1918 (Hartman, 2003). To engage the public and shape the public sphere, suffragettes also established a dress code that required supporters to dress in the Women's Social and Political Union (WSPU) colors of purple, white, and green (Parkins, 1997). Their objective extended beyond mere involvement in political activities within the existing public sphere; they aimed to transform the public sphere itself by introducing new perspectives and embracing new ways of life. Notably, debates on women's rights, commonly referred to as "the sex" debates, gained significant attention in the late nineteenth century. Major mainstream newspapers such as the *Nineteenth Century*, *Fortnightly Review*, *Contemporary Review*, *National Review*, and *Westminster Review* engaged in a "national and commercial debate about female suffrage" from various political standpoints (Brake, 2004).

Alternative media outlets emerged as communication tactics to counter the mainstream media's attempts to downplay the progressive agenda of the suffragette movement. For instance, *The Englishwoman*, a monthly journal dedicated to progressive causes, serves as an excellent example of such alternative media outlets, which also garnered respect from their opponents. A reviewer from *The Men's League*, as noted in *Women's Franchise*, acknowledged that it was "likely to receive a hearing where exclusively Suffrage journals have no opening" (June 10, 1909, cited in DiCenzo et al., 2010, p. 121). One crucial section of this journal, titled "Points for Reflection," encouraged criticism of the movement and provided an open platform for discussion to facilitate progress. Similarly, The Freewoman, a weekly magazine, offered a space for contemplating the dynamics of the movement and envisioning new avenues of activism. This contribution played a significant role in shaping new collective identities within the suffragette movement (DiCenzo et al., 2010).

The Freewoman introduced several authors to the public and published pieces that had been rejected by more prestigious journals like the *Nineteenth Century* or "serious" women's movement periodicals such as *The Englishwoman*. The paper delved into topics such as sexual morality, women's economic independence, and cultural criticism, captivating readers. It openly discussed sexual morality and practices, sexual pleasure, and offered a fresh perspective on prostitution as a potentially necessary aspect of human sexuality, sparking contested debates on these previously unspoken matters. The editors of *The Freewoman* actively sought to engage in extended dialogues with other journals, and their discussions with daily newspapers like *The Times* and *The Morning Post* demonstrated a commitment to reaching larger audiences, thereby challenging the existing public sphere.

The emerging public sphere gained momentum, characterized by a broader range of voices, more disagreement, and diversity of opinions. Several factors contributed to this shift, with one significant aspect being the resistance exhibited by women themselves, leading to the emergence of the anti-suffrage movement. Furthermore, suffragettes faced mistreatment in prison, including force-feeding as a means to break their hunger strikes.

Violet Markham, a social reformer and opponent of women's suffrage, succinctly expressed her opposition to the suffragette movement by emphasizing the clear distinctions between men and women, grounded in undeniable facts and legal frameworks. The anti-suffrage argument served as a grave warning, asserting that the pursuit of superficial equality with men would inevitably lead to a fundamental misunderstanding of women's true dignity and unique purpose (Bush, 2002). This statement was featured in the *Nineteenth Century* magazine under the title "An Appeal against Female Suffrage." In response to such articles, suffragettes also contributed to these magazines, further fueling the public discourse.

Vessey (2021) discusses the suffragettes' hunger strikes and how the government reacted by forcibly feeding them. The author highlights the role of mainstream media, specifically the *Daily Mail*, the *Daily Express*, and the *Daily Mirror*, in shaping the public sphere in early twentieth century. The author argues that the Women's Social and Political Union (WSPU) aimed to utilize the correspondence columns and prisoner testimonies in these newspapers to generate empathy and advance their own agenda regarding forcible feeding and women's suffrage. This strategic approach sought to co-opt newspapers into the suffragettes' campaign and generate publicity for their cause by capturing the public's attention and garnering support for their cause.

As evident from the discussion above, the suffragette movement, including its repertoire of protests and alternative media, as well as its interaction with mainstream media, paved the way for women's inclusion in the public sphere and challenged the dichotomy of the private and public spheres for women.

Women's Liberation Movement

The women's liberation movement emerged, predominantly in the industrialized countries of the Western world in response to the widespread discrimination and oppression faced by women, aiming to achieve equality and autonomy in society. It encompassed various objectives, including political, economic, and social equality, reproductive rights, and the eradication of violence against women. Considered the second phase of women's movements, it brought about significant changes by providing women access to previously male-dominated jobs and challenging gender stereotypes in the media (Epstein, 2001).

The women's liberation movement comprised both liberal and radical aspects. The liberal perspective recognized the interconnectedness of women's oppression with race and class, while the radical side viewed gender inequality as the root cause of all other forms of oppression. The movement involved national organizations advocating for reproductive rights and reforms, as well as women's liberation and consciousness-raising groups, along with grassroots projects (ibid.).

Consciousness-raising groups played a crucial role in recruiting participants to the women's liberation movement. These groups provided a non-hierarchical and loosely structured setting for women to discuss their experiences and politics, aiming to reshape their understanding of the world (Whittier, 1995). Instead of resorting to violent actions, the movement employed communication tactics focused on building support through networking. Consciousness-raising facilitated the development of critical awareness of societal culture through informal meetings where personal experiences were shared and generalized. It also addressed various forms of oppression and facilitated the organization of new consciousness-raising groups. By creating a safe space for members to critique their own actions and seek improvement, consciousness-raising empowered women within the movement (Sowards & Renegar, 2004).

Campbell (1973) emphasizes the importance of consciousness-raising, highlighting the affirmation of personal experience, self-exposure, self-criticism, dialogue, and autonomous decision-making. Criticisms were raised regarding the predominantly White, middle-class membership, which neglected the experiences of women of color, the working class, and marginalized individuals. Sowards and Renegar (2004) note that consciousness-raising, fueled by mass media, popular culture, and education, challenged gender inequities in the public sphere (please see Chapters 8–10 on Intersectionality). These consciousness-raising groups disrupted binaries and bridged the realms of the public and private, political and personal, encapsulated in the feminist slogan "personal is political" (Nachescu, 2006).

It is worth noting the significant achievement of the Women's Liberation Movement in creating consciousness-raising groups, which became one of the primary educational and organizing programs for women in the 1960s and 1970s. These groups were designed to uncover radical truths about the situation of women in order to inspire radical action (Sarachild, 1978). Consciousness-raising groups continue to exist today and are used by different audiences for various goals, such as multicultural awareness or conflict resolution, illustrating their enduring power and effectiveness (Leonard, 1996; Nan, 2011).

It is noteworthy to acknowledge the counter movements and backlashes that emerged in response to the Women's Liberation Movement. Faludi (1991) examines the challenges and setbacks faced by women in the United States during the 1980s, as societal and political forces contributed to a backlash against women's rights and gender equality.

Faludi argues that despite significant progress made by the feminist movement in previous decades, deliberate and concerted efforts were made to undermine women's achievements and push back against their advancements. She identifies various sources of this backlash, including conservative media, political campaigns, and societal expectations. Focusing on mainstream media, she reports on how women were portrayed during this time, perpetuating stereotypes and reinforcing traditional gender roles. Faludi contends that the media played a significant role in shaping public opinion and disseminating anti-feminist sentiments. She criticizes the portrayal of women in the media, often reducing them to narrow stereotypes, such as the "career woman" (p. 48), which undermined the progress made by women and dismissed their concerns. Faludi argues that mainstream media, including newspapers, magazines, television, and advertising, played a part in promoting the idea that women's liberation had gone too far and that a return to traditional gender roles was necessary. She highlights how media outlets sensationalized stories and manipulated statistics to create a sense of crisis, presenting feminism as a threat to traditional values and family structures. This backlash coincided with the rise of the "new traditionalist" movement, which aimed to reassert traditional family values and push women back into more traditional roles as wives and mothers, echoing the patterns observed in the earlier suffragette movement.

The women's liberation movement differed from suffragette and suffragist movements in that it lacked centralized leadership and structure.

There were no designated leaders or spokespeople, yet certain individuals attracted media and public attention and assumed these roles by default. This highlighted the tendency to seek leaders even in leaderless movements (Keshtiban et al., 2023). The absence of a clear structure, as criticized by Freeman (1972), led to confusion within the movement. While a formalized structure would not necessarily eliminate the informal structure, it could hinder the predominance of the informal structure. Consequently, by the early 1980s, the movement lacked a single core and struggled to agree on a unified strategy or analysis. However, this did not deter activists from pursuing their own strategies for empowerment within the movement. For instance, the Greenham Common Women's Peace Camp had a radical feminist ethos and attracted supporters from various segments of the women's liberation movement, which I will discuss in the next section.

The Greenham Common Women's Peace Camp

In September 1981, a group of approximately 35 activists, predominantly women, marched from Cardiff to the Greenham Common US Air Force base in Newbury to protest against the NATO decision in 1979 that permitted the housing of US nuclear Cruise missiles at military bases in Europe (Feigenbaum, 2013). The Greenham Common Women's Peace Camp stands as a significant example of a peace movement, with peace marches and demonstrations garnering a greater number of participants than any other type of movement and leaving a major impact on British politics. It even contributed to the fragmentation of the Labour Party, leading to the formation of the Social Democrats in the early 1980s, and had implications for the 1987 UK general election (Byrne, 2013).

The women at the camp decided to exclude the small number of men involved in the action, asserting that a women-only protest camp would highlight the contrast between female peace protesters and male military and civil authorities. Over the following years, the camp thrived and welcomed women participants from the United Kingdom and around the world. Their repertoire of protest included large-scale demonstrations, such as when 30,000 women encircled the base in 1983, and 40,000 in 1984. They also employed smaller, localized tactics, such as breaking into the base to paint slogans and leave reminders of their presence. The occupation of the RAF Greenham Common base emerged as the most impactful pillar of their movement's repertoire when the first missiles arrived at the end of 1983.

Similar to the suffragette movement discussed earlier, the Greenham Common women also created their own media. Throughout their years of protest, they became media producers, crafting their own newsletters, booklets, and other ephemeral media. Their diverse forms of media, including poetry, cartoons, sketches, songs, intricate drawings, and haphazard doodles, portrayed Greenham as a place abundant in creativity, spontaneity, political experimentation, and self-reflection (Feigenbaum, 2013). Remarkably, the Greenham protest endured from 1981 to 2001 (Feigenbaum et al., 2013) as a place-based protest, distinct geographically and ideologically from other spaces (Feigenbaum, 2010).

According to Couldry (1999), the Greenham Common movement challenged various social divisions within the public sphere, including the formal distinction between men and women in social space, and the power dynamics between the general public and the state that created insiders and outsiders within the public sphere. Like the suffragette and women's liberation movements, the Greenham Common Peace movement faced criticism from the mainstream media. The media and local villagers, emphasizing women's domestic roles within traditional UK families, labeled the activists as neglectful of their daily caregiving duties to protest, or depicted them as unclean and sexually deviant due to the camp's substantial lesbian population, aiming to challenge the status quo (Cresswell, 1996; Feigenbaum, 2013). While the movement utilized mainstream media to further their cause, they also utilized their own leaflets and media work in parallel to mobilize and recruit new participants, as well as challenge the public sphere. Their communications addressed "ordinary people" and "ordinary women," using specific language to engage with a broader audience (ibid.: p. 346). The extraordinary actions taken by ordinary people challenged the public sphere, attracting international mainstream media coverage and making the movement a global reference point for concerns about nuclear weapons. Similar to the suffragette movement, the Greenham Women aimed to be open to criticism and consistently provided diverse perspectives in their newsletters, info sheets, and booklets (Feigenbaum, 2013). The content they created for alternative media encompassed creative writing and artworks, including sketches, drawings, and cartoons of various sizes with predominantly political contexts.

The alternative media and occupied space provided the Greenham Common women with the means to contest the public sphere by challenging established norms, whether pertaining to the traditional concept of family or the division between the government and ordinary people in decisions concerning national security. Although these movements made significant strides in challenging the public sphere and creating a new one for future generations, the current state of affairs indicates that there is still much work to be done to move away from traditional notions of family. This is particularly evident with the recent overturning of Roe v. Wade by the US Supreme Court in June 2022, which revoked the constitutional right to abortion. The #MeToo movement in 2017 represents the most recent social movement that seeks to challenge the public sphere by addressing forms of domination, patriarchy, SH, and sexism.

#MeToo Movement

The #MeToo movement aims to empower victims of sexual abuse and harassment, particularly in the workplace, by encouraging them to speak out and share their experiences. Through empathy and solidarity, the movement challenges the public sphere surrounding SH. Tarana Burke, the founder of the campaign, describes the empathy within the #MeToo movement as transformative, fostering active listening and self-reflection to potentially change one's own beliefs (Rodino-Colocino, 2018).

While the campaign was established in 2006, it gained significant attention in 2017 following the widely publicized SH allegations against Harvey Weinstein. Actress Alyssa Milano's tweet urging individuals to respond with "me too" if they had experienced SH or assault garnered extensive reactions from prominent figures, sparking global media coverage and discussions on the prevalent issue of workplace SH and assault. Like other movements discussed in this chapter, the #MeToo movement faced criticism from some of its own supporters, who perceived it as limited to elite individuals and reflective of a bourgeois public sphere, as described by Habermas (1974). Zarkov and Davis (2018) argue that the involvement of wealthy celebrities, TV personalities, journalists, and political elites on X contributed to the movement's momentum. However, it is worth noting that mainstream media has shifted its portrayal of accusers, showing more support compared to the past. This shift can be attributed to the decentralized nature of Twitter (now called X), allowing users to employ various tactics to make a hashtag trend and initiate meaningful debates. The #MeToo movement shares similarities with earlier movements in terms of its tactics. Like the Suffragettes and the Greenham movement, it employed provocative communication strategies, including directly naming perpetrators, which was a novel approach.

The decentralized nature of X also bears resemblance to the leaderless Women's Liberation Movement, allowing for organic and collective mobilization of individuals. In response to the #MeToo movement, counter movements and criticisms emerged, such as the "NotAllMen" movement and #HimToo. These movements reacted against social movements that do not promote masculine dominance and White supremacy. Their supporters argued that the #MeToo movement unfairly portrayed all men as perpetrators of sexual misconduct, emphasizing the importance of focusing on individual actions rather than making broad generalizations about gender.

Critics raised the issue of backlash and false accusations within the #MeToo movement (Flood, 2019, Maricourt & Burrell, 2022). They expressed concerns about the potential for false allegations and the negative impact they could have on the lives and reputations of those accused. They argued that the movement could create a climate of distrust and lead to unfair consequences for individuals who are wrongly accused. Similar to the suffragette and other movements discussed in this chapter, criticism of the #MeToo movement is not limited to men but also includes conservative women who backlash against it. Their argument is grounded in the belief that the proliferation of the #MeToo movement could trigger a defensive reaction, leading to changes in men's behavior that, ironically, might worsen existing gender inequalities (Lisnek et al., 2022). Similar to the movements discussed earlier, the critics also voiced opposition to the feminist foundations of the #MeToo movement. They believed that it undermined traditional gender roles and relationships, advocating for the preservation of more traditional views of gender dynamics (Hindes & Fileborn, 2020).

Another criticism centered around the need for due process and fairness when addressing allegations of SH and assault. Critics contended that some accusations within the #MeToo movement were treated as guilty verdicts without sufficient evidence or proper legal procedures (Clarke, 2019). They emphasized the importance of upholding principles of due process to ensure fairness in dealing with such sensitive matters, which is in line with what the Select Task Force on Harassment recommends, which is against so-called zero-tolerance policies, instead opting for what Porter (2018, p. 59) describes as "fair and proportional responses to report of harassment (after fair and thorough investigations)."

The #MeToo movement, which began on the X platform, served as a consciousness raising platform not just for survivors but also for anyone who wanted to confront the public sphere on matters such as SH, media handling of SH charges, and so on. As discussed earlier, due to the nature of X as an online platform, it facilitated the transformation of consciousness-raising groups from local, internal, and centralized audiences into a decentralized forum with diverse public audiences. According to Brunner and Partlow-Lefevre (2020), users employed various tactics to promote the #MeToo hashtag on X, ultimately making it a trending topic on X/Twitter. This, in turn, propelled it into everyday conversations across various media channels, including newspapers, magazines, television, podcasts, and radio. Users achieved this by sharing stories with the hashtag #MeToo, using the hashtag without accompanying stories, and engaging with these posts through comments, shares, and reposts.

What is evident from this discussion is the fact that although the #MeToo movement on X is created by the elite people (as discussed earlier), ordinary people took advantage of this initiative and got themselves involved into the debate around SH. This was made possible by the decentralized nature of the X platform and other social media platforms. They open up new avenues for reviving and revitalizing the public sphere, not as a single, one-dimensional space, but as a more complex system of distinct and diverse yet interconnected and overlapping mediums, each representing different topics and approaches to mediated communication (Bruns & Highfield, 2015). This allows everyone to get involved in discussions in real-time, quickly and without constraints (Colleoni et al., 2014).

Positioning #MeToo Within Discussed Social Movements

As previously discussed, the #MeToo movement shares similarities with the social movements examined in this chapter. What these movements, including #MeToo, accomplished was not a direct opposition to or creation of an alternative public sphere, but rather a reshaping of the public sphere to foster greater openness in discussing challenging or taboo subjects. While different from past movements that employed methods like breaking windows or physical occupations, the #MeToo movement sought to challenge the public sphere by employing a consciousness-raising agenda through the X platform.

The engagement with the public sphere through X offers a foundation for both action and discussion, with the capacity to motivate feminist movements that go beyond mere criticism and validation. To ensure the creation and global development of these new consciousness-raising groups, it is crucial to emphasize the decentralization of online platforms such as X. The importance of this issue is amplified when we consider recent events that have unfolded. For instance, the alarming attack on the US Capitol and the transformation of Twitter into a platform known as X have raised significant concerns. These developments have sparked worries about the potential emergence of a novel kind of mainstream media in the future, one that operates within the context of decentralized online platforms like X. This concern arises due to the growing influence of various algorithms and the introduction of manual censorship practices for tweets. Such a shift the could significantly impact the dynamics of information dissemination, public sphere, and the overall landscape of media and communication.

Future Research

Future research can be directed toward examining the influence of social movements, such as the #MeToo movement, in reconfiguring the public sphere. This research can focus on the manner in which these movements challenge and reshape the public sphere, fostering more open discussions surrounding sensitive and taboo subjects, including SH, gender equity, and related topics.

Moreover, further exploration can be undertaken to understand how social movements facilitate transformational empathy and experiential learning. This investigation can delve into the ways in which these movements promote empathy and learning through shared stories and experiences. It is noteworthy to mention that this effort to promote empathy was done in person in the women's movement (consciousness raising groups) and at Greenham (where they lived together). Will empathy building work in an online world, where there is abundant opportunity for immediate backlash and negative feedback? Additionally, the impact of these elements on cultivating healthy communities and enhancing individual well-being can be explored.

Furthermore, research can be conducted to analyze the role of social media platforms in feminist movements. This examination can assess the effectiveness of various strategies employed by social movements, such as the utilization of hashtags and consciousness-raising agendas via platforms like X. Additionally, as the investigation delves into the transformative power of these movements, what is the significance of decentralizing online platforms in facilitating the formation and advancement of consciousness-raising groups? How do these platforms enable both local and global connections within feminist networks?

The implications arising from algorithmic control and censorship on online platforms warrant investigation, especially considering the potential replacement of mainstream media by decentralized online platforms. It is crucial to explore the consequences of algorithmic control and manual censorship on platforms like X, identifying and addressing the associated risks and challenges. The research can also propose strategies to mitigate the negative effects of such developments while taking into account positive implications, such as improved content quality and protection from harmful content.

Finally, future research can build upon the discussion of the #MeToo movement by exploring the concept of intersectionality within social movements. This exploration can investigate how different movements intersect and mutually support one another, while addressing issues related to critical analysis, embodied inter-corporeality, and personal development. The interconnectedness and collaborative nature of diverse movements for social change can be examined in this context.

References

Bode, L., Vraga, E. K., Borah, P., & Shah, D. V. (2014). A new space for political behavior: Political social networking and its democratic consequences. *Journal of Computer-Mediated Communication, 19*(3), 414–429.

Brake, L. (2004). Writing women's history: 'The sex' debates of 1889. In *New woman hybridities: Femininity, feminism and international consumer culture, 1880–1930*. Routledge.

Brunner, E., & Partlow-Lefevre, S. (2020). # MeToo as networked collective: Examining consciousness-raising on wild public networks. *Communication and Critical/Cultural Studies, 17*(2), 166–182.

Bruns, A., & Highfield, T. (2015). Is Habermas on Twitter?: Social media and the public sphere. In *The Routledge companion to social media and politics* (pp. 56–73). Routledge.

Bush, J. (2002). British women's anti-suffragism and the forward policy, 1908–14. *Women's History Review, 11*(3), 431–454.

Byrne, P. (2013). *Social movements in Britain*. Routledge.

Caine, B. (1997). *English feminism 1780–1980*. Oxford University Press.

Calhoun, C. (1993). "New social movements" of the early nineteenth century. *Social Science History, 17*(3), 385–427.

Campbell, K. K. (1973). The rhetoric of women's liberation: "An oxymoron". *Quarterly Joumai of Speech, 55*(1), 74–86.

Castells, M. (2008). The new public sphere: Global civil society, communication networks, and global governance. *The ANNALS of the American Academy of Political and Social Science, 616*(1), 78–93. https://doi.org/10.1177/0002716207311877

Clarke, J. A. (2019). The rules of #MeToo. *University of Chicago Legal Forum, 2019*, Article 3. https://chicagounbound.uchicago.edu/uclf/vol2019/iss1/3

Colleoni, E., Rozza, A., & Arvidsson, A. (2014). Echo chamber or public sphere? Predicting political orientation and measuring political homophily in Twitter using big data. *Journal of Communication, 64*(2), 317–332.

Couldry, N. (1999). Disrupting the media frame at Greenham Common: A new chapter in the history of mediations? *Media, Culture & Society, 21*(3), 337–358.

Cresswell, T. (1996). *In place/out of place: Geography, ideology, and transgression*. University of Minnesota Press.

Della Porta, D., & Diani, M. (2009). *Social movements: An introduction*. John Wiley & Sons.

Diani, M. (1992). The concept of social movement. *The Sociological Review, 40*(1), 1–25. https://doi.org/10.1111/j.1467-954X.1992.tb02943.x

DiCenzo, M., Ryan, L., & Delap, L. (2010). *Feminist media history: Suffrage, periodicals and the public sphere*. Springer.

Eckersley, R. (1989). Green politics and the new class: Selfishness or virtue? *Political Studies, 37*(2), 205–223.

Edwards, G. (2004). Habermas and social movements: What's "new"? *The Sociological Review, 52*(1_suppl), 113–130.

Edwards, G. (2013). Infectious innovations? The diffusion of tactical innovation in social movement networks, the case of suffragette militancy. *Social Movement Studies, 13*(1), 48–69. https://doi.org/10.1080/14742837.2013.834251

Epstein, B. (2001). What happened to the women's movement? *Monthly Review, 53*(1), 1–13.

Eyerman, R., & Jamison, A. (1991). *Social movements: A cognitive approach*. Penn State Press.

Faludi, S. (1991). *Backlash: The undeclared war against women*. Chatto & Windus.

Feigenbaum, A. (2010). *Tactics and technology: Cultural resistance at the Greenham common women's peace camp*. Library and Archives Canada.

Feigenbaum, A. (2013). Written in the mud: (Proto)zine-making and autonomous media at the Greenham Common women's peace camp. *Feminist Media Studies*, 13(1), 1–13.

Feigenbaum, A., Frenzel, F., & McCurdy, P. (2013). *Protest camps*. Zed Books.

Flood, M. (2019). Men and #MeToo: Mapping men's responses to anti-violence advocacy. In B. Fileborn & R. Loney-Howes (Eds.), *#MeToo and the politics of social change*. Palgrave Macmillan. https://doi.org/10.1007/978-3-030-15213-0_18

Fraser, N. (1996). Multiculturalism and gender equity: The U.S. "difference" debates revisited. *Constellations*, 3, 61–72. https://doi.org/10.1111/j.1467-8675.1996.tb00043.x

Freeman, J. (1972). The tyranny of structurelessness. *Berkeley Journal of Sociology*, 17, 151–164. *Constellations*, 3(1), 61–72. https://doi.org/10.1111/j.1467-8675.1996.tb00043.x

Garnham, N. (2007). Habermas and the public sphere. *Global Media and Communication*, 3(2), 201–214.

Goodwin, J., & Jasper, J. M. (2015). *The social movements reader: Cases and concepts*. Wiley.

Habermas, J. (1974). The public sphere: An encyclopedia article (1964). *New German Critique*, 3, 49–55.

Habermas, J. (1981). New social movements. *Telos*, 49, 33–37.

Hall, C. (1990). Private persons versus public someones: Class, gender and politics in England, 1780–1850. In T. Lovell (Ed.), *British feminist thought*. A Reader.

Hartman, K. (2003). "What made me a suffragette": The new woman and the new (?) conversion narrative. *Women' History Review*, 12(1), 35–50. https://doi.org/10.1080/09612020300200346

Hetland, G., & Goodwin, J. (2013). The strange disappearance of capitalism from social movement studies. *Marxism and Social Movements*, 46, 86–98.

Hindes, S., & Fileborn, B. (2020). "Girl power gone wrong":# MeToo, Aziz Ansari, and media reporting of (grey area) sexual violence. *Feminist Media Studies*, 20(5), 639–656.

Jacobs, R. N. (1999). Race, media and civil society. *International Sociology*, 14(3), 355–372. https://doi.org/10.1177/0268580999014003008

Johannessen, M. R., Sæbø, Ø., & Flak, L. S. (2016). Social media as public sphere: A stakeholder perspective. *Transforming Government: People, Process and Policy*, 10(2), 212–238.

Keshtiban, A. E., Callahan, J. L., & Harris, M. (2023). Leaderlessness in social movements: Advancing space, symbols, and spectacle as modes of "Leadership". *Human Resource Development Quarterly*, 34(1), 19–43.

Kluge, A., & Negt, O. (1972). *Public sphere and experience: Toward an analysis of the bourgeois and proletarian public sphere*. University of Minnesota Press.

Kruse, L. M., Norris, D. R., & Flinchum, J. R. (2018). Social media as a public sphere? Politics on social media. *The Sociological Quarterly*, 59(1), 62–84.

Lance, K. C. (1979). Strategy choices of the British women's social and political union, 1903–18. *Social Science Quarterly*, 60(1), 51–61.

Leonard, P. J. (1996). Consciousness-raising groups as a multicultural awareness approach: An experience with counselor trainees. *Cultural Diversity and Mental Health*, 2(2), 89.

Lisnek, J. A., Wilkins, C. L., Wilson, M. E., & Ekstrom, P. D. (2022). Backlash against the# MeToo movement: How women's voice causes men to feel victimized. *Group Processes & Intergroup Relations*, 25(3), 682–702.

Maricourt, C. de, & Burrell, S. R. (2022). #MeToo or #MenToo? Expressions of backlash and masculinity politics in the #MeToo Era. *The Journal of Men's Studies, 30*(1), 49–69. https://doi.org/10.1177/10608265211035794

Melucci, A. (1980). The new social movements: A theoretical approach. *Information (International Social Science Council), 19*(2), 199–226.

Nachescu, V. (2006). *Becoming the feminist subject. Consciousness-raising groups in second wave feminism.* State University of New York at Buffalo.

Nan, S. A. (2011). Consciousness in culture-based conflict and conflict resolution. *Conflict Resolution Quarterly, 28*(3), 239–262.

Offe, C. (1985). New social movements: Challenging the boundaries of institutional politics. *Social Research, 52*(4), 817–868.

Parkins, W. (1997). Taking Liberty's, breaking windows: Fashion, protest and the suffragette public. *Continuum: Journal of Media & Cultural Studies, 11*(3), 37–46. https://doi.org/10.1080/10304319709359451

Piccato, P. (2010). Public sphere in Latin America: A map of the historiography. *Social History, 35*(2), 165–192.

Porter, N. B. (2018). Ending harassment by starting with retaliation. *Stanford Law Review Online, 71*, 41–61.

Rodino-Colocino, M. (2018). Me too,# MeToo: Countering cruelty with empathy. *Communication and Critical/Cultural Studies, 15*(1), 96–100.

Salter, L. (2013). Democracy, new social movements, and the Internet: A Habermasian analysis. In *Cyberactivism* (pp. 127–154). Routledge.

Sarachild, K. (1978). Consciousness-raising: A radical weapon. In *Feminist revolution* (pp. 144–50). Random House.

Scott, A. (1990). *Ideology and the new social movements.* Unwin Hyman.

Sowards, S. K., & Renegar, V. R. (2004). The rhetorical functions of consciousness-raising in third wave feminism. *Communication Studies, 55*(4), 535–552.

Tierney, T. (2013). *The public space of social media: Connected cultures of the network society.* Taylor & Francis.

Vessey, D. (2021). Words as well as deeds: The popular press and suffragette hunger strikes in Edwardian Britain. *Twentieth Century British History, 32*(1), 68–92.

Whittier, N. (1995). *Feminist generations: The persistence of the radical women's movement.* Temple University Press.

Zarkov, D., & Davis, K. (2018). Ambiguities and dilemmas around# MeToo:# ForHow long and# WhereTo? *European Journal of Women's Studies, 25*(1), 3–9.

2

AMBIGUOUS SPACES

#MeToo in the Digital Realm

Jennifer Lundquist and Kaitlynn Mendes

> Posting a hashtag is easy. It is putting your own vulnerability out there in public that is hard.
>
> (#MeToo Participant cited in Mendes and Ringrose 2019)

The Power of Digital Technologies

In recent years, scholars have noted the power of digital technologies in fostering social change—from the Arab Spring uprisings to anti-capitalist, LGBTQ+, anti-colonialism, and feminist movements (see Brown et al., 2017; Gerbaudo, 2012; Jackson et al., 2020; Mendes et al., 2019; Raynauld et al., 2018). There is ample evidence of the ways digital technologies have been empowering, particularly for marginalized groups. In the context of feminist activism, digital technologies have enabled consciousness-raising and developed a new language to understand oppressive and patriarchal social practices, becoming a space for discursive activism in which people's minds are changed about feminist issues (Clark-Parsons, 2022; Dey, 2018; Mendes, 2015; Mendes et al., 2019; Shaw, 2012). Despite these promises, digital technologies have also facilitated trolling, hateful comments, rape and death threats, and much more misogyny (see Jane, 2016) that breeches the boundaries of digital spaces and traverses to offline contexts (see Regehr, 2022).

Research shows how this *technology-facilitated* (Powell & Henry, 2017) abuse and misogyny has significant consequences for many groups, including activists and those identifying as women or fem-presenting—terrifying, censoring, and silencing them (see Ging & Siapera, 2018; Loewen Walker,

DOI: 10.4324/9781003300953-3

2022; Mendes et al., 2019). One of the less appreciated—and more controversial—legacies of movements such as #MeToo and others that came before it (see Loney-Howes et al., 2021), as this book shows, is the way these movements have broadened the way we think about sexual violence and harassment. Despite its initial focus on harassment in the workplace, as the #MeToo movement went mainstream a significant shift occurred in public debates regarding misogyny occurring *outside* the physical bounds of the workplace (Durham, 2021). These conversations extend to spaces with unclear boundaries demarcating the private from the public and the professional from the personal. In this chapter, we define online spaces as ambiguous spaces for harassment, focusing specifically on online comments sections, social media, Internet dating, and gaming platforms. By harassment, we mean abusive, hateful, and/or sexualizing commentary or threats. Harassment is often obscured in online spaces because such spaces are viewed by much of the public as a less authentic, or a less *real*, experience than face-to-face interactions. Operating between and outside of familiar physical institutions, such as the workplace and school or social networks of one's community or friend groups, online spaces lack formally and informally defined cultural norms and have little to no accountability mechanisms in place.

The Internet plays a major role in our everyday work and personal lives. Across the globe, people spend an average of almost seven hours a day on the Internet, 2.5 hours of which are spent on social media (Statistica, 2023a, 2023b). Boundaries delineating online activity between the private/public and personal/work divide on social media are increasingly porous. Some occupations that operate entirely online make this distinction especially challenging, ranging from social media influencing to content creation and professional gaming. Journalists and writers routinely rely on social media to distribute their intellectual work and receive feedback. Universities encourage their faculty to engage the public in their scholarship; as such, the use of academic "altmetrics," the measurement of scholarly impact based on online attention, is a growing way to assess such public engagement (Arroyo-Machado & Torres-Salinas, 2023). Moreover, the workplace is an increasingly hybridized location, with the average firm or business having a web and social media presence, increasing variation in virtual work norms, and employees using personal social media to enhance their professional standing and connection with others in their field. Although social media is commonly thought to be used primarily to communicate non-work personal and political opinions and updates, one study found that almost 40% of posts on private X accounts were work-related (Van Zoonen et al., 2016). This blurred relationship also goes in the other direction, with up to 70% of employers using social media to screen potential hires (HBR, 2021). Furthermore, workplace colleagues commonly "friend" or follow one another on private social media accounts (Leonardi & Vaast, 2017), which may reveal personal information and unvarnished disclosures that spill beyond the typical boundaries of workplace settings. Social media has introduced the dilemma of "context collapse," in which self-presentation becomes more challenging before an undifferentiated audience made up of friends, colleagues, acquaintances, and family (Marwick & Boyd, 2011).

With a focus on harassment in online ambiguous spaces, the chapter unfolds as follows. We begin by laying out research showing the ubiquity of online gendered and sexual harassment (SH) in general before delving into how it manifests across the following spaces: online comments sections, social media, online dating, and video gaming. We end the chapter with thoughts on what steps need to be taken to create safer, more equitable spaces that are free from harassment.

Sexual Violence, Harassment, and Misogyny in Digital Spaces

An example of how the #MeToo movement began to move outside the boundaries of the workplace and into less clear-cut interactions outside of sexual assault was the viral account of Aziz Ansari's behavior during a date, published on babe.net (see also Durham, 2021). This story sparked mainstream discussions about male entitlement and predatory behaviors in intimate relations that were previously seen as normative masculine behaviors (Gunnarsson, 2018). We argue that #MeToo not only has enabled a new contextual and spatial shift in the way we think critically about SH and misogyny but is also raising awareness of how digital technologies facilitate these outcomes.

As our digital sphere continues to expand, we have moved into a *post-digital* age, in which "the divide between the digital and non-digital is no longer binary and oppositional" (Jordan, 2019, p. 1). Misogynistic harassment has extended beyond face-to-face encounters and proliferated unabated in women's online public and online private lives. #MeToo's very identity as a digital movement starting in 2006 on Myspace and then going viral on X (formerly Twitter)[1] in 2017, and the (digital) backlash that followed, primes us to make this leap (see also Chapter 1). One of the strengths of the #MeToo movement is that it has allowed us to begin asking how much it matters *where* misogynistic harassment takes place, whether on the factory line, a video date, or one's social media feed. While sexual discrimination in the workplace has very real implications for women's career advancement and economic equality, sexual discrimination outside of the workplace also has material consequences for women's equal participation in the public sphere and their overall wellbeing as citizens and individuals. Furthermore, outside the workplace, there is little in the way of discrimination protection or legal recourse, and the blurred online boundaries of professional relationships between what is work and what is not has made adjudicating even work-related harassment challenging. The Internet is often heralded as being more accessible and liberating for disadvantaged voices. This belief ignores a flourishing online culture that polices and silences some individuals' expression on these channels more than others, often based on intersecting identity characteristics. Two factors, anonymity and the online disinhibition effect, which empowers people to impulsively say things online they would not otherwise say face to face, hasten the prevalence of online harassment (see Lai & Tsai, 2016; Suler, 2004). For women and girls, online harassment is typically focused on their gender characteristics (Dunn, 2020; Jane, 2016; Loewen Walker, 2022; Henry & Powell, 2016). Nearly half of Americans have experienced online harassment, with 83% of women ages 18–29 recognizing it as a major problem, compared to 55% of men in the same age group (Duggan, 2017). Young adult women in the United States report online SH at more than three times that reported by young men (Ibid.). These networked instances of SH often include comments about their bodies and appearance, lewd references, and gendered insults and abuse. An Amnesty International (2017) report finds that 27% of women users who experienced misogynistic abuse received physical or sexual assault threats. And while it is common to tell victims to simply disconnect, digital technologies and online spaces have become so integrated in our daily lives that it is more of a basic public utility, like telephone service—one, however, that is run by unregulated for-profit companies with no obligation for social responsibility.

Technology-facilitated abuse spans from repeat ad hominem personal and identity-based attacks, the sending of explicit content without consent, doxxing (posting addresses and private data), and other direct threats of physical harm. Online misogynistic harassment occurs most commonly via social media, but notably also in article comments sections and web fora, gaming platforms, online dating, and more. Indeed, 47% of women worldwide report experiencing misogynistic online comments directed against them, and 26% report experiencing online sexual or physical threats against them (Amnesty International, 2017). These comments and threats have become normal, everyday experiences for many women as they use digital technologies in their personal lives. These occurrences also constitute a professional issue given the boundary-blurring facets of modern digital life, with many people's work identities expanding to include roles as public intellectuals and expectations that they post work-related products and events on social media and other fora. This is the case for broadcasters, journalists, academics, and many more.

The Ubiquity and Ambiguity of Harassment

Perhaps because it is so routine, many people around the world don't see online harassment as a problem (see Ging & da Silva, 2022). In a Pew survey (2017), 73% of men ages 18–29 believe people take online harassment too seriously, compared to 49% of same-age women respondents. This is likely because the ambiguity of its virtual nature makes online harassment seem less real. But it is real for its victims. An Amnesty International survey (2017) shows that 55% of women who reported online harassment said it caused them stress, anxiety, or panic attacks, and 36% said they feared for their physical safety as a result. Loewen Walker (2022, p. 5) writes that misogyny is affective and "lingers in the body; it haunts us long after impact." This statement rings true regardless of its online or offline origins.

In interviews with women about their experiences of online SH and abuse, Sarah Sobieraj (2020) identifies online misogyny as a threat to democracy, an often-successful attempt to silence and discredit women who use their voices to speak publicly. Attacks are most vicious against women who speak out against sexist and/or racist treatment and who challenge norms in male-dominated online spaces (see Chapter 8). Misogynoir, the intersecting oppressions of both race and gender, is prevalent online, with Black women's online presence frequently questioned and challenged (Bailey, 2021).

Some forms of technology-facilitated harassment, particularly those presenting clear and tangible physical threats, are increasingly recognized as cyberstalking, cyberharassment, or cyberbullying by many US states and nations and can carry the same legal penalty as in-person stalking and harassment (see Cyberbullying Research Centre, n.d; Hosani et al., 2019). However, most online threats are disembodied—anonymous and untraceable—presenting jurisdictional challenges when the perpetrator and target are located in different state or national contexts (see Dunn, 2020). Even when the perpetrator is identifiable, general threats of sexual and physical violence without details on the where and when do not rise to a legal security concern (see Adorjan et al., 2022; Dodge & Spencer, 2018; Mendes & Jeong, 2023). Much abusive technology-facilitated harassment consists instead of hateful language and name-calling, which is often protected under free speech laws. Because misogynistic harassment happens at a distance, it is often dismissed as what women must expect when they "put themselves out there" online. Calls to "ignore the trolls" and "grow a thicker skin" indicate widespread acceptance both of the ubiquity and the ambiguous context of online abuse. But the digital sphere is not divorced from real life; in modernity, the two bleed into one another (Cramer, 2015). Nathan Jurgenson (2011) calls this false assumption of separateness "digital dualism." We call for a *postdigital* way of thinking that "allows for that previously coded as 'digital' to be woven into the wider discussion of social dialects" (Cormier et al., 2019, p. 478).

Pointing to the tendency to trivialize, victim-blame, individualize, and otherwise accept online abuse as inevitable, Sobieraj (2020) draws a connection between online harassment and rape culture. Indeed, it is telling that although the gunman, who in May 2022 killed 19 children in Uvalde, Texas, had a history on social media of sexually aggressive messaging and threats of rape and sexual assault, many of his victims did not think his behavior stood out from the usual angry misogyny they encountered every day, with one teen explaining that's just "how online is" (Foster-Frau et al., 2022; see also Regehr, 2022).

How have people grappled with the growing toxicity of their online lives? Some grassroots efforts have arisen to fill the void by offering support to people experiencing online abuse and harassment.[2] Individuals sometimes also attempt to challenge online bystander effect norms by reacting to online abuse when they see it, also known as bystander intervention (Latané & Darley, 1970; see also Chapter 3). In a 2017 Pew Hispanic survey, 30% of respondents reported engaging in bystander efforts, most often by responding to the attacker directly, flagging or reporting the content, or offering support to the victim. In digital spaces, research shows that younger people and those with higher empathy and family support are most likely to intervene (Herry et al., 2021; Markey, 2000; Van Cleemput et al., 2014), but more research is still needed in this area.

Online Comments Sections

One seemingly benign area of digital life that is now widely seen as problematic are comments sections in news and other websites (see Gardiner, 2018; Harmer & Lewis, 2022). While originally considered an admirable innovation in allowing important issues of the day to be democratically discussed and debated (Papacharissi, 2002), in practice, comments sections commonly devolve into misogynistic and abusive spaces (Electronic Frontier Foundation, n.d.). Such behaviors would not be tolerated in town halls and community meetings, but online comments sections represent an in-between space, one of ambiguity. Platform after platform, from Reuters to National Public Radio have disbanded comments sections altogether due to unregulated sexist and hateful behavior. Indeed, it has become a cliché among publicly engaged academics to warn their colleagues and mentees, "Just don't read the comments."

The *New York Times* is one of the most notable holdouts on this practice. However, the resources needed for AI and human moderation to weed out the invective requires *NYT* to limit the number of articles it can open for comment. Despite its heavy moderation, as well as other effective interventions, such as requiring a log-in and public identity, abuse flagging options, and highlighting posts earning *NYT* 'Picks status,' moderator Marie Tessier (2021) laments that significantly fewer women than men post comments there. Although online comments on news have become a primary form of political discourse in the twenty-first century, online antagonism against women across the Internet has led to the silencing of women's voices even in these theoretically empowering spaces.

Publications like *The Conversation*, founded in Australia in 2011 but with an international reach, have employed similar tactics—only opening a small percentage of articles for comments. This is due to a 2020 decision by the High Court of Australia, which placed responsibility for comments on the publication or platform where they appear. Placing a greater onus on corporations to keep their spaces safe has meant increased investment in moderation. While abusive comments are less likely to pass muster, it also means there are fewer chances for the public to weigh in on issues. This is a trade-off in establishing safer and abuse-free spaces that society will likely continue to debate into the future.

Social Media

Social media is another ambiguous space that lacks agreed upon user norms and accountability mechanisms found in organizations and operating informally in smaller social networks. As a result, the social media environment is an especially toxic space for women (Jane, 2016; Jurgenson, 2011). In the United States, hate speech is legally protected under constitutional First Amendment free-speech rights; however, social media operate on private platforms, which are free to create their own rules and policies. Until very recently, US corporations have had little incentive to enforce behavioral norms on their platforms because Section 230 of the 1996 Communications Decency Act (CDA) protects them from being held legally responsible for the behaviors and speech of their users (Electronic Frontier Foundation, n.d.). This is in contrast to the ruling in Australia noted earlier, showing diversity in how nations conceptualize and operationalize the right to free speech versus protecting people from abuse. Moreover, in a political economy where social media companies encourage "clicks" and engagement, toxic and abusive behaviors online are not only accepted but profitable (Shepherd et al., 2015).

But in 2017 after #MeToo went viral, then Twitter publicized a new policy that, for the first time, expressly condemned nonconsensual SH, such as sexual objectification of other users, the sending of unwanted sexual imagery, unwanted sexual textual content, and so forth (X Blog, 2017).[3] Increasing evidence about the power of social media mis/disinformation to threaten democracy and public health is also changing the seriousness with which the public views the influence of social media from one of ambiguity to clear alarm bells (Pew, 2020). In response, many platforms have developed more robust community guidelines and codes of conduct explicitly condemning hate speech and disinformation (see Bateman et al., 2021). By extension, online misogyny on these platforms has also been increasingly acknowledged as a problem to be addressed.

Beginning about a decade ago and picking up steam during the #MeToo movement, social media platforms almost universally introduced features allowing users to report and flag problematic content, warn violators, remove posts, and suspend or even deplatform accounts.[4] One example of an in-house fix is an Instagram tool, Hidden Words. Introduced in 2021, if turned on, this feature can automatically filter direct message (DM) requests that contain offensive words, phrases, and emojis. However, it is difficult to know how effective such sanctions are against harassing behaviors given that Instagram does not release related data. Data-based analyses indicate that far more material that should be censored escapes screening (Angwin & Grassegger, 2017). In any case, many such new-found screening and anti-harassment policies adopted by platforms over the last decade are now being reversed. At the time this book went to press, Meta, following X, had begun rolling back its hateful conduct policies and moderation standards in anticipation of the second Trump term (Ortutay, 2025). The Center for Countering Digital Hate, a watchdog organization partnering with platform users to collect data on their online experiences, employs teams to report abusive posts to track what sort of action, if any, platforms take. In one study of the X platform following the passage of an anti-LGBTQ+ bill in Florida, a large majority of related posts violating X's hateful conduct policy faced no consequence (CCDH, 2022b). In another study of Meta's Instagram (which also owns Facebook and WhatsApp), the organization worked with prominent women in the media, such as American Actress Amber Heard, and found that despite Instagram's (2021) pledge to also apply its anti-harassment protocols to private messages (DMs), the platform failed to act on 90% of sexually harassing and sexually abusive messages sent to the study participants (CCDH, 2022a).

Even if abusive treatment happens less often than supportive or neutral interactions online, these experiences accumulate daily given that online interactions are such an integral part of women's everyday lives (see Chapter 7). In Canada and the United States, large majorities of the public use social media (Statistica, 2022; Auxier & Anderson, 2021). Larger proportions of women than men use TikTok, Facebook, Instagram, Nextdoor, and Snapchat, while about equal numbers of men and women use X and YouTube. Majorities of social media users report visiting social media sites at least once a day (Auxier & Anderson, 2021). And yet, normalized abuse on these channels alters the way women are able to participate. Thirty-two percent of women who had experienced online abuse stopped posting their opinions on specific issues (Amnesty, 2017). Most reported unease in subsequently engaging with social media. This is a problem when social media and digital technologies are used in daily life for leisure and socializing, work, education, and more in our increasingly digital landscape.

Online Dating

The harassment that occurs on comments sections and social media platforms is very public; however, dating platforms are less visible online platforms that are nevertheless notorious for SH. While harassment is more privatized, occurring in digital conversations among two people, dating sites also blur the distinction between private and public in that the dating profiles, which can contain very private information, are often available for large numbers of people to view.

Unlike traditional dating markets where couples meet through known social networks, dating sites bring together strangers with potentially intimate aims. The Aziz Ansari #MeToo controversy in early 2018 brought a critical eye to heterosexual intimate interactions that fall outside of clear abuse and threats. It triggered mainstream conversation around why male aggression, coercion, and entitlement are so often normalized in the dating world.

As of 2013, online dating sites became the single most common way straight couples meet (Rosenfeld et al., 2019), and the pandemic drove those numbers even higher, bringing singles who had never used online dating sites before into the fold (Curington & Lundquist, 2021). While misogyny and sexism are key issues on these sites, it's important not to forget the ways this violence and abuse interconnects with other identity characteristics. For example, the term "digital sexual racism" was coined to describe the ways that fast-evolving digital dating technologies interact with and intensify forms of intersectional sexism and racism (Curington et al., 2021). Online platforms can foster the expression of aggressive and direct forms of sexual racism that occur much more often than in face-to-face courtship markets due to the combined effects of (a) more people of differing backgrounds coming into contact with one another online than offline; (b) the online disinhibition effect; and (c) the dehumanizing effects of mass online dating markets.

The vast majority of women report experiencing abusive interactions on dating sites on a regular basis (Curington & Lundquist, 2021). In a review of studies to date, 57% to 89% of daters report at least one instance of harassment on dating apps (Gewirtz-Meydan et al., 2023). Because of the immense scale of potentially hundreds of online interactions in a short period, even a minority of abhorrent messages can still feel like a jarring blitz. One dater described the process with a sense of resignation:

> [F]irst they start like "hi very beautiful girl" or something like that. . . . And then they'll want to maybe get explicit pictures . . . and you don't respond . . . They get angry and send you a bunch of threatening messages . . . like hi, hi, hi. They'll keep on spamming you. And they'll be like, "Oh, hello are you there?" Then it'll be like, "Oh, dumb bitch. Oh, stupid bitch." And they'll go, "I hope you get raped." Things like that.

Another woman recounted being stalked by a dater across the digital ecosphere on multiple other platforms after she blocked him on the dating app. Women of color have the unique disadvantage of being subjected to an added layer of intersectional harassment, experiencing both racialized and gendered objectification from men whose inner prejudices often flourish in a disassociated online space (see Chapters 8 and 9). As one woman of color interviewee summed up dating online: "It's a lot of men just being like . . . 'I just want to degrade you.'" (Curington et al., 2021; see also Loewen Walker, 2022).

The experience of harassment on dating apps is so prevalent that several social media pages have been established to both highlight this as an issue and "talk back" (hooks, 1989) to the online harassment and misogyny that women experience (Tweten, 2018; Shaw, 2016). Sites like @ByeFelipe and Fedoras of OkCupid where people share harassing experiences exemplify strategies of digital feminist resistance in response to online harassment and misogyny. These forms of "discursive activism" (Shaw, 2016) intervene at the level of speech and enable women to see these actions as structural and political rather than personal. However, it was not until #MeToo that many dating platforms rushed to create community guidelines, reporting, flagging options, and penalties for those who violate the terms. As an example, OkCupid has the most extensive sections on harassment behaviors and consent among dating platforms, in which they state:

> We expect everyone on OkCupid to treat each other respectfully, with kindness and compassion. We do not tolerate hateful, hurtful, or harassing content on OkCupid. We consider unwanted sexual content and messages to be sexual harassment. . . . Exposing other people to your sexual fantasies without their consent is rude and inappropriate, and it's not what most people on OkCupid are looking for.
>
> *(OkCupid, 2022a)*

Notably, the platform stands out in its attention to consent. OkCupid has a guide on affirmative consent, educating users on its definition and providing examples and best practices. For example, the platform asks, "How good are you at hearing 'No'? Does being turned down make you visibly upset or angry? If so, keep in mind that this can make the other person feel unsafe. Practice responding in a kind and easygoing way" (OkCupid, 2022b). These interventions are direct indications of a significant societal shift in recognizing and problematizing toxic masculinities as a form of SH.

Newly introduced interventions range from the seemingly ineffective—that is, "reactions" emojis for daters to respond to annoying messages, like eye rolling and a drink thrown in the face—to ones with more teeth. Some platforms cut daters off after contacting a match multiple times without a response, while others try to interrupt bad behavior, such as sending a pop-up warning to daters that their match may find the message they are about to send offensive. In the last case, data shows that inappropriate messages were reduced by 10% after an offender saw the pop-up (Lovine, 2021).

Like social media, most dating platforms give users the option to block others and report harassing behaviors. Some platforms use AI to detect inappropriate language, inviting recipients to file a report. When reported behavior is found to violate guidelines, platforms will ban the violator from the platform. Like with social media, this is an invisible process to the public. It is difficult to know how often membership termination happens, as platforms have little incentive to publicly acknowledge harassment ban rates for fear of losing clientele. However, one app, Stroovy, recognized this vacuum and provides a peer-rating system of daters sourced across dating platforms (Bell, 2016). Other dating apps have adopted features allowing women to leave public reviews directly on men's profiles (Urwin, 2016; White, 2016) to incentivize users to stay "civil." Some women have migrated to more woman-centered platforms. Bumble, for example, is often celebrated as a "feminist" dating app that allegedly attracts fewer misogynists because it requires women to initiate the dating interaction and has enhanced privacy features, such as hiding a user's name, photo verification, and rapid reporting (Prokopets, 2022). Yet, since companies do not release data to the public, many question how much safer these apps are (Suddath, 2020). Recently working with the Rape, Abuse & Incest National Network (RAINN), Tinder has added trauma-informed processes to its reporting procedure, allowing users more agency over how the reporting happens and recommending contacting local authorities if required (Thompson, 2022).

Despite widespread complaints about the misogyny and abuse in online dating, many women say they will nevertheless put up with it over the risks inherent in meeting drunk at a party or out at a bar (Lundquist & Curington, 2019). There is also evidence that #MeToo has made some meaningful impact on the way daters conduct themselves. A 2019 Match.com survey of singles found that 40% of men report that the #MeToo movement has caused them to become more cautious and reserved at work, 34% on dates, and 28% on their social media (Garcia, 2019).

Video Gaming

Video gaming is another ambiguous space where pervasive misogynistic abuse is prevalent but largely accepted as part of the user experience. Fifty-nine percent of women in China, Germany, and the United States say they intentionally hide their gender while gaming online; 77% of the women said they had experienced SH while playing games online, including misogynistic comments about their video gaming ability as well as exclusionary, gatekeeping commentary and abusive comments (Sinclair, 2021). In another survey, 10% of women gamers reported rape threats (Valentine, 2018). Although online gaming is still considered to be a largely male domain, 45% of video gamers are women (Clement, 2022). Taken together, large majorities of women are experiencing abuse while simply seeking leisure and relaxation in their private lives. Yet the ambiguity of the space makes it easy for the gaming community to dismiss threats and abuse as not real, just as the battle arenas of gameplay are not real.

Despite the large female audience, 76% of game designers are men, most games target a male audience, and 80% of video game characters are male-presenting (Ellington, 2021; Input, 2022). When women participate in these spaces, sexist treatment is the norm; when women push back against this treatment, hostility toward them is incandescent (see Cote, 2017; Salter & Blodgett, 2012). Anita Sarkeesian, a video game and media critic who frequently comments on the depiction of women in popular culture, experienced this when she pointed out sexist themes in the gaming community with her series Tropes vs. Women in Video Games. Her critique in 2012 unleashed Gamergate, an intense and abusive hate campaign organized by toxic online men's groups with ties to profoundly anti-feminist internet communities.[5] Leaving no doubt as to the depth of the misogyny Sarkeesian was highlighting, those who dared to speak out in Sarkeesian's defense were subjected to relentless rape and death threats, swatting, doxxing, and public shaming that went on for years with little response or condemnation from the gaming community. Given this backdrop, it is not surprising that women gamers often feel unwelcome (McLean & Griffiths, 2019). Hotlines specifically for gamers dealing with harassment, such as Feminist Frequency's Games and Online Harassment Hotline, provide emotional support for what is a notoriously toxic environment for women gamers.

In a viral tweet showing a recording of a typical reaction when she revealed her voice during a multiplayer game, the woman streamer Annemunition was called vile slurs and told to "kill herself" for doing nothing more than existing as a woman in these spaces (Grayson, 2018). Although we have focused so far on gaming as a leisure pursuit, Annemunition's experience calls attention to the fact that gaming is not just a hostile space for leisure but also a hostile place of work. Her experience is confirmed by experimental research that alternated neutral comments in female and male voices during gameplay; female voices elicited three times as much abuse (Kuznekoff & Rose, 2013). It is common for women to seek out advice from other women gamers and develop strategies on how to pursue their hobby in the face of so much online hate (see Cote, 2017; McLean & Griffiths, 2019). The Reddit group Girl Gamers, for example, has a thread asking how other gamers cope with constant online harassment. The main piece of advice gamers give one another is to essentially silence themselves if they want to be able to participate fully (Reddit, 2022). Strategies for self-censorship range from muting so that people do not know they are women (a disadvantage since teams need to communicate and collaborate), purchasing a voice changer, using a male or gender-neutral avatar, or limiting themselves to single-player games. Research on multiplayer online games (with primarily male samples) shows significant psychosocial benefits to online group engagement and game interaction (Kaye et al., 2017). Women are less able to benefit in the same way from these activities.

Like social media and dating platforms, game streaming platforms began adopting anti-harassment community guidelines and terms of service policies in the aftermath of #MeToo. In 2018, Amazon's Twitch, one of the largest streaming video game platforms, adopted policies prohibiting harassment that could lead to account suspension and removal. However, as with the other platforms already discussed, it is unclear how well these policies are enforced, especially when so many users are able to simply adopt new accounts under anonymous identities.

What steps can be taken to improve these spaces for women? Women's representation among game designers and promoters to match the demographics of their participants would be a good start. Gaming industry executives largely escaped #MeToo accountability at the time, perhaps in part because of the wake of fear Gamergate activists inflicted on women in the industry. More recently, however, the industry has been experiencing its own #MeToo moment with allegations on X and a lawsuit uncovering rampant misogynistic and discriminatory behavior toward women (Browning & Isaac, 2021; Lorenz & Kellen, 2021). These events may help begin to dismantle the strong currents of misogyny that course through the gaming world.

Conclusion and Future Research Topics

While acknowledging the important ways #MeToo has raised consciousness around sexual violence and led to legal, cultural, and policy changes, this chapter surveys the extent of online harassment and misogyny in ambiguous online spaces. We have highlighted some efforts to curb the abuse directed toward women, but as we enter the second Trump administration, it will be a long road ahead. The Global Partnership for Action on Gender-Based Online Harassment and Abuse has been a hopeful sign of change, bringing together Australia, Denmark, Sweden, Korea, the United Kingdom, and the United States to better understand technology-facilitated gender-based violence and develop domestic and international interventions (U.S. Dept. of State, 2023). Looking to the future, we outline what we would like to see change and what new research and knowledge we think it will take to get us there.

Many of the important changes made by digital platforms in response to #MeToo are proving to be ephemeral. We should dispense with expectations that platforms and social media companies will enact profound changes on their own accord. Political economists such as José van Dick (2013) have written about how all online interactions—positive or not—are profitable for social media companies, and that the drive to create more interactions undergirds their business models. As such, it is naive to expect any private corporation, which is mandated to generate profit for its shareholders, to prioritize social well-being over profit. Existing laws protect this structure. Alternative networked spaces known as "citizens'" social media (see Gehl, 2015, 2022; Rodriguez, 2001), those that are not imbued with or connected to capital, present a promising alternative to the corporate social media that dominates our media landscape. This might mean, for example, applying the model of publicly funded media already used in radio and television (think BBC, NPR, PBS, etc.) to the

Internet. It also means the development of small private nonprofit plat-forms that organize themselves around a set of nonmonetary principles and serve a variety of communities. One example is Mastodon, whose motto is, "Your home feed should be filled with what matters to you most, not what a corporation thinks you should see. Radically differ-ent social media, back in the hands of the people" (Mastodon, 2022). Such platforms are locally moderated and allow users to choose their server according to the degree of code of conduct management and user terms. Alternative social media allows users to share content and connect with one another while denying the commercialization of their speech, allowing users to radically experiment with surveillance models (Gehl, 2015). As Ethan Zuckerman notes, "Facebook and Twitter can be such unpleasant places because strong emotions lead to high engagement, and engagement sells ads. Engineer a different social network around dif-ferent principles, and it's possible that the deliberation and debate we might hope from a digital public sphere could happen within a platform" (Zuckerman, 2018). Yet, while these alternative platforms sound prom-ising, empirical evidence is needed to assess what sorts of models and designs will make material changes. Some scholars have started exploring this (see Mannell & Smith, 2022; Zulli et al., 2020), but it is too soon to draw firm conclusions.

While encouraging the growth of public digital media platforms offers great potential, all digital spaces, monetized or not, operate within a patri-archal system. Cultural change is slow. Regulation is an important inter-vention that speeds the pace of change. Regulation must hold corporations responsible by requiring user guidelines and enforcing them effectively, otherwise facing fines and legal sanction, and provide algorithmic and pol-icy transparency to the public. In the United States, where platforms enjoy blanket immunity protecting them from content risk under the 1996 CDA, there is no legislation to this effect. As a result, the Internet has become a veritable digital Wild West given how many of the largest platforms oper-ate from the United States. However, change is underway.

The EU's landmark 2022 Digital Services Act will require Big Tech to take action against the posting of illegal or harmful content on their plat-forms, including cyberviolence against women, and increase transparency in how their platforms operate. Such action is likely to impact even coun-tries that lack regulatory oversight, as it will be most efficient for multina-tional corporations to implement compliance policies universally. In the interim, while there is widespread variation in how platforms are regulated across the world, it is an opportune time to collect cross-national data to evaluate the before and after regulatory impacts on the problems we have outlined in this chapter. Equipping policymakers with evidence-based research about the nature and scope of this problem is one tool that could be used as a lever to push for radical change.

Another potential area of research is better understanding whether and how digital SH spills into face-to-face behaviors. Are people who engage in digital SH also likely to be in-person harassers? Is such a relationship causal or associative? In reference to workplace harassment scholarship, one might ask how work-related digital technologies, such as Microsoft Teams or company social media groups, might intensify and layer SH already occurring at the office (see Chapter 6).

Furthermore, given the need for cultural change, there are potentially compelling research opportunities to study Bystander Effects in a digital context (see Chapter 3). How can people deploy bystander behavior in an online context, and do the most effective strategies for in-person action differ for online action? We recommend that best practices be tested and developed for such scenarios with an eye toward disseminating norms to the public on how to be good digital citizens.

In our constantly changing digital environment, progress will also require dynamism and flexibility to respond to the challenges ahead. For example, the Metaverse, a 3D digital world that Meta describes as a place where people play, work, learn, socialize, and shop, one that will "help you connect with people when you aren't physically in the same place and get us even closer to that feeling of being together in person." What does that "feeling of being together in person" mean in the context of the widespread online sexual abuse and misogyny that we have documented throughout these pages? As our day-to-day existence moves more fully into this fourth dimension, these issues are likely to worsen. Indeed, it is when platforms first emerge that they are often the least safe. As such, scholars must continue to study these ambiguous spaces with the understanding that what separates the online and offline worlds is no longer a bright line but rather an increasingly blurred, ambiguous one, making online harassment and misogyny as urgent and as tangible there as anywhere else.

Notes

1 We refer to Twitter as X henceforth.
2 In the United States, some examples of nongovernmental organizations among many are Crash Override, Heartmob, and Block Party, while Canada has Cyberscan, which supports victims of online harassment.
3 These guidelines are still in place upon the transition from Twitter to X, although they have been redefined. The Center for Countering Digital Hate (CCDH) has documented a rise in hate speech on X, however, which appears to be correlated to the platform's changes in content moderation policies and reduced oversight. www.nytimes.com/2023/10/27/technology/elon–musk-twitter-year.html and https://counterhate.com/topic/twitter/

4 There has been a backlash to deplatforming and censorship efforts by social media companies due to concerns about free speech. As of this writing, a series of lawsuits are suing the US federal government for its collaboration with social media platforms to moderate COVID mis/disinformation and over the removal of Trump from Twitter after January 6, 2021. Some US states have forbidden social media companies from banning users for their speech, and some disinformation scholars are being sued by Elon Musk as a "scare campaign to drive away advertisers."
5 For example, Reddit and 4chan/8chan are imageboard websites characterized by their anonymity and the controversies associated with their content, such as far-right extremism, violent images, child pornography, misinformation, and origins of conspiracy theories.

References

Adorjan, M., Ricciardelli, R., & Huey, L. (2022). "Facebook is the devil": Exploring officer perceptions of cyber-based harms facing youth in rural and remote communities. *International Journal of Rural Criminology, 7*(1), 71–95.

Amnesty International. (2017, November 7). Social media can be a dangerous place for UK women. *Amnesty International.* www.amnesty.org.uk/files/Resources/Online-abuse-briefing.pdf

Angwin, J., & Grassegger, H. (2017, June 28). Facebook's secret censorship rules protect White men from hate speech but not Black children. *ProPublica.* www.propublica.org/article/facebook-hate-speech-censorship-internal-documentsalgorithms

Arroyo-Machado, W., & Torres-Salinas, D. (2023). Evaluative altmetrics: Is there evidence for its application to research evaluation? *Frontiers in Research Metrics and Analytics, 8.*

Auxier, B., & Anderson, M. (2021, April 7). Social media use in 2021. *Pew Hispanic Research Center.* www.pewresearch.org/internet/2021/04/07/social-media-use-in-2021/

Bailey, M. (2021). Misogynoir transformed: Black women's digital resistance. *New York University Press.* https://nyupress.org/9781479865109/misogynoir-transformed/

Bateman, J., Thompson, N., & Smith, V. (2021, April 1). How social media platforms' community standards address influence operations. *Carnegie Endowment for International Peace.* https://carnegieendowment.org/2021/04/01/how-social-media-platforms-community-standards-address-influence-operations-pub-84201

Bell, K. (2016, May 4). There's another app for rating people—if they're using dating sites. *Mashable.* https://mashable.com/article/stroovy-app

Brown, M., Ray, R., Summers, E., & Fraistat, N. (2017). # SayHerName: A case study of intersectional social media activism. *Ethnic and Racial Studies, 40*(11), 1831–1846.

Browning, K., & Isaac, M. (2021). Activision, facing internal turmoil, grapples with #MeToo reckoning. *The New York Times.* www.nytimes.com/2021/07/29/technology/activision-walkout-metoo-call-of-duty.html

Center for Countering Digital Hate. (2022a, April 6). *Hidden hate: How Instagram fails to act on 9 in 10 reports of misogyny in DMs.* https://counterhate.com/research/hidden-hate/

Center for Countering Digital Hate. (2022b, August 10). *Digital hate: Social media's role in amplifying dangerous lies about LGBTQ+ people.* https://counterhate.com/research/hidden-hate/

Clark-Parsons, R. (2022). *Networked feminism: How digital media makers transformed gender justice movements.* University of California Press. www.ucpress.edu/book/9780520383845/networked-feminism

Clement, J. (2022). Distribution of video gamers in the United States from 2006 to 2022, by gender. *Statista*. www.statista.com/statistics/232383/gender-split-of-us-computer-and-video-gamers/#:~:text=U.S.%20video%20gaming%20audiences%202006%2D2021%2C%20by%20gender&text=In%202021%2C%20women%20accounted%20for,women%20during%20the%20previous%20year

Cormier, D., Jandrić, P., Childs, M., Hall, R., White, D., Phipps, L., Truelve, I., Hayes, S., & Fawns, T. (2019). Ten years of the postdigital in the 52group: Reflections and developments 2009–2019. *Postdigital Science and Education*, 1(2), 475–506.

Cote, A. C. (2017). "I can defend myself" women's strategies for coping with harassment while gaming online. *Games and Culture*, 12(2), 136–155.

Cramer, F. (2015). What is 'post-digital'? In *Postdigital aesthetics* (pp. 12–26). Palgrave Macmillan.

Curington, C., & Lundquist, J. (2021). *Challenging, internalizing and transforming gendered courtship norms in online dating*. ASA 2021 Online Conference. American Sociological Association. https://convention2.allacademic.com/one/asa/asa21/

Curington, C. V., Lundquist, J. H., & Lin, K. H. (2021). *The dating divide: Race and desire in the era of online romance*. University of California Press. www.ucpress.edu/book/9780520293458/the-dating-divide

Cyberbullying Research Centre. (n.d.). *Bullying laws across America*. Cyberbullying Research Centre. https://cyberbullying.org/bullying-laws

Dey, A. (2018). *Nirbhaya, new media and digital gender activism*. Emerald Group Publishing. https://books.emeraldinsight.com/page/detail/Nirbhaya-New-Media-and-Digital-Gender-Activism/?k=9781787545304

Dodge, A., & Spencer, D. C. (2018). Online sexual violence, child pornography or something else entirely? Police responses to non-consensual intimate image sharing among youth. *Social & Legal Studies*, 27(5), 636–657.

Duggan, M. (2017, July 11). Online harassment 2017. *Pew Research Center*. www.pewresearch.org/internet/2017/07/11/online-harassment-2017/Technology-facilitated gender-based violence: An overview. Centre for International Governance Innovation: Supporting a Safer Internet Paper, (1). www.cigionline.org/static/documents/documents/SaferInternet_Paper%20no%201_0.pdf

Durham, M. G. (2021). *MeToo: The impact of rape culture in the media*. Wiley Press.

Dunn, S. (2020, December 7). Technology-facilitated gender-based violence: An overview. *Suzie Dunn, "Technology-facilitated gender-based violence: An overview" (2020) centre for international governance innovation: Supporting a safer internet paper*, 1. Retrieved from: https://www.cigionline.org/publications/technology-facilitated-gender-based-violence-overview/

Electronic Frontier Foundation. (n.d.). CDA 230: The most important law protecting internet speech. *Electronic Frontier Foundation*. www.eff.org/issues/cda230#:~:text=Section%20230%20says%20that%20%22No,%C2%A7%20230.

Ellington, A. J. (2021). Nearly 80% of video game characters are male, according to new diversity study. *Newsweek*. www.newsweek.com/nearly-80-video-game-characters-are-male-according-new-diversity-study-1616389

Foster-Frau, S., Zakrzewski, C., Nix, N., & Harwell, D. (2022, May 28). Before massacre, Uvalde gunman frequently threatened teen girls online. *The Washington Post*. www.washingtonpost.com/technology/2022/05/28/uvalde-texas-gunman-online-threats/

Garcia, J. (2019). Has #MeToo changed modern dating? Half of single men say yes. *Heartbeat*. https://blog.match.com/post/has-metoo-changed-modern-dating-half-of-single-men-say-yes

Gardiner, B. (2018). "It's a terrible way to go to work": What 70 million readers' comments on the Guardian revealed about hostility to women and minorities online. *Feminist Media Studies, 18*(4), 592–608. https://doi.org/10.1080/14680777.2018.1447334

Gehl, R. W. (2015). The case for alternative social media. *Social Media + Society, 1*(2). https://doi.org/10.1177/20563051156043

Gehl, R., W. (2022, October 25). Citizens' social media, like Mastodon, can provide an antidote to propaganda and disinformation. *The Conversation.* https://theconversation.com/citizens-social-media-like-mastodon-can-provide-an-antidote-to-propaganda-and-disinformation-192491

Gewirtz-Meydan, A., Volman-Pampanel, D., Opuda, E., & Tarshish, N. (2024). Dating Apps: A New Emerging Platform for Sexual Harassment? A Scoping Review. *Trauma, Violence, & Abuse, 25*(1), 752–763. https://doi.org/10.1177/15248380231162969

Gerbaudo, P. (2012). *Tweets and the streets: Social media and contemporary activism.* Pluto Press. www.plutobooks.com/9780745332482/tweets-and-the-streets/

Ging, D., & da Silva, R. (2022). *Young people's experiences of sexual and gender-based harassment and abuse during the Covid-19 pandemic in Ireland: Incidence, intervention and recommendations.* Dublin City University. https://antibullyingcentre.ie/wp-content/uploads/2022/10/Young-Peoples-Experiences.pdf

Ging, D., & Siapera, E. (2018). Special issue on online misogyny. *Feminist Media Studies, 18*(4), 515–524. https://doi.org/10.1080/14680777.2018.1447345

Grayson, N. (2018). Popular Twitch streamer makes an example of her harassers. *Kotaku.* https://kotaku.com/popular-twitch-streamer-makes-an-example-of-her-harasse-1826499663

Gunnarsson, L. (2018). "Excuse me, but are you raping me now?" Discourse and experience in (the grey areas of) sexual violence. *NORA-Nordic Journal of Feminist and Gender Research, 26*(1), 4–18. https://doi.org/10.1080/08038740.2017.1395359

HBR. (2021). Stop screening job candidates' social media. September-October issue. *Harvard Business Review.* https://hbr.org/2021/09/stop-screening-job-candidates-social-media

Harmer, E., & Lewis, S. (2022). Disbelief and counter-voices: A thematic analysis of online reader comments about sexual harassment and sexual violence against women. *Information, Communication & Society, 25*(2), 199–216. https://doi.org/10.1080/1369118X.2020.1770832

Henry, N., & Powell, A. (2016). Sexual violence in the digital age: The scope and limits of criminal law. *Social & Legal Studies, 25*(4), 397–418.

Herry, E., Gönültaş, S., & Mulvey, K. L. (2021). Digital era bullying: An examination of adolescent judgments about bystander intervention online. *Journal of Applied Developmental Psychology, 76*, 101322. https://doi.org/10.1016/j.appdev.2021.101322

hooks, B. (1989). *Talking back: Thinking feminist, thinking black* (Vol. 10). South End Press.

Hosani, H. A., Yousef, M., Shouq, S. A., Iqbal, F., & Mouheb, D. (2019). *A comparative analysis of cyberbullying and cyberstalking laws in the UAE, US, UK and Canada.* 2019 IEEE/ACS 16th International Conference on Computer Systems and Applications (AICCSA), 1–7. doi: 10.1109/AICCSA47632.2019.9035368.

Input. (2022). Data shows the gaming industry still has a pressing diversity problem. *Input.* www.inverse.com/input/features/data-shows-the-gaming-industry-still-has-a-pressing-diversity-problem

Instagram. (2021, February 11). An update on our work to tackle abuse on Instagram. *Instagram.* https://about.instagram.com/blog/announcements/an-update-on-our-work-to-tackle-abuse-on-instagram inst

Jackson, S. J., Bailey, M., & Welles, B. F. (2020). # *HashtagActivism: Networks of race and gender justice*. MIT Press. https://mitpress.mit.edu/9780262043373/hashtagactivism/

Jane, E. A. (2016). *Misogyny online: A short (and brutish) history*. Sage. https://uk.sagepub.com/en-gb/eur/misogyny-online/book245572

Jordan, S. (2019). *Postdigital storytelling: Poetics, praxis, research*. Routledge. www.routledge.com/Postdigital-Storytelling-Poetics-Praxis-Research/Jordan/p/book/9781032087702

Jurgenson, N. (2011). Digital dualism versus augmented reality. *The Society Pages, 24*. https://thesocietypages.org/cyborgology/2011/02/24/digital-dualism-versus-augmented-reality/

Kaye, L. K., Kowert, R., & Quinn, S. (2017). The role of social identity and online social capital on psychosocial outcomes in MMO players. *Computers in Human Behavior, 74*, 215–223.

Kuznekoff, J. H., & Rose, L. M. (2013). Communication in multiplayer gaming: Examining player responses to gender cues. *New Media & Society, 15*(4), 541–556.

Lai, C. Y., & Tsai, C. H. (2016, August). Cyberbullying in the social networking sites: An online disinhibition effect perspective. In *Proceedings of the 3rd multidisciplinary international social networks conference on social informatics 2016, data science 2016* (pp. 1–6). https://doi.org/10.1145/2955129.2955138

Latané, B., & Darley, J. M. (1970). *The unresponsive bystander: Why doesn't he help?* Prentice Hall.

Leonardi, P. M., & Vaast, E. (2017). Social media and their affordances for organizing: A review and agenda for research. *Academy of Management Annals, 11*, 150–188.

Loewen Walker, R. (2022). Call it misogyny. *Feminist Theory*. https://doi.org/10.1177/14647001221119995

Loney-Howes, R., Mendes, K., Fernández Romero, D., Fileborn, B., & Núñez Puente, S. (2021). Digital footprints of# MeToo. *Feminist Media Studies, 22*(6), 1345–1362. https://doi.org/10.1080/14680777.2021.1886142

Lorenz, T., & Browning, K. (2021). Dozens of women in gaming speak out about sexism and harassment. *The New York Times*. www.nytimes.com/2020/06/23/style/women-gaming-streaming-harassment-sexism-twitch.html

Lovine, A. (2021, May 20) Tinder releases "are you sure?" Feature to stop harmful messages before they happen. *Mashable*. https://mashable.com/article/tinder-are-you-sure

Lundquist, J. H., & Curington, C. V. (2019). Love me Tinder, love me sweet. *Contexts, 18*(4), 22–27.

Mannell, K., & Smith, E. T. (2022). Alternative social media and the complexities of a more participatory culture: A view from scuttlebutt. *Social Media + Society, 8*(3). https://doi.org/10.1177/20563051221122448

Markey, P. M. (2000). Bystander intervention in computer-mediated communication. *Computers in Human Behavior, 16*(2), 183–188. https://doi.org/10.1016/S0747-5632(99)00056-4

Marwick, A. E., & Boyd, D. (2011). I tweet honestly, I tweet passionately: Twitter users, context collapse, and the imagined audience. *New Media & Society, 13*(1), 114–133.

Mastodon. (2022). Social networking that's not for sale. *Mastodon*. https://join-mastodon.org/

McLean, L., & Griffiths, M. D. (2019). Female gamers' experience of online harassment and social support in online gaming: A qualitative study. *International Journal of Mental Health and Addiction, 17*(4), 970–994.

Mendes, K. (2015). *SlutWalk: Feminism, activism and media*. Palgrave Macmillan. https://link.springer.com/book/10.1057/9781137378910

Mendes, K., & Jeong, E. (2023). Digital feminist activism. In K. Boyle & S. Berridge (Eds.), *Routledge companion to gender, media & violence*. Routledge.

Mendes, K., & Ringrose, J. (2019). Digital feminist activism: #MeToo and the everyday experiences of challenging rape culture. In B. Fileborn & R. Loney-Howes (Eds.), *#MeToo & the politics of social change*. Palgrave Macmillan.

Mendes, K., Ringrose, J., & Keller, J. (2019). *Digital feminist activism: Girls and women fight back against rape culture*. Oxford University Press. https://academic.oup.com/book/5871?login=false

OkCupid. (2022a). Community guidelines. *OkCupid*. https://help.okcupid.com/hc/en-us/articles/5221229275405-Community-Guidelines

OkCupid. (2022b). Consent and dating. *OkCupid*. https://help.okcupid.com/hc/en-us/articles/5221215810829-Consent-and-Dating

Ortutay, B. (2025). *Meta rolls back hate speech rules as Zuckerberg cites 'recent elections' as a catalyst*. Associated Press. https://apnews.com/article/meta-facebook-hate-speech-trump-immigrant-transgender-41191638cd7c720b950c-05f9395a2b49

Leonardi, P. M., & Vaast, E. (2017). Social media and their affordances for organizing: A review and agenda for research. *Academy of Management Annals, 11*, 150–188.

Papacharissi, Z. (2002). The virtual sphere: The internet as a public sphere. *New Media and Society, 4*(1), 9–27. https://doi.org/10.1177/14614440222226244

Pew. (2020, January 29). *Republicans and Democrats distrust social media sites for political and election news*. www.pewresearch.org/journalism/2020/01/29/an-oasis-of-bipartisanship-republicans-and-democrats-distrust-social-media-sites-for-political-and-election-news/

Powell, A., & Henry, N. (2017). *Sexual violence in a digital age*. Springer.

Prokopets, E. (2022, July 22). How Bumble is building a better world of online dating. *Latana*. https://latana.com/post/how-bumble-is-building-a-better-world-of-online-dating/

Raynauld, V., Richez, E., & Boudreau Morris, K. (2018). Canada is# IdleNoMore: Exploring dynamics of Indigenous political and civic protest in the Twitterverse. *Information, Communication & Society, 21*(4), 626–642. https://doi.org/10.1080/1369118X.2017.1301522

Reddit. (2022). How do you guys cope with constant online harassment? *Reddit*. www.reddit.com/r/GirlGamers/comments/uysrgm/how_do_you_guys_cope_with_constant_online/

Regehr, K. (2022). In (cel) doctrination: How technologically facilitated misogyny moves violence off screens and on to streets. *New Media & Society, 24*(1), 138–155. https://doi.org/10.1177/14614448209590

Rodriguez, C. (2001). *Fissures in the mediascape: An international study of citizens' media*. Hampton Press

Rosenfeld, M. J., Thomas, R. J., & Hausen, S. (2019). Disintermediating your friends: How online dating in the United States displaces other ways of meeting. *Proceedings of the National Academy of Sciences, 116*(36), 17753–17758.

Salter, A., & Blodgett, B. (2012). Hypermasculinity & dickwolves: The contentious role of women in the new gaming public. *Journal of Broadcasting & Electronic Media, 56*(3), 401–416. https://doi.org/10.1080/08838151.2012.705199

Shaw, F. (2012). The politics of blogs: Theories of discursive activism online. *Media International Australia, 142*(1), 41–49. https://doi.org/10.1177/1329878X121420010

Shaw, F. (2016). "Bitch I said hi": The Bye Felipe campaign and discursive activism in mobile dating apps. *Social Media+ Society*, 2(4). https://doi.org/10.1177/2056305116672889

Shepherd, T., Harvey, A., Jordan, T., Srauy, S., & Miltner, K. (2015). Histories of hating. *Social Media + Society*, 1(2), 1–10. https://doi.org/10.1177/2056305115603997

Sinclair, B. (2021, May 19). Survey says 59% of women hide gender to avoid harassment while gaming online. *GamesIndustry.Biz*. www.gamesindustry.biz/survey-says-59-percent-of-women-hide-gender-to-avoid-harassment-while-gaming-online

Sobieraj, S. (2020). *Credible threat: Attacks against women online and the future of democracy*. Oxford University Press. https://doi.org/10.1093/oso/9780190089283.001.0001

Statistica. (2022, October 18). Social media usage in Canada—statistics & facts. *Statista*. www.statista.com/topics/2729/social-networking-in-canada/#topicHeader__wrapper

Statistica. (2023a, October). *Average daily time spent using the internet by online users worldwide from 3rd quarter 2015 to 2nd quarter 2023*. www.statista.com/statistics/1380282/daily-time-spent-online-global/

Statistica. (2023b, January). *Daily time spent on social networking by internet users worldwide from 2012 to 2023*. www.statista.com/statistics/433871/daily-social-media-usage-worldwide/

Suddath, C. (2020, January 17). For Bumble, the future isn't female, it's female marketing. *Bloomberg*. www.bloomberg.com/news/features/2020-01-17/for-bumble-the-future-isn-t-female-it-s-female-marketing?leadSource=uverify%20wall

Suler, J. (2004). The online disinhibition effect. *Cyberpsychology & Behavior*, 7(3), 321–326.

Tessier, M. (2021, October 25). Comments sections have a sexism problem. This is by design. *Fast Company*. www.fastcompany.com/90688891/comments-sections-have-a-sexism-problem-this-is-by-design. https://doi.org/10.1177/095935351772022

Thompson, R. (2022, January 26). Tinder launches significant redesign to its sexual violence reporting system. *Mashable*. https://mashable.com/article/tinder-sexual-violence-reporting-update

Tweten, A. (2018). *Bye Felipe: Disses, dick pics, and other delights of modern dating*. Running Press Adult. www.runningpress.com/titles/alexandra-tweten/bye-felipe/9780762463749/

US Dept. of State. (2023). 2023 roadmap for the global partnership for action on gender-based online harassment and abuse. *US Dept. of State*. https://www.state.gov/2023-roadmap-for-the-global-partnership-for-action-on-gender-based-online-harassment-and-abuse/

Urwin, R. (2016, June 24). How dating apps are changing in the #MeToo era. *The Times*. www.thetimes.co.uk/article/how-dating-apps-are-changing-in-the-metoo-era-hlcj9pzgn

Valentine, R. (2018, June 5). One-third of UK women gamers report abuse or discrimination from male gamers. *GAMESINDUSTRY.BIZ*. https://perma.cc/ZPA7-9YTG

Van Cleemput, K., Vandebosch, H., & Pabian, S. (2014). Personal characteristics and contextual factors that determine "helping," "joining in," and "doing nothing" when witnessing cyberbullying. *Aggressive Behavior, 40*(5), 383–396. https://doi.org/10.1002/ab.21534

Van Dijck, J. (2013). *The culture of connectivity: A critical history of social media.* Oxford University Press. https://academic.oup.com/book/9914?login=false

Van Zoonen, W., Verhoeven, J. W., & Vliegenthart, R. (2016). How employees use Twitter to talk about work: A typology of work-related tweets. *Computers in Human Behavior, 55,* 329–339.

White, D. (2016, January 6). Women on this dating app feel safer thanks to "Peer Review" feature. *Global Dating Insight.* www.globaldatinginsights.com/news/06022016-the-grade-study-peer-reviews-makes-users-feel-safer/

X Blog. (2017, December 18). https://blog.twitter.com/en_us/topics/company/2017/safetypoliciesdec2017

Zuckerman, E. (2018). Six or seven things social media can do for democracy. *Medium.* https://medium.com/trust-media-and-democracy/six-or-seven-things-social-media-can-do-for-democracy-66cee083b91a

Zulli, D., Liu, M., & Gehl, R. (2020). Rethinking the "social" in "social media": Insights into topology, abstraction, and scale on the Mastodon social network. *New Media & Society, 22*(7), 1188–1205. https://doi.org/10.1177/1461444820912533

3

BYSTANDERS IN THE #METOO MOVEMENT

Lynn Bowes-Sperry, Ho Kwan Cheung and Jennifer Griffith

Those in the Know: The Role of Apathetic, Avoidant, Allied, and Adversarial Bystanders in the MTM

> *In the aftermath of the Weinstein story, much of the subsequent report-ing focused on . . . find(ing) out who knew what and when, and who failed to act on the information . . . the question of "who knew?" forces powerful people . . . to grapple with their complicity.*
> Fortmueller (2022, p. 21)

We refer to the people described in the quote above *"who knew"* as sex-ual harassment (SH) bystanders, that is, individuals who were not directly involved as the initiator or target of SH but who witnessed an incident first-hand or acquired secondhand information later in time (Bowes-Sperry & O'Leary-Kelly, 2005). Before the MeToo movement (MTM), targets and initiators of SH took on starring roles under the spotlight, even though the importance of SH bystanders and their reluctance to intervene had been acknowledged in the management literature for quite some time (Bowes-Sperry & Powell, 1999; Miner-Rubino & Cortina, 2004; Reich & Hersh-covis, 2015). The MTM helped move SH bystanders out of the shadows as mass media outlets such as the *New York Times* (e.g., Kantor, 2017) revealed story after story, illuminating two realities associated with work-place SH. The first reality is that many people knew about SH and abuse within their organizations and industries, and the second is that these bystanders frequently chose to avoid taking action within the boundaries of these institutions.

DOI: 10.4324/9781003300953-4

These stories confirm what scholars who study workplace SH knew *before* the MTM went viral in 2017 and have known for decades—that SH bystanders typically do not take action to stop workplace SH despite having the ability to make a difference in terms of outcomes for SH targets (e.g., McDonald et al., 2016; McMahon, 2022; Moschella & Banyard, 2020), and that bystanders' failure to act serves to perpetuate SH (Bowes-Sperry & Powell, 1999). While it is undeniable that many bystanders *"failed to act"* in response to the information they had, in an ideal world, SH bystanders would not have been called upon to resolve situations for which their organizations were morally and legally responsible. It is due to widespread failure of organizational leadership[1] and governmental institutions across the globe to address SH[2] (e.g., Zinshteyn, 2022) that bystanders often found themselves in untenable situations and thus opted to remain in the shadows rather than taking action that could thrust themselves into the spotlight. Thus, it is institutions more so than individuals that need *"to grapple with their complicity"* in perpetuating SH (e.g., Daley et al., 2019; Feldblum & Lipnic, 2016). And while there are numerous examples of institutional failure to grapple with complicity, there have also been some successes. For instance, the United States passed the Speak Out Act (2022), a law nullifying nondisclosure agreements (NDAs) associated with sexual assault and harassment incidents, which had been used in institutional settings to silence targets of workplace SH (Barmes, 2023).

Now that the role of SH bystanders has begun to emerge from the shadows, our primary goal with this chapter is to illuminate the centrality of SH bystanders leading up to and during the MTM. As described previously, bystanders' lack of action in response to workplace SH contributed to the need for SH targets to seek recognition and justice outside the boundaries of their organizations through a social movement like the MTM. Perhaps paradoxically, it was also bystanders' actions that allowed the MTM to flourish. From a sociological perspective, social movements are bystander events, and this was true for the MTM as SH bystanders were front and center in ways that were both positive (e.g., supporting SH targets who disclosed their experiences) and negative (e.g., trolling those who disclosed their experiences as well as bystanders who supported them) with regard to addressing workplace SH.

We use past research on SH bystanders' behavior[3] (BB) inside their work organizations to examine their behavior outside these organizations in MTM spaces, that is, any space in which MTM-related activity takes place. We then "loop back" to utilize lessons learned from BB in MTM spaces to see how it has (or could) impact BB inside organizational spaces as well as what it means for future research on the topic of BB in workplace SH. Shining the light on bystanders in the MTM has allowed us to contribute to the literature by developing a typology of SH bystanders (i.e., apathetic, avoidant, allied, or adversarial) and a framework of BB in workplace SH that expands existing models to include the dimensions of: (a) the location in which bystanders take action, (b) the intention driving bystanders' action, and (c) the communication channels bystanders use to take action.

Reconceptualizing Workplace SH Bystander Behavior

The publicity regarding workplace SH generated by digital media (e.g., X, formerly known as Twitter) and news outlets (e.g., the *New York Times*) during the MTM was staggering. For example, in less than three months, more than 24 million people were active on Facebook in conversations about SH "posting, reacting, and commenting over 77 million times,"[4] and in the first year after Alyssa Milano's iconic tweet, the #MeToo hashtag had been used on Twitter more than 19 million times.[5] This dramatically increased the number of individuals with access to information regarding particular SH incidents that only would have been available in the past to those with a personal or work-related connection to the incident. In other words, the MTM exponentially increased the number of individuals who can be considered SH bystanders and subsequently the potential for increased occurrences of BB, making it even more important that we understand the factors that influence bystanders' actions, the types of actions they take and the spaces in which they take them, and the impact of their actions on individuals (including themselves), organizations, and societies.

Before we begin our analysis of SH bystanders, we provide a brief comparison of our typology of SH bystanders to that of Bowes-Sperry and O'Leary-Kelly (2005).[6] Both models are adapted from Latané and Darley's (1970) decision-making framework, which considers BB as the outcome of a process that includes recognizing a situation as requiring action and then deciding what action, if any, to take in response to the situation.[7] While the underlying decision-making processes in both models of BB in workplace SH remain the same, the idea of SH bystanders taking action in a computer-mediated environment via mechanisms such as social media was inconceivable when Bowes-Sperry and O'Leary-Kelly (2005) developed their model. These technological changes have complicated the notion of who becomes a bystander, what types of actions they can take, and where and when they can take them. As a result of these changes, our analysis expands the 2005 model to include where and how BB takes place, which can be conceptualized in terms of (a) organizational spaces (i.e., inside and/or outside workplace organizations), and (b) communication spaces (i.e., physical, virtual, and/or digital channels).

Prior to the MTM, most BB in workplace SH occurred within organizational spaces (i.e., spaces in which work occurs, Stephenson et al., 2020) or those closely affiliated with them such as governmental spaces like the Equal Employment Opportunity Commission and the judicial system focused on adjudicating SH in the United States. The MTM made it clear that BB can also take place in spaces entirely *outside* the organizations in which SH occurs. While BB in spaces outside of organizations has been the topic of previous research,[8] it has not been conceptualized in terms of a nomological network of BB in workplace SH despite the MTM going viral because of workplace SH and its potential for enriching current frameworks.

Similarly, before the MTM, much research focused on BB in *physical* spaces such as office buildings or off-site social outings related to work. In today's workplace, however, BB in response to workplace SH can occur in *virtual* (e.g., Zoom meetings) and *digital* (e.g., social media) spaces as well as physical spaces. Given that many employees shifted to work from home arrangements during (and after) the pandemic, SH in virtual (e.g., exposing one's self during virtual meetings) and digital (e.g., texting unwanted

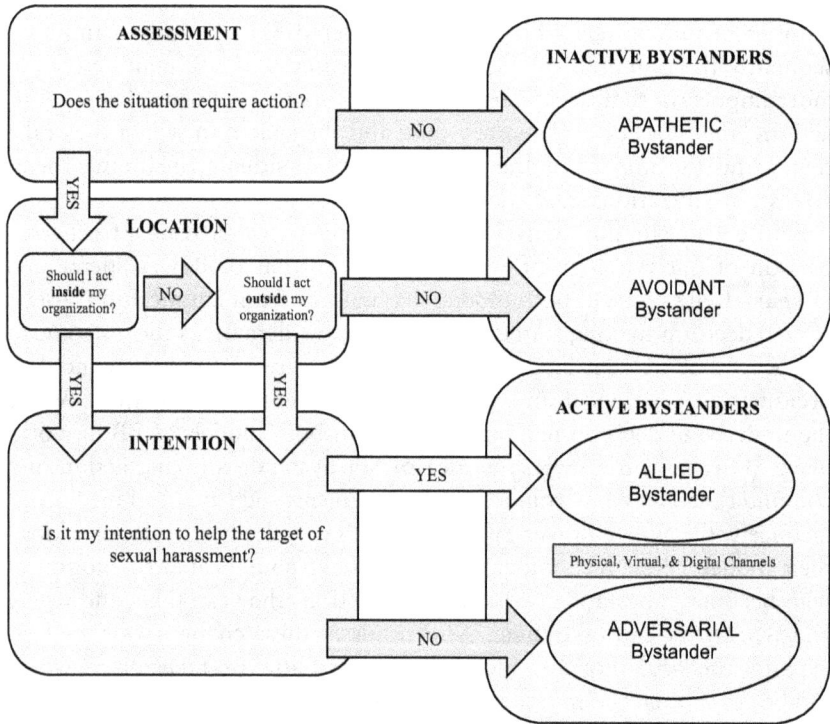

FIGURE 3.1 Paths travelled by inactive and active bystanders.

sexual images) spaces increased dramatically (Elsesser, 2020; Fathimah et al., 2023; Karami et al., 2021), thus offering more opportunities for bystander intervention in organizational spaces that are not physical.

In addition to spotlighting the expansion of spaces in which BB occurs, we also focus on how this expansion provided more avenues and opportunities for what we call "adversarial bystanders" to undermine not only particular targets of SH but also women in general (e.g., Dodson et al., 2023; Gentile, 2017). Our model of BB in response to workplace SH is depicted in Figure 3.1.

Shining the Spotlight on Types of Bystanders

When considering the time periods leading up to and during the MTM, it becomes clear that there are several types of bystanders. In the next sections of this chapter, we delineate four types of BB in response to workplace SH. We conceptualize bystanders as falling into two broad categories, that is, inactive or active. Within the inactive category, there are two types of bystanders to which we refer as "apathetic bystanders" who refrain from taking action because they lack concern or do not believe action is required and "avoidant bystanders" who refrain from taking action despite believing that action is required. Similarly, there are two types of bystanders in the active category. We refer to these as "allied bystanders" who take action intended to help SH targets and "adversarial bystanders" who take action intended to undermine or harm SH targets. Bystander type is determined by the outcome of a series of decision points beginning with the decision as to whether or not the SH incident is a situation that requires action and ending with the decision regarding the communication channel(s) they will use to take action.

Category One: Inactive Bystanders

Type One: Apathetic Bystanders

We define "apathetic bystanders" as those who refrain from taking action due to a lack of concern because they do not believe action is required. Early research on BB emerged in response to societal beliefs that individuals who chose not to intervene in emergency situations were morally deficient and lacking concern for those around them, and perhaps even humanity in general. Latané and Darley's (1969) commentary in response to the lack of BB in the infamous Kitty Genovese murder captures the public outcry against these bystanders. They noted that the story of Ms. Genovese's murder was the "journalistic sensation of the decade" generating condemnation by "preachers, professors, and other sermonizers . . . columnists and commentators" who made claims of apathy, indifference, moral callousness, and dehumanization. Fast forward more than 50 years later to the MTM, and there was a similar outcry by many in response to egregious and pervasive workplace SH as reporters demanded to know "who knew what and when, and who failed to act on the information" (Fortmueller, 2022, p. 21).

As the media began asking such questions in an attempt to force those in the know "to grapple with their complicity," the role of bystander inaction in perpetuating SH moved bystanders from the shadows to the spotlight. Film director Quentin Tarantino provides what appears to be a prototypical example of an apathetic bystander. When asked what he knew about Weinstein's behavior, he admitted that he "knew enough to do more than [he] did"[9] and that "[e]veryone who was close to Harvey had heard of" his predatory behavior toward women in the entertainment industry before it became public knowledge (Kantor, 2017). In addition to admissions such as Tarantino's, there were other indicators that Weinstein's behavior was an "open secret" (Garber, 2017) that had been tolerated by those in the know who had avoided taking action. Interesting questions arise with regard to bystander apathy in response to workplace SH. One question is whether the MTM changed the proportion of apathetic bystanders. It is likely that the magnitude and egregiousness of SH revealed by the MTM jolted many people out of their apathy, similar to the way the George Floyd incident and Black Lives Matter (BLM) movement did. However, given the counter-movements that arose in response to the BLM (e.g., All Lives Matter) and the MTM (#HimToo), jolting bystanders out of apathy does not necessarily imply that they will take action to support targets of harassment and discrimination.

Another question is whether SH bystanders are more likely to be apathetic inside organizational spaces associated with their work or outside of them in spaces like the MTM. On the one hand, bystanders could perceive SH targets who went public with their experiences during the MTM as more removed or distant and thus less relevant to their lives than SH targets in one's workplace leading to more apathy toward the MTM. On the other hand, there is substantial overlap between the roles of SH target and SH bystander—like actors on a stage, individuals involved in the drama of SH overtime can play many parts (Shakespeare, 1599). Research on SH bystanders in the workplace indicates that many individuals who had been in the role of target take action if they "come to know" about other incidents of SH as bystanders (Liang & Park, 2022; Ryan & Wessel, 2012), and that the roles of target and bystander are often amorphous with indirect exposure to SH (i.e., ambient SH) resulting in the same types of negative outcomes as direct exposure (Glomb et al., 1997). Given this, we do not believe that individuals with these overlapping roles are likely to be apathetic in any context.

Although the impetus for initial research (e.g., Latané & Darley, 1969) on the topic of inactive bystanders was the public's assumption that bystanders were inactive due to apathy, in reality, many were not apathetic at all. We now turn our attention to bystanders who were inactive for reasons other than apathy, that is, avoidant bystanders.

Type Two: Avoidant Bystanders

We define "avoidant bystanders" as those who refrain from taking action *despite* believing that action is required. The following quote in response to the failure of numerous bystanders to take action in the infamous murder case of Kitty Genovese captures what we believe to be the essence of avoidant bystanders—"Although it is unquestionably true that witnesses in emergencies have often done nothing to save the victims, 'apathy,' 'indifference,' and 'unconcern' are not entirely accurate descriptions of their reactions . . . their behavior was neither helpful nor heroic; but it was not indifferent or apathetic either" (Latané & Darley, 1969, p. 244). Similar to research in emergency situations occurring outside the workplace, research on SH bystanders in the workplace finds that many who avoid taking action are not apathetic (i.e., lacking interest or concern). This research suggests that a bystander's failure to take action in response to workplace SH may stem from other less sinister sources such as perceiving the situation as ambiguous or not likely to reoccur, questioning the social appropriateness of taking action, not knowing what action to take, and perhaps most importantly, fear of negative consequences for taking action (e.g., Bowes-Sperry & O'Leary-Kelly, 2005; Griffith et al., 2022; Ng et al., 2022; Pouwelse et al., 2021; Ryan & Wessel, 2012).

In addition to empirical evidence, there is a great deal of anecdotal evidence indicating that bystanders' failure to act is not always motivated by apathy. The following quote provides an excellent example—"The scandals sending shockwaves through Hollywood, . . . have left in their wake people who have expressed remorse for failing to do more to stop the inappropriate behavior of powerful men" (Olson, 2017). People who are apathetic are unlikely to express remorse. Let's revisit our previous example of Quentin Tarantino. He says he wished he had taken responsibility for addressing Weinstein's behavior and regretted his failure to act. Most interesting perhaps, is that even though Tarantino is considered a "heavy hitter" in the entertainment industry, he called "on the other guys who knew more to *not be scared*" (emphasis added) to "do better by our sisters" (Kantor, 2017).[10] If people with such high levels of power and status in their industries express apprehension about negative consequences for calling out SH, imagine how difficult it is for people in lower level jobs lacking power.[11]

Indeed, bystanders in the context of workplace SH are frequently retaliated against by management and ostracized by coworkers (Flecha, 2021; Medeiros & Griffith, 2019; Moschella & Banyard, 2021; Olson, 2017). This is why it took a social movement occurring outside the employment context to free SH bystanders who wanted to help from the constraints of organizational-level factors[12] such as organizational culture and social networks. Other than organizational factors that inhibit bystander intervention, we believe that many of the reasons for not taking action within one's workplace when one is "in the know" about SH also apply to avoidant (and apathetic) bystanders during the MTM. Although many SH bystanders are apathetic or avoidant, some bystanders choose action over inaction. In the next section, we provide an overview of types of actions available to bystanders during the MTM.

Category Two: Active Bystanders

Active bystanders are those who take *some* action in response to workplace SH, i.e., they engage in bystander intervention.[13] "Intervention" is "the act of interfering with the outcome or course, especially of a condition or process, as to prevent harm or improve functioning."[14] In accordance with this definition, intervention by SH bystanders could entail "interfering" (a) to prevent harm in the course of an SH incident that is currently in process, or (b) to improve the "functioning" of targets, harassers, organizations, and/ or societies in the wake of SH. This definition is consistent with Bowes-Sperry and O'Leary-Kelly's (2005) typology of BB,[15] which categorizes BB along two dimensions; level of involvement (i.e., how deeply bystanders immerse themselves in the SH incident) and timing of actions (i.e., how quickly bystanders respond to the SH incident). Both types of bystanders in the active bystander category can engage in actions ranging from low to high involvement and from quick to slow timing.

There is a substantial body of research in the context of organizational spaces (such as the workplace and educational institutions) indicating how SH bystanders take action (i.e., typically with a low level of involvement) and when they take action (i.e., typically after the incident has occurred) but we know little about BB outside of organizational spaces. In addition to knowing how and when SH bystanders are likely to intervene, it is important to understand *where* and through *which channels* they are likely to intervene. Thus, we have incorporated the dimensions of bystander location and communication channel in our theoretical framework (see Figure 3.1). Whether a bystander takes action in support of an SH target (as an allied bystander) or against an SH target (as an adversarial bystander), they have choice regarding: (1) the location in which they take action (i.e., inside and/or outside of organizational spaces), and (2) the communication channel they utilize to take action (i.e., physical, virtual, and/or digital).

Type Three: Allied Bystanders

We define "allied bystanders" as those who take action intended to help SH targets. Most research on SH bystanders in the workplace has focused on allied bystanders, that is, those who intervened with the intention of helping targets. Bystanders who aligned themselves with the goals of the MTM (e.g., increasing awareness of the magnitude of workplace SH, holding harassers accountable)[16] were integral to its success. For example, people who had not personally experienced Harvey Weinstein or other high-status harassers became outraged and acted for social change[17] on behalf of those who had by taking actions such as participating in social media campaigns[18] and physical protests, pressuring employers to hold harassers accountable,[19] and "outing" of long-known perpetrators. It was the willingness of bystanders to take action online in the very public environment of social media during the MTM that provided the fuel required for turning a single tweet into a flourishing social movement as SH bystanders engaged in actions related to building community, engaging in advocacy, and allowing SH targets to seek justice (Brown & Battle, 2019; Rentschler, 2017).

Allied bystanders can take action that ranges from low to high with regard to involvement (e.g., Bowes-Sperry & O'Leary-Kelly, 2005). A prime example of bystanders who enact low-level involvement are those participating in the "whisper network," in which "those in the know" share information about SH incidents quietly among themselves (Hershcovis et al., 2021; Meza, 2017). Although the whisper network often has negative connotations stemming from underlying assumptions that it is a form of bystander complicity, it has been used in positive ways such as protecting newcomers from known harassers. The whisper network can serve as a form of low involvement/low immediacy bystander intervention, contributing to the larger conversation by exposing "bad actors" within organizations and/or industries and spreading the word of such harassers to a wider global audience through mechanisms such as crowdsourced documents (e.g., Blair, 2019; Haritos, 2018). In cases when the "whisper" network is used in digital private spaces, it represents a higher level of involvement because it leaves a digital footprint or shadow that can be accessed by those for whom it was not intended. Thus, taking such action is not without risk. For instance, Moira Donegan initiated the creation of the Shitty Media Men list, a compilation of anonymously submitted accounts detailing alleged instances of sexual misconduct within the media industry. Despite not actively contributing to the list, Donegan found herself entangled in a personal legal dispute when an individual mentioned on the list filed a lawsuit against her. Eventually, Donegan reached a settlement with the individual, agreeing to pay a six-figure sum (Cartwright, 2023).

Another example of what might be considered moderate-level involvement allied bystander intervention occurred during the 2013 Oscars, four years prior to the MTM going viral. While announcing nominees for best supporting actress, comedian Seth MacFarlane joked, "Congratulations, you five ladies no longer have to pretend to be attracted to Harvey Weinstein" (Smith, 2017). Instead of being met with dismay, his comment received raucous laughter from the audience. While McFarlane opted to publicly acknowledge Weinstein's behavior and implicitly call out Hollywood's role in facilitating the behavior, the audience's laughter in response can be interpreted as passive acceptance of Weinstein's behavior, rendering them complicit. In accordance with their passive acceptance, the audience members would be classified as inactive bystanders who laughed either because they thought the situation was comical (making them apathetic bystanders) or because they were afraid to applaud McFarlane despite thinking that his calling out Weinstein was appropriate (making them avoidant bystanders). If even one person had yelled "Bravo!" or stood up and started clapping rather than laughing in response to MacFarlane calling out the problem, a groundswell of bystander action could have ensued rather than casual (if not callous) acceptance of what was clearly a widely known, problematic situation plaguing the entertainment industry as well as many others. If anyone had stood up they would have "played the part" of allied bystander.

This incident took on a second life after the MTM erupted and MacFarlane was faulted for joking about Weinstein's behavior rather than taking stronger measures. In response to these criticisms, MacFarlane explained his joke by noting that he "couldn't resist the opportunity to take a hard swing in [Weinstein's] direction" and that his action "came from a place of loathing and anger" in response to knowledge that Jessica Barth, one of his friends, was harassed by Weinstein. In response to those criticizing MacFarlane for not "doing" anything, Barth told them "please STOP! He stood by me and respected my wishes that he not retaliate in any way" (Smith, 2017). It is important to note that the simple act of MacFarlane standing by Barth is also a form of allied bystander action exhibiting a low-level of involvement (Bowes-Sperry & O'Leary-Kelly, 2005). As

Barth's statement indicates, even allied bystander actions that don't result in disciplinary actions against harassers can be useful in helping SH targets (Moschella & Barnyard, 2020) and thus should not be discounted (see also Griffith et al., 2022).

There are, however, bystanders who took more substantive actions in the workplace as well as those who did so during the MTM despite being apprehensive. One prime example of an allied bystander taking more substantive action is Carrie Fisher, who confronted a Hollywood producer who had sexually assaulted one of her friends; Fisher handed him a box containing a cow tongue and a note stating, "if you ever touch . . . any other woman again, the next delivery will be something of yours in a much smaller box!"(Carrie Fisher . . ., 2017). Fisher's intervention could have emanated from factors such as outrage over SH, moral courage, and/or her position of power in the industry (e.g., Dodson et al., 2023; Goodwin et al., 2020). The contrasting behavior of Tarantino (inaction) and Fisher (high involvement action), both of whom had high levels of power and access to the individuals enacting SH, is likely the result of (social) network silence (e.g., Hershcovis et al., 2021) given that Tarantino acknowledged his "father-son closeness" with Weinstein (Kantor, 2017).

Another example of an SH bystander who took substantive action before the MTM is Christopher Partee, who was fired from his job as a forklift operator for serving as a witness in an SH complaint against his supervisor. He stated "I was thinking about not getting involved because I had a feeling that something like this would happen . . . But if a woman is crying . . . I'm not going to walk away . . . I'm just not that type of person." Partee's comment that he's not that "type of person" is indicative of allyship, which despite having some overlap with bystander intervention, is often conceptualized as an identity rather than as a behavior (Selvanathan et al., 2020). Nonetheless, allyship, by definition, requires advantaged group members[20] engaging in *actions* that can improve treatment or circumstances of a marginalized group (Radke et al., 2020). As such, we address the relationship between BB and allyship in more detail in the last section of this chapter as a topic for future research.

Type Four: Adversarial Bystanders

We define "adversarial bystanders" as those who take action intended to undermine or harm SH targets. Although SH bystanders could intervene with various beneficiaries in mind, including SH initiators (Bowes-Sperry & O'Leary-Kelly, 2005; McDonald et al., 2016), the majority of research on BB in workplace SH has focused on bystanders who were inactive or took action to *help* targets of SH. Nonetheless, empirical research conducted before and after the MTM found that in addition to bystanders who fail to take action or who take action that helps SH targets, some bystanders take action in opposition to SH targets, often with the intention of harming them. McDonald et al. (2016) provide evidence of adversarial bystanders in the workplace engaging in behavior that harmed targets. For example, they quote an SH target who described the behavior of a company director who started "laughing his head off" after another director exposed himself at a work-related lunch in a hotel room. The laughing company director described earlier is a common example of an "adversarial bystander."

Gentile (2017) provides several prototypical examples of adversarial bystanders such as Roman Polanski, who "lamented about a world he sees as having been taken over by "female mass hysteria" (Desta, 2018), and Woody Allen, who "declared #metoo to be a witch hunt, but this time of men, by women." It is noteworthy, and perhaps not surprising given our previous discussion of the existence of overlapping roles, that Polanski had been found guilty of sex-related crimes, and Allen has been alleged to have committed such crimes. Thus, just as SH targets often become allied bystanders, SH initiators (or those accused of SH) can become adversarial bystanders. And as Gentile (2017)) notes, some women also take on the role of adversarial bystander as she mentions Daphne Merkin's (2018, p. 241) *New York Times* op-ed, "describing her fears that women, embolden (sic) by the #MeToo campaign, are creating an atmosphere of patronizing protectionism at best, a new form of censorship at worst."

Given that the digital realm provides exponentially more opportunities for bystanders to engage in adversarial behaviors, it is not surprising that so much of it occurred during the MTM, which played out, in large part, within digital spaces (see Chapter 2 for more detail). Like other digital spaces, the public nature of digital MTM spaces facilitates the ability of individuals within these spaces to violate societal expectations of general civility because there are fewer avenues for holding them accountable relative to the workplace.[21] This lack of accountability poses a risk to anyone in a digital MTM space but as in most other digital spaces, women experience higher levels of online harassment and bullying (Vogels, 2021). And given that most individuals sharing their SH experiences in digital MTM spaces (as well as those supporting them) were women and that the topic of SH is often seen as "feminist," it is not surprising that backlash was quick and extensive in nature (Ayanian et al., 2024; Boyle & Rathnayake, 2020; Flecha, 2021; Nutbeam & Mereish, 2022). Adversarial bystanders worked to extinguish the efforts of allied bystanders as they rebelled against the MTM by joining counter movements such as #HimToo, in an attempt to derail the MTM through actions such as questioning the credibility of those who publicly shared their SH experiences and claiming that the MTM was a witch hunt that was persecuting innocent men, whose behavior should not have been considered harassment (Morris, 2018).[22] We now turn our attention to sharing ideas for future research on SH bystanders to workplace SH.

Potential Areas for Future Research

We use Figure 3.1 to generate a series of questions emanating from our analysis that we believe can lead to meaningful research on the topic of SH bystanders in relation to the MTM. The first step delineated in Figure 3.1 is the SH bystander's determination regarding whether or not the situation of which they are aware requires action. We believe the most relevant aspect of the MTM with regard to this decision is the increased access to information generated by the movement, leading to question one.

Question one: "Does increased access to information about SH in general brought about by the MTM influence bystanders' perceptions that a particular incident of SH in the workplace requires action?"

We expect that there may be important moderators to consider when investigating this topic such as SH bystanders' ideologies (e.g., van der Linden & Panagopoulos, 2019) and their perceptions that SH is an unethical behavior (e.g., O'Leary-Kelly & Bowes-Sperry, 2001). It is important to remember that believing a situation requires action is not enough, SH bystanders must still be willing to take action, otherwise they remain "avoidant bystanders."

The second step delineated in Figure 3.1 deals with the location (i.e., inside or outside organizational spaces) in which SH bystanders contemplate taking action. Given that SH bystanders often refrain from taking action due to organizational-level factors,[23] we believe that providing an alternative avenue—outside of organizational spaces—for SH bystanders to take action is one of the most significant accomplishments of the MTM. Thus, we pose the following questions:

Question two: Has the MTM led to increases in allied bystander actions *within* organizational spaces?

Question three: Has the MTM led to increases in adversarial bystander actions *within* organizational spaces?

Question four: Are bystanders who took action outside organizational spaces (as opposed to those who did not) during the MTM more likely to take action inside organizational spaces after the MTM?

The third step delineated in Figure 3.1 involves the intention of SH Bystanders. As stated previously, most research on BB in workplace SH focuses on what we call "allied bystanders," leading us to consider two avenues for future research. The first is examining "allied bystanders" in light of the research on allyship, and the second avenue is examining "adversarial bystanders" in light of existing research on allied bystanders.

Despite the conceptual alignment between SH bystanders and allyship, discussion of allyship within the workplace SH context has been limited. Even though allyship and what we refer to as allied bystander action are traditionally conceptualized as discrete behaviors, increasing attention from both researchers and practitioners has called for allyship as an identity (Carlson et al., 2020). Specifically, rather than seeing allyship as one-off actions, individuals should view allyship as an ongoing developmental process to understand one's privilege and learning to support those who are disadvantaged by existing societal structure (Bergkamp et al., 2022). As noted previously, when describing why he took action, Christopher Partee stated he could not just walk away when asked to serve as a witness because he is "just not that type of person" (Olson, 2017), in essence invoking the concept of allyship as an identity. Integrating ideas from the allyship literature can potentially enhance our understanding on why individuals choose to get involved (or not) in SH incidents. This conceptualization can be extended to allied bystanders within the SH context, wherein bystanders may be more motivated to get directly involved when viewing any given incident or even discussion of an incident within the larger societal context and through the lens of allyship. This leads to interesting questions, one of which we encapsulate in question five.

Question five: For SH bystanders who identify as men, is an identity of
   ally a stronger predictor of allied bystander action than factors found in
   previous research to predict SH bystander behavior such as perceptions
   of the situation?

The second avenue related to type of bystander is examining "adversarial bystanders" in light of existing research on (allied) bystanders. For example, the perceived moral intensity of an incident of SH (Bowes-Sperry & Powell, 1999; Jones, 1991) could motivate both allied *and* adversarial bystanders to take action but with allied bystanders perceiving an incident as high in moral intensity and adversarial bystanders perceiving the same incident as low in moral intensity. This dichotomy with regard to perceptions is consistent with research finding that moral disengagement in response to SH decreases sympathy and prosocial behavioral intentions toward SH targets and increases happiness about the SH incident and victim-blaming (Page et al., 2016). This informs our next question:

Question six: Are the factors that motivate allied bystanders the same as those that motivate adversarial bystanders to take action?

Another interesting topic to explore is the idea of allyship in the context of adversarial bystanders. We imagine that individuals whom we categorize as "adversarial bystanders" do not see themselves as adversarial, which leads to question seven:

Question seven: How do adversarial bystanders perceive themselves and their own actions?

When contemplating this question, one word that comes to mind is "patriot," which Michael Edison Hayden, senior investigative reporter and spokesman for the Southern Poverty Law Center, states has been co-opted "for the purpose of doing harm" (Vera, 2021). Thus adversarial bystanders are likely to frame their actions in ways akin to patriotism, fighting the "good fight" to protect "innocent men" from undeserved persecution rather than as action to harm SH targets. And, Peter Sokolowski, editor-at-large for Merriam-Webster dictionary, notes that being a patriot is an "identity . . . that touches people deeply" (Vera, 2021). Thus, both patriot and ally are terms associated with one's self-concept or identity. And yet another interesting idea is to apply the Bowes-Sperry and O'Leary-Kelly (2005) typology to adversarial bystanders, leading to our next two questions.

Question eight: Do adversarial bystanders use low-involvement actions similar to those used by allied bystanders such as privately offering support to individuals but to those accused of SH rather than to their targets?
Question nine: What types of actions are used most frequently by adversarial bystanders?

The final step in Figure 3.1 deals with the type of communication channels SH bystanders chose (i.e., physical, virtual, and/or digital), leading to our final two questions:

Question ten: Do allied bystanders tend to use different communication channels than adversarial bystanders: (a) inside organizational spaces, and/or (b) outside organizational spaces?

Question 11: What role, if any, does the strength of an organization's SH policy play on the communication channels that allied and adversarial bystanders use inside organizational spaces?

In conclusion, the MTM impacted many aspects of BB in workplace SH. First, it created more bystanders by providing access to information about SH incidents to anyone who wanted to know about it. Second, it gave these people, who became "those in the know" as well as others who had known about SH within their workplaces before the MTM a space outside of the organizations which employed them to make their voices heard, some voicing support for SH targets and others for those accused of harassing them. And finally, we hope, it forced organizations that had been complicit in perpetuating SH to "do better" so that fewer individuals within these organizations have the chance to become "those in the know."

Notes

1 See Chapter 4 for detail on organizational failures with regard to addressing SH.
2 It is important to note that some countries have done better than others in terms of creating and enforcing anti-harassment legislation.
3 We use the term "behavior" rather than "intervention" when speaking generally because it is a more accurate description of the phenomenon given that many bystanders do not intervene. We do, however, use "intervention" when describing the behavior of *active* bystanders.
4 www.cnn.com/2017/11/09/world/metoo-hashtag-global-movement/index.html
5 www.pewresearch.org/short-reads/2018/10/11/how-social-media-users-have-discussed-sexual-harassment-since-metoo-went-viral/
6 We use this model because it "is the root of multiple models" (Griffith et al., 2022), which extend the original focus beyond workplace SH harassment and because it has been used to empirically explore other topics such as BB in harassment based on sexual-orientation (Ryan & Wessel, 2012).
7 Latané and Darley's (1970) framework includes additional steps that we chose to exclude because they are not central to our model.
8 See Chapter 2 for more detail on MTM in the digital realm.
9 This response implies that Tarantino actually "did" something helpful but that something may have been to downplay or ignore SH of which he was aware, which may have been helpful to SH initiators but not their targets.
10 While Tarantino may regret his actions and thus could be considered an avoidant bystander, there is evidence indicating he was an adversarial bystander before the MTM, taking actions such as euphemistically labelling the "sexual assault of a 13-year-old girl in 1977," saying she was "down with it" (Carroll, 2018).
11 See Chapter 10 for details about the role of SES in #MeToo.
12 See Chapter 4 for detail about the role of organizational factors in the MTM.
13 We use the term "intervention" (rather than "behavior") for active bystanders because their behavior can be considered intervention whereas that of inactive bystanders cannot.
14 www.merriam-webster.com/dictionary/intervention

15 Some literature refers to bystanders who intervene as "upstanders," that is, individuals who do not simply "stand by" in the face of injustices such as SH but rather "stand up" by taking action to improve the situation (e.g., Bond & Haynes-Baratz, 2022; Grantham, 2011).
16 www.britannica.com/topic/Me-Too-movement
17 See Chapter 1 for detail on the MTM as a form of social activism.
18 See Chapter 2 for detail on the importance of social media during the MTM.
19 See Chapter 11 for detail regarding accountability for harassers.
20 Although Christopher Partee is Black, his gender (i.e., man) places him in an "advantaged group" with regard to gender-related issues such as SH.
21 Although most organizations have policies and procedures for holding harassers accountable, these mechanisms are often not utilized effectively—hence, necessitating the MTM
22 See Chapter 6 for detail about less severe social-sexual behaviors that are not considered to be SH by many individuals.
23 See Chapter 4 for detail about organizational-level factors in SH.

References

Ayanian, A. H., Uluğ, Ö. M., Radke, H. R., & Zick, A. (2024). The social psychological predictors of men's backlash responses to the# MeToo movement. *Group Processes & Intergroup Relations*, 13684302231210492.

Barmes, L. (2023). Silencing at work: Sexual harassment, workplace misconduct and NDAs. *Industrial Law Journal*, 52(1), 68–106.

Bergkamp, J., Olson, L., & Martin, A. (2022). Before allyship: A model of integrating awareness of a privileged social identity. *Frontiers in Psychology*, 13, 7714.

Blair, E. (2019, September 4). When the "whisper network" goes public: The shitty media men list, 2 years on. *National Public Radio*. www.npr.org/2019/09/04/757282973/when-the-whisper-network-goes-public-the-s-y-media-men-list-2-years-on

Bond, M. A., & Haynes-Baratz, M. C. (2022). Mobilizing bystanders to address microaggressions in the workplace: The case for a systems-change approach to getting a (Collective) GRIP. American *Journal of Community Psychology*, 69(1–2), 221–238.

Bowes-Sperry, L., & Powell, G. N. (1999). Observers' reactions to social-sexual behavior at work: An ethical decision making perspective. *Journal of Management*, 25(6), 779–802.

Bowes-Sperry, L., & O'Leary-Kelly, A. M. (2005). To act or not to act: The dilemma faced by sexual harassment observers. *Academy of Management Review*, 30(2), 288–306.

Boyle, K., & Rathnayake, C. (2020). # HimToo and the networking of misogyny in the age of# MeToo. *Feminist Media Studies*, 20(8), 1259–1277.

Brown, S. E., & Battle, J. S. (2019). Ostracizing targets of workplace sexual harassment before and after the# MeToo movement. *Equality, Diversity and Inclusion: An International Journal*, 39(1), 53–67.

Carrie Fisher gave a cow tongue to predatory producer. (2017, October 17). www.bbc.com/news/entertainment-arts-41650345

Carlson, J., Leek, C., Casey, E., Tolman, R., & Allen, C. (2020). What's in a name? A synthesis of "allyship" elements from academic and activist literature. *Journal of Family Violence*, 35, 889–898.

Carroll, R. (2018, February 7). *"I think people are really disgusted"—Quentin Tarantino faces Hollywood backlash.* www.theguardian.com/film/2018/feb/07/quentin-tarantino-hollywood-baclash-uma-thurman-roman-polanski

Cartwright, L. (2023, March 6). Ugly battle over "Shitty Media Men" list ends in six-figure payout. *Daily Beast.* www.thedailybeast.com/ugly-battle-over-shtty-media-men-list-ends-in-six-figure-payout

Daley, L. P., Travis, D. J., & Shaffer, E. S. (2019). Sexual harassment in the workplace: How companies can prepare, prevent, respond, & transform their culture. *Catalyst.* www.catalyst.org/wp-content/uploads/2019/01/sexual_harassment_in_the_workplace_report.pdf

Desta, Y. (2018, May 9). Roman Polanki thinks the #metoo movement is just "mass hysteria". *Vanity Fair.* www.vanityfair.com/hollywood/2018/05/roman-polanski-opinion-me-too-movement

Dodson, S. J., Goodwin, R. D., Graham, J., & Diekmann, K. A. (2023). Moral foundations, sympathy, and punishment following organizational sexual misconduct allegations. *Organization Science, 34*(5), 1651–1996.

Elsesser, K. (2020, December 21). Covid's impact on sexual harassment. *Forbes.* www.forbes.com/sites/kimelsesser/2020/12/21/covids-impact-on-sexual-harassment/

Fathimah, S., Malihah, E., Wiyanarti, E., Munthe, D. P., & Suarjana, I. W. G. (2023). "From workspace to virtual space": The impact of cyber sexual harassment on women workers' well-being. *Journal of Public Health,* fdad225.

Feldblum, R., & Lipnic, V. A. (2016). *Select task force on the study of harassment in the workplace.* US Equal Employment Opportunity Commission.

Flecha, R. (2021). Second-order sexual harassment: Violence against the silence breakers who support the victims. *Violence Against Women, 27*(11), 1980–1999.

Fortmueller, K. (2022). Vintage furniture: The significance of the casting couch as industry gossip and rumor. *NECSUS_European Journal of Media Studies, 11*(1), 18–40.

Garber, M. (2017, October 11). In the valley of the open secret. *The Atlantic.* www.theatlantic.com/entertainment/archive/2017/10/harvey-weinstein-latest-allegations/542508/

Gentile, K. (2017). Playing with shame: The temporal work of rape jokes for the cultural body. *Studies in Gender and Sexuality, 18*(4), 287–293.

Glomb, T. M., Richman, W. L., Hulin, C. L., Drasgow, F., Schneider, K. T., & Fitzgerald, L. F. (1997). Ambient sexual harassment: An integrated model of antecedents and consequences. *Organizational Behavior and Human Decision Processes, 71*(3), 309–328.

Goodwin, R., Graham, J., & Diekmann, K. A. (2020). Good intentions aren't good enough: Moral courage in opposing sexual harassment. *Journal of Experimental Social Psychology, 86,* 103894.

Grantham, T. C. (2011). New directions for gifted Black males suffering from bystander effects: A call for upstanders. *Roeper Review, 33*(4), 263–272.

Griffith, J., Malone, M. F. T., & Shea, C. M. (2022). From bystander to ally among faculty colleagues: Construction and validation of the bystander intervention behavior scale. *Equality, Diversity and Inclusion: An International Journal, 41*(2), 273–293. doi:10.1108/edi-02-2021-0050

Haritos, A. (2018, January 5). Whisper network: A dozen university cases logged in sexual misconduct database. *Michigan Daily.* www.michigandaily.com/news/academics/whisper-network-university-michigan-academics-logged-sexual-misconduct-database/

Hershcovis, M. S., Vranjes, I., Berdahl, J. L., & Cortina, L. M. (2021). See no evil, hear no evil, speak no evil: Theorizing network silence around sexual harassment. *Journal of Applied Psychology, 106*(12), 1834.

Jones, T. M. (1991). Ethical decision making by individuals in organizations: An issue-contingent model. *Academy of Management Review, 16*(2), 366–395.

Kantor, J. (2017, October 19). Tarantino on Weinstein: "I knew enough to do more than I did". *New York Times*. www.nytimes.com/2017/10/19/movies/tarantino-weinstein.html

Karami, A., Spinel, M. Y., White, C. N., Ford, K., & Swan, S. (2021). A systematic literature review of sexual harassment studies with text mining. *Sustainability*, *13*(12), 6589.

Latané, B., & Darley, J. M. (1969). Bystander "apathy". *American Scientist*, *57*(2), 244–268.

Latané, B., & Darley, J. M. (1970). *The unresponsive bystander: Why doesn't he help?* Appleton-Century-Crofts.

Liang, Y., & Park, Y. (2022). Because I know how it hurts: Employee bystander intervention in customer sexual harassment through empathy and its moderating factors. *Journal of Occupational Health Psychology*, *27*(3), 339–348.

Medeiros, K. E., & Griffith, J. A. (2019). Double-edged scalpels: The trials and triumphs of women surgeons. *Narrative Inquiry in Bioethics*, *9*(3), 221–227.

McDonald, P., Charlesworth, S., & Graham, T. (2016). Action or inaction: Bystander intervention in workplace sexual harassment. *The International Journal of Human Resource Management*, *27*(5), 548–566.

McMahon, S. (2022). How helpful is bystander intervention? Perspectives of dating and sexual violence survivors. *Violence Against Women*, 10778012221117596.

Merkin, D. (2018, January 5). Publicly, we say #metoo. Privately, we have misgivings. *New York Times*. www.nytimes.com/2018/01/05/opinion/golden-globes-metoo.html

Miner-Rubino, K., & Cortina, L. M. (2004). Working in a context of hostility toward women: Implications for employees' well-being. *Journal of Occupational Health Psychology*, *9*(2), 107–122.

Morris, A. (2018, October 11). #HimToo: Left and right embrace opposing takes on the same hashtag. *National Public Radio*. www.npr.org/2018/10/11/656293787/-himtoo-left-and-right-embrace-opposing-takes-on-same-hashtag

Moschella, E. A., & Banyard, V. L. (2020). Reactions to actions: Exploring how types of bystander action are linked to positive and negative consequences. *The Journal of Primary Prevention*, *41*(6), 585–602.

Moschella, E. A., & Banyard, V. L. (2021). Action and reaction: The impact of consequences of intervening in situations of interpersonal violence. *Journal of Interpersonal Violence*, *36*(7–8), NP3820–NP3843.

Meza, S. (2017, November 22). What is a whisper network? How women are taking down bad men in the #metoo age. *Newsweek*. www.newsweek.com/what-whisper-network-sexual-misconduct-allegations-719009

Ng, K., Niven, K., & Notelaers, G. (2022). Does bystander behavior make a difference? How passive and active bystanders in the group moderate the effects of bullying exposure. *Journal of Occupational Health Psychology*, *27*(1), 119–135.

Nutbeam, M., & Mereish, E. H. (2022). Negative attitudes and beliefs toward the# MeToo movement on Twitter. *Journal of Interpersonal Violence*, *37*(15–16), NP13018–NP13044.

O'Leary-Kelly, A. M., & Bowes-Sperry, L. (2001). Sexual harassment as unethical behavior: The role of moral intensity. *Human Resource Management Review*, *11*(1–2), 73–92.

Olson, A. (2017, December 17). For witnesses, calling out sexual harassment is complicated. *Associated Press*. https://apnews.com/article/239a0f62b30642a78 058fbb1b3df1f7e

Page, T. E., Pina, A., & Giner-Sorolla, R. (2016). "It was only harmless banter!" The development and preliminary validation of the moral disengagement in sexual harassment scale. *Aggressive Behavior*, *42*(3), 254–273.

Pouwelse, M., Mulder, R., & Mikkelsen, E. G. (2021). The role of bystanders in workplace bullying: An overview of theories and empirical research. In P. D'Cruz, E. Noronha, E. Bailien, B. Catley, K. Harlos, A. Høgh & E. G. Mikkelsen (Eds.), *Pathways of job-related negative behaviour* (pp. 385–422). Springer Singapore.

Radke, H. R., Kutlaca, M., Siem, B., Wright, S. C., & Becker, J. C. (2020). Beyond allyship: Motivations for advantaged group members to engage in action for disadvantaged groups. *Personality and Social Psychology Review, 24*(4), 291–315

Reich, T. C., & Hershcovis, M. S. (2015). Observing workplace incivility. *Journal of Applied Psychology, 100*(1), 203–215.

Rentschler, C. A. (2017). Bystander intervention, feminist hashtag activism, and the anti-carceral politics of care. *Feminist Media Studies, 17*(4), 565–584.

Ryan, A. M., & Wessel, J. L. (2012). Sexual orientation harassment in the workplace, when do observers intervene? *Journal of Organizational Behavior, 33*(4), 488–509.

Selvanathan, H. P., Lickel, B., & Dasgupta, N. (2020). An integrative framework on the impact of allies: How identity-based needs influence intergroup solidarity and social movements. *European Journal of Social Psychology, 50*(6), 1344–1361.

Shakespeare, W. (2000). *As you like it* (Rev. ed.). Yale University Press. (Original work published 1599)

Speak Out Act, Public Law No. 117–224. (2022). www.congress.gov/bill/117th-congress/senate-bill/4524/text

Smith, L. (2017, October 12). Seth McFarland explains joke about Harvey Weinsten from 2013. *The Independent.* www.independent.co.uk/news/world/americas/seth-macfarlane-harvey-weinstein-2013-joke-jessica-barth-a7995821.html

Stephenson, K. A., Kuismin, A., Putnam, L. L., & Sivunen, A. (2020). Process studies of organizational space. *Academy of Management Annals, 14*(2), 797–827.

van der Linden, S., & Panagopoulos, C. (2019). The O'Reilly factor: An ideological bias in judgments about sexual harassment. *Personality and Individual Differences, 139*, 198–201.

Vera, A. (2021, January 30). What exactly does it mean to be a patriot? Experts say it's not easy to define. *CNN.* www.cnn.com/2021/01/30/us/patriot-definition-trnd/index.html

Vogels, E. A. (2021, January 13). The state of online harassment. *Pew Research Center.* www.pewresearch.org/internet/2021/01/13/the-state-of-online-harassment/

Zinshteyn, M. (2022, February 17). Cal State chancellor resigns under fire over how he handled sexual harassment complaints. *Cal Matters.* https://calmatters.org/education/higher-education/2022/02/cal-state-chancellor-resigns/

4

EXPOSING ORGANIZATIONAL CULTURE THROUGH THE PROCESS OF SENSEMAKING

Angela Workman-Stark

Introduction: Making the Invisible Visible

More than 10 years ago, I was a Chief Superintendent in the Royal Canadian Mounted Police (RCMP) overseeing the organization's response to complaints of sex-based discrimination and harassment, which eventually included a class action lawsuit involving over 3,000 women and costing nearly $150 million in damages. During a meeting on culture and organizational change, Commissioner Paulson characterized the RCMP culture as a "High School Boys' locker room" in Arkansas. While no one at the meeting had ever been in this type of locker room, the analogy was clear—the kind of language used, the antics played, and the types of guys who dominated or got picked on. Essentially, what Commissioner Paulson described was a masculinity contest culture in which people vie for status by proving their ability to "man up" and demonstrate they are physically strong, emotionally tough, and socially ruthless (Berdahl et al., 2018).

Masculinity contest cultures harm both women and men (Glick et al., 2018; Regina & Allen, 2023; Workman-Stark, 2021; Xie & Zheng, 2022), but like other sexual harassment (SH) class action lawsuits, the RCMP lawsuit was limited to women victims only. The internal RCMP narrative followed this same theme with many action items focused on advancing women, such as mentoring and changes to selection processes. Additionally, as the Commissioner tended to define the problem as the actions of a few "rotten apples," this characterization not only downplayed the seriousness of the harassment issue but also ignored the influence of organizational culture. In short, these depictions illustrate the efforts of top RCMP leaders to

DOI: 10.4324/9781003300953-5

create a reality that was "given" to employees as opposed to allowing them to share their own interpretations of events. While influencing employees' understanding is an important element of organizational change (Maitlis & Christianson, 2014), these top-down efforts were unlikely to convey an adequate sense of reality because they did not capture the perceptions and experiences of employees. As a result, RCMP leaders lacked a sufficient understanding of key contextual factors, such as the persistence of masculinity contest norms, focusing instead on person-level solutions.

In this chapter, I use the example of the RCMP to illustrate how organizational sensemaking—a social process in which members interpret their environment through interactions with others (Maitlis & Christianson, 2014)—can help identify the nature of SH and provide important insights into organizational culture, including how it enables harassment to persist and how it might be effectively addressed. Drawing from more than 20 years of experience in the RCMP and hundreds of pages of data, I show how masculinity contest cultures (MCCs) operate to reinforce status based on sex, race, and other identities with negative implications for both men and women. I also demonstrate how MCCs perpetuate sex-based and other forms of harassment through social networks that protect abusers and compel victims and bystanders to remain silent (Hershcovis et al., 2021). Importantly, I illustrate that conventional interventions that focus on the actions of individuals are not going to be effective in MCCs.

Throughout this chapter, I consider what the #MeToo movement has helped to illuminate and what remains hidden in the shadows about the nature and causes of SH. For instance, numerous studies have highlighted the prevalence of SH (e.g., Ilies et al., 2003; Leskinen et al., 2011; Wilson, 2018), with as many as 58% of women having experienced harassment at work (Ilies et al., 2003). Yet it took the #MeToo movement to create a reckoning for organizations and individual harassers. What is even more surprising is that despite this renewed focus on SH, interventions continue to target individuals and not the broader system. In this chapter, I advocate for employee sensemaking as a critical resource for exposing organizational culture and informing differing perceptions of reality about the nature and scope of harassment. In addition to highlighting the value of sensemaking in both preventing and addressing SH, I suggest the need for future research to address key questions about what works, what does not.

#MeToo and Sexual Harassment Research

Sexual harassment refers to behavior that demeans or humiliates others based on sex (Berdahl, 2007a) and encompasses three primary types of misconduct: sexual coercion, unwanted sexual attention, and gender harassment (Fitzgerald et al., 1997). As the most common form of SH (e.g., Cortina & Areguin, 2021), gender harassment involves gender put-downs that can take the form of misogynist comments and behaviors against women. Against men it can consist of comparing men to women and suggesting they are "not man enough" (Berdahl & Moore, 2006). Unwanted sexual attention is the second most common form of harassment that includes sexual behaviors such as touching, attempts to draw someone into sex-related conversations, and repeated requests for dates. Sexual coercion is rarest and involves job-related threats or promises to coerce sexual cooperation.

To date, SH research has largely explored individual contributors, including the motives and actions of the perpetrators, the demographic characteristics of both harassers and their targets (e.g., Cortina & Berdahl, 2008; Lengnick-Hall, 1995; O'Leary-Kelly et al., 2009; USMSPB, 2018; Welsh, 1999), or the reasons why victims fail to report harassment (Bergman et al., 2002), such as concerns that no action will be taken, they will not be believed, or they will retaliated against for speaking up (e.g., Bergman et al., 2002; Cortina & Magley, 2003; Clair et al., 2019; Fernando & Prasad, 2018; Ford et al., 2021; Scarduzio et al., 2020).

Whereas individual factors can motivate individuals to harass others (Cortina & Areguin, 2021), increasingly, studies show that organizational factors are more likely to predict SH. For instance, male-dominated organizations, particularly those with strong masculine identities and those with men occupying greater positions of power, are associated with higher rates of SH (e.g., Bell et al., 2002; Berdahl, 2007b; Fitzgerald et al., 1997; Kabat-Farr & Cortina, 2014; McLaughlin et al., 2012). Organizational tolerance has also been shown to be significant predictor of SH (e.g., Hulin et al., 1996; Willness et al., 2007).

Organizational climates with a high tolerance for SH are characterized by perceptions that it is risky to make a formal complaint, that complaints will not be taken seriously, that victims will face retaliation, or that harassers will not be held accountable (Williams et al., 1999). This reality was captured in the early stages of the #MeToo movement in a public letter from Monica Ramirez, who, on behalf of an organization of farmworker women, called out the similar circumstances for victims across different environments. Namely, the common experience of "being preyed upon by individuals who have the power to hire, fire, blacklist and otherwise threaten [their] economic, physical and emotional security" (Corbett, 2022, para. 14).

Another prominent contributor is organizational culture, which is expected to play a critical role in how SH is interpreted and responded to (Keyton et al., 2001). Male dominated occupations, such as the military and policing, are expected to have higher rates of SH due to hierarchical, organizational cultures that endorse traditional forms of masculinity (Fitzgerald et al., 1999), including "competitiveness, assertiveness, physical strength, aggression, risk-taking, courage, heterosexuality, and lack of feminine traits" (Willer et al., 2013, p. 983).

Despite the influence of these contextual factors, organizational leaders continue to adopt individualized responses to SH with a specific focus on mandatory harassment training as well as identifying and weeding out those individuals who sexually harass others (e.g., Cortina & Areguin, 2021). While sanctioning individual harassers is a necessary response to SH, this approach prevents organizations from seeing the uncomfortable truth about the factors that enable SH in the first place. As a result, the narrative of the "few rotten apples" prevails and alternate realties are blocked from emerging. Worse still, SH continues, unchecked. To effectively respond to SH requires shifting from the rotten apple narrative to the "bad barrels" of workplace contexts that generate and tolerate SH (e.g., Tenbrunsel et al., 2019; Zimbardo, 2004).

From Rotten Apples to Rotten Barrels

A classic case of the rotten apple focus is the prosecution and conviction of Harvey Weinstein for sexual assault against multiple victims. No doubt, actress Alyssa Milano's #MeToo call to action can be credited with helping take Weinstein and others down, but what about the environment that enabled this behavior to continue for so long? In this section of the chapter, I move beyond person-level factors (e.g., sexist beliefs) to the organizational context that helps facilitate SH. In particular, I focus on a dysfunctional culture that endorses and promotes dominance over others: the masculinity contest culture.

Masculinity Contest Cultures

Masculinity contest cultures (MCCs) are characterized by zero-sum competitions in which mostly men "compete at work for dominance, by showing no weakness, demonstrating a single-minded focus on professional success, displaying physical endurance and strength, and engaging in cutthroat competition (Berdahl et al., 2018, p. 430). Engaging in masculinity contests requires individuals to play by rules that endorse hegemonic, masculine norms (Berdahl et al., 2018), specifically, favoring masculinity over femininity and traits that men should possess (e.g., aggression, ambition, and strength versus sensitivity, insecurity, uncertainty, and other forms of perceived weakness; see Rudman et al., 2012). The outcome of these contests is the establishment of gendered hierarchies that reinforce inequalities for women and men who fail to conform (Bridges & Pascoe, 2014). In short, these hierarchies place White, heterosexual, physically fit and able-bodied men at the top with all other marginalized identities relegated to lower social status within the workplace (e.g., Berdahl et al., 2018; Connell & Messerschmidt, 2005).

Once MCC norms are embedded into an organization's culture, both men and women are expected to play the game to be successful. This means proving that they are "man enough" through hypercompetitive contests, such as maintaining heavy workloads and working long hours, stepping on others to get ahead, or taking unreasonable risks (Berdahl et al., 2018). For some individuals, proving masculinity might involve displays of bravado or aggressiveness (Bosson et al., 2009) or avoiding behaviors and people deemed as feminine and weak (Kupers, 2005; Vandello & Bosson, 2013). For women, this might mean avoiding the "pink jobs" (roles that are deemed more suited to women), distancing themselves from other women, or failing to support women in general (Derks et al., 2011).

Other individuals might feel pressured to downplay or hide marginalized identities, such as those based on race, ability, or sexuality. Because women and men from these marginalized groups tend to be perceived as having lower social status, playing the game may lead to backlash due to social norms that object to traditional masculine behaviors enacted by women and minority men (e.g., Amanatullah & Tinsley, 2013; Livingston & Pearce, 2009; Rudman et al., 2012; Williams & Tiedens, 2016). Winning the contest means dominating others; therefore, women, gay men, men of color, men with lessor physical abilities, and other types of "non-conforming" men and women are more likely to be the "losers" of the masculinity contest.

At the more extreme end of the contest, masculinity beliefs can compel some men to preserve and protect their identities as "real men" by challenging the heterosexuality of other men (Maass et al., 2003), harassing both men and women (Alonso, 2018; Berdahl, 2007b; Maass et al., 2003), and/or silencing individuals who speak out against harassment (e.g., Hershcovis et al., 2021). These and other behaviors may also be enacted by men who have had their masculinity threatened and feel the need to reassert their manhood.

In recent years, I have collected hundreds of stories from police personnel about their experiences of working in masculinity contest cultures. One of the more memorable stories came from a constable who shared the fallout from his decision to attend a Pride event with one of his work colleagues. Although it was well known that he was heterosexual, when he returned to work for his next shift, he was completely ostracized by most members of his team. Over the next several weeks, the isolation continued, including the refusal of his colleagues to back him up when he responded to high-risk situations. Through association with members of the gay community this constable had violated the masculine norms of his unit and was no longer seen as "man enough." Whereas his colleagues chose to preserve their masculine identities by distancing themselves from him, he frequently put himself at risk during dangerous situations involving violent offenders or used excessive force to compel cooperation in attempts to prove his masculinity (Workman-Stark, 2017).

Diagnosing MCCs

To assist with diagnosing MCCs, Jennifer Berdahl and colleagues (2018) developed a 20-item measure that assesses four distinct, but related dimensions: (1) *Show No Weakness* (avoiding displays of vulnerability, such as admitting mistakes or doubt, and feminine emotions); (2) *Strength and Stamina* (endorsing physical strength and ability to work long hours without rest); (3) *Put Work First* (putting work ahead of external obligations, such as family, and not taking leave or breaks); and (4) *Dog-Eat-Dog* (a cutthroat environment in which employees are pitted against each other to become the "top dog").

While MCCs can exist in multiple sectors they are expected to be more pronounced in male-dominated, physical occupations. For example, firefighters tend to emphasize their muscular physique as evidence of status and legitimacy. Until recently, a primary outlet for these displays has been the firefighters' annual calendar with images depicting firefighters' "hardened bodies" and the heroic nature of their work. Because of the importance of physicality, less active and older firefighters are more likely to be stigmatized and vulnerable to isolation and harassment (Perrott, 2019). Research also shows how garbage collectors highlight their status over others through demonstrations of physical strength and the ability to run an entire collection route while lifting heavy bags of garbage, and by comparing themselves to workers who were viewed as lazy and less committed (Slutskaya et al., 2016). In policing, *strength and stamina* can be a significant source of social status and worth.

> *I've looked at physical fitness as synonymous with a good cop. If you weren't physically fit, I instantly would look down on you. I had already formed an opinion of who you are and what your abilities were.*
> *(Male police officer; Workman-Stark, 2022, p. 1251)*

Consistent with the importance placed on strength and physical fitness, not showing any weakness is another element of the contest that can be revealed through the actions of occupational members, such as condemning others for showing emotion. "There's no time for this . . . boys don't cry. Get the job done. Suck it up" (Workman-Stark, 2022, p. 1248). At the same time, pressure to constantly prove oneself can cause individuals to refrain from disclosing any issues with physical and mental health due to fears of being perceived as weak and potentially rejected by others.

> *I suffer from PTSD ADD and Mild depression. The only member who knows this is my current supervisor. I dare not tell anyone else for fear of persecution in some way or another . . .*
> *(Male police officer; Workman-Stark, 2021, p. 313)*

In my research involving Canadian police organizations, the dog-eat-dog and put work first dimensions of the MCC have been found to be more prominent (e.g., Rawski & Workman-Stark, 2018; Workman-Stark, 2021; Workman-Stark et al., 2023). These results are consistent with frequent depictions of the police workplace as a high school, bullying culture in which some people seek to dominate and/or isolate others who are seen as weaker or less committed.

The Harmful Outcomes of MCCs

The numerous lawsuits involving corrections, policing, firefighting, and military service (for example) suggest that MCCs promote the normalization of SH and other negative behaviors. Survey studies show that workplaces characterized as MCCs have significantly higher rates of harassment (Workman-Stark, 2021), including SH, co-worker bullying, and ethnic harassment (Glick et al., 2018). Employees also suffer more burnout, poorer mental and physical health, and significantly lower levels of psychological safety (Glick et al., 2018; Koc et al., 2021).

Beyond these outcomes, MCCs can influence the type of leadership that is embraced and the associated policies and practices for how leaders are selected. Taking policing as an example, the macho culture has tended to emphasize an aggressive, competitive, and performance-driven leadership style (Silvestri, 2003, 2007). Therefore, it is not surprising that depictions of MCCs within policing highlight the prevalence of selection processes that pit employees against each other to get ahead (Workman-Stark, 2021). While the relationship between MCCs and leadership practices may be circular, in that MCCs influence leadership and vice versa, MCCs, regardless of occupational sector, are related to a more toxic form of leadership (Matos et al., 2018) and have fewer women in leadership positions (Glick et al., 2018).

Sandy Hershcovis and colleagues (2021) introduced the idea that MCCs can also cause harassment-related silence. That is, MCC norms compel members of workplace networks (victims, bystanders, authority figures) to be silent (e.g., not speak up about SH), silence others (e.g., advise against making a formal complaint), or to refrain from taking action (e.g., dismiss or trivialize those who speak up about their experiences).

Janet Merlo, a former member of the Royal Canadian Mounted Police (RCMP), is well known for her lead role in successfully bringing forth a class action lawsuit against the RCMP. In her book, published years after her experiences of harassment, she describes the great wall of silence that emerged after she formally reported the abuse.

> *The investigator told me that none of the members named in my statement—neither perpetrators nor bystanders—could recall any of the incidents I mentioned . . . No one could remember having seen a blow-up doll in a watch commander's office, though it had been legend around the detachment . . . Nobody remembered the dildos or requests to kiss it better or a multitude of other vulgar incidents. Nobody substantiated any of my claims . . . [it was] the wall of silence.*
>
> *(Merlo, 2013)*

I was at an executive meeting soon after Merlo's lawsuit was filed and her book was released. Just like the third dimension of silence (not hearing; not taking action), some individuals sought to invalidate her and her experiences because she was not a "real mountie." They didn't believe she really wanted to become one. She just showed up at a recruiting session with someone else and decided to apply, implying she did not have the same level of commitment as others. Therefore, her concerns were not worthy of attention.

As previously indicated, organizations with MCCs not only contribute to SH and other forms of misconduct, they also influence how organizations respond to complaints of SH. Whereas the widespread endorsement of MCC norms pressures people to conform by engaging in and perpetuating the contest, it also compels protection of harassers and the promotion of harassment-related silence. Yet none of this harsh reality means anything if leaders persist with individualistic, "fixed" solutions and allow MCCs to remain hidden and unchallenged.

Exposing and Confronting MCCs

For winners of the masculinity contest or individuals who have significantly adapted their behaviors to survive, MCC norms may have become so entrenched that people either are unaware of them or simply accept that they exist. Just like fish may not recognize they are swimming in water, individuals who have been long-term winners of the masculinity contest may not even realize there is a dominant culture that awards winners and punishers losers. Given the emphasis on competitiveness and avoidance of weakness in many western organizations, people may even fail to see there are better ways to organize and interact with others, such as treating them fairly and confronting unethical issues like SH. In this section of the chapter, I present a process for exposing MCCs and other dominant cultures. I then highlight the potential of ethical leadership to counteract these problematic cultures.

Organizational Sensemaking

Jennifer Freyd (2018) suggests that senior leaders require *institutional courage* to engage in a transparent process of self-study and to accept accountability and make reparations where needed. The need for this type of courage may be particularly important for MCCs in which admitting mistakes and acknowledging problems are often viewed as weaknesses and where efforts to confront entrenched norms are pushed back against. Yet without exposing and challenging these toxic norms, organizations will continue with ineffective solutions that are likely to make matters worse. Organizational sensemaking is a valuable mechanism to facilitate these goals as it is a social process by which individuals assign meaning to their experiences through interactions with others (Maitlis & Christianson, 2014). It allows people to develop plausible explanations for situations or events that have occurred and to apply this knowledge to future action (Weick, 1995, 2001). Through the telling and retelling of these shared experiences, sensemaking not only illuminates organizational culture but also how it is created and sustained (Weick, 1995).

In their interactional framing theory of work social sexual behavior, Rawski and colleagues (2022b) propose that culture and sensemaking are intertwined processes in that sensemaking develops norms and values that are taught to organizational members while culture helps sets the boundaries for acceptable behavior (Daft & Weick, 1984). In other words, sensemaking can provide a critical theoretical lens through which the relationship between culture and SH can be examined and understood (Dougherty & Smythe, 2004; Rawski et al., 2022a).

Weick's (1995, 2001) seven core properties of sensemaking can help shape an understanding of culture and its relationship to SH in several ways. First, sensemaking is about identity and identity construction, and involves the sensemaker developing a sense of who they are based on their own experiences and the experiences of others. How people see themselves in a given situation influences how they make sense of these situations through interactions with others. For example, early in my policing career I came to see myself as an interloper, someone who was trespassing on the domain of men. Therefore, when my male colleagues made fun of a female constable who complained about SH, I joined in on the laughter rather than call out their behavior.

Sensemaking is also *retrospective* in that interpretations of past experiences and events will be used to make sense of or predict future events. This retrospective process involves developing plausible reasons that rationalize what people are doing or have done (Weick et al., 2005). It attempts to create order from ambiguity and chaos by asking, "What is the story here?" followed by the question of "Now what?" (i.e., actions that could/should be taken), which can include self-talk, undertaken individually, or through the sharing of narratives in conversations with others. The intent is to assign meaning to these experiences (Brown et al., 2008; Weick, 1995).

The properties of *enactment* and *enacting cues* suggest that employees are part of an environment as well as actors within it who rely on cues from their environment to associate meaning with events. From these interpretations, people can respond to these cues in ways that either reinforce or resist these environmental pressures. Sensemaking is also primarily *social* in that sensemaking processes are influenced by others. In other words, when people interpret situations or events, they are expected to consider what they have been told by others along with how others think about or demand from them. For example, someone who has experienced SH is likely to reflect on the experiences of others who have reported harassment as well as the expectations from their social environment when making a decision about speaking up.

Lastly, sensemaking is an *ongoing* process through which people constantly make sense of themselves and their environment, thereby influencing their understanding of organizational culture and expectations for behavior during a given situation. As it is driven by *plausibility* rather than accuracy, sensemaking may also cause some information to be eliminated or distorted to achieve a sense of coherence. This latter property helps explain why sensemaking can lead to different understandings of the same situation or events, compelling individuals to reinforce or reject a prevailing narrative about the nature of SH.

Exposing Dominant Norms in the RCMP

Following numerous harassment complaints, including a class action lawsuit, and national broadcasts sharing the stories of women, the RCMP was pressured to take action. The outcome was the development of an action plan that emphasized mandatory harassment training, strengthening harassment policies and practices, and increasing the representation of women and other minority employees. A few months after the action plan was shared with employees, a survey was undertaken to assess employee perceptions of key themes, such as ethics, supervision, and job satisfaction, along with open-ended questions about the working environment.

Nearly a decade after the data were collected, responses to the open-ended questions were analyzed through a sensemaking lens to develop a better understanding of organizational culture and its relationship to SH and other forms of misconduct (Workman-Stark & Jones, 2023). This data subset ($N = 3,769$) comprised participants who were mainly White (92.3%), male (80.4%) officers, who were between the ages of 30 and 39 years (37.3%), and had been working for the RCMP for between 5 and 14 years (45.7%).

Two key questions guided the analysis of the data: (1) How did RCMP members make sense of the numerous disclosures of harassment and how the organization has responded?; (2) How did this sensemaking potentially reinforce or challenge dominant norms about harassment? For brevity, I focus on two key themes to illustrate the value of a sensemaking process: (1) employee interpretations of SH, and (2) the relationship between culture and silence.

Interpreting Sexual Harassment

Like the aftermath of the Harvey Weinstein affair, there was so much public discourse about SH within the RCMP it was impossible to escape it. Because of the intensity of media coverage, organizational sensemaking was both inherently social and retrospective. From the survey data, it was evident that the public nature of the harassment complaints created a shared experience that people attempted to make sense of.

The Commissioner says he wants to create a harassment-free environment, but when I watched the television show about what happened in the west to the women in the RCMP who spoke out against harassment, he did nothing to help them. That's the culture of the RCMP, women are tolerated.
                    (Female, White, 50–54 years of age, 25–29 years of service)

This is an organization that does not practice what it preaches. I know of many members who have suffered from bullying, harassment, and sexual harassment. Instead of punishing the bullies and harassers we

seem to promote them to a higher rank ... We have a commissioner who believes that our problems can be attributed to a "few rotten apples" as opposed to institutional problems.
                    (Male, Indigenous, 35–39 years of age, 5–9 years of service)

For a larger group of respondents, the survey provided an opportunity to communicate their interpretations of harassment, including their own experiences of bullying and harassment. While the majority of comments pertained to gender harassment, some respondents confronted the prevailing harassment narrative through shared experiences of bullying and discrimination and harassment based on race, sexuality, and physical and mental health. The implication was that the RCMP was "[n]ot a place for people who care about themselves and their families, but for those who are A types, can't stop working and competing for promotions or jobs." In other words, the RCMP environment was consistent with a masculinity contest culture.

We have a high percentage of members that are medicated for anxiety, and depression. We eat our own at the first sign of weakness and do not properly support those members that have legitimate workplace injuries. There are members that abuse the system but there is also a high percentage of members who are and have been off duty sick that are painted with the same brush. These members have been there to answer the call for the RCMP and when they look for help from the organization they receive a blank stare. I believe that the organization does not want to leave these members in the wind but they are too ignorant to the true problems to effectively change and help their walking wounded.
                    (Male, White, 30–34 years of age, 5–9 years of service)

For many respondents, a key part of the initial sensemaking process was to assess the plausibility of the SH complaints and media depictions of what was happening in the RCMP. The majority indicated that harassment, primarily gender harassment and discrimination, were common issues experienced across the RCMP, yet others rejected the idea that SH was even an issue.

The whole sexual harassment issue needs to be put to rest. We are no different than any other large company or organization.
                    (Male, White, 25–29 years old, 5–9 years of service)

I find that the whole sexual harassment scandals in the media are really tiresome for morale. I don't believe that it happens quite the way that these female members are reporting it and it makes the other female members look like idiots. I think that management should fight against the allegations that are not legit and do it publicly. I think that the majority of these allegations are baseless and they have done more harm than good for the rest of the female membership.

(Female, White, 40–44 years old, 15–19 years of service)

The Relationship Between Culture and Silence

In a previous section of this chapter, I discussed how MCCs can influence silencing behaviors, such that people choose to remain silent about harassment, discourage others from speaking up, or fail to address complaints once they have been reported. Drawing from two of Weick's (1995, 2001) sensemaking properties (social cues and enactment), the survey data showed how respondents relied upon cues from their social environment or their own experiences, which influenced how they had responded or might respond to future experiences of harassment.

I have only one personal experience of trying to use the internal processes to deal with a harassing supervisor. I am an older and experienced member. Reporting it only made my life hell. I hope things go better in the future for others who choose to run against the herd.

(Female, 45–49 years of age, 20–24 years of service)

Contrary to what commissioner has been saying there is still a lot of sexual harassment toward female members. And there is NO incentive for women to fill out a form and lay a formal complaint against a co-worker or supervisor. Who in their right mind would do that given the organization's track record?

(Male, White, 35–39 years old, 10–14 years of service)

Like previous depictions of MCCs, cues extracted from the work environment exposed a culture that not only compelled people to remain silent but to discourage them from speaking up. These cultural expectations of behavior were not limited to SH; they seemingly pertained to reporting misconduct in general.

They say all the right things in their emails and videos, but do not practice them. They claim that they will listen if an employee has concerns, but I have seen firsthand that the person who speaks up gets hammered down for opening their mouth.

(Male, White, 40–44 years of age, 5–9 years of service)

I was told to be quiet as nothing good would happen if I was to make a complaint, so I was transferred a few times from a job that I loved doing, just because my supervisor hated me and made my life miserable. Many of my co-workers and others that knew of the situation told me that I should have made a complaint, but I was advised not to. Since then, I have been very disappointed with the RCMP.
(Male, White, 40–44 years of age, 15–19 years of service)

Expectations or experiences of how formal complaints would be addressed relied upon the same social cues that were suggestive of dominant group norms to preserve and protect those in positions of power and influence. These norms primarily included protecting prominent group members from allegations of misconduct through discouraging of reporting, retaliating against complainants, and inadequate efforts to investigate complaints and impose sanctions on perpetrators.

I would be a policeman for free. There is nothing else I would have done in my life. I have for the most part enjoyed my postings, the challenges of general duty policing. What grinds my gears is watching the organization implode because of employees and supervisors who have been dishonorable in their pursuit of self advancement and perpetuating the old boys club. They protect each other and squash those who would stand up to them.
(Male, White, 45–49 years of age, 20–24 years of service)

The harassment system is completely ineffective and again relies on members of the same "old boys club" to investigate the allegations which are almost always dismissed.
(Male, White, 35–39 years of age, 10–14 years of service)

Implications of the RCMP Experience

The brief description of the RCMP experience demonstrates how organizational sensemaking can expose a dominant and toxic form of organizational culture and its implications for the workplace, specifically as it relates to SH. Whereas a minority of survey respondents contested the narrative that SH was an issue to be addressed, the majority perceived harassment to be a systemic problem seemingly driven by MCC norms that endorsed a competitive environment in which members of the "boys' club" were more likely to be elevated to positions of status while lower status individuals were potentially subjected to bullying and harassment. When victims complained, attempts were made to silence them to protect club members (i.e., the dominant majority). In short, this sensemaking process highlights that person-level solutions, such as simply revising reporting mechanisms, will do little to confront the culture that keeps people quiet in the first place or ignores their complaints of harassment. At the same time, it illustrates that while top leaders may ignore or be oblivious to the toxic culture, many people are not only likely to call it out for what it is but also have experienced its effects. By doing so, this sensemaking process exposes the bad barrel problem and challenges the narrative that a few rotten individuals are to blame.

Although this case study pertains to a policing environment, the same sensemaking process can be applied in other sectors. Additionally, these same themes have been identified through #MeToo. For example, the walkout of thousands of Google employees following lofty payouts to senior executives accused of SH, exposed the fallacy of the claim that a "few bad apples" were to blame and a deeper issue in which individuals in positions of power exploited policy gaps, protected harassers from facing consequences, and retaliated against those who complained (Elias, 2020). Like the RCMP and countless other organizations who had also implemented SH policies, the toxic culture rendered these policies ineffective.

Summary and Future Research

There is no denying that the #MeToo movement has further exposed the persistence of SH across many jurisdictions and the harms it has caused for those targeted. It has also helped spur additional research, enhancing our collective understanding of the situational factors that contribute to SH. More importantly, it has reinforced the concern that failure to expose and challenge existing cultural norms is unlikely to lead to any substantive change because the root causes remain hidden and harassment-related silence is allowed to continue, thus, the need for culturally based solutions.

In this chapter, I demonstrate that confronting toxic cultures can be particularly challenging in organizations characterized as MCCs due to the desire to avoid demonstration of weaknesses and to protect masculinity contest winners. Exposing systemic issues can also open organizations to legal and financial jeopardy. Yet substantively addressing SH requires institutional and leader courage, namely, courage to engage in a process of self-study, acknowledge the results, and accept responsibility to address them. To facilitate this process, I demonstrate how sensemaking can reveal dominant norms as well as challenge attempts by leaders to explain SH as the actions of a few problematic individuals.

As highlighted throughout this chapter, making toxic cultures visible is an important step in preventing and responding to SH; however, further research is required to test the efficacy of culturally based interventions. Without such research, organizations are likely to continue to adopt "best practice" interventions without evidence that these practices will make a difference. In other words, #MeToo has substantially moved the marker on SH, but more research is needed.

Preliminary results from studies involving Canadian police organizations suggest that ethical leadership can counteract the effects of MCCs and the climate of silence that is influenced by them. That is, leaders who exemplify ethical values, treat people fairly, listen to what employees have to say, communicate expectations for behavior, and hold people accountable for harassing others should have lower levels of harassment within their teams (Workman-Stark et al., 2023, 2024). These results are encouraging and provide an opportunity to explore additional research questions: Are ethical leaders more likely to intervene in SH (see Chapter 3 on Bystanders in SH)? How can organizations select for or develop ethical leaders? At what level of leadership should organizations intervene? To confront norms that keep problems hidden, future study could also explore how organizations can develop *institutional courage*.

References

Alonso, N. (2018). Playing to win: Male–male sex-based harassment and the masculinity contest. *Journal of Social Issues, 74*(3), 477–499.

Amanatullah, E. T., & Tinsley, C. H. (2013). Punishing female negotiators for asserting too much . . . or not enough: Exploring why advocacy moderates backlash against assertive female negotiators. *Organizational Behavior and Human Decision Processes, 120*(1), 110–122.

Bell, M. P., Mclaughlin, M. E., & Sequeira, J. M. (2002). Discrimination, harassment and the glass ceiling: Women executives as change agents. *Journal of Business Ethics, 37*(1), 65–76.

Berdahl, J. L. (2007a). Harassment based on sex: Protecting social status in the context of gender hierarchy. *Academy of Management Review, 32*(2), 641–658.

Berdahl, J. L. (2007b). The sexual harassment of uppity women. *Journal of Applied Psychology, 92*(2), 425–437.

Berdahl, J. L., Cooper, M., Glick, P., Livingston, R. W., & Williams, J. C. (2018). Work as a masculinity contest. *Journal of Social Issues, 74*(3), 422–448.

Berdahl, J. L., & Moore, C. (2006). Workplace harassment: Double jeopardy for minority women. *Journal of Applied Psychology, 91*(2), 426–436.

Bergman, M. E., Langhout, R. D., Palmieri, P. A., Cortina, L. M., & Fitzgerald, L. F. (2002). The (un)reasonableness of reporting: Antecedents and consequences of reporting sexual harassment. *Journal of Applied Psychology, 87*(2), 230–242.

Bosson, J. K., Vandello, J. A., Burnaford, R. M., Weaver, J. R., & Wasti, S. A. (2009). Precarious manhood and displays of physical aggression. *Personality and Social Psychology Bulletin, 35*(5), 623–634.

Bridges, T., & Pascoe, C. J. (2014). Hybrid masculinities: New directions in the sociology of men and masculinities. *Sociology Compass, 8*(3), 246–258.

Brown, A. D., Stacey, P., & Nandhakumar, J. (2008). Making sense of sensemaking narratives. *Human Relations, 61*(8), 1035–1062.

Clair, R. P., Brown, N. E., Dougherty, D. S., Delemeester, H. K., Geist-Martin, P., Gorden, W. I., Sorg, T., & Turner, P. K. (2019). #MeToo, sexual harassment: An article, a forum, and a dream for the future. *Journal of Applied Communication Research*, 47(2), 1–19.

Connell, R. W., & Messerschmidt, J. (2005). Hegemonic masculinity: Rethinking the concept. *Gender & Society*, 19(6), 829–859.

Corbett, H. (2022, October 27). *#MeToo five years later: How the movement started and what needs to change*. www.forbes.com/sites/hollycorbett/2022/10/27/metoo-five-years-later-how-the-movement-started-and-what-needs-to-change/?sh=b9f3ec5afe4a

Cortina, L. M., & Areguin, M. A. (2021). Putting people down and pushing them out: Sexual harassment in the workplace. *Annual Review of Organizational Psychology and Organizational Behavior*, 8(1), 285–309.

Cortina, L. M., & Berdahl, J. L. (2008). Sexual harassment in organizations: A decade of research in review. In C. L. Cooper & J. Barling (Eds.), *Handbook of organizational behavior* (pp. 469–97). Sage.

Cortina, L. M., & Magley, V. J. (2003, January 1). Raising voice, risking retaliation: Events following interpersonal mistreatment in the workplace. *Journal of Occupational Health Psychology*, 8(4), 247–265.

Daft, R. L., & Weick, K. E. (1984). Toward a model of organizations as interpretation systems. *Academy of Management Review*, 9(2), 284–295.

Derks, B., Ellemers, N., van Laar, C., & de Groot, K. (2011). Do sexist organizational cultures create the Queen Bee? *British Journal of Social Psychology*, 50(3), 519–535.

Dougherty, D., & Smythe, M. J. (2004). Sensemaking, organizational culture, and sexual harassment. *Journal of Applied Communication Research*, 32(4), 293–317.

Elias, J. (2020, September 29). Google's $310 million sexual harassment settlement aims to set new industry standards. *CNBC*. www.cnbc.com/2020/09/29/googles-310-million-sexual-misconduct-settlement-details.html

Fernando, D., & Prasad, A. (2018). Sex-based harassment and organizational silencing: How women are led to reluctant acquiescence in academia. *Human Relations*, 72(10), 1–30.

Fitzgerald, L. F., Drasgow, F., Hulin, C. L., Gelfand, M. J., & Magley, V. J. (1997). Antecedents and consequences of sexual harassment in organizations: A test of an integrated model. *Journal of Applied Psychology*, 82(4), 578–589.

Fitzgerald, L. F., Magley, V. J., Drasgow, F., & Waldo, C. R. (1999). Measuring sexual harassment in the military: The sexual experiences questionnaire. *Military Psychology*, 11(3), 243–263.

Ford, J. L., Ivancic, S., & Scarduzio, J. (2021). Silence, voice, and resilience: An examination of workplace sexual harassment. *Communication Studies*, 72(4), 513–530.

Freyd, J. J. (2018, July 12). When sexual assault victims speak out, their institutions often betray them. *The Conversation* [Internet]. http://theconversation.com/when-sexual-assault-victims-speak-out-their-institutions-often-betray-them-87050

Glick, P., Berdahl, J. L., & Alonso, N. M. (2018). Development and validation of the masculinity contest culture scale. *Journal of Social Issues*, 74(3), 449–476.

Hershcovis, M. S., Vranjes, I., Berdahl, J. L., & Cortina, L. M. (2021). See no evil, hear no evil, speak no evil: Theorizing network silence around sexual harassment. *Journal of Applied Psychology*, 106(12), 1834–1847.

Hulin, C. L., Fitzgerald, L. F., & Drasgow, F. (1996). Organizational influences on sexual harassment. In M. Stockdale (Ed.), *Sexual harassment in the workplace* (Vol 5, pp. 127–150). Sage.

Ilies, R., Hauserman, N., Schwochau, S., & Stibal, J. (2003). Reported incidence rates of work-related sexual harassment in the United States: Using meta-analysis to explain reported rate disparities. *Personnel Psychology*, 56(3), 607–631.

Kabat-Farr, D., & Cortina, L. M. (2014). Sex-based harassment in employment: New insights into gender and context. *Law and Human Behavior*, 38(1), 58–72.

Keyton, J., Ferguson, P., & Rhodes, S. C. (2001). Cultural indicators of sexual harassment. *Southern Communication Journal*, 67(1), 33–50.

Koc, Y., Gulseren, D., & Lyubykh, Z. (2021). Masculinity contest culture reduces organizational citizenship behaviors through decreased organizational identification. *Journal of Experimental Psychology-Applied*, 27(2), 408–416.

Kupers, T. A. (2005). Toxic masculinity as a barrier to mental health treatment in prison. *Journal of Clinical Psychology*, 61(6), 713–724.

Lengnick-Hall, M. L. (1995). Sexual harassment research: A methodological critique. *Personnel Psychology*, 48(4), 841–864.

Leskinen, E. A., Cortina, L. M., & Kabat, D. B. (2011). Gender harassment: Broadening our understanding of sex-based harassment at work. *Law and Human Behavior*, 35(1), 25–39.

Livingston, R. W., & Pearce, N. A. (2009). The teddy-bear effect: Does having a baby face benefit black chief executive officers? *Psychological Science*, 20(10), 1229–1236.

Maass, A., Cadinu, A., Guarnieri, G., & Grasselli, A. (2003). Sexual harassment under social identity threat: The computer harassment paradigm. *Journal of Personality and Social Psychology*, 85(5), 853–870.

Maitlis, S., & Christianson, M. (2014). Sensemaking in organizations: Taking stock and moving forward. *The Academy of Management Annals*, 8(1), 57–125.

Matos, K., O'Neill, O., & Lei, X. (2018). Toxic leadership and the masculinity contest culture: How "win or die" cultures breed abusive leadership. *Journal of Social Issues*, 74(3), 500–528.

McLaughlin, H., Uggen, C., & Blackstone, A. (2012). Sexual harassment, workplace authority and the paradox of power. *American Sociological Review*, 77(4), 625–647.

Merlo, J. (2013). *No one to tell: Breaking my silence on life in the RCMP*. Breakwater Books.

O'Leary-Kelly, A. M., Bowes-Sperry, L., Bates, C. A., & Lean, E. R. (2009). Sexual harassment at work: A decade (plus) of progress. *Journal of Management*, 35(3), 503–536.

Perrott, T. (2019). Doing hot and "dirty" work: Masculinities and occupational identity in firefighting. *Gender, Work and Organization*, 26(10), 1398–1412.

Rawski, S. L., O'Leary-Kelly, A. M., & Breaux-Soignet, D. (2022a). It's all fun and games until someone get hurts: Interactional framing theory of work social sexual behavior. *Academy of Management Review*, 47(4), 617–636.

Rawski, S., Foster, J., & Bailenson, J. (2022b). Sexual harassment bystander training effectiveness: Experimentally comparing 2D video to virtual reality practice. *Academy of Management Annual Meeting Proceedings*, 2022(1), 1–16.

Rawski, S. L., & Workman-Stark, A. L. (2018). Masculinity contest cultures in policing organizations and recommendations for training interventions. *Journal of Social Issues*, 74(3), 607–627.

Regina, J., & Allen, T. D. (2023). Masculinity contest culture: Harmful for whom? An examination of emotional exhaustion. *Journal of Occupational Health Psychology*, 28(2), 117–128.

Rudman, L. A., Moss-Racusin, C. A., Phelan, J. E., & Nauts, S. (2012). Status incongruity and backlash effects: Defending the gender hierarchy motivates prejudice against female leaders. *Journal of Experimental Social Psychology*, 48(1), 165–179.

Scarduzio, J. A., Malvini Redden, S., & Fletcher, J. (2020). Everyone's uncomfortable but only some people report: An exploration of emotional discomfort and thresholds in reporting decisions. *Journal of Applied Communication Research*, 49(1), 66–85.

Silvestri, M. (2003). *Women in charge: Policing, gender and leadership*. Willan Publishing.

Silvestri, M. (2007). Doing police leadership: Enter the "new smart macho". *Policing and Society*, 17(1), 38–58.

Slutskaya, N., Simpson, R., Hughes, J., Simpson, A., & Uygur, S. (2016). Masculinity and class in the context of dirty work. *Gender, Work and Organization*, 23(2), 165–182.

Tenbrunsel, A. E., Rees, M. R., & Diekmann, K. A. (2019). Sexual harassment in academia: Ethical climates and bounded ethicality. *Annual Review of Psychology*, 70, 245–270.

U.S. Merit Systems Protection Board (USMSPB). (2018). *Update on sexual harassment in the federal workplace*. Office of Policy and Evaluation, USMSPB. www.mspb.gov/studies/researchbriefs/Update_on_Sexual_Harassment_in_the_Federal_Workplace_1500639.pdf

Vandello, J. A., & Bosson, J. K. (2013). Hard won and easily lost: A review and synthesis of theory and research on precarious manhood. *Psychology of Men and Masculinity*, 14(2), 101–113.

Weick, K. E. (1995). *Sensemaking in organizations*. Sage.

Weick, K. E. (2001). *Making sense of the organization*. Blackwell Publishing.

Weick, K. E., Sutcliffe, K. M., & Obstfeld, D. (2005). Organizing and the process of sensemaking and organizing. *Organization Science*, 16(4), 409–421.

Welsh, S. (1999). Gender and sexual harassment. *Annual Review of Sociology*, 25, 169–190.

Willer, R., Rogalin, C. L., Conlon, B., & Wojnowicz, M. T. (2013). Overdoing gender: A test of the masculine overcompensation thesis. *American Journal of Sociology*, 118(4), 980–1022.

Williams, J. H., Fitzgerald, L. F., & Drasgow, F. (1999). The effects of organizational practices on sexual harassment and individual outcomes in the military. *Military Psychology*, 11(3), 303–328.

Williams, M. J., & Tiedens, L. Z. (2016). The subtle suspension of backlash: A meta-analysis of penalties for women's implicit and explicit dominance behavior. *Psychological Bulletin*, 142(2), 165–197.

Willness, C. R., Piers, S., & Kibeom, L. (2007). A meta-analysis of the antecedents and consequences of workplace sexual harassment. *Personnel Psychology*, 60(1), 127–162.

Wilson, L. C. (2018). The prevalence of military sexual trauma: A meta-analysis. *Trauma Violence & Abuse*, 19(5), 584–597.

Workman-Stark, A. (2017). *Inclusive policing from the inside out*. Springer Publishing International.

Workman-Stark, A., Hershcovis, S., Cortina, L., Vranjes, I., Lyubykh, Z., Berdahl, J., & Chrusch, C. (2024, August 9–13). *Sexual harassment and silence: Getting in the way of healthier workplaces*. Paper presented at the Academy of Management Annual Meeting, Chicago, IL.

Workman-Stark, A., & Jones, K. (2023, April 19–21). *A question of trust: Meaning making in the aftermath of a sexual harassment scandal*. Paper presented at the human relations 75th anniversary conference, London, UK.

Workman-Stark, A., Vranjes, I., Lyubykh, Z., Hershcovis, S., Cortina, L., Chrusch, C., & Berdahl, J. (2023, July 6–8). *Sexual harassment and silence: Getting in the way of a good life in organizations.* Paper presented at the EGOS annual conference, Cagliari, Italy.

Workman-Stark, A. L. (2021). Exploring differing experiences of a masculinity contest culture in policing and the impact on individual and organizational outcomes. *Police Quarterly, 24*(3), 298–324.

Workman-Stark, A. L. (2022). "Real men" doing dirty work: Implications for change. *Policing and Society: An International Journal of Research and Policy, 32*(10), 1242–1257.

Xie, L., & Zheng, Y. (2022). A moderated mediation model of masculinity contest culture and psychological well-being: The role of sexual harassment, bullying, organizational tolerance and position in organization. *Sex Roles, 88*(1/2), 86–100.

Zimbardo, P. G. (2004). A situationist perspective on the psychology of evil: Understanding how good people are transformed into perpetrators. In A. Miller (Ed.), *The social psychology of good and evil: Understanding our capacity for kindness and cruelty* (pp. 21–50). Guilford.

5

SOCIETAL CULTURE AND GENDER-BASED VIOLENCE

Jana L. Raver and Jessie Kim

Bridging Disciplines to Expand the Study of Sexual Harassment at Work

Although the #MeToo movement originated in the United States, it ignited victims of *gender-based violence (GBV)*—that is, harmful acts directed at an individual based on their gender (United Nations Refugee Agency, 2022)—around the world to unify and speak up. In some countries (e.g., France, Mexico), the spark became a raging fire leading to public debate and decreased normative tolerance for GBV. In others (e.g., India, Japan, Austria), the initial fire began to fade as institutions (e.g., government, media, law) and cultural ideologies (e.g., shared beliefs, traditions) suppressed the movement and facilitated backlash against those who spoke out. In still others (e.g., China, Saudi Arabia), the movement quietly simmered underground due to institutional constraints (The Washington Post, 2020). This cross-cultural variation within the #MeToo movement mirrors the nuanced differences in how sexual harassment and violence are perpetuated across cultural contexts (Toker, 2016; Wasti et al., 2000). Unfortunately, organizational scholars have scantly examined cultural influences on sexual harassment in recent years (Latcheva, 2017; Raver, 2024). Sexual harassment (SH) is one specific form of GBV, and evidence on the sociocultural antecedents of GBV has been the focus of much research in recent years. Given organizational scholars' decline in attention to societal culture and SH, it is important to turn our attention to neighboring disciplines where attention to the societal culture and GBV is more abundant and offers many insights that can inspire future scholarship on SH.

DOI: 10.4324/9781003300953-6

In this chapter, we synthesize multidisciplinary literatures on how societal culture—including ideologies as well as the institutions that embody them—contributes to and perpetuates GBV. Culture has been broadly defined as "the man-made part of the human environment" (Triandis et al., 1973, p. 355), which includes both subjective culture—a society's "characteristic way of perceiving its social environment" (Triandis, 1972, p. viii, 3)—as well as the societal institutions that embody and reinforce these perceptions through rules and structures (Thornton et al., 2012). Scholarly work on culture and GBV has occurred in many disciplines including organizational behavior, organizational and cross-cultural psychology, sociology, gender studies, public health, legal studies, and international development studies, among others. However, these disparate bodies of work have not heretofore been integrated in a way that can guide future theory, research, and policy on societal culture and GBV. In integrating this work, we unroot the societal institutions and ideologies that collectively uphold gender hierarchies and the normalization of gendered aggression. By doing so, we emphasize that all organizational agents' actions—either toward or against GBV—must be understood as culturally reified patterns. To change these deeply rooted patterns of behavior, scholars must shift their attention beyond merely individuals, teams, dyads, and even organizations to our societal institutions and the shared belief systems that uphold them.

This synthesis of the literature on societal culture and gender-based violence will unfold as follows. First, we define GBV and highlight its prevalence, scope, and nature around the world. After providing an overview of our literature review process, we begin by summarizing the research on societal culture and SH, highlighting this specific form of GBV in work settings. Given that the organizational literature has limited attention to societal influences on GBV, we next integrate insights by synthesizing the multidisciplinary research and theory on socio-structural determinants of GBV. In our review of this broader literature, we first unpack ideologies—messages that are taught and reinforced through cultural values and beliefs—that perpetuate masculine dominance and feminine subjugation, and how they are linked with GBV. Although several gender ideologies exist (Davis & Greenstein, 2009), the most widely cited as a determinant of GBV is hegemonic masculinity (e.g., Connell, 2005). Next, we turn our attention to institutions and how they serve as structural constraints that reinforce messages about the normalization of gender hierarchies and help to justify GBV. Throughout this review, we show the pervasiveness of messaging regarding the subjugation of femininity in many cultures' ideologies and institutions, which serves to justify GBV as part of a cultural system that prevents the achievement of gender equality, including in organizations. The final section of the paper is dedicated to recommendations for future research and intervention stemming from the conceptual synthesis, with a focus on using this knowledge to help make gains toward gender equality.

Gender-Based Violence and Its Prevalence Around the World

Gender-based Violence (GBV) is an umbrella term that encompasses many forms of harassment and violence, which are unified because these harmful acts are directed at an individual because of their gender (United Nations Refugee Agency, 2022). Bloom (2008) provided a more comprehensive definition of GBV as "violence that occurs as a result of the normative role expectations associated with each gender, along with unequal power relationships between the two genders, within the context of a specific society" (p. 14). More specific constructs and terms that are used to describe forms of GBV include sexual harassment, sex-based harassment, sexual assault, intimate partner violence, street harassment, and violence against those who are LGBTQ2+, trans-gender, and/or non-binary, among others. Throughout this chapter, we use the term GBV to describe all forms of harmful acts directed someone because of their gender, and during the literature review we specify the particular form of GBV that authors studied in the research. We note here that much of the research describes GBV as a problem that predominantly affects women, and thus much of the research and theory in this review will focus upon women's experience of GBV. Although men and non-binary people are less often studied, our review will highlight evidence on how GBV is perpetrated against those who violate hegemonic masculinity.

Well before the recent #MeToo movement shone a spotlight on GBV, the United Nations identified GBV as a major global and development issue (United Nations, 1989) and undertook a host of public education programs and policies around the world to reduce GBV. Despite substantial increases in legislation and policies against GBV around the world since the 1980s, GBV still persists at disturbingly high levels. For example, in work contexts, 60% of women in the United States and 55% of women in the European Union were sexually harassed at least once at work (European Union Agency for Fundamental Rights, 2014; Feldblum & Lipnic, 2016). In non-work contexts, World Health Organization data shows that globally 31% of women aged 15–49 have been subjected to physical and/or sexual violence from an intimate partner, from a non-partner, or from both (WHO, 2021).

In 2015, the UN committed to achieving 17 Sustainable Development Goals (SDGs) and goal #5— "Achieve gender equality and empower all women and girls"—pertains to eliminating GBV (United Nations, 2015). Each year since that commitment, the UN has published GBV statistics and a report on progress toward achieving this SDG (United Nations, 2021a; United Nations Women, 2022). Little progress has occurred. UN data from 106 countries show that 18% of women and girls have experienced physical and/or sexual violence in the prior year alone; in the least developed countries, this number was a staggering 24% (UN, 2019). GBV became even worse with the COVID-19 pandemic, which saw increased levels of GBV and a return to more traditional gender roles, so the world is not on-track to achieve the gender equality SDG by 2030 (UN Women, 2022). The UN progress reports emphasize the pervasive nature of GBV and the need for continued global efforts to combat violence and promote gender equality. They also underscore the importance of integrating cultural and local contexts into global strategies to effectively address GBV. Dramatically reducing GBV is a global goal of utmost importance for achieving gender equality and creating healthy and safe spaces for people of all genders to work and play without fear of harassment or violence. We seek to inspire future research and education programs based upon the review provided next in our chapter.

The Current Literature

We began our review by first discovering the broad body of research on societal cultural and GBV, in both work and non-work settings. We conducted literature searches in PsycInfo, EBSCOhost, and Business Source Premier for papers on the intersection of societal culture and GBV (and its constituent constructs). We specified "culture," along with "gender" and/or "sex," numerous terms that refer to forms of GBV, including "violence," "harassment," "aggression," "assault," "hostility," "abuse," and "bullying." We conducted supplemental literature searches that further specified "organization" and/or "work" as search terms to uncover research on GBV in work settings in particular. Potentially relevant articles resulting from these searches were then parsed down further by applying these criteria: (a) the research or theory needed to be focused on societal (country-level) culture, not organizational culture or ethnocultural groups within a country; (b) the research or theory needed to focus on gender-based violence, not only violence or aggression more broadly; (c) the focal population of the work needed to be adults or older adolescents, in alignment with our focus on the working population; (d) the paper needed to be published in a journal or book; and (e) the paper needed to be published in and/or translated to English. We also focused on papers published since 2000, but we highlight a few papers published before this date where earlier work provides an important foundation. These criteria resulted in 47 papers on societal culture and GBV, which are reviewed below. The study details provided in this review are necessarily selective due to space constraints, but we have tried to highlight the papers that align most closely with key themes and developments; the full set of papers included in this review are provided in the references.

In alignment with most of the chapters in this edited volume, our scholarly focus was first on SH in work settings, and thus we begin our review there. However, the bulk of the papers reviewed in this chapter come from other disciplines, many of which have investigated societal culture and GBV in more depth. For example, key works from sociology highlight the social structures, norms and power dynamics that contribute to the construction of gender ideologies, which shape societal attitudes toward violence and gender roles (e.g., Beasley, 2008; Davis & Greenstein, 2009). Contributions from gender studies provide a critical lens and examine how GBV is a product of cultural and gendered expectations (e.g., Conway, 2011; Hearn et al., 2012). Public health research addresses the implications of GBV for health and well-being and also looks at the effectiveness of interventions and policies (Heise et al., 2002; Montesanti & Thurston, 2015). Legal studies examines how laws and legal frameworks address GBV, including the effectiveness and limitations of legal responses (e.g., Maxwell et al., 2022; Merry, 2006). International development studies address how GBV intersects with development issues and policies, including efforts to combat GBV within global and regional frameworks (e.g., OECD, 2021; United Nations, 2021a, 2021b). Each discipline contributes unique insights into the causes, manifestations, and responses to GBV, highlighting the need for an integrative approach to understanding and preventing GBV.

Societal Culture and Sexual Harassment at Work

Organizational scholars have dedicated substantial research attention to understanding SH at work (for reviews, see Berdahl & Raver, 2011; Chawla et al., 2021; Fitzgerald & Cortina, 2018), but much of the extant scholarship on this topic neglects societal culture as a more macro influence on this phenomenon. With that said, there was early promise in this area of scholarship in the late 1990s and 2000s through examinations of the cross-cultural generalizability and manifestations of SH. One of the first challenges of studying SH across cultures was establishing whether the construct had more universal and generalizable meanings (i.e., *etic*) or whether it was culture-specific and must be understood as a local phenomenon that does not generalize (i.e., *emic*; Triandis, 1994). This important question was addressed in research by Gelfand et al. (1995) and Wasti et al. (2000) in their examinations of the cross-cultural generalizability of SH, as assessed behaviorally via the Sexual Experiences Questionnaire (SEQ; Fitzgerald et al., 1988). Both studies established that the measurement of SH at work was cross-culturally generalizable; furthermore, Wasti et al. (2000) discovered that the antecedents and consequences of SH at work were also parallel. Nonetheless, these authors and several others (e.g., Cortina & Wasti, 2005; Merkin, 2008a, 2008b; Sigal et al., 2005; Wasti, 2005, 2014; Wasti & Cortina, 2002) highlighted that several emic elements of SH may not be captured within etic measures, and they called for additional research to explore cultural influences on SH at work.

Despite this early robust attention to culture and workplace SH, research slowed substantially in the subsequent decade (Raver, 2024). Two studies explored cross-cultural differences in perceptions and reports of SH, in Pakistan (Merkin & Shah, 2014) and in Turkey (Toker, 2016), respectively. In both, participants from the United States reported a higher likelihood of perceiving and/or reporting SH compared to those in other countries. Toker (2016) discussed how US culture tends to emphasize individual rights, which may lead to a lower tolerance for ambiguous harassment, whereas Turkish culture emphasizes collective social norms and relationships, which can lead targets to downplay its seriousness. Merkin and Shah (2014) found that although US participants reported a higher frequency of harassment, Pakistani participants reported more severe consequences, which may be due to cultural stigmas surrounding reporting it. Thus, there is evidence on emic manifestations of SH as well as more nuanced attention to cultural influences on perceiving and reporting harassment.

Much of the conceptual work and reviews on what perpetuates workplace SH points to the fact that organizations are embedded within larger societal contexts, which reinforce and perpetuate gender inequality (Berdahl & Raver, 2011; Fitzgerald & Cortina, 2018; Latcheva, 2017; Luthar & Luthar, 2002, 2007). Nonetheless, little recent research has examined the macro socio-structural cultural environment, which we believe is concerning and is a motivation for the current review. To more fully understand the root causes of how and why workplace SH persists, scholars must look beyond the walls of the organizations to the larger socio-structural environment in which organizations are embedded. Doing so may inspire future research on SH at work that is more aligned with established concepts and evidence from disciplines that have dedicated more attention to socio-structural influences. As such, the next focus in our review is the larger, multidisciplinary literature on GBV and societal culture.

Societal Cultural Ideologies and Gender-Based Violence

Hegemonic Masculinity and Gender Ideologies

One key theme from the multidisciplinary literature on societal culture and GBV is the central importance of cultural values and beliefs—that is, cultural ideologies—that teach and reinforce constraining messages about gender roles. Most prominent is *hegemonic masculinity*, an ideology where men are socialized to believe they are supposed to be dominant and to achieve this goal, and women must be subjugated to maintain men's power (Connell, 2005; Gallagher & Parrott, 2011; Smith et al., 2015). Hegemonic masculinity beliefs vary around the world and have been argued by many to be a key cultural ideology that perpetuates GBV globally. There are many empirical and conceptual papers that have adopted this focus on hegemonic masculinity and its related manifestations (Alcalde, 2010; Beasley, 2008; Conway, 2011; Dabby & Yoshihama, 2021; Davis & Greenstein, 2009; Eslen-Ziya & Koc, 2016; Gallagher & Parrott, 2011; Grunow et al., 2018; Hearn et al., 2012; Javaid, 2017; Jewkes & Morrell, 2018; Kersten, 1996; Kubai & Ahlberg, 2013; Lease et al., 2013; Levant & Richmond, 2008; Morrell et al., 2012; OECD, 2021; Russo & Pirlott, 2006; Smith et al., 2015; Spector-Mersel, 2006; Wang et al., 2019). Below, we have clustered this body of work into main themes to illustrate (a) how hegemonic masculinity and related ideologies have been culturally constructed, (b) their relationships with GBV in specific cultural contexts, and (c) interventions to change ideologies to reduce GBV.

Unpacking Hegemony Masculinity and Gender Ideology

It is first important to understand the nature of hegemonic masculinity and gender ideologies; however, clarifying these terms is challenging as they are culturally nuanced and dynamic. Indeed, the first set of studies and conceptual papers focuses on unpacking the meaning of hegemonic masculinity and related ideologies across cultures. Both Beasley (2008) and Conway (2011) provided critical analyses of hegemonic masculinity from socio-political and cultural perspectives, highlighting how the term can have multiple meanings (i.e., masculinities) that are constructed as part of public discourse within a particular cultural context. Consistent with this position on masculinities, Gallagher and Parrott (2011) conceptualized hegemonic masculinity as having several manifestations (including beliefs about maintaining one's superior status, toughness, and antifemininity); they examined how these facets were linked with masculine gender role stress and hostility toward women for men in the United States. They found that the toughness aspect of masculinity was directly linked to hostility toward women, but the effects of status and antifemininity were mediated through masculine gender role stress. This study is notable in that it shows the mechanisms through which hegemonic masculinity are linked with GBV, namely through men experiencing stress following violations of their traditional male role beliefs and lashing out to reinforce their superior status. These results are further corroborated by Smith et al. (2015), who found that the masculine gender role stress associated with violations of hegemonic masculinity—antifemininity norms in particular—were associated with sexual aggression toward an intimate partner. Taken together, these findings help to explain why GBV against women is more likely when the masculine ideology of inherent superiority over women is threatened (see also Davis & Greenstein, 2009). These findings are also aligned with workplace SH research showing that "uppity women"—who threaten masculine superiority—are targeted for SH (Berdahl, 2007).

A related line of work has focused on gender ideologies, which is a larger construct that includes hegemonic masculinity, but the research on gender ideology has focused mostly on work/family responsibilities, with less emphasis on gendered oppression and GBV. One early exception is in Davis and Greenstein's (2009) influential sociology literature review. They describe gender ideology as a social construction that reflects one's level of support for a division of responsibilities based upon a belief in gendered separate spheres. They review evidence linking gender ideology with wife abuse, noting that women who earn a larger share of the household's earnings are more likely to be abused, but only if they are married to husbands with a traditional gender ideology. We also mention one more paper on gender ideologies because of its cross-cultural focus, albeit they did not study GBV. Specifically, Grunow et al. (2018) problematize the unidimensional conceptualization and measurement of gender ideologies. They instead introduce a multidimensional framework that conceptualizes one's beliefs about gender roles as having three parts: (a) whether only the male should bring in earnings or if both partners bring in earnings; (b) whether only the woman should engage in caring activities or if both partners are involved; and (c) whether gender roles are due to personal choice or gendered (inherent) traits. Egalitarian ideologies are those that combine these three beliefs to reflect joint responsibility for both earnings and childcare, and personal choice. In their study of eight European countries, they found different combinations of these beliefs across countries, which were linked to countries' work-family policies. We would recommend future extensions of this framework to studying GBV.

Spector-Mersel (2006) provides a unique examination of Western hegemonic masculinity scripts from a temporal perspective, making a strong case for the need to take into consideration age as part of the construction of masculinity. She argues against a homogeneous view of masculinity, integrating evidence on how there are many context-dependent masculinities, and makes the case that divergent masculinities can exist *within-person* over time, not just between people. She argues that "each culture, in a given time and place, offers its men hegemonic masculinity scripts that attach masculine 'social clocks' to men's life courses" (p. 67). For example, young men may engage hegemonic masculinity scripts of physical toughness and domination of women, but as they age, these scripts of what constitutes a "real man" transition (e.g., financial success, career status). The implication for GBV is that violations of different aspects of masculinity may not have the same meaning across the lifespan as men age. Although this lifespan view is not present within other papers, it would be insightful for scholars to pursue more work on masculinities as they pertain to age and aging across cultures.

In addition to these preceding papers that focused on the meaning of these ideologies, a few studies have examined how cultures vary in their endorsement of hegemonic masculinity and related ideologies. Levant and Richmond (2008) reviewed research on masculinity ideologies based upon the gender role strain paradigm (Pleck, 1981, 1995), which asserts that gender ideology is a cultural script that varies according to social location and cultural context, and is used to uphold gender-based power structures. Their review of early comparative studies concluded that cultural differences were strong; indeed, country differences in the endorsement of masculine ideologies were often even larger than gender differences in endorsement of these ideologies. Finally, Lease et al. (2013) compared the endorsement of masculinity ideology among Turkish, Norwegian, and US men. Like Gallagher and Parrott (2011), they also assessed three aspects of masculinity (i.e., status, toughness, and antifemininity) and compared cultures on their endorsement of these aspects. Norwegian men were significantly less likely than Turkish and US men to endorse all three aspects of masculinity, but the latter groups did not differ from each other. This study's evidence supports the conclusion that masculinities are socially constructed, such that cultures proscribe different gender role attitudes that influence their enactment.

Masculinities and GBV in Specific Cultural Contexts

A second cluster of studies that we review here go beyond unpacking the meaning or endorsement of these ideologies; instead, they provide in-depth, emic examinations of how these ideologies influence the enactment of GBV in specific cultural contexts. One subset within this cluster is a group of studies that describe links between hegemonic masculinity and intimate partner/family violence. Specifically, Alcalde (2010) examined the experiences of Latina immigrants from Peru and Mexico, examining in detail through several cases how their experiences of GBV were linked back to cultural ideologies around hegemonic masculinity, self-sacrificing femininity, and feminism. Wang et al. (2019) explored links between hegemonic masculinity and GBV in central China, finding that approximately half of men had perpetrated physical or sexual violence against their partners. The authors describe Chinese cultural constructions of hegemonic masculinity as contributors to this GBV, including male decision-making, reputation concerns, violence, and heterosexuality. Finally, Dabby and Yoshihama (2021) provide an in-depth analysis of several forms of intimate partner and family violence (e.g., forced marriage, abuse by in-laws, marry-and-dump, transnational abandonment) within Asian and Pacific Islander communities. They highlight the root causes of GBV as mechanisms of gender oppression, patriarchy, and exclusionary social structures, among others. These papers each provide compelling, emic evidence on the ways that oppressive masculinities are contributing to sexual aggression against partners, which is a major global health concern.

Although much of the research is focused on women's experiences of GBV, two studies have linked culture, masculinities, and GBV as experienced by men. First, Eslen-Ziya and Koc (2016) examine the experiences of gay men in Turkey via interviews that asked about their constructions of masculinities. Their findings highlight how the pervasive cultural masculinity norms contribute to these men's experiences of stigma and discrimination, including hiding their sexuality and even endorsing homophobic acts toward other gay men. All of the participants exhibited prejudice toward gay men with feminine dispositions as well as those who were outspoken; many internalized hegemonic masculinity ideals, which led to internal conflict and tensions. Within the UK cultural context, Javaid's (2017) qualitative study examined how male sexual victimization is downplayed or ignored by social services and police officers, resulting in the "othering" of male rape victims, who ultimately suffer a masculinity crisis. The results highlight how hegemonic masculinity plays an important role in the discourse of male sexual victimization, leading to victims not being taken seriously and being placed at the bottom of the gender hierarchy. These findings emphasize that restrictive and oppressive masculinities can result in gender-nonconforming men being "othered" and/or targeted with GBV as well.

Three final studies in this cluster have provided emic examinations of hegemonic masculinity in Sweden and South Africa. Specifically, Hearn et al. (2012) review 40 years of research on hegemonic masculinity in Sweden. The authors profile the diverse approaches that have been pursued in gender equality projects, and how the concept of hegemonic masculinity has been used, adapted, and not used in different and complex ways across projects. Within the context of South Africa, Morrell et al. (2012) provide a historical narrative account of masculinities in South Africa, highlighting how constructions of masculinity have shifted as a function of political role models and national programs and policies over time. They highlight how public discourse over hegemonic masculinity has led to backlash and resistance to gender equality efforts. In a more recent extension of their work in South Africa, Jewkes and Morrell (2018) conducted latent class analysis on a sample of men to classify them into three groups based upon variables previously associated with violent, sexually risky and antisocial behaviors (e.g., illegal gun, transactional sex, drug use). Men categorized into the most violent and antisocial category were more likely to be more gender inequitable, been more controlling in their relationships, and been more likely to have raped a partner. The authors discussed these findings as a function of hegemonic masculinity, which prescribes strength, toughness and the capacity to use violence as part of the normative masculine gender role in South Africa.

Interventions to Change Ideologies

A few papers describe interventions (e.g., development initiatives, policies, education programs) that have attempted to change hegemonic masculinity and/or gender ideology. One compelling narrative by Kubai and Ahlberg (2013) helps to illustrate the complexities of social change, given the inter-weaving of culture and gender ideologies with social realities and policies. The authors conducted interviews and focus groups in Rwanda to exam-ine cultural beliefs and practices in relation to the new gender equality policy and the Girinka program, which sought to facilitate gender equality and improve poverty by giving a cow to poor families. The authors' nar-rative unpacks nuances of how national programs, inspired by develop-ment goals, can be misaligned with social realities and cultural values on the ground and may actually make matters worse for women. The gender equality policy and Girinka program challenge cultural beliefs and notions of masculinity, which codify the subjugation of women, even disallowing them from milking cows. Without better attention to how cultural gender ideologies resist change, programs can backfire and result in even greater GBV when women are seen to be inappropriately challenging gender hierarchies.

Another large-scale program aimed at tracking and changing masculine norms has been underway by the OECD Development Centre, with data provided by the Social Institutions and Gender Index (SIGI) being used to track countries' progress toward women's empowerment over time. The comprehensive OECD (2021) report provides a detailed examination of restrictive masculinities that obstruct women's empowerment. Beliefs that comprise restrictive masculinities include be the breadwinner, be financially dominant, work in "manly" jobs, be the "ideal worker," be a "manly" leader, have a final say in household decisions, control household assets, protect and exercise guardianship of family members, dominate sexual and reproductive choices, and not do unpaid care or domestic work. Data from the SIGI over time has shown that these norms of restrictive masculinities have direct negative consequences for women, including devaluing women's economic and labor force contributions and minimizing agency in household decision-making (OECD, 2021). The OECD is continuing to monitor social change toward gender-equitable masculinities, and their data is influential for public policy and for informing the development of many education and outreach programs on transforming masculinities (see Ruane-McAteer et al., 2020).

Taken together, these articles highlight the cultural constructions of hegemonic masculinity and other gender ideologies, and how these masculinities are associated with the perpetuation of GBV across societal contexts. Masculinity is best understood as a multifaceted construct that is socially embedded and enacted within a particular cultural context, and when it has hegemonic elements, it is used as a logic for the oppression of women and perpetuation of gender inequalities, including GBV. These articles also hint at culture-specific challenges with socio-political and institutional constraints that reinforce existing gender ideologies and resist change imposed through well-intentioned policies and efforts at building gender equality (e.g., Kubai & Ahlberg, 2013). As such, we now turn our attention to societal institutions.

Societal Cultural Institutions and Gender-Based Violence

There is also work that has provided empirical and conceptual analyses of how societal cultural institutions can serve as structural constraints that either constrain or perpetuate GBV. This literature is diverse, comes from multiple disciplines, and can be broadly categorized into three domains of scholarship that have been linked with GBV: (1) laws and policies, (2) public health, and (3) the media. Throughout this work, authors illustrate how these institutions create socio-structural constraints that prevent the achievement of gender equality, including in organizations. Although other cultural institutions have been discussed as contributors to GBV (e.g., religion, sports), evidence from a cross-national perspective is not yet sufficient to draw robust conclusions about links to societal culture. In addition, it is important to keep in mind that organizations are institutions in and of themselves, and we encourage readers to see Chapter 4 in this volume for more attention to how masculinity can influence organizational institutions.

Laws and Policies on Gender-Based Violence

Several scholars have discussed and synthesized legal frameworks and policies for GBV across societal contexts, often with a goal of informing the development of transnational legal frameworks and/or comparing the effectiveness of governmental responses. A key theme in this literature is that legal and policy interventions are motivated by a goal to constrain GBV; however, the implementation of policies is often ineffective and may instead perpetuate it if local realities are ignored. Lazarus-Black and Merry (2003) was an early paper that explored the politics of gender violence globally, informing their analysis with case studies in divergent cultural contexts. They argued that global frameworks for GBV can be helpful and create alignment with international pressure for legal reforms, yet it is essential to consider local cultural contexts, power structures, resource availability, and political will when implementing laws against GBV. Merry (2006) commented on the rise of international systems of human rights law and how they can be overly prescriptive. Merry advocated for engaging with local communities to understand their perspectives on GBV and to incorporate their local traditions and meanings into intervention strategies. Klugman (2017) provided a detailed summary of legislative actions against GBV around the world and concluded that laws against violence are indeed effective and serve to communicate a policy commitment, yet she echoed similar concerns regarding the need to dedicate more attention to local social norms and gender ideologies, as legal interventions are not effective if misaligned with gender attitudes. These arguments are further supported by Maxwell et al. (2022) and Sanz-Barbero et al. (2018), both of which concluded that laws must be part of a larger framework that pursues gender equity and GBV prevention through multiple, aligned social policies and interventions.

In a different vein, Alldred and Biglia (2015) reviewed GBV policies (which they termed gender-related violence) for four countries in the European Union (i.e., Italy, Ireland, Spain, and the United Kingdom) to help inform policy development in more than one country. They conducted a linguistic/content analysis of relevant legal texts across these EU countries to compare and integrate laws in relation to GBV, also incorporating an intersectional lens (including race, class, age, sexual orientation, and ability). They first noted the absence of any comprehensive coverage of GBV by the EU Directive; indeed, the Council of Europe provisions that aim to protect women from violence had not yet been ratified in Ireland (ratified in 2019) or the United Kingdom (ratified in 2022). However, British and Irish legislation includes frequent mention of domestic violence, whereas it rarely occurs in Italian or Spanish legislation. They conclude that the existing legislation does not deal with GBV in a comprehensive way, but instead treats it as an individualized matter. Thus, "legislation frequently misses important structural and normalized cultural forms of violence" (Alldred & Biglia, 2015, p. 670).

Most recently, Gordon et al. (2022) analyzed 60 countries' government responses to GBV during the COVID-19 pandemic, during which women reported alarming levels of GBV, with an estimated additional 31 million cases of GBV globally by six months into the pandemic. Governmental responses varied substantially; the authors coded countries' responses based upon (a) whether GBV-specific policies were introduced as part of the COVID-19 response, (b) whether there was COVID-specific GBV funding, and (c) whether there was a government-supported COVID GBV awareness campaign. Their review points to substantial cross-cultural variation in the effectiveness of governmental responses to GBV. Most countries responded with an awareness campaign, and this was the sole response for many low- and middle-income countries. Just over one-third of countries implemented pandemic-specific GBV legislation, but most of these initiatives were under-funded, leading to new measures that are hampered by the lack of funds. One of the best predictors of whether governments responded proactively was whether there was an active civil society organization that campaigned for gender issues, which highlights the importance of activism and social movements (see Chapter 1, this volume), as governmental responses alone were often ineffective and exacerbated existing vulnerabilities.

Public Health and Gender-Based Violence

In addition to legal and policy frameworks, scholars have discussed GBV from the perspective of public health, both with regard to the implications for women's health as well as a more proactive approach of designing public health interventions. Heise et al. (2002) provided an early integrative review of several forms of GBV (e.g., intimate partner violence, sexual coercion) and health outcomes that women experience. In particular, GBV has been linked with a wide array of health outcomes including problems pertaining to physical health, reproductive health, mental health, negative health behaviors, chronic conditions, and even fatal outcomes. The authors especially called for increased care and responsiveness to GBV among reproductive health professionals, as a means to encourage health professionals to adopt more proactive and systematic approaches to intervening to prevent further harm to victims of GBV.

In their critical public health commentary, Scott-Samuel and colleagues (2009) also adopt an advocacy position to address health inequalities by targeting hegemonic masculinity as a key driver of deleterious health outcomes. They first describe how health inequalities emerge as a function of structural inequalities in power, prestige, finances, knowledge, and social connections. They go on to position hegemonic masculinity as being a type of structural violence, as it is abstracted from individuals' actions and part of a wider set of culturally reified systems of oppression faced by individuals, communities and societies as a whole. They conclude that "from a public health perspective, what is required is evidence and debate around the notion that hegemonic masculinity is a 'preventable disease'" (p. 291), and that action to remediate the public health harm caused by hegemonic masculinity is long overdue.

Montesanti and Thurston (2015) build upon this discussion of structural violence, which emerges from systemic inequalities and social injustices, and present evidence of how structural violence often exacerbates the risks of women experiencing interpersonal violence (including GBV). They assert that many public health interventions currently fall short, and must instead go beyond the individual to address social determinants of health that contribute to GBV. They propose a multifaceted and collaborative approach to public health interventions that bridge disciplines (i.e., healthcare, social services, law enforcement) and incorporate education, community-based strategies, and advocacy to change societal norms.

Ruane-McAteer and colleagues (2020) synthesize the robust body of evidence on public health intervention studies that aimed to improve sexual and reproductive health and rights (SRHR) through gender-transformative programming. Gender-transformative programming involves education and social reform initiatives that seek to challenge and change oppressive or restrictive masculinities (OECD, 2021) that contribute to inequities in sexual and reproductive health. Gender-transformative programming involves men and boys in SRHR initiatives with the goal of fostering more equitable relationships and improving health outcomes for all genders. This large-scale systematic review of randomized controlled trials and quasi-experimental studies ($n > 80,000$ participants) demonstrated positive or mixed efficacy of gender-transformative programming interventions on attitudinal and behavioral outcomes, consistent with challenging gender inequality and reducing GBV. Their focus was on involving men and boys within gender-transformative interventions, and their findings strongly supported the benefits of involving men and boys more systematically in gender-transformative programming and SRHR initiatives. Finally, these studies also align with Montesanti and Thurston's (2015) arguments that the most effective interventions will be multifaceted, as the most robust interventions included persuasion, modeling, and enablement approaches over time. Taken together, this body of evidence from public health is demonstrating promise for reducing GBV by intervening to reduce the underlying gender ideologies and hegemonic masculinity that fosters it.

The Media and Gender-Based Violence

The final cultural institution that we explore in relation to GBV is the media. Interest in the media has grown following the #MeToo movement, but earlier research also explored how cultural representations and media narratives shape societal attitudes toward masculinity. For example, Charlebois (2009) analyzed cultural constructions of hegemonic masculinity within a film in Japan and in its US remake, focusing on how the film reflects cultural narratives of masculinity. In Japan, hegemonic masculinity entailed social role conformity, yet in the US remake, hegemonic masculinity entailed dominance, control, and emotional suppression. Without greater societal awareness of how films reinforce potentially undesirable discourses, these images of hegemonic masculinity stay central within the cultural narratives. Tan and colleagues (2013) examined constructions of masculinity in a different media source, namely men's lifestyle magazines. They examined 636 magazine ads from Taiwan, China, and the United States to determine how masculinities are portrayed in these contexts. They argue that a defining characteristic of global hegemonic masculinity is commodity consumption, which aligns well with what they describe as a "refined and sophisticated" depiction of masculinity as being financially and occupationally successful. This "refined and sophisticated" masculinity was the most popular media portrayal across all three cultures, which the authors argue constitutes the modern masculinity that is taught and reinforced in the media as the hegemonic ideal.

Since the #MeToo movement was ignited in 2017, there has been substantial interest in better understanding the role of the media, including social media, in influencing GBV. The media-induced SH framework proposed by Galdi and Guizzo (2021) emerged amidst the post-#MeToo surge of attention to the media. This conceptual framework proposes that exposure to sexually objectifying media can elicit cognitive and affective changes (i.e., dehumanization, disruption of empathy, and shift in gender norms) in perpetrators, victims, and bystanders, which can result in increased levels of GBV. In discussing the implications of their findings, the authors emphasize the need for media literacy interventions that educate audiences about the impacts of sexual objectification. Another study that emerged following the #MeToo movement is Rimjhim and Dandapat's (2022) large-scale, ethnographic study using social media data to establish links between culture and GBV. They conclude that there is a robust link between culture (especially uncertainty avoidance, indulgence, and individualism) and GBV as manifested in tweet content. The authors note that it would be possible to reveal more culture-specific traits of GBV for each country, which could be used to target interventions to curb GBV on social media. We leave the reader to delve into evidence on social media in more depth in Chapter 2 of this volume. Overall, these papers underscore the need for critical engagement with media content and cultural practices to address the root causes of GBV.

Discussion

Throughout this chapter, we have examined societal cultural influences on the prevalence and perpetuation of SH and GBV more broadly through a multidisciplinary lens. Given that most SH research focuses upon workplace settings and our own disciplinary backgrounds aligns with that focus on organizations, it can be tempting to maintain a narrow focus on the ways in which harassment and gender inequalities are enacted at work. However, we hope that the preceding review has shed new light on a well-established problem by shifting the level of focus up to the more macro, societal environment with insights garnered from scholarly evidence in neighboring disciplines (e.g., sociology, public health, legal studies, development studies, gender studies). Organizational scholars have often noted that SH at work reflects the broader societal norms and beliefs of the contexts where harassment occurs (Berdahl & Raver, 2011; Fitzgerald & Cortina, 2018; Latcheva, 2017), yet recent research on societal culture has been scarce. We hope that this chapter will inspire renewed attention to conducting cross-national and emic studies on the role of culture and SH. Moreover, we have expanded the focal construct beyond SH to focus upon GBV, which is a broader construct that includes SH as one of many forms of gendered aggression (e.g., violence in public, street harassment, intimate partner violence, sexual assault) that emerge from oppressive gender ideologies and norms. There is a great deal of overlap between workplace SH and other forms of GBV, so we assert that it is important to be informed by the broader literature on antecedents and consequences of GBV. In the remainder of this discussion, we seek to provide a bridge between the macro-, socio-structural evidence described throughout this review and the ways in which it can help to inform future research and practice in organizational settings.

The most discussed and researched area of scholarship from the preceding GBV literature review focused upon hegemonic masculinities and related gender ideologies. Knowledge about the extant evidence on cultural constructions of masculinities is foundational for understanding this body of work and the interventions (e.g., policies, laws, development initiatives, training) that are underway to promote changes to achieve the UN's SDG #5 to "achieve gender equality and empower all women and girls" (United Nations, 2015). As discussed earlier, there is recognition of multiple aspects of hegemonic masculinity (e.g., Beasley, 2008; Gallagher & Parrott, 2011; Smith et al., 2015), different cultures endorse different masculinities (e.g., Lease et al., 2013), and some scholars even focus on other gender ideologies that focus on norms and roles (e.g., Davis & Greenstein, 2009; Grunow et al., 2018). It is now well-established that there are multiple masculinities, some of which covary and are restrictive (OECD, 2021), but that the evidence does not support the view of hegemonic masculinity as a uniform and static construct. Masculinities are socially constructed and dynamic (e.g., Hearn et al., 2012; Tan et al., 2013), and they vary across cultures in alignment with local cultural beliefs and narratives (e.g., Morrell et al., 2012). Given this evidence, it is surprising that more of this scholarship and evidence has not been incorporated into research and theory on SH at work. There is a growing interest in masculinity as it pertains to SH (see Chapter 4, this volume), but the predominant conceptualization of masculinity in the organizational literature has been of the "masculinity contest" (Berdahl et al., 2018; Glick et al., 2018; Rawski & Workman-Stark, 2018). This highly competitive aspect of masculinity is certainly important and research on this topic is valuable, yet when one looks at the evidence in the broader literature, it begs the question of why the organizational literature has not also unpacked and studied multiple aspects of masculinity and other gender ideologies in relation to GBV. Given the evidence on masculinity as a cultural construction, it also begs the question of whether comparative studies on masculinities and GBV at work will show cross-cultural equivalence of this construct. We encourage future work on these topics.

Related to the preceding point, a few studies in this review (e.g., Gallagher & Parrott, 2011; Smith et al., 2015) examined how specific aspects of hegemonic masculinity were linked to GBV through their relationship with masculine gender role stress, as theorized by the gender role stress paradigm (Pleck, 1981, 1995). This paradigm provides one of the rare theoretical frames within which to investigate gender ideologies and GBV from a cultural perspective. Much of the literature reviewed in this chapter lacks theoretical grounding and there is only minimal conceptual development in most papers. Therefore, another avenue for future attention is to bolster the theoretical grounding of research in this area. An integrative conceptual framework would be highly valuable for making sense of discrepant findings about culture, gender ideologies and GBV and also building a body of knowledge. There has been more attention to gender ideologies than to the ways in which they are culturally embedded; incorporating theory and research on cultural values could be one viable path forward (e.g., Luthar & Luthar, 2002, 2007).

One of the most promising and socially impactful lines of research described in this review is that on gender-transformative programming (Ruane-McAteer et al., 2020). There are many large-scale societal public health interventions underway that are aimed at not merely studying restrictive masculinities (OECD, 2021) but actually changing them in multifaceted and collaborative ways that involve several interventions and supports over time (Ruane-McAteer et al., 2020). These interventions are showing good promise for attitude and behavior change at the societal level, so might it be possible for organizational scholars studying SH to borrow key principles and practices from gender-transformative programming for the workplace? If so, what would gender-transformative programming look like in an organizational context, and how might these programs be supported and sustained? Research is also needed (along with well-designed interventions) to track their effectiveness, as is done at the societal level, and document shifts in gender ideologies and harassment over time. As noted earlier, it is also crucial to ensure that attempts to change gender ideologies do not backfire (e.g., Kubai & Ahlberg, 2013) by adapting them to local cultural and organizational realities, resources, and policies.

The UN identified GBV as a major global and development issue many years ago (United Nations, 1989) and many initiatives and programs have been pursued as a way to promote the empowerment of women and reduction of GBV. More than 20 years later, rates of GBV are still disturbingly high, they got worse during the pandemic, and the world will not achieve gender equality by 2030 (UN Women, 2022). The existing research and interventions on societal cultural ideologies and institutions are beginning to show gains in developing healthier and more egalitarian gender roles. We hope that this synthesis of the multidisciplinary literatures on societal cultural ideologies and institutions has helped to inspire future work that brings many of these insights and programs into organizational settings as well. Everyone deserves to work and play in a harassment-free space without the constraints of oppressive gender ideologies.

References

Alcalde, M. (2010). Violence across borders: Familism, hegemonic masculinity, and self-sacrificing femininity in the lives of Mexican and Peruvian migrants. *Latino Studies, 8,* 48–68.

Alldred, P., & Biglia, B. (2015). Gender-related violence and young people: An overview of Italian, Irish, Spanish, UK and EU legislation. *Children & Society*, *29*(6), 662–675.

Beasley, C. (2008). Rethinking hegemonic masculinity in a globalizing world. *Men and Masculinities*, *11*(1), 86–103.

Berdahl, J. L. (2007). The sexual harassment of uppity women. *Journal of Applied Psychology*, *92*(2), 425.

Berdahl, J. L., Cooper, M., Glick, P., Livingston, R. W., & Williams, J. C. (2018). Work as a masculinity contest. *Journal of Social Issues*, *74*(3), 422–448.

Berdahl, J. L., & Raver, J. L. (2011). Sexual harassment. In S. Zedeck (Ed.), *APA handbook of industrial and organizational psychology, Vol. 3. Maintaining, expanding, and contracting the organization* (pp. 641–669). American Psychological Association.

Bloom, S. S. (2008). *Violence against women and girls: A compendium of monitoring and evaluation indicators*. MEASURE Evaluation.

Charlebois. (2009). Cross-cultural representations of hegemonic masculinity in Shall we dance. *Intercultural Communication*, *19*, 1–16.

Chawla, N., Gabriel, A. S., O'Leary Kelly, A., & Rosen, C. C. (2021). From #MeToo to #TimesUp: Identifying next steps in sexual harassment research in the organizational sciences. *Journal of Management*, *47*(3), 551–566.

Connell, R. W. (2005). *Masculinities* (2nd ed.). University of California Press.

Conway, J. (2011). Analysing hegemonic masculinities in the anti-globalization movement(s). *International Feminist Journal of Politics*, *13*(2), 225–230.

Cortina, L. M., & Wasti, S. A. (2005). Profiles in coping: Responses to sexual harassment across persons, organizations and cultures. *Journal of Applied Psychology*, *90*, 182–192.

Dabby, C., & Yoshihama, M. (2021). Gender-based violence and culturally specific advocacy in Asian and Pacific Islander communities. In G. Geffner et al. (Eds.), *Handbook of interpersonal violence and abuse across the lifespan: A project of the National Partnership to End Interpersonal Violence Across the Lifespan (NPEIV)* (pp. 2675–2703). Springer International Publishing.

Davis, S., & Greenstein, T. N. (2009). Gender ideology: Components, predictors, and consequences. *Annual Review of Sociology*, *35*(1), 87–105.

Eslen-Ziya, H., & Koc, Y. (2016). Being a gay man in Turkey: Internalised sexual prejudice as a function of prevalent hegemonic masculinity perceptions. *Culture, Health & Sexuality*, *18*(7), 799–781.

European Union Agency for Fundamental Rights. (2014). *Violence against women: An EU-wide survey—Fundamental rights agency*. Retrieved December 30, 2022, from https://fra.europa.eu/sites/default/files/fra-2014-vaw-survey-at-a-glance-oct14_en.pdf

Feldblum, C. R., & Lipnic, V. A. (2016, June). Select task force on the study of harassment in the Workplace. *US EEOC*. Retrieved December 30, 2022, from www.eeoc.gov/select-task-force-study-harassment-workplace

Fitzgerald, L. F., & Cortina, L. M. (2018). Sexual harassment in work organizations: A view from the 21st century. In C. B Travis, J. W. White, A. Rutherford, W. S. Williams, S. L. Cook & K. F. Wyche (Eds.), *APA handbook of the psychology of women: Perspectives on women's private and public lives* (pp. 215–234). American Psychological Association.

Fitzgerald, L. F., Shullman, S. L., Bailey, N., Richards, M., Swecker, J., Gold, Y., Ormerod, A. J., & Weitzman, L. (1988). The dimensions and extent of sexual harassment in higher education and the workplace. *Journal of Vocational Behavior*, *32*, 152–175.

Galdi, S., & Guizzo, F. (2021). Media-induced sexual harassment: The routes from sexually objectifying media to sexual harassment. *Sex Roles, 84*(11), 645–669.

Gallagher, K. E., & Parrott, D. J. (2011). What accounts for men's hostile attitudes toward women? The influence of hegemonic male role norms and masculine gender role stress. *Violence Against Women, 17*(5), 568–583.

Gelfand, M. J., Fitzgerald, L. F., & Drasgow, F. (1995). The structure of sexual harassment: A confirmatory factor analysis across cultures and settings. *Journal of Vocational Behavior, 47*, 164–177.

Glick, P., Berdahl, J. L., & Alonso, N. M. (2018). Development and validation of the masculinity contest culture scale. *Journal of Social Issues, 74*(3), 449–476.

Gordon, R., Cheeseman, N., Rockowitz, S., Stevens, L. M., & Flowe, H. D. (2022). Government responses to gender-based violence during COVID-19. *Frontiers in Global Women's Health, 3*, 857345–857345.

Grunow, D., Begall, K., & Buchler, S. (2018). Gender ideologies in Europe: A multidimensional framework. *Journal of Marriage and Family, 80*(1), 42–60.

Hearn, J., Nordberg, M., Andersson, K., Balkmar, D., Gottzen, L., Klinth, R., Pringle, K., & Sandberg, L. (2012). Hegemonic masculinity and beyond: 40 years of research in Sweden. *Men and Masculinities, 15*(1), 31–55.

Heise, L., Ellsberg, M., & Gottmoeller, M. (2002). A global overview of gender-based violence. *International Journal of Gynecology & Obstetrics, 78*, S5–S14.

Javaid, A. (2017). The unknown victims: Hegemonic masculinity, masculinities, and male sexual victimisation. *Sociological Research Online, 22*(1), 28–47.

Jewkes, R., & Morrell, R. (2018). Hegemonic masculinity, violence, and gender equality: Using latent class analysis to investigate the origins and correlates of differences between men. *Men and Masculinities, 21*(4), 547–571.

Kersten, J. (1996). Culture, masculinities and violence against women. *The British Journal of Criminology, 36*(3), 381–395.

Klugman, J. (2017). *Gender based violence and the law*. Retrieved December 30, 2022, from https://thedocs.worldbank.org/en/doc/232551485539744935-0050022017/original/WDR17BPGenderbasedviolenceandthelaw.pdf

Kubai, A., & Ahlberg, B. M. (2013). Making and unmaking ethnicities in the Rwandan context: Implication for gender-based violence, health, and wellbeing of women. *Ethnicity & Health, 18*(5), 469–482.

Latcheva, R. (2017). Sexual harassment in the European Union: A pervasive but still hidden form of gender-based violence. *Journal of Interpersonal Violence, 32*(12), 1821–1852.

Lazarus-Black, M., & Merry, S. E. (2003). The politics of gender violence: Law reform in local and global places. *Law & Social Inquiry, 28*(4), 931–939.

Lease, S. H., Montes, S. H., Baggett, L. R., Sawyer, R. J., Fleming-Norwood, K. M., Hampton, A. B., Ovrebo, E., Çiftçi, A., & Boyraz, G. (2013). A cross-cultural exploration of masculinity and relationships in men from Turkey, Norway, and the United States. *Journal of Cross-Cultural Psychology, 44*(1), 84–105.

Levant, R. F., & Richmond, K. (2008). A review of research on masculinity ideologies using the male role norms inventory. *The Journal of Men's Studies, 15*(2), 130–146.

Luthar, H. K., & Luthar, V. K. (2007). A theoretical framework explaining cross-cultural sexual harassment: Integrating Hofstede and Schwartz. *Journal of Labor Research, 28*, 169–188.

Luthar, V. K., & Luthar, H. K. (2002). Using Hofstede's cultural dimensions to explain sexually harassing behaviours in an international context. *International Journal of Human Resource Management, 13*, 268–284.

Maxwell, L., Khan, Z., & Yount, K. M. (2022). Do laws promoting gender equity and freedom from violence benefit the most vulnerable? A multilevel analysis of women's and adolescent girls' experiences in 15 low- and-middle-income countries. *Health Policy and Planning, 37*(1), 33–44.

Merkin, R. (2008a). Cross-cultural differences in perceiving sexual harassment: Demographic incidence rates of sexual harassment/sexual aggression in Latin America. *North American Journal of Psychology, 10*(2), 277–290.

Merkin, R. S. (2008b). The impact of sexual harassment on turnover intentions, absenteeism, and job satisfaction: Findings from Argentina, Brazil and Chile. *Journal of International Women's Studies, 10,* 73–91.

Merkin, R. S., & Shah, M. K. (2014). The impact of sexual harassment on job satisfaction, turnover intentions, and absenteeism: Findings from Pakistan compared to the United States. *Springer Plus, 3,* 1–13.

Merry, S. E. (2006). Human rights and transnational culture: Regulating gender violence through global law. *Osgoode Hall LJ, 44,* 53.

Montesanti, S. R., & Thurston, W. E. (2015). Mapping the role of structural and interpersonal violence in the lives of women: Implications for public health interventions and policy. *BMC Women's Health, 15*(1), 1–13.

Morrell, R., Jewkes, R., & Lindegger, G. (2012). Hegemonic masculinity/masculinities in South Africa: Culture, power, and gender politics. *Men and Masculinities, 15*(1), 11–30.

OECD. (2021). *Man enough? Measuring masculine norms to promote women's empowerment.* Social Institutions and Gender Index, OECD Publishing, Paris. https://doi.org.proxy.queensu.ca/10.1787/6ffd1936-en

Pleck, J. H. (1981). *The myth of masculinity.* MIT Press.

Pleck, J. H. (1995). The gender role strain paradigm: An update. In R. F. Levant & W. S. Pollack (Eds.), *A new psychology of men* (pp. 11–32). Basic Books.

Raver, J. L. (2024). Culture and workplace deviance. In M. J. Gelfand & M. Erez (Eds.), *The Oxford handbook of cross-cultural organizational behavior* (pp. 268–297). Oxford University Press.

Rawski, S. L., & Workman-Stark, A. L. (2018). Masculinity contest cultures in policing organizations and recommendations for training interventions. *Journal of Social Issues, 74*(3), 607–627.

Rimjhim, R., & Dandapat, S. (2022). Is gender-based violence a confluence of culture? Empirical evidence from social media. *Peer J Computer Science, 8,* e1051–e1051.

Ruane-McAteer, E., Gillespie, K., Amin, A., Aventin, A., Robinson, M., Hanratty, J., Khosla, R., & Lohan, M. (2020). Gender-transformative programming with men and boys to improve sexual and reproductive health and rights: A systematic review of intervention studies. *BMJ Global Health, 5,* 1–17.

Russo, N. F., & Pirlott, A. (2006). Gender-based violence concepts, methods, and findings. *Annals of the New York Academy of Sciences, 1087*(1), 178–205.

Sanz-Barbero, B., Corradi, C., Otero-García, L., Ayala, A., & Vives-Cases, C. (2018). The effect of macrosocial policies on violence against women: A multilevel study in 28 European countries. *International Journal of Public Health, 63*(8), 901–911.

Scott-Samuel, A., Stanistreet, D., & Crawshaw, P. (2009). Hegemonic masculinity, structural violence and health inequalities. *Critical Public Health, 19*(3–4), 287–292.

Sigal, J., Gibbs, M. S., Goodrich, C., Rashid, T., Anjum, A., Hsu, D., Perrino, C. S., Boratav, H. B., Carson-Arenas, A., van Baarsen, B., van der Pligt, J., & Pan, W. K. (2005). Cross-cultural reactions to academic sexual harassment: Effects of individualist vs. collectivist culture and gender of participants. *Sex Roles, 52,* 201–215.

Smith, P., D. J., Swartout, K. M., & Tharp, A. T. (2015). Deconstructing hegemonic masculinity: The roles of antifemininity, subordination to women, and sexual dominance in men's perpetration of sexual aggression. *Psychology of Men & Masculinity, 16*(2), 160–169.

Spector-Mersel, G. (2006). Never-aging stories: Western hegemonic masculinity scripts. *Journal of Gender Studies, 15*(1), 67–82.

Tan, Y., Shaw, P., Cheng, H., & Kim, K. K. (2013). The construction of masculinity: A cross-cultural analysis of men's lifestyle magazine advertisements. *Sex Roles, 69*(5–6), 237–249.

Thornton, P. H., Ocasio, W., & Lounsbury, M. (2012). *The institutional logics perspective: A new approach to culture, structure and process.* OUP Oxford.

Toker, Y. (2016). Perception differences in ambiguous forms of workplace sexual harassment: A comparison between the United States and Turkey. *The Journal of Psychology, 150,* 625–643.

Triandis, H., Malpass, R. S., & Davidson, A. R. (1973). Psychology and culture. *Annual Review of Psychology, 24*(1), 355–378.

Triandis, H. C. (1972). *The analysis of subjective culture.* Wiley.

Triandis, H. C. (1994). *Culture and social behavior.* McGraw-Hill.

United Nations. (1989). *Violence against women in the family.* United Nations.

United Nations. (2015). *Transforming our world: The 2030 agenda for sustainable development.* Retrieved December 30, 2022, from https://sdgs.un.org/2030agenda

United Nations. (2019). *UN sustainable development goals report of the secretary-general.* Retrieved December 30, 2022, from https://unstats.un.org/sdgs/report/2019/

United Nations. (2021b). *Progress of the world's women 2019–2020.* United Nations. Retrieved June 4, 2022, from www.unwomen.org/sites/default/files/Headquarters/Attachments/Sections/Library/Publications/2020/UN-Women-annual-report-2019-2020-en.pdf

United Nations. (2021a). *The sustainable development goals report 2021.* United Nations. Retrieved June 4, 2022, from https://unstats.un.org/sdgs/report/2021/

United Nations Refugee Agency. (2022). *Gender-based violence.* Retrieved July 2, 2022, from www.unhcr.org/gender-based-violence.html

United Nations Women (2022). *Progress on the sustainable development goals: The gender snapshot 2022.* Retrieved December 30, 2022, from www.unwomen.org/en/digital-library/publications/2022/09/progress-on-the-sustainable-development-goals-the-gender-snapshot-2022

Wang, X., Fang, G., & Li, H. (2019). Gender-based violence and hegemonic masculinity in China: An analysis based on the quantitative research. *China Population and Development Studies, 3*(1), 84–97.

The Washington Post. (2020). #MeToo is at a crossroads in America. Around the world, it's just beginning. *The Washington Post, Opinions.* Retrieved July 2, 2022, from www.washingtonpost.com/opinions/2020/05/08/metoo-around-the-world/

Wasti, S. A. (2005). The role of cultural values in the perception and reporting of sexual harassment in Turkey. *Journal of Cross-Cultural Psychology, 36*(6), 708–729.

Wasti, S. A. (2014). Organizational culture, national culture, and sexual harassment: A comparative study. *International Journal of Cross-Cultural Management, 14*(1), 25–48.

Wasti, S. A., Bergman, M. E., Glomb, T. M., & Drasgow, F. (2000). Test of the cross-cultural generalizability of a model of sexual harassment. *Journal of Applied Psychology, 85*, 766–778.

Wasti, S. A., & Cortina, L. M. (2002). Coping in context: Sociocultural determinants of responses to sexual harassment. *Journal of Personality and Social Psychology, 83*, 394–405.

World Health Organization. (2021, March 9). Violence against women prevalence estimates. *World Health Organization.* Retrieved December 30, 2022, from www.who.int/publications/i/item/9789240022256

PART II

Sexual Harassment Issues in the Shadows

6

AMBIGUOUSLY SEXUAL INTERACTIONS

Chloe Grace Hart and Ivana Vranjes

The #MeToo movement has brought global attention to issue of sexual harassment (SH) and has been credited with many beneficial effects, such as increased public awareness (Szekeres et al., 2020), better legislation (Tippett, 2018), and a decrease in harassment prevalence (Johnson et al., 2019). Notwithstanding these positive effects, the movement has also been criticized for its over-emphasis on prototypical forms of harassment (Hart, 2023; Kessler et al., 2020; Saguy & Rees, 2021). Harassment can take many forms (Gelfand et al., 1995; Fitzgerald et al., 1988) that differ in their prevalence and conspicuousness. In that regard, Johnson et al. (2019) found in their study that while blatant SH declined in the aftermath of the #MeToo movement, there was simultaneously an increase in reports of more subtle forms of harassment.

When SH plays out in the workplace, it often begins with interactions that are ambiguous, rather than explicitly sexual. As detailed in Hart (2021), *ambiguously sexual interactions* are those that can be interpreted as subtle sexual advances or efforts to otherwise make sexuality salient but can just as plausibly be interpreted as non-sexually motivated. For example, a coworker's invitation to get coffee, efforts to connect on social media, or inquiries about a romantic partner are all ambiguously sexual interactions in that they may or may not carry sexual intent. Furthermore, because of their subtle and undetermined nature and the fact that they can potentially develop into something more serious, adaptively dealing with unwanted ambiguously sexual interactions in the workplace can pose great challenges for people (Hart, 2021). We lift this phenomenon from the shadows of the #MeToo movement by elucidating unique challenges

DOI: 10.4324/9781003300953-8

associated with dealing with unwanted, ambiguously sexual interactions. Namely, when the proactive work that people do to *avoid* SH from unfolding (what Hart terms *trajectory guarding*) is taken into account, the true costs of the phenomenon of SH grow larger than what scholars have previously documented.

The concept and costs of unwanted, ambiguously sexual interactions are documented in detail in Hart (2021). That study drew on data from interview-based research with 84 women, men, and nonbinary people working in the Silicon Valley tech industry, recruited primarily via LinkedIn invitations, who were asked about sexual interactions they had experienced in the workplace. Throughout the interviews Hart (2021) documented the ambiguous origins of many SH experiences and people's laborious coping strategies that aimed to prevent SH from unfolding. In this chapter, we build on Hart's (2021) concepts of *ambiguously sexual interactions* and *trajectory guarding* and a number of ways. First, we contextualize the concepts within the management and psychology literatures, framing trajectory guarding as a form of coping. Second, we develop a model of coping with ambiguously sexual interactions in which we distinguish three forms of trajectory guarding strategies (avoidance, distancing, and protective shielding) and consider multiple costs of trajectory guarding on individual, relational, professional, and societal levels. Third, we outline areas of further research necessary in this domain. Finally, we consider the practical implications: how might the costs of trajectory guarding against unwanted, ambiguously sexual interactions be mitigated?

Unwanted, Ambiguously Sexual Interactions as a Harbinger of Sexual Harassment

In its broadest sense, SH refers to behavior that derogates, humiliates, or demeans people based on sex or gender (Berdahl, 2007). It encompasses three categories of behavior: unwanted sexual attention, sexual coercion, and gender harassment, (Fitzgerald et al., 1995, 1988). The first category refers to a wide range of unwanted sexually loaded verbal and non-verbal behaviors (e.g., unwanted touching). The second category describes behaviors where favorable professional treatment is conditioned on sexual activity (e.g., promotion in exchange for sexual favors). Finally, the third category encompasses behaviors that convey hostility, objectification, exclusion, or second-class status toward members of one gender or those who violate gender norms (e.g., sexists remarks). SH thus encompasses behaviors that are both sexual (unwanted attention and sexual coercion) and nonsexual (gender harassment). While both sexual and nonsexual harassing behaviors are harmful for people who experience them (Sojo et al., 2016), in this chapter, we specifically focus on behaviors that are problematic because they are potentially sexually motivated—that is, behaviors that hint at unwanted sexual attention or sexual coercion (rather than behaviors that fit or foreshadow gender harassment). We term these behaviors unwanted, ambiguously sexual interactions.

How do unwanted, ambiguously sexual interactions play out? One example of the link between ambiguously sexual interactions and SH, as described in Hart (2021), comes from Melanie,[1] a product marketing manager in her forties. Melanie described how her conversations with her boss in a previous job began with interactions that were initially ambiguously sexual, making her boss's intentions hard to parse. Specifically, in casual conversation her boss began asking her about her boyfriend and how they had spent time together recently. Although this touched on an intimate topic—activities she had done with her romantic partner—it was not clear at this point that her boss had intended to make sexuality salient. Asking about time spent with a romantic partner, after all, is relatively common fodder for platonic conversation. Yet in this case, the boss's questions were the first in an increasingly sexually explicit line of questioning about Melanie's personal life that evolved into questions about Melanie's masturbation habits and porn use. In this case, then, asking about her partner was the first step in a trajectory toward explicit SH. Similarly, other reports of harassment following the #MeToo era also described how personal conversations in the professional context turned into harassment over time, suggesting that in some cases, efforts to get coworkers to talk about their personal lives may be a way of testing and pushing their boundaries.

A second example detailed in Hart (2021) came from Catalina, a data scientist in her thirties, who described a similar trajectory of SH that began with ambiguously sexually motivated behaviors from her manager. Catalina's experience started with her manager sending her casual text messages on a weekend night, talking about what she described as "random stuff." This behavior, too, is ambiguously sexual: while initiating impromptu conversation—over text or otherwise—may at times be a flirtatious gesture, it may also represent an overture of platonic friendship. At the point when Catalina's manager sent the first weekend message, then, a trajectory toward explicit SH was possible but not certain. But in Catalina's case, like Melanie's, her manager moved toward increasingly sexually coded behavior. He began texting her every day and telling her that he wanted to see her. Then, on a work trip, he offered to let her lead a high-profile presentation but demanded that they work together in his hotel room to prepare the presentation. Once in the hotel room, he attempted to get Catalina on the bed. At this point, she left the room, and he retaliated by withdrawing the opportunity to let her give the presentation. As in Melanie's case, an ambiguously sexual interaction—here, casual texts on the weekend—foreshadowed more explicit SH.

As is clear from the above examples, unwanted, ambiguously sexual interactions can start with actions that are not clearly sexually motivated (e.g., questions about private life and text messages during off-work time). Although such actions may simply represent efforts to build a friendship with a coworker, they may also represent interactional moments that will escalate into clearly harassing behavior (e.g., inquiring into sexual habits and attempting to initiate unwanted sexual activity). Ambiguously sexual interactions, then, sometimes presage explicit SH.

Unwanted Ambiguously Sexual Interactions and Related Phenomena

The phenomenon of unwanted ambiguously sexual interactions has parallels with the concepts of workplace incivility (rude, condescending, and isolating acts that breach workplace norms of respect but otherwise look normal; Andersson & Pearson, 1999; Cortina et al., 2001) and microaggressions (verbal, behavioral, or environmental slights that are brief and frequent on a daily basis, whether they are intended or not; Sue et al., 2007). Unwanted and ambiguously sexual interactions, workplace incivility, and microaggressions are linked by the fact that each can appear mundane, unremarkable, and ambiguous, yet may be disruptive and detrimental to those who experience them (Hart, 2021; Lui & Quezada, 2019; Schilpzand et al., 2016; see also Chapter 7). Unlike workplace incivility and microaggressions, however, unwanted, ambiguously sexual interactions are typically carried out through gestures that are not in-and-of-themselves offensive, or not even necessarily sexual (e.g., efforts to find opportunities for conversation, to communicate outside of the office, or to invite a fellow employee to spend time together). Indeed, many employees *want* to connect with their coworkers through interactions like these. Although such interactions at times foreshadow SH, at other times, they can lay the groundwork for building platonic friendships. Thus, whereas workplace incivility and microaggressions are generally regarded as harmful despite the actor's motive, the potentially sexually motivated nature of the behavior is what makes ambiguously sexual interactions harmful and difficult to navigate.

Ambiguously sexual interactions are in some ways analogous to workplace social sexual behavior. Whereas ambiguously sexual interactions are, by definition, ambiguous, social sexual behavior describes more plainly sexual behavior, which may or may not be perceived as harassing and may be enjoyed by some employees (Berdahl & Aquino, 2009).

In their recent work, Rawski et al. (2022) build on the Goffman's framing principles (1974) to propose an interactional model of social sexual behavior, highlighting its subjective and volatile nature. A key postulation of their model is that through sustained interacting cycles of sensemaking and engrossment groups can define an interaction of social sexual behavior as benign or positive (the play frame), but that such sensemaking can change dramatically when the same interaction becomes perceived as serious or malignant (the SH frame). Just as social sexual behavior can create interaction vulnerability—where there is the potential for interactants to interpret the same sexual behavior as either playful or harassment—ambiguously sexual interactions also represent interaction vulnerability, in that more than one frame of behavior—sexual or nonsexual—is plausible. However, social sexual behavior is already clearly sexual in nature: the ambiguity in this behavior lies in whether interactants interpret the behavior as playful or offensive. In contrast, with ambiguously sexual interactions it is unclear whether the behavior should be construed as sexual to begin with.

What is potentially problematic about ambiguously sexual interactions, then, is not the content of the interaction itself, but its possible intent: that it may be a signal of unwanted sexual interest and a harbinger of escalating harassment. Unwanted ambiguously sexual interactions are often not forms of mistreatment themselves, but rather send a warning sign that future mistreatment may be imminent. We next explain why such interaction are particularly stressful and how they can evolve into protective coping strategies that may be potentially costly for individuals.

Model of Coping With Ambiguously Sexual Interactions

In what follows, we propose a model of coping with ambiguously sexual behaviors at work. Our model describes a taxing process in which people deploy a significant investment of resources into deciphering whether or not certain behavior is threatening and select coping strategies. We further describe how due to the ambiguous nature of such behaviors, people may resort to trajectory guarding strategies (strategies such as avoidance, distancing, and protective shielding, as we detail below) as a form of coping. However, although trajectory guarding strategies that might shield people from harm in the short term, they may carry costs on an individual, relational, professional, and societal level. The main ideas of this model are summarized in Figure 6.1. Below, building on the transactional theory of stress (Lazarus & Folkman, 1984), we discuss different parts of this model, including people's primary appraisal process, their secondary appraisal process and the outcomes of people's coping efforts.

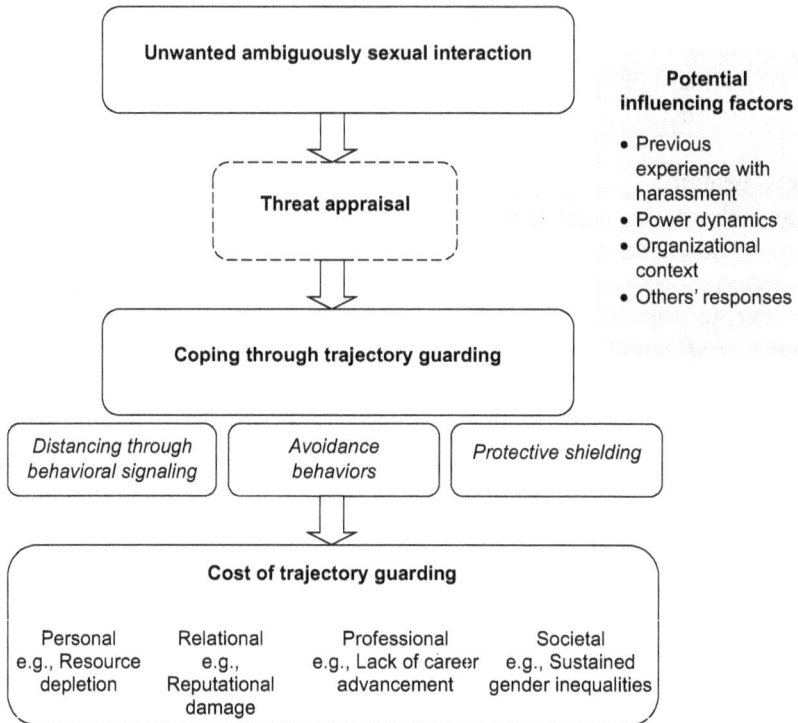

FIGURE 6.1   A model describing how people cope with unwanted sexually ambiguous interactions at work.

Appraising Ambiguously Sexual Interactions as a Potential Threat

According to the transactional theory of stress (Lazarus & Folkman, 1984), stress is a result of an ongoing transaction between individuals and their environment, during which a person determines an event to be significant and potentially harmful (i.e., primary appraisal) and subsequently assesses one's options and possibilities for coping (i.e., secondary appraisal). The primary appraisal phase is critical for the development of effective coping strategies. Yet, in the case of unwanted ambiguously sexual interactions, this phase is complicated due to the lack of clarity regarding the initiator's intent for the behavior (sexual or not) and thus the potential of the behavior to escalate into SH.

Many theories document people's aversion toward ambiguous situations (see Curley et al., 1986) and role ambiguity is seen as a common stressor experienced in the workplace (Jackson & Schuler, 1985; Tubre & Collins, 2000). This can be attributed to the threatening subjective experience of not having all relevant knowledge to make a decision (Frisch & Baron, 1988). Ambiguity creates confusion around the clarity, priority, and coherence of a situation (March, 1988) and is often paired with feelings of self-blame (Curley et al., 1986; Frisch & Baron, 1988). Therefore, appraising ambiguously sexual interactions can be a mentally and emotionally taxing process. Indeed, in Hart's data, interviewees described carefully monitoring ambiguously sexual interactions as effortful "cognitive load" or "mindshare that's having to go to solve that problem." (Hart, 2021)

Determining Strategies to Cope With the Threat

Since unwanted ambiguously sexual interactions may escalate into explicit harassment and thus pose harm to an individual, these interactions prompt people to find ways to cope with the behavior (i.e., secondary appraisal stage; Lazarus & Folkman, 1984). Ambiguity tied to a negative behavior may make people more likely to resort to avoidance-oriented behaviors (Meral et al., 2023), which are a dominant strategy for coping in other contexts, such as in response to blatant SH (Cortina & Wasti, 2005; Diekmann et al., 2013; Fitzgerald et al., 1995; Woodzicka & LaFrance, 2001).

In Hart (2021), in response to ambiguously sexual interactions many interviewees engaged in what Hart termed *trajectory guarding*: carefully monitoring future interactions with the person and deploying a range of strategies to prevent further SH from unfolding or continuing. We build on that prior work by identifying three distinct categories of trajectory guarding: *distancing through behavioral signaling, avoidance behaviors,* and *protective shielding.*

First, some interviewees adopted a chilly demeanor toward coworkers who initiated interactions that were plausibly sexually motivated: what we call distancing through behavioral signaling. For example, as detailed in Hart (2021), after the SH experience with her manager Catalina described being "completely, blatantly cold with any man that would approach me strangely," and refusing to answer messages she received on the weekend from coworkers. Second, other interviewees described trying to actively avoid the person who had initiated the ambiguously sexual interaction: what we term avoidance behaviors. For example, interviewees described leaving work early to avoid being alone in the office with the person who had initiated an unwanted, ambiguously sexual interaction, or avoiding professional development or team-building activities in which they may be expected to interact closely with the person. Finally, when it was an option, some interviewees signaled their lack of sexual availability: what we call protective shielding. For example, one interviewee described intentionally mentioning her romantic partner during a conversation; another recounted gesturing in ways that displayed her wedding ring.

People find it hard to address ambiguous negative behavior because of fear that their interpretation of the behavior may differ from the person enacting the negative behavior (Robinson et al., 2013). This is true of ambiguously sexual interactions, which come with plausible deniability: there are always multiple interpretations of the interaction, including a conceivable interpretation that it was not sexually motivated.

In Hart (2021), interviewees typically found ambiguously sexual interactions difficult to clarify with others. They offered three reasons for why they were reluctant to address unwanted, ambiguously sexual interactions with the initiator directly, and instead engaged in trajectory guarding strategies. First, interviewees worried that they would be perceived as presumptuous or paranoid for suggesting that the interaction was sexually motivated if the initiator had not intended it to be. This is in line with harassment literature indicating that victims of SH are often met with disbelief from others, even when the behavior they experienced was overtly sexual (Hershcovis et al., 2021). The backlash toward confronting behavior is likely to be more pronounced when it is not clear that the behavior is sexual to begin with. As one interviewee, Eddie, explained in Hart (2021): "The difficult part is that it's almost impossible to bring up [ambiguously sexual interactions] for discussion if there isn't like clear evidence of it, [like] a specific action that occurs that you can reference in a conversation as to why it's inappropriate or that can't happen, or things like that."

Second, interviewees worried that explicitly, in confronting an ambiguously sexual interaction directly, expressing their lack of sexual interest in the initiator might damage that person's ego and potentially lead to retaliation from them. Indeed, people who speak up about SH in the workplace often experience retaliatory behaviors (Bergman et al., 2002; Buchanan et al., 2014; Marshall, 2005; McDonald, 2012). Finally, people expressed apprehension that addressing an interaction as sexually motivated would unduly stigmatize the initiator as a "creep." Despite the prevalent myth that many harassment claims are motivated by a desire to damage another person's reputation (Lonsway et al., 2008), victims of harassment actually sometimes remain silent about their experiences to protect the harasser (Gutek, 1985; Maitindale, 1990). Such prosocial motives are likely to be even more prevalent when the behavior in question can be potentially construed as friendly and nonsexual.

Interviewees who worried that unwanted, ambiguously sexual interactions foreshadowed SH thus tended to avoid confronting the initiators directly because of this set of concerns, and instead embrace trajectory guarding strategies. Over time, however, the use of coping strategies can potentially progress into feelings of alienation, depression, and loneliness and may hamper people on many levels, which is what we discuss next.

Costs of Trajectory Guarding Strategies

The effectiveness of any given coping strategy is dependent on how well the coping strategy fits within the context (Dewe & Cooper, 2007; Folkman & Moskowitz, 2004). While avoidance-focused strategies for coping can be effective in the moment as they can help shield a person from harm, continual reliance on these strategies does not help tackle the underlying source of stress (Ben-Zur, 2009) and potentially depletes people's cognitive and emotional resources (Maslach & Leiter, 2008). Thus, although deployed for good reason, trajectory guarding as a way of dealing with ambiguous sexual interactions may be quite costly. Indeed, Hart (2021) identified several costs associated with trajectory guarding strategies. Here, we consider how these costs play out on individual, relational, professional, and societal levels.

On an *individual* level, engaging in trajectory guarding can be quite cognitively and emotionally tasking. As indicated before, deciphering whether an ambiguously sexual behavior is threatening or not requires an investment of energy and resources, which can leave people feeling depleted. Further, trajectory guarding can be a useful tool to defend against SH, but it is difficult to wield the tool with precision. Not every ambiguously sexual interaction is actually intended as an initial step toward increasingly explicit sexual behavior, yet the people on the receiving end of such interactions have no straightforward way to parse the initiator's intent. When a coworker sends a casual text over the weekend, for example, this could be a gesture signaling a desire to initiate a romantic or sexual relationship, but it may also be a gesture of platonic friendship. Inevitably, those who are wary of SH unfolding from ambiguously sexual interactions will sometimes invest energy into trajectory guarding in cases when it is not necessary—for example, toward a coworker sending a platonically motivated text—thus proactively defending against ambiguously sexual interactions that were never destined to become SH.

On a *relational* level, engaging in trajectory guarding strategies can negatively impact people's working relationships and professional reputations. Because the interactions that prompt trajectory guarding are typically ambiguous and subtle, other people in a workplace may not recognize when an employee is engaging in trajectory guarding. For example, if Catalina had treated her manager coldly after he began texting her on the weekend, her coworkers would be unlikely to pinpoint the source of her chilly demeanor to his possible romantic overture, and so may well attribute the behavior to her deficient social skills rather than his behavior. Thus, trajectory guarding can operate as a hidden interactional maneuver, and those who use it may simply be read as unfriendly, antisocial, or distracted. While harassers often occupy central positions within their social networks—giving them power, access to resources, and freedom to act as they please—people who experience harassment often occupy more peripheral positions that make them vulnerable (Hershcovis et al., 2021). A person's position in a social network therefore plays an important role in the likelihood that others in that network will be motivated to support them and engage with them. When a peripheral person starts engaging in trajectory guarding, this can lead to isolation from, or a loss of reputation with, colleagues, outcomes that may further diminish one's credibility when attempting to report behavior in the future.

On a *professional* level, many of these trajectory guarding strategies complicated interviewees' efforts to carry out their work. Interviewees described carefully monitoring interactions as a distracting endeavor that robbed them of attention that could otherwise be directed toward their work tasks. Minimizing one's presence in the workplace makes it difficult to gain visibility at work and build a professional network. Leaving work early to avoid being alone with the person may be read by others as a lack of commitment to the job. Thus, although trajectory guarding strategies are a logical means of seeking to minimize the possibility of SH, many simultaneously present barriers to career advancement.

Finally, at a broader *organizational* and *societal* scale, trajectory guarding may sustain existing gender inequalities in the workplace. The interviewees who engaged in trajectory guarding were those who were most wary of SH, often because they had prior experience with it. Prior research shows that women disproportionately experience SH in their lives relative to men (e.g., Kearl, 2018), and this was true in Hart's (2021) interview sample as well. As a result, Hart found that women were also more likely to *anticipate* SH, reading ambiguously sexual interactions as possible early signs of SH. Thus, women were far more likely to deploy trajectory guarding strategies to deter SH. Such avoidant-focused strategies can disadvantage women's societal position, maintaining the status quo in which men disproportionately occupy the most influential positions across fields (Huang et al., 2019). That the costs of engaging in trajectory guarding disproportionately fall upon women can subtly hinder societal attempts to advance gender equality in the workplace.

Unwanted, Ambiguously Sexual Interactions: Future Research Opportunities

It is well documented that experiencing SH is linked to wide-ranging negative impacts on the mental and physical health, work performance and outcomes, and financial wellbeing of the people who experience it (Hart, 2019; McLaughlin et al., 2017; Willness et al., 2007). Yet, as described earlier, anticipating and working to proactively defend against SH can also be costly. It is important to understand what factors could potentially influence the above-described process of coping with ambiguously sexual behaviors through trajectory guarding strategies. We highlight several research avenues to explore.

First, there is a need for more research on SH as an ongoing day-to-day exchange which can be influenced by people's experiences and their organizational context (Chawla et al., 2021). People's past exposure to SH may affect how they perceive and handle ambiguously sexual interactions at work (e.g., Gowan & Zimmermann, 1996), by making people more sensitive to potential threats related to ambiguously sexual behaviors in the workplace. In Hart's data, people who described engaging in trajectory guarding to manage ambiguously sexual interactions had typically experienced SH before. Thus, the potential costs associated with trajectory guarding appear to fall most on those who have already been harmed by prior experiences of harassment, compounding the costs of harassment. Further research should more directly explore how prior SH experience subsequently shapes how people respond to unwanted, ambiguously sexual behavior. If people have previous experiences of SH that were left unresolved or in which more active forms of coping such as confronting the perpetrator or reporting the behavior backfired, might this further increase a sense of threat and thus encourage people to engage in trajectory guarding in the future? In addition, such research could examine whether prior experiences of other types of harassment—for example, racial harassment—make a person more likely to engage in trajectory guarding (see Chapter 8).

The power dynamic between individuals also merits further inquiry. When an individual experiences ambiguously sexual behaviors from a coworker, the coworker's organizational power may shape a person's likelihood of perceiving such interactions as threatening and, therefore, their likelihood of employing trajectory guarding to manage the threat. SH can be seen as an expression of power and dominance and a mechanism for protecting or enhancing one's gender-based status (Berdahl, 2007). People may be more likely to fear escalation of ambiguously sexual behaviors into explicit SH when the initiator of the behavior has greater organizational power to wield—that is, when the initiator is in a superordinate position. In general, people are more likely to feel threatened and engage in avoidance coping when they feel powerless or unable to control a situation (Holahan & Moos, 1987), as they may fear retaliation from people holding a position of power (Cortina & Magley, 2003). Thus, ambiguously sexual behaviors initiated by more powerful individuals may be perceived as particularly threatening and difficult to cope with. Although prior work implies that the respective organizational power held by the initiator and recipient might play a role in whether the recipient engages in trajectory guarding, future research should examine this issue directly.

The context of the organization may also influence how people decide to respond to unwanted, ambiguously sexual interactions. In interviews, people who engaged in trajectory guarding typically did so with the expectation that if they were to experience SH, their organization would do little to help them. Similarly, previous research has found that coping with SH is particularly difficult in organizations with a high tolerance for harassment—a powerful predictor of harassment occurrence (Fitzgerald & Cortina, 2018). Would people feel less threatened, and therefore less of a need to trajectory guard, in an organization with a climate in which employees perceive that targets of SH are supported? In such a workplace, the stakes of waiting to see if unwanted, ambiguously sexual interactions indeed evolve into SH—rather than proactively engaging in trajectory guarding—may be lower.

Finally, it might also be relevant to explore how responses to unwanted, ambiguously sexual interactions are perceived by others and what types of responses are the most effective. As described earlier, many people interviewed described a sense that confronting ambiguously sexual interactions directly—that is, clarifying in the moment with the interaction's initiator whether an interaction was sexually motivated or not—would seem presumptuous and awkward. Research could examine whether there are effective strategies for communicating about ambiguously sexual interactions when they occur. If there is indeed backlash for asking directly whether an interaction is sexually motivated—as many interviewees intuited—does the way that the inquiry is made matter? For example, if a person asks directly whether an ambiguous interaction is sexually motivated, but uses humor or acknowledges in their question that this may seem presumptuous and awkward, would such approaches help to defray the risk of being perceived negatively?

A low-cost way of directly establishing the intent of an unwanted, ambiguously sexual interaction might allow people to reach a shared agreement that a relationship is platonic, thus removing the need to engage in trajectory guarding. Of course, though, such individual strategies do not eliminate the risk that SH may stem from ambiguously sexual interactions. Some people will go on to harass even after clarifying that their initial, ambiguously sexual interactions are not sexually motivated. Thus, better understanding the consequences of individual strategies to address SH may be instructive in some ways, but cannot be taken as a panacea.

The Practical Implications of Unwanted, Ambiguously Sexual Behaviors at Work

As described earlier, unwanted ambiguously sexual interactions at work can threaten individuals and lead them to engage in trajectory guarding strategies, which in turn carry many costs to individuals, organizations and to the society as a whole. This raises the question of how these interactions are best addressed by individuals, organizations, and society.

On the individual level, SH in all forms is difficult to cope with, and moreover, there is no individual response to SH that is guaranteed to resolve it (Cortina & Magley, 2003; Firestone & Harris, 2003). People experiencing SH face contradictory expectations about confronting the behavior: do nothing and appear less credible and more blameworthy (Balogh et al., 2003; Hart, 2023), report and have your character called into question (Lonsway et al., 2008), or face retaliation (Bergman et al., 2002).

Similarly, interviewees who experienced unwanted, ambiguously sexual interactions with coworkers worried about being perceived negatively if they attempted to clarify the motive of such interactions. This points to the importance of the research examining whether low-cost strategies for clarifying if an interaction is sexually motivated exist, as outlined earlier. At the same time, people seeking to signal their interest in establishing friendships with coworkers might also work to make the motivation behind their behavior more plainly platonic, for example, by proposing spending time together in a group of people, rather than one on one.

When people engage in trajectory guarding at work, it is potentially costly not only to their own careers but also to the organizations in which they work. Organizations benefit when employees can focus, attend workplace functions freely, and have positive relationships with their coworkers; trajectory guarding, by Hart's (2021) interviewees' accounts, interferes with these aims. It is in organizations' interest, then, to mitigate the harms of trajectory guarding. One approach that may spring to mind is for organizations to simply mandate that employees do not initiate interactions that are ambiguously sexual. Yet, this approach is both unfeasible and likely to backfire. First, much of human communication is ambiguous: when people communicate, the intent, meaning, and emotional content of what they say is often open to multiple interpretations (Stivers et al., 2022). This is true of ambiguously sexual interactions too: gestures like dropping by someone's workstation to chat, or smiling or making eye contact with a coworker, may be done to convey sexual interest but may also be done merely to convey friendliness. Asking employees to avoid these sorts of interactions because they could be interpreted as sexually motivated would make for a sterile and unenjoyable workplace culture (see also Berdahl & Aquino, 2009). Moreover, employees may well develop other subtle, ambiguous gestures to convey sexual interest if the current set of gestures recognized as ambiguously sexual were banned. Promoting workplace cultures in which employees perceive that SH is taken seriously and that there is organizational support for those who experience it could also make employees feel less of a need to engage in trajectory guarding, as described earlier.

Offering training to employees about unwanted, ambiguously sexual interactions and their link to SH may further be used to make employees more cognizant of their possible harms. However, such an approach comes with risks. Although some SH trainings have shown positive outcomes, many have proven ineffective or elicited backlash effects (Dobbin & Kalev, 2020; Roehling & Huang, 2018). For example, one large-scale study of organizations that implemented SH trainings found that in the years after training was implemented, the representation of White women in management declined and the representation of Black, Latina, and Asian American women remained flat (Dobbin & Kalev, 2019). This suggests that SH trainings for employees do not help to remove barriers women face in advancing up the corporate ladder, and in some cases may heighten such barriers. Other research finds that SH trainings may also activate unequal gender beliefs, unconscious gender bias, and negative perceptions of women (Tinkler, 2013; Tinkler et al., 2007). A training for an organization's workforce about unwanted, ambiguously sexual interactions, rather than SH, may have similar unintended consequences.

Importantly, research on SH trainings suggests that not all trainings backfire. Trainings specifically for managers and trainings framed around bystander intervention have shown signs of efficacy. For example, manager trainings for explicit SH appear to be more effective at creating conditions in which women can rise into management positions (Dobbin & Kalev, 2019). The effectiveness of these types of trainings may stem from the fact that, whereas general employee trainings about SH imply that those taking the training are likely to engage in SH themselves (thus the need for the training), bystander intervention and manager SH trainings position the people taking the training as those who will *solve,* rather than perpetrate, SH (Dobbin & Kalev, 2020). Given the parallels with SH, there is good reason to think that addressing unwanted, ambiguously sexual interactions by training in which the participants are assumed to be allies trying to limit possible harm done would be a promising avenue. For instance, coworkers could be trained to monitor and check in with each other about ambiguously sexual interactions that they observe. However, as we currently know little about the efficacy of the specific interventions that such a training might provide, it would be reckless to roll out an untested training about unwanted, ambiguously sexual interactions to an organization's workforce on a large scale; instead, trainings in this vein should be piloted and their efficacy carefully tested before they are scaled up.

Could efforts to raise public consciousness toward unwanted, ambiguously sexual interactions, and the possibility that SH might spring from them, help to build momentum toward recognizing, and perhaps addressing, their harms? The gains won by heightened attention to the harms of SH outlined earlier suggest that this could indeed be impactful. Yet, seeking public recognition of sexual interactions that are ambiguous also has the potential to generate backlash. Indeed, one of the most hotly debated cases of unwanted sexual behavior discussed during the MeToo movement—an unwanted sexual encounter with the comedian Aziz Ansari, as described by an unnamed young woman to the publication *Babe.net*—was contentious because of its perceived ambiguity (see Way, 2018). The (debatably) ambiguous interactions in question were the woman's efforts to indicate her disinterest in having sex. Rather than stating her disinclination directly, she used indirect forms of communication like repeatedly disengaging from sexual activity that he initiated, emphasizing her desire to instead just "relax" or "chill," and at one point saying "no, I don't think I'm ready to do this." The publicization of the case triggered contentious debate: while some argued that Ansari should have understood the woman's refusals, others disparaged her for not communicating with Ansari more emphatically or simply leaving (e.g., Flanagan, 2018; Weiss, 2018; West, 2018).

That the Aziz Ansari case was controversial *because* it was more ambiguous than other MeToo accounts suggests that efforts to create greater public consciousness of unwanted, ambiguously sexual interactions could be similarly divisive. Moreover, there is a risk that efforts to bring attention to unwanted, ambiguously sexual interactions and the trajectory guarding they often spur could inadvertently result in a conflation between ambiguously sexual interactions and SH in public discourse. Such a conflation could fuel the perspective that SH is typically ambiguous, vague, and may be explained away as simple misunderstandings. This perspective could dilute disapproval toward SH, leading to greater tolerance and less social sanctioning against it. Broadening social awareness of the sometimes subtle origins of SH may thus be counterproductive.

Ultimately, the best way to reduce the harms of trajectory guarding is to lessen the need to trajectory guard at all, by reducing the prevalence of

SH. People engage in trajectory guarding when they experience unwanted, ambiguously sexual interactions only because they have learned that escalating SH often follows these interactions. This need not be the case. In fact, among the people interviewed, many men recounted experiencing unwanted, ambiguously sexual interactions but rarely described SH unfolding from these interactions, consistent with other research demonstrating that women experience SH far more often than men (Kearl, 2018). When they were not wary of SH, these men simply ignored unwanted, ambiguously sexual interactions, and eventually, the possible sexual overtures that they sensed dissipated. These men offer a compelling glimpse of a world in which, without the looming threat of SH, there is no need to guard one's interactional trajectory from SH when unwanted, ambiguously sexual interactions arise.[2]

Conclusion

People may engage in proactive labor, termed trajectory guarding, to try to prevent SH from unfolding when they experience clues—unwanted, ambiguously sexual interactions—that are sometimes harbingers of escalating SH. The potential costs of this labor suggest that the true costs of SH are greater than has previously been documented. Moreover, the costs of trajectory guarding may deepen other inequalities: women appear to disproportionately engage in trajectory guarding, and thus disproportionately bear its potential career costs (Hart, 2021). Developing a research program to better understand and mitigate the harms of trajectory guarding is thus critical.

Notes

1 All names in this chapter are pseudonyms.
2 Although men experience sexual harassment at lower rates than women, men can and do experience sexual harassment—and engage in trajectory guarding (Hart, 2021). Indeed, men who are targets of harassment face a host of unique challenges because they are not the prototypical harassment targets (see Chapter 9).

References

Andersson, L. M., & Pearson, C. M. (1999). Tit for tat? The spiraling effect of incivility in the workplace. *Academy of Management Review, 24*(3), 452–471.
Balogh, D. W., Kite, M. E., Pickel, K. L., Canel, D., & Schroeder, J. (2003). The effects of delayed report and motive for reporting on perceptions of sexual harassment. *Sex Roles, 48*(7–8), 337–348.
Ben-Zur, H. (2009). Coping styles and affect. *International Journal of Stress Management, 16*(2), 87–101.

Berdahl, J. L. (2007). Harassment based on sex: Protecting social status in the context of gender hierarchy. *Academy of Management Review, 32*(2), 641–658.

Berdahl, J. L., & Aquino, K. (2009). Sexual behavior at work: Fun or folly? *Journal of Applied Psychology, 94*(1), 34.

Bergman, M. E., Langhout, R. D., Palmieri, P. A., Cortina, L. M., & Fitzgerald, L. F. (2002). The (un) reasonableness of reporting: Antecedents and consequences of reporting sexual harassment. *Journal of Applied Psychology, 87*(2), 230.

Buchanan, N. T., Settles, I. H., Hall, A. T., & O'Connor, R. C. (2014). A review of organizational strategies for reducing sexual harassment: Insights from the U.S. military. *Journal of Social Issues, 70*(4), 687–702.

Chawla, N., Gabriel, A. S., O'Leary Kelly, A., & Rosen, C. C. (2021). From# MeToo to# TimesUp: Identifying next steps in sexual harassment research in the organizational sciences. *Journal of Management, 47*(3), 551–566

Cortina, L. M., & Magley, V. J. (2003). Raising voice, risking retaliation: Events following interpersonal mistreatment in the workplace. *Journal of Occupational Health Psychology, 8*(4), 247–265.

Cortina, L. M., Magley, V. J., Williams, J. H., & Langhout, R. D. (2001). Incivility in the workplace: Incidence and impact. *Journal of Occupational Health Psychology, 6*(1), 64–80. https://doi.org/10.1037/1076-8998.6.1.64

Cortina, L. M., & Wasti, S. A. (2005). Profiles in coping: Responses to sexual harassment across persons, organizations, and cultures. *Journal of Applied Psychology, 90*(1), 182.

Curley, S. P., Yates, J. F., & Abrams, R. A. (1986). Psychological sources of ambiguity avoidance. *Organizational Behavior and Human Decision Processes, 38*(2), 230–256.

Dewe, P., & Cooper, C. L. (2007). Coping research and measurement in the context of work related stress. In G. Hodgkinson & J. Kevin Ford (Eds.). *International Review of Industrial and Organizational Psychology 22*, 141–191.

Diekmann, K. A., Sillito Walker, S. D., Galinsky, A. D., & Tenbrunsel, A. E. (2013). Double victimization in the workplace: Why observers condemn passive victims of sexual harassment. *Organization Science, 24*(2), 614–628. https://doi.org/10.1287/orsc.1120.0753

Dobbin, F., & Kalev, A. (2019). The promise and peril of sexual harassment programs. *Proceedings of the National Academy of Sciences, 116*(25), 12255–12260. https://doi.org/10.1073/pnas.1818477116

Dobbin, F., & Kalev, A. (2020). Why sexual harassment programs backfire, and what to do about it. *Harvard Business Review*.

Firestone, J. M., & Harris, R. J. (2003). Perceptions of effectiveness of responses to sexual harassment in the US military, 1988 and 1995. *Gender, Work and Organization, 10*(1), 42–64. https://doi.org/10.1111/1468-0432.00003

Fitzgerald, L. F., & Cortina, L. M. (2018). Sexual harassment in work organizations: A view from the 21st century. In C. B. Travis & J. W. White (Eds.), *APA handbook of the psychology of women*. American Psychological Association.

Fitzgerald, L. F., Shullman, S. L., Bailey, N., Richards, M., Swecker, J., Gold, Y., Ormerod, M., & Weitzman, L. (1988). The incidence and dimensions of sexual harassment in academia and the workplace. *Journal of Vocational Behavior, 32*(2), 152–175.

Flanagan, C. (2018, January 14). The humiliation of Aziz Ansari. *The Atlantic*. www.theatlantic.com/entertainment/archive/2018/01/the-humiliation-of-aziz-ansari/550541/

Folkman, S., & Moskowitz, J. T. (2004). Coping: Pitfalls and promise. *Annual Review of Psychology, 55*(1), 745–774.

Frisch, D., & Baron, J. (1988). Ambiguity and rationality. *Journal of Behavioral Decision Making, 1*(3), 149–157.

Gelfand, M. J., Fitzgerald, L. F., & Drasgow, F. (1995). The structure of sexual harassment: A confirmatory analysis across cultures and settings. *Journal of Vocational Behavior, 47*(2), 164–177.

Goffman, E. (1974). *Frame analysis: An essay on the organization of experience.* Harvard University Press.

Gowan, M. A., & Zimmermann, R. A. (1996). Impact of ethnicity, gender, and previous experience on juror judgments in sexual harassment cases. *Journal of Applied Social Psychology, 26*(7), 596–617.

Gutek, B. A. (1985). *Sex and the workplace.* Jossey-Bass.

Hart, C. G. (2019). The penalties for self-reporting sexual harassment. *Gender & Society, 33*(4), 534–559. https://doi.org/10.1177/0891243219842147

Hart, C. G. (2021). Trajectory guarding: Managing unwanted, ambiguously sexual interactions at work. *American Sociological Review, 86*(2), 256–278. https://doi.org/10.1177/0003122421993809

Hart, C. G. (2023). Is there an idealized target of sexual harassment in the MeToo era? *Social Problems.* Advance online publication. https://doi.org/10.1093/socpro/spad016

Hershcovis, M. S., Vranjes, I., Berdahl, J. L., & Cortina, L. M. (2021). See no evil, hear no evil, speak no evil: Theorizing network silence around sexual harassment. *Journal of Applied Psychology, 106*(12), 1834.

Holahan, C. J., & Moos, R. H. (1987). Personal and contextual determinants of coping strategies. *Journal of Personality and Social Psychology, 52*(5), 946.

Huang, J., Krivkovich, A., Starikova, I., Yee, L., & Zanoschi, D. (2019). *Women in the workplace 2019.* www.mckinsey.com/featured-insights/gender-equality/women-in-theworkplace-2019.

Jackson, S. H., & Schuler, R. S. (1985). A meta-analysis and conceptual critique of research on role ambiguity and role conflict in work settings. *Organizational Behavior and Human Decision Processes, 36*, 16–78.

Johnson, S. K., Keplinger, K., Kirk, J. F., & Barnes, L. (2019). Has sexual harassment at work decreased since# MeToo? *Harvard Business Review.*

Kearl, H. (2018). The facts behind the #MeToo movement: A national study on sexual harassment and assault. *Stop Street Harassment.* www.stopstreetharassment.org/wp-content/uploads/2018/01/Full-Report-2018-National-Study-on-Sexual-Harassment-and-Assault.pdf

Kessler, A. M., Kennair, L. E. O., Grøntvedt, T. V., Bjørkheim, I., Drejer, I., & Bendixen, M. (2020). The effect of prototypical #MeToo features on the perception of social-sexual behavior as sexual harassment. *Sexuality & Culture, 24*, 1271–1291.

Lazarus, R. S., & Folkman, S. (1984). *Stress, appraisal, and coping.* Springer

Lonsway, K. A., Cortina, L. M., & Magley, V. J. (2008). Sexual harassment mythology: Definition, conceptualization, and measurement. *Sex Roles, 58*, 599–615.

Lui, P. P., & Quezada, L. (2019). Associations between microaggression and adjustment outcomes: A meta-analytic and narrative review. *Psychological Bulletin, 145*(1), 45.

Maitindale, M. (1990). *Sexual harassment in the military: 1988.* Defense Manpower Data Center.

March, J. G. (1988). *Decisions and organizations.* Basil Blackwell.

Marshall, A.-M. (2005). Idle rights: Employees' rights consciousness and the construction of sexual harassment policies. *Law & Society Review, 39*(1), 83–124.

Maslach, C., & Leiter, M. P. (2008). Early predictors of job burnout and engagement. *Journal of Applied Psychology, 93*(3), 498.

McDonald, P. (2012). Workplace sexual harassment 30 years on: A review of the literature. *International Journal of Management Reviews*, *14*(1), 1–17. https://doi.org/10.1111/j.1468-2370.2011.00300.x

McLaughlin, H., Uggen, C., & Blackstone, A. (2017). The economic and career effects of sexual harassment on working women. *Gender & Society*, *31*(3), 333–358. https://doi.org/10.1177/0891243217704631

Meral, E. O., Vranjes, I., van Osch, Y., Ren, D., van Dijk, E., & van Beest, I. (2023). Intensity, intent, and ambiguity: Appraisals of workplace ostracism and coping responses. *Aggressive Behavior*, *49*(2), 127–140.

The National Academies of Sciences Engineering and Medicine. (2018). *Sexual harassment of women: Climate, culture, and consequences in academic sciences engineering, and medicine*. The National Academies Press.

Rawski, S. L., O'Leary-Kelly, A. M., & Breaux-Soignet, D. (2022). It's all fun and games until someone gets hurt: An interactional framing theory of work social sexual behavior. *Academy of Management Review, 47*(4), 617–636. https://doi.org/10.5465/amr.2019.0316.

Robinson, S. L., O'Reilly, J., & Wang, W. (2013). Invisible at work: An integrated model of workplace ostracism. *Journal of Management*, *39*(1), 203–231.

Roehling, M. V., & Huang, J. (2018). Sexual harassment training effectiveness: An interdisciplinary review and call for research. *Journal of Organizational Behavior*, *39*(2), 134–150. https://doi.org/10.1002/job.2257

Saguy, A. C., & Rees, M. E. (2021). Gender, power, and harassment: Sociology in the #MeToo era. *Annual Review of Sociology*, *47*, 417–435.

Schilpzand, P., De Pater, I. E., & Erez, A. (2016). Workplace incivility: A review of the literature and agenda for future research. *Journal of Organizational Behavior*, *37*(Suppl 1), S57–S88.

Sojo, V. E., Wood, R. E., & Genat, A. E. (2016). Harmful workplace experiences and women's occupational well-being: A meta-analysis. *Psychology of Women Quarterly*, *40*(1), 10–40.

Stivers, T., Rossi, G., & Chalfoun, A. (2022). *Ambiguities in action ascription*. Social Forces.

Sue, D. W., Capodilupo, C. M., Torino, G. C., Bucceri, J. M., Holder, A. M. B., Nadal, K. L., & Esquilin, M. (2007). Racial microaggressions in everyday life: Implications for clinical practice. *American Psychologist*, *62*(4), 271–286.

Szekeres, H., Shuman, E., & Saguy, T. (2020). Views of sexual assault following #MeToo: The role of gender and individual differences. *Personality and Individual Differences*, *166*, 110203.

Tinkler, J. E. (2013). How do sexual harassment policies shape gender beliefs? An exploration of the moderating effects of norm adherence and gender. *Social Science Research, 42*(5), 1269–1283.

Tinkler, J. E., Eatenson, J. E., Li, Y., & Mollborn, S. (2007). Can legal interventions equalize interactions? The effect of sexual harassment policies on gender beliefs. *Social Psychology Quarterly*, *70*(4), 480–494. https://doi.org/10.1177/019027250707000413

Tippett, E. C. (2018). The legal implications of the MeToo movement. *Minnesota Law Review*, *103*, 229–302.

Tubre, T. C., & Collins, J. M. (2000). Jackson and Schuler (1985) revisited: A meta-analysis of the relationships between role ambiguity, role conflict, and job performance. *Journal of Management*, *26*(1), 155–169.

Way, K. (2018). I went on a date with Aziz Ansari. It turned into the worst night of my life. *Babe.net*. https://babe.net/2018/01/13/aziz-ansari-28355

Weiss, B. (2018). Aziz Ansari is guilty. Of not being a mind reader. *The New York Times*. www.nytimes.com/2018/01/15/opinion/aziz-ansari-babe-sexual-harassment.html

West, L. (2018). Aziz, we tried to warn you. *The New York Times*. www.nytimes.com/2018/01/17/opinion/aziz-ansari-metoo-sex.html

Willness, C. R., Steel, P., & Lee, K. (2007). A meta-analysis of the antecedents and consequences of workplace sexual harassment. *Personnel Psychology*, *60*(1), 127–162. https://doi.org/10.1111/j.1744-6570.2007.00067.x

Woodzicka, J. A., & LaFrance, M. (2001). Real versus imagined gender harassment. *Journal of Social Issues*, *57*(1), 15–30.

7

A TRAUMA-INFORMED PERSPECTIVE ON SEXUAL HARASSMENT

Sandra L. Bloom and Shannon L. Rawski

Introduction

The #MeToo movement put a spotlight on horrific details of sexual harassment (SH) incidents and the magnitude of the shared experience of SH across the human population (Le Bars, 2022). In the wake of this movement, we are left wondering what toll SH leaves on its targets and the society that failed to prevent it. SH is a form of sexual violence (Grosser & Tyler, 2022), and in this chapter, we argue that workplace SH is a potentially traumatic event that can cause long-lasting harm, including post-traumatic stress disorder or PTSD (Willness et al., 2007). The purpose of this chapter is to shine a spotlight on a "trauma-informed" perspective of workplace SH. We first define trauma and make our case that SH is a potentially traumatic event. Then, we describe common responses to trauma and how these might relate to workplace SH. Finally, we will offer a possibility for trauma-informed work organizations and the new research questions that follow from this perspective.

Trauma and Sexual Harassment

Traumatic stress refers to extreme psychophysiological responses under specific circumstances (i.e., potentially traumatic events) characterized by exposure to actual or threatened death, serious injury, or sexual violence in the following ways: (1) through direct experience, (2) through observing another person's direct experience, (3) through another close person's account of their direct or observed experience, and/or (4) through repeated

DOI: 10.4324/9781003300953-9

or extreme exposure to aversive details related to a traumatic experience (Bloom, 1997). Traumatic stress causes maladaptive and dysfunctional changes in a person's biology, psychology, and behavior (Christopher, 2004). We contend that SH (i.e., behavior appraised as unwanted, offensive, or threatening that derogates, demeans, or humiliates an individual based on that individual's sex; Fitzgerald et al., 1997; Berdahl, 2007) should be regarded as a potentially traumatic event. First, SH can involve very severe conduct, including serious injury, sexual violence, or in rare cases actual or threatened death. SH can occur through various modes including (but not limited to) physical, verbal, and virtual/digital. Physical SH can include unwanted touching, groping, assault, or rape (Fitzgerald et al., 1997), which maps on to the "actual . . . serious injury or sexual violence" component of the definition of potentially traumatic events. While verbal and virtual harassment do not involve physical contact, verbal harassment often involves threats of gender-based violence or other demeaning gender-based comments intended to push targets (usually women and gender minorities) out of certain spaces like workplaces or online spaces (see Chapter 2). These forms of SH represent the "threatened . . . serious injury or sexual violence" from the definition of potentially traumatic events. Further, different forms of SH often co-occur (Schneider et al., 1997), so it is likely that physical harassment is associated with verbal and/or virtual harassment as well. While actual or threatened death is not typically part of the definition of SH, there are case studies of SH in particular industries (e.g., policing) whereby the target of SH was at risk of death in addition to other sexually harassing experiences. For example, one woman in the Royal Mounted Canadian Police was denied backup while on a dangerous and potentially life-threatening call as a form of retaliation for reporting SH (Workman-Stark, 2017; see also Chapter 4).

Second, similar to other potentially traumatic events, SH can have broad and dispersed effects. Most commonly, SH directly effects a target, but research shows that SH also influences observers in the workplace, often causing them harm similar to that of targets (Glomb et al., 1997; Schneider, 1996). In the #MeToo movement, widespread disclosure of SH may have resulted in collective sensemaking in the general public that women and other gender minorities were especially at risk for SH at work. This collective sensemaking spotlighted a societal problem but also created the unintended consequence of vicarious trauma (via hyperarousal stress responses) among those highly targeted groups. SH also often involves repeated and severe exposure, characteristics that are common in both playful social sexual work behavior and sexually harassing hostile work environments (Rawski et al., 2022). As such, SH meets the various experiences component of the definition of trauma provided earlier.

Finally, SH can result in extreme psychophysiological stress responses. Research shows that the experience of SH is associated with decreased physical and mental health, decreased life satisfaction, decreased health satisfaction, increased psychological distress, and even an increased likelihood of being diagnosed with PTSD (Gettman & Gelfand, 2007; Willness et al., 2007). Because SH can involve serious injury, broad and dispersed effects, and repeated exposure, this experience can fit within the core tenets of a traumatic experience that can lead to traumatic stress.

Types of Trauma and Sexual Harassment

Trauma can be categorized in various ways. First, the stage of life in which trauma occurs (childhood vs. adulthood) can be an important factor. Childhood trauma can be especially debilitating given its effect on the developing brains of children, especially from birth to age five (Shonkoff & Garner, 2012). Childhood trauma is commonly assessed via the Adverse Childhood Experiences (ACEs) Questionnaire (Centers for Disease Control and Prevention, 2010), which categorizes types of potentially traumatic events children may experience into three categories: Household (e.g., physical, sexual, verbal abuse, physical or emotional neglect, losing a parent to incarceration, deportation, separation, divorce, or death, living with a mentally ill or addicted parent, etc.), Community (e.g., living in an unsafe neighborhood, living in a warzone, race- or gender-discrimination, bullying, poverty, substandard schools or housing, lack of employment opportunities, etc.), and Climate (e.g., frequent extreme weather events such as tornados, fires, earthquakes, hurricanes, and floods). ACEs are disturbingly common with nearly two-thirds of adults having experienced at least one ACE (Felitti et al., 1998). Those who have at least one ACE are also 87% more likely to have two or more ACEs (Felitti et al., 1998). So, potentially traumatic experiences are likely to co-occur in childhood. Further, these experiences are associated with dramatically worse lifetime outcomes such as addiction, mental illness, chronic illness, suicide, and otherwise shortened lifespans (Felitti et al., 1998).

In the context of workplace SH, child workers (whether legal in some countries or illegal in others) and teenage workers are increasing within the workforce (Kaori Gurley, 2023) and are at significant risk to developmental harm if exposed to SH or sexual abuse while at work. This harm may be especially prolonged if the minor is required to work due to family financial need and cannot easily leave their employer. To date, very little management research has investigated the workplace SH of minors in the United States or other countries, though popular media has documented its occurrence (Weber, 2024). We also know that childhood trauma, especially sexual abuse, is associated with the experience of SH later in life (Campbell et al., 2008; Miron & Orcutt, 2014; Pinchevsky et al., 2020).

Potentially traumatic experiences can also occur in either chronic or acute ways. For instance, children raised in abusive home or soldiers enduring the atrocities of war for an entire tour of duty are examples of chronic trauma, prolonged exposure to potentially traumatic events. Alternatively, a tragic car accident or active shooter event is more acute in that the potentially traumatic event is short lived and does not usually reoccur to the same person. Chronic trauma is also commonly referred to as relentless trauma in adults and toxic trauma in children (McEwen, 2012; Shonkoff & Garner, 2012) due to the mind and body being repeatedly exposed to the over-activity of the psychophysiological stress response. In terms of SH research, we know that the most common form of SH is gender harassment and that more severe and physical forms of SH, such as unwanted sexual attention and sexual coercion, tend to co-occur with gender harassment (Cortina & Areguin, 2021). Though acute instances of SH are possible, it is more probable for most targets to experience SH in a chronic way, with many instances of different forms of harassment occurring over time.

Lastly, trauma can be conceptualized in terms of its scope across time and groups of people. Trauma can be collective, cultural, or historical. Collective trauma is a potentially traumatic event experienced by a large group of people, often causing disruptions to or breakdowns of society and creating a crisis of meaning the motivates collective sensemaking about the event and the group's identity (Erikson, 1994; Hirschberger, 2018). Cultural trauma is a form of collective trauma that also undermines or overwhelms essential aspects of a group's culture (Alexander, 2004; Smelser, 2004), and historical trauma (sometimes called intergenerational trauma) is a form of collective trauma and often cultural trauma that has occurred in the past but still has a profound impact on subsequent generations of the group that directly experienced the traumatic event (Casey et al., 2019; Fitzgerald, 2020). We know from SH research that, in addition to targets, observers of SH are negatively affected (Glomb et al., 1997; Schneider, 1996). So, the occurrence of SH may have the potential to be a collective trauma. We also know that women of color (and other marginalized intersectionalities) are more likely to be targeted by SH (Berdahl & Moore, 2006; see also Chapter 8). This targeting of marginalized communities may manifest in cultural trauma, especially if the SH co-occurs with other forms of mistreatment (e.g., racial/ethnic harassment, homophobia, religious harassment, etc.). Considering the microcosm of organizational culture within a larger societal culture, SH may also pose a threat to the artifacts, values, and assumptions that informally control organizational behavior (Schein,

1992). In other words, SH may lead to cultural trauma at the organizational level, such as in cases of masculinity contest cultures (see Chapter 4). Finally, SH may lead to historical trauma through both organizational and non-organizational pathways. Networks of silence within organizations may rationalize, dismiss, or silence past incidents of SH (Hershcovis et al., 2021). Passing on these silencing tactics to organizational newcomers may perpetuate the tolerance or acceptance of SH within an organization over time. Outside the organization, cultural events like #MeToo may prompt new collective sensemaking that reframes old experiences as SH (see Chapters 1 and 4), validating those experiences as traumatic for many targets simultaneously.

Responses to Trauma

To understand why trauma is so damaging, it is necessary to understand more about the human body and the exquisite balancing act that living systems have evolved over the millennia, to keep our bodies functioning within an optimal range while maintaining equilibrium, a process known as "homeostasis" (Goldstein, 2019). It is important to emphasize that this internal balancing act happens automatically and outside of consciousness. So, reactions to trauma are largely not within conscious control. These automatic reactions primarily involve the autonomic nervous system as it constantly responds to demands for activation or relaxation. The two main divisions of the autonomic nervous system are known as the sympathetic nervous system and the parasympathetic nervous system.

In reaction to an environmental threat, the sympathetic nervous system releases powerful neurochemicals and neurohormones that then stimulate the release of adrenaline, cortisol, beta-endorphin, glucagon and others (Bloom, 1997). All of these substances have powerful effects on the body and the brain. Then, when the need to respond to the stressor has passed, the parasympathetic nervous system calms that response down, so the organism can return to restoring energy and growth, and to repair any damage that has occurred. The variable response to a stressor is influenced by three levels of the brain: automatic responses to survival threats in the brainstem, emotionally based responses originating in the limbic system, and eventually more complex and even conscious responses that originate in the cerebral cortex (van der Kolk, 2014).

The extensive and automatic variation in the control mechanisms that promote internal, physiological balance helps us understand what can go so wrong in our modern world. We still respond to any kind of survival threat as our ancient ancestors and other mammals do. However, we are more complex than most other creatures so that this automatic response to threats is also evoked by anything we perceive as emotionally or culturally threatening. In the human world, we require not just a sense of physical safety, but also psychological safety, social safety, moral safety and cultural safety (Bloom, 2023). Therefore, the stress response can be evoked by threats to any level of safety including threats to our status, to our individual and group identities (Petriglieri, 2011), and to our beliefs and ideological frameworks.

Because SH is a potentially traumatic event, we can conceptualize responses to SH as trauma responses. This trauma-informed perspective may add clarity and insight into the response behaviors of SH targets, bystanders, and even perpetrators.

Fight-Flight Responses to Trauma

The fight-flight response to environmental threats is well documented (McCarty, 2016). These responses are activated by the sympathetic nervous system, which prepares the body to fight off or run away (i.e., take flight) from a threat. During fight-flight, a person is likely to experience increases in blood pressure, heart rate, breathing, accelerated delivery of nutrients to muscles, blunted pain perception, increased blood clotting, activation of the immune system, and a brain that is on alert. At the same time, long-term digestion, growth, tissue repair, and reproduction are all turned off. Because we are so programmed to respond quickly and below the level of conscious thought, our amygdalae can trigger the full fight-flight response instantaneously after a threat is perceived.

Cognitively, as soon as the alarm phase is triggered, rational mode thinking that is high quality, multidimensional, integrative, and creative takes too much time and so routinely shifts to experiential thinking that is automatic, outside of consciousness, and very rapid (Epstein, 1994). Under such conditions, the perceptual field narrows to focus only on the immediate threat with an accompanying loss of peripheral vision and altered sounds while the visual clarity of some details may be heightened and other details lost (Grossman & Christiansen, 2012). The person may experience a wide variety of distortions in time, distance, color, facial recognition, and lighting (Artwhol, 2002).

The consequence of these cognitive distortions is that memory is fragmented. Traumatic experiences profoundly affect normal memory function. During the traumatic event, for all or part of the experience, our verbal capacities go "off-line," and yet, survival depends on retaining memories of any dangerous circumstance. Because the trauma target is unable to encode anything in words, the elements of traumatic memories are likely to be stored in a nonverbal form—as images, all varieties of sensations, and associated with strong and negative emotions (Schore, 2001, 2002, 2009). This is why it is so difficult for a trauma survivor to accurately describe what happened to them even while they may be enduring vivid images, sensations, and emotions accurately portraying the trauma but without language—these experiences are known as "flashbacks." Cognitive distortions due to threat responses also explains why traumatic events are so frequently associated with "traumatic amnesia"—the person has no words for the worst aspects of their experience, so in their later more verbally conscious state, they do not remember what happened. Evidence exists to indicate that the over-secretion of neurohormones at the time of the trauma may deeply imprint the fragmented, non-verbal, and emotional traumatic memory, so deeply that it may be permanent and quite difficult if not impossible to entirely eliminate, although the higher centers of the brain can suppress the disturbance up to a point. This "engraving" of trauma has been noted by many researchers studying various survivor groups (van der Kolk et al., 1996; LeDoux, 1996).

While the fight-flight response is essential for protecting a person from present danger, this response can also be "hijacked" by stimuli that are not actually dangerous (Goleman, 1995). For instance, someone can be "triggered" by an environmental cue that reminds them of an original traumatic event even when no real danger is present. This is referred to as "fear-conditioning" and creates a network of ever-expanding neural pathways that trigger the fight-flight response (LeDoux, 1992; LeDoux, 1994). People who have been previously sexually abused or harassed may be triggered by a cologne, or a physical resemblance or a tone of voice, basically by anything in the present that reminds them—usually unconsciously—of the previous traumatic event. People to whom this happens are not aware of the connections their minds are making, but their bodies are still reacting as if the same traumatic event is happening again. This response is evident in trajectory guarding responses to ambiguous sexual behaviors at work (see Chapter 6).

Due to fear-conditioning, trauma can also result in dysfunctional emotional expression in response to harmless environmental triggers associated with the original trauma. These emotions are deeply felt but not consciously understood by the trauma survivor and are often inappropriate in their current situation. As a result, traumatized people cannot predictably rely on their emotions to provide accurate evaluative information (van der Kolk, 1996a). Emotional states then are disconnected and are no longer available as warning signals that promote some kind of adaptive action (LeDoux, 1994; Krystal, 1978). This is all so disturbing that when this happens repeatedly, people lose the capacity to modulate their level of emotional arousal and tend to stay irritable, jumpy and on-edge with powerful negative emotions that are beyond their control.

The fight-flight response, guided by the sympathetic nervous system, has a significant impact on many bodily functions (Sapolsky, 1998). When the body experiences these extreme levels of arousal very frequently, as in the case of chronic trauma, a person will develop "chronic hyperarousal." Consequently, the effectiveness of the stress response diminishes, and the body becomes desensitized to the effects of some neurohormones, and hypersensitive to others. The entire system can become dysregulated in multiple ways. This then results in a set of highly dysfunctional and mala-daptive brain activities (Perry & Pate, 1994).

The fight-flight response to trauma adds insight to the experience of SH in the workplace. The inability to verbally communicate past traumas could make reporting SH difficult or even impossible for targets. This effect may also be exacerbated by a lack of support from bystanders and cow-orkers who struggle to make sense of the target's nonverbal reactions to SH. Dysfunctional emotional expression, regulation, or suppression could lead to further social problems with coworkers or superiors. Often, targets who do report SH are transferred or fired after reporting (McCann et al., 2018). This may be evidence of a punitive response to the failure of the target to regulate after the traumatic experience of SH. Misunderstand-ings and mismanagement of emotional dysfunction resulting from SH or other past trauma should be investigated as a potential explanatory fac-tor for the removal of reporting targets from the workforce. Additionally, chronic hyperarousal may account for the common strain outcomes associ-ated with experiencing and witnessing SH, including lower mental health, greater symptoms of post-traumatic stress disorder, lower life satisfaction, and decreased physical health (Willness et al., 2007; Glomb et al., 1997; Schneider, 1996). It is likely these results would occur more often for targets with a previous history of trauma exposure (from childhood or outside the workplace) and for targets working in organizations with a high tolerance for SH, where harassment behaviors are frequent and often permitted or even encouraged (Fitzgerald et al., 1997; Hulin et al., 1996; Williams et al., 1999). Other individual outcomes of SH such as trajectory guarding (see Chapter 6), absenteeism, and turnover (Willness et al., 2007; Gettman & Gelfand, 2007) may also be characterized as flight responses, whereby the target disengages from the work environment in order to avoid the trauma of SH. More research is needed to determine how coworkers, leaders, and organizations make sense of targets' fight-flight responses to SH and how these attributions predict behaviors toward targets of SH in the workplace.

Freeze-Fawn Responses to Trauma

The next set of trauma responses is governed by the parasympathetic nerv-ous system, the system that slows down the body. The freeze response to a traumatic event is characterized by a slowing heart rate, preserving blood flow, and even simulating death (i.e., freezing in the presence of danger). In nature the freeze response may be especially effective for preventing or surviving attacks from predators, that may be less interested in prey that seems already dead (Levine, 1997). This response is an animal's best survival strategy when it is impossible to fight off or flee from the threat of danger.

The freeze response also involves immediate shock or dissociation, the "temporary breakdown in continuous, interrelated processes of perception, memory, or identity" (Brewin, 2011, p. 211). Humans frequently do not fully emerge from the dissociative state spontaneously and may stay internally separated from memories, feelings, and physical sensations associated with the traumatic events for their entire lives. Dissociation is common in response to child abuse, especially sexual abuse, emanating from a close and trusted other such as a parent. In these situations, dissociation becomes an adaptive mechanism that allows the victim to preserve a relationship upon which the victim depends (Freyd, 1996; Freyd & Birrell, 2013).

Dissociation can further complicate the emotional experiences of trauma survivors. Dissociation serves to buffer the central nervous system against hyperarousal when in danger. One way that dissociation can occur is a separation of the emotions associated with the actual experience. When this happens repeatedly, the person may develop *alexithymia*, the inability to identify specific emotions and put those emotions into words. This was first described in concentration camp survivors (Krystal, 1988). It is now widely recognized that what cannot be put into words is often expressed through bodily symptoms (van der Kolk, 1996b, 2014). People who develop alexithymia are more likely to experience a wide range of physical symptoms (Lumley, 1996). The emotional numbing of alexithymia may also interfere with successful treatment (Harber & Pennebaker, 1992), and people may also try to avoid traumatic reminders and their own emotions to the extent that they withdraw from everyday life and become "dead to the world."

Another result of alexithymia is the behavioral expression of emotions and memories that cannot be put into words (van der Kolk, 1996b, 2014). Survivors of traumatic life events are very likely to reenact their traumatic experiences overtly or symbolically. Both Sigmund Freud and his contemporary, Pierre Janet, noted in the nineteenth century that traumatized people compulsively reenact trauma. Both men believed that it was the presence of mute, unsymbolized, and unintegrated experiences that drove this repetition (van der Kolk & Ducey, 1989). The fragmented, non-verbal, and emotional memories created by trauma drive these *traumatic reenactments*, behaviors that mirror those enacted during the original trauma. As Rogers (2006) has written, "the unsayable could be 'spoken' through unconscious reenactments but at a terrible cost." (p. 72).

In the case of chronic trauma, the body's endorphin response system may operate in overdrive. Because endorphins act like painkillers, similar to opiates, trauma survivors may unconsciously seek out risky situations or people in order to reenact trauma behaviors and trigger the release of endorphins. However, when the trauma reenactment stops, it can feel like opiate withdrawal (Butler & Finn, 2009). This means that some people can become addicted to their own endorphin responses without even realizing this is happening and then must put themselves into stressful and risky experiences repeatedly as a method of self-regulation in order to evoke an internal chemical response (van der Kolk et al., 1985; Stanley et al., 2010).

The reenactment of trauma is especially problematic when the original trauma occurred in childhood at the hands of a parent or caregiver because the child must bond with the source of their own maltreatment to survive. The result is known as trauma-bonding, the attachment bond that is created through repeated abusive or traumatic childhood experiences with the caregiver, whereby this relationship pattern becomes internalized as a learned pattern of behavior for attachment into adulthood (James, 1994). Even as adults, we need to attach to others, particularly when exposed to stress or danger. If you experienced abuse from a caregiver who also loved you, then you learned to associate love with abuse to the extent that abuse feels like love. Trauma-bonding, therefore, is a part of the complicated picture for battered spouses, abused children, prisoners, and victims of torture, and any other situation in which the abuse is prolonged and repeated (Herman, 2015). Knowledge about this phenomenon occurring in previously apparently healthy people came out of a bank robbery in Sweden, hence the term "Stockholm Syndrome" (Strenz, 1982; Graham, 1994).

Trauma reenactments can persist until they are reintegrated with the verbally conscious parts of the brain, overcoming the past dissociation to properly encode and store the memory of trauma (van der Kolk, 1989; Bloom, 1996). This was how and why Freud and others developed "the talking cure," as psychotherapy came to be called. It was the linking of nonverbalized experiences with words that allowed the memories of the traumatic experiences to become conscious and once consciousness prevailed, the compulsive repetition ceased. This is why it is so important to understand dysfunctional behavior as (potentially) a form of symbolic communication of past trauma. From a social interactionist perspective (Dewulf et al., 2009), behavioral reenactments are a meta-communicative cry for help and compassion.

Unfortunately, when bystanders and leaders are not "trauma-informed," they may harshly judge a trauma survivor's inappropriate emotions, decisions, and behaviors and their inability to coherently explain them. Even when a trauma survivor is able to verbally disclose their trauma experience, the phenomenon of emotional contagion compels listeners to disrupt the stories by switching topics, by pressing their own perspective on the person, or by avoiding them altogether (Coates et al., 1979). This response on the part of others then forces the survivor to inhibit their own emotions and avoid discussing the trauma but that puts the survivor at increased risk for physical illness, impaired information processing, a loss of social support and therefore opportunities for healing and recovery (Coates et al., 1979). Survivors who are unable to communicate or cope with their trauma experiences are driven to relieve their symptoms. When social support diminishes, many turn to alcohol, drugs, food, sex, self-harm, or other compulsive behaviors as a form of temporary relief (van der Kolk, 2014).

A lesser-known trauma response is the fawn response, characterized by attempts to please and appease the source of the threat in order to avoid harm, abandonment, or conflict (Walker, 2013) This response often involves acquiescing to the demands of the threat in order to secure one's own safety while also sacrificing one's own needs and desires (e.g., complying with the unreasonable demands of an abusive partner to avoid physical violence). Unfortunately, this response often strengthens connections with abusers, making those who fawn more "attractive" targets for future abuse (Walker, 2013). In addition to susceptibility to future abuse, fawning can also disrupt development of a coherent identity and healthy boundaries in other relationships. Fawning may also lead to the trauma reenactments and trauma bonding discussed previously. Because the target has learned to survive by appeasing and tolerating their abuser, they are frequently drawn into future cycles of abuse in other contexts (Walker, 2013). For instance, an adult with a history of fawn responses to prior child abuse may be more likely to attempt to appease and tolerate abusive supervision or SH from their leader in a workplace context.

Both the freeze and fawn responses are learned overtime based on the need to survive chronic trauma, especially toxic childhood trauma where the child cannot enact autonomy to end or escape the threat through fighting or fleeing. In these chronic circumstances, the best strategy is to avoid the threat by appeasing or survive the threat by freezing as well as psychologically protecting oneself from the memories of abuse via dissociation. When these strategies do lead to survival and harm reduction, many trauma survivors develop "learned helplessness," in which they routinely respond to future threats (or similar but non-dangerous triggers) by freezing or fawning even when fight or flight responses (or other less activated responses such as negotiation) are possible or advantageous (Bloom, 1997).

The freeze and fawn responses have many implications for SH research. First, these responses may explain some targets' reluctance to identify unwanted social sexual behaviors as SH. The dissociation from one's own experience and feelings accompanied by a disruption to identity may make it difficult for a person to identify their own wants and "unwants" as well as their own boundaries, values, and roles associated with their core identities. If chronic trauma has damaged one's self concept, it may be genuinely difficult to identify when the self is being harmed. It may also be difficult for freezers and fawners to accurately report SH if they suffer from dissociation-induced memory disruption. Further, due to the inaction and cooperation associated with freezing and fawning, claims of SH may appear less credible to bystanders (see Chapter 3), especially if harassers cite targets' freeze and fawn behavior as evidence that the harassment was welcome. Freezing and fawning may also make a person more susceptible to frequent harassment, as the tolerance of harassment and acquiescence to power may encourage a serial harasser to form a stronger "connection" with a target.

Trauma reenactments may predispose childhood trauma survivors to form dysfunctional or abusive connections with others in the workplace. Though most of our discussion has been on the targets of harm, trauma can also result from being the perpetrator of harm, as is the case for many war veterans (van der Kolk, 2014). Chronic trauma may also involve a combination of being both target and perpetrator, such as when a physically abused child physically aggresses against a sibling or a schoolmate. Men often experience being both target and perpetrator in masculinity contest cultures (i.e., workplace cultures characterized by the social dominate of masculine norms; Berdahl et al., 2018), where they are under constant threat of losing their status as a man and must dominate other, weaker individuals (e.g., women, minorities, and non-masculine men) in order to hold on to their social status. In this way, masculinity contest cultures require men to victimize each other and women via gender harassment, creating complex networks of abuse throughout a workforce (see Chapters 4 and 9).

Learned helplessness also has implications in the realm of SH, such that the effects of organizational intolerance for SH may be less influential for targets who have developed learned helplessness. These individuals may be less likely to use organizational mechanisms (e.g., reporting) even when these mechanisms are well-supported and high functioning. It is also possible that high organizational tolerance for SH, characterized by the degree to which an organization's structure lacks policies, procedures, and routines to effectively identify, investigate, manage, prevent, and prohibit SH (Fitzgerald et al., 1997; Hulin et al., 1996; Williams et al., 1999), will predispose individuals to cope with SH via freeze and fawn responses and to potentially develop learned helplessness since the organization has created an environment from which SH cannot be escaped.

Fawning responses to SH, in particular, should be examined in light of the literature on strategic sexual performance (i.e., a combination of verbal, nonverbal, and artifactual behaviors that can be overtly or subtly sexual and are enacted for the purpose of ingratiation; Baskerville Watkins et al., 2013). While it is possible that some individuals truly desire to engage in social sexual behaviors at work, it is also possible that this behavior, when performed "strategically" to earn job benefits, may also be an example of fawning (i.e., enacting sexual behaviors to appease those who would otherwise harm the employee by denying those same benefits). Indeed, strategic sexual performance may very well be a learned coping strategy to avoid hostile sexism at work and instead reap the relatively safer treatment of benevolent sexism (Glick & Fisk, 1996).

We also know that compulsive sexual behavior may be a behavioral result of past trauma, especially sexual trauma, such that survivors become addicted to endorphins released in response to risky sex or unconsciously seek to reenact prior sexual abuse as nonverbal communication about their trauma. So, it is possible that trauma survivors may be predisposed to being both targets and perpetrators of SH in the workplace. While prior trauma does not excuse SH behavior, and we should not interpret trauma reenactments as a form of victim-blaming, a trauma-informed perspective does add complexity to our understanding of SH and may offer new methods for preventing SH in the workplace.

Post-Traumatic Stress Disorder

When adaptation to potentially traumatic events causes prolonged traumatic stress responses (i.e., the fight-flight-freeze-fawn responses discussed previously) long after the event is over, an individual may meet the DSM-5 diagnostic criteria for post-traumatic stress disorder (PTSD; American Psychiatric Association, 2013), which is characterized by reexperiencing the traumatic event in nightmares, flashbacks, or intrusive thoughts, avoidance of people or places that are reminders of the traumatic event, and chronic hyperarousal (e.g., overactive startle responses, irritability, emotion dysregulation, and sleep problems). It is important to note that the immediate experience of a fight-flight-freeze-fawn response to a traumatic event does not necessarily constitute a diagnosis of PTSD. Rather it is the prolonged experience of these responses far after the original event has occurred and to the extent that normal, day-to-day functioning is disrupted (e.g., the ability to work, maintain relationships, care for oneself) that determines a diagnosis of PTSD. Additionally, it is also noteworthy that potentially traumatic events do not always result in PTSD. It is possible for individuals to heal and grow from a traumatic stress experience (Tedeschi et al., 1998).

Though, the occurrence of post-traumatic growth is also not an excuse for the allowance of *preventable* potentially traumatic events. In the SH literature, there is evidence that SH experiences can result in a diagnosis of PTSD (Willness et al., 2007), but even when this diagnosis is not present, SH is still a potentially traumatic experience that should be prevented by organizations and their leaders.

A Trauma-Informed Approach to Sexual Harassment in Work Organizations

Organizations are imbedded in societies and as such reflect the assumptions, values, and artifacts of those societies (Hofstede, 1980). In the public health discipline, the term "traumatogenic" has been used to describe societies in which the perpetration of trauma is deeply embedded and normalized through childrearing practices such as corporal punishment, lack of parental supports (e.g., paid leaves, access to daycare), lack of developmental and educational supports (e.g., poorly funded schools and poorly trained teachers), and other policies and practices that do not adequately support the safety and needs of all members of a society. A traumatogenic culture produces trauma-organized individuals, families, organizations, and communities (Bloom & Reichert, 1998). A trauma-organized system is one that is fundamentally and unconsciously organized around the impact of chronic and toxic stress, even when this undermines the essential mission of the system (Bloom & Farragher, 2010; Bentovim, 1992; Bloom, 2011, 2012). This idea of the pathology of cultural communities has yet to be fully explored by social science (Freud, 1930), including organizational science. Organizations perpetuate traumatogenic societies by promoting productivity over human needs. Concepts such as burnout (i.e., a prolonged response to chronic emotional and interpersonal stressors on the job, characterized by the three dimensions of exhaustion, cynicism, and professional inefficacy; Maslach & Leiter, 2016) would likely not exist if not for the reproduction of trauma within organizational life.

As we have previously argued, SH is a potentially traumatic event. So, to the extent that SH exists within work organizations (in addition to other workplace traumas; e.g., accidents, violence), we can say that the modern work organization is traumatogenic (Office of the Surgeon General, 2024). We can see the effects of traumatogenic systems at play in our work organizations in much of the SH research that already exists. For instance, Hershcovis's and colleagues' (2021) recent work of networks of silence clearly depict complex systems that protect harassers, dismiss the harassment experiences of targets, and perpetuate the reproduction of SH at work. Rawski and colleagues' (2022) work of the interactional framing of

SH shows how complex social sensemaking tactics allow for and encourage social sexual behavior at work under the guise of play and how these same mechanisms prevent the reframing of this behavior as harassment. Roehling and colleagues' (2022) meta-analysis on SH training calls into question the effectiveness of common training tactics at changing attitudes and behaviors, showing how our "prevention" systems pale in comparison to our traumatogenic systems. Reviews of SH research conclude that SH is insidious, affects all types of people, though mostly women and gender/racial minorities, and continues to occur despite decades of research, intervention, and legislation, again demonstrating the fortitude of traumatogenic systems to prevail in spite of efforts to understand and dismantle them.

How then should organizations become "trauma-informed"? This shift will likely require a new paradigm of organizing work (Bloom, 2023). We will have to expand our typical ways of conceptualizing and modeling organizations. One thought-provoking approach aligns well with trauma as a violation to the physical and psychological human body. This approach frames organizations as biocracy or a "complex adaptive system"—a living system made of people. In 1940, Harvard physiologist, Dr. Walter B. Cannon, asserted that the most efficient and stable human society would be a "biocracy in which the myriad of differentiated cells would be organized into functional organs all cooperating in a dynamic democracy in which any form of dictatorship would lead to degeneration and death" (Laurence, 1940, p. 1). Using our own bodies as an example, an organization that functions as a biocracy must be thought of as a living being that can grow, adapt and change, and become universally "trauma-informed" by synthesizing and integrating all the knowledge we now have available about the widespread impact of adversity and trauma (Bloom, 2023). In a biocracy, one member of the organization is not forsaken to harassment from another, just as in a body, one hand does not cut off the other, the heart does not suffocate the lungs, nor do the muscles seek to destroy the skeleton. Rather all the systems work synergistically, and if injury does occur, the body has special systems to protect and repair that injury. In a biocratic organization, all members are looked after so they can perform at their best and there would be specific departments and job roles assigned to monitor, preserve, and protect employee wellness. SH would not be tolerated, and those who experience and perpetrate SH would be cared for to stop the harassment and repair the effects of the trauma that it causes or that caused it.

This description may seem unrealistic and utopian, but it is an ideal to strive toward. Small changes in organizational routine could make progress toward a more biocratic organization. For instance, benefits related to mental health care and trauma-informed training for organizational leaders could be one place to start. Another avenue, more specifically related to SH, might be trauma-informed response procedures that prioritize care and compassion toward targets and rehabilitation of perpetrators. In the public health realm, the P.R.E.S.E.N.C.E. model (Bloom, 2021) has been demonstrated as a way to reorient organizations to be trauma-informed. P.R.E.S.E.N.C.E. is an acronym for a series of trauma-informed concepts and values (i.e., Partnership-Power, Reverence-Restoration, Emotional Wisdom-Empathy, Safety-Social Responsibility, Embodiment-Enactment, Nature-Nurture, Culture-Complexity, and Emergence-Evolution) that are meant to consistently inform and anchor all personal, interpersonal, and organizational processes. In the implementation process, each value is actualized through the acquisition of individual and organizational knowledge, practices and skills that are tailored to specific needs of the organization and the role of the individual within the organization. The overarching purpose in the P.R.E.S.E.N.C.E. model is to provide the knowledge base and skill development for collective change starting at the organizational level and gradually impacting every member of the organizational culture through the acquisition of knowledge and experience with coaches and with each other (Bloom, 2021). We encourage readers to learn more about P.R.E.S.E.N.C.E. via the website, www.creatingpresence.net/, or the podcast series, Creating P.R.E.S.E.N.C.E. (creatingpresence.net/podcast). While this program is designed for public health organizations with a particular focus on clients' or patients' trauma experiences, similar values, knowledge and skill development, and programming may be adapted for business organizations with a focus on employees' trauma experiences. This shift in the realm of business would change workplaces into a community pillar of healing for those who have endured trauma in other realms of life.

In the post-#MeToo era, organizations that cultivate trauma-informed cultures may be employers of choice, especially for women and gender minorities. This would result in the attraction and retention of highly talented workers who seek out socially responsible employers. Trauma-informed organizations would also likely benefit from increased productivity and development as their leaders advance in skills related to conflict resolution and empathy. So, there is a probable competitive advantage to adopting trauma-informed practices in work organizations.

Directions for Future Research

A trauma-informed lens provides many new insights and directions for SH research in the post-#MeToo era (see Table 7.1). Several themes have emerged through this chapter. First, SH is a potentially traumatic event.

TABLE 7.1 Directions for future research on sexual harassment (SH) as trauma

Theme	*Questions*
SH is trauma	What forms of SH (e.g., verbal vs. physical, quid pro quo vs. hostile work environment) are most trauma-inducing?
	How does SH interact with other experienced traumas within and outside of the workplace (e.g., childhood trauma, workplace violence, cultural trauma) to predict outcomes?
	Could current therapies for trauma help SH targets or perpetrators?
SH leads to Flight-fight-freeze-fawn responses and PTSD	How do trauma responses such as Fight-Flight-Freeze-Fawn affect dynamic work interactions after a SH incident?
	Do targets experience dissociation, trauma reenactment, hyperarousal, and learned helplessness in response to SH?
	How can knowledge of common trauma responses be integrated into our organizational response systems for SH (e.g., protocols for interacting with targets and perpetrators during investigations)?
	Is the perpetration of SH a possible reenactment of past trauma (e.g., childhood sexual abuse, SH from others)?
Trauma-informed leaders and bystanders	Does trauma-informed training change leaders' and bystanders' attitudes and behaviors in reaction to SH (e.g., belief and support of targets, efforts to rehabilitate harassers)?
	Do the trauma histories of leaders' and bystanders' affect their reactions to SH in the workplace?
	Did the #MeToo movement constitute a cultural trauma, and if so, how did this event affect leaders' and bystanders' reactions to SH?
Traumatogenic and trauma-informed biocratic organizations	What are the key defining features of traumatogenic and biocratic organizational forms?
	Do biocractic organizations exist anywhere currently?
	Can we develop or redesign organizations to be more biocratic and trauma-informed, especially in reaction to SH incidents?
	Do the key features of traumatogenic or biocratic organizations predict the occurrence of SH or other outcomes (e.g., target wellbeing, perpetrator rehabilitation, healthy culture maintenance) after SH has occurred?

Second, because SH is traumatic, it is likely to lead to trauma responses, including the fight-flight-freeze-fawn responses and even PTSD. Third, organizational leaders and bystanders may interpret SH and responses to it differently depending on their own trauma-informed perspective (or lack thereof). Finally, we can reexamine our organizations from a traumatogenic lens to identify systems that perpetuate SH and reimagine these organizations as trauma-informed biocracies with different ways of organizing that prevent and heal the harms of SH.

It is our hope that the integration of trauma research with organizational science can better inform SH researchers and practitioners, advancing work to better understand, prevent, and treat SH in the workplace.

References

Alexander, J. C. (2004). Toward a theory of cultural trauma. In J. C. Alexander, R. Eyerman, B. Giesen, N. J. Smelser, & P. Sztompka (Eds.), *Cultural trauma and collective identity*. University of California Press.

American Psychiatric Association. (2013). *Diagnostic and statistical manual of mental disorders* (5th ed.). https://doi.org/10.1176/appi.books.9780890425596

Artwhol, A. (2002). Perceptual and memory distortion during officer involved shootings. *FBI Law Enforcement Bulletin*, 71(10), 18–24.

Baskerville Watkins, M., Smith, A. N., & Aquino, K. (2013). The use and consequences of strategic sexual performances. *Academy of Management Perspectives*, 27, 173–186. https://doi.org/10.5465/amp.2010.0109

Bentovim, A. (1992). *Trauma-organized systems: Physical and sexual abuse in families* (1st ed.). Routledge. https://doi.org/10.4324/9780429484315

Berdahl, J. L. (2007). Harassment based on sex: Protecting social status in the context of gender hierarchy. *The Academy of Management Review*, 32(2), 641–658. https://doi.org/10.2307/20159319

Berdahl, J. L., Cooper, M., Glick, P., Livingston, R. W., & Williams, J. C. (2018). Work as a masculinity contest. *Journal of Social Issues*, 74, 422–448. https://doi.org/10.1111/josi.12289

Berdahl, J. L., & Moore, C. (2006). Workplace harassment: Double jeopardy for minority women. *Journal of Applied Psychology*, 91(2), 426–436. https://doi.org/10.1037/0021–9010.91.2.426

Bloom, S. L. (1996). Every time history repeats itself, the price goes up: The social reenactment of trauma. *Sexual Addiction & Compulsivity*, 3(3), 161–194. https://doi.org/10.1080/10720169608400111

Bloom, S. L. (1997). *Creating sanctuary: Toward the evolution of sane societies*. Routledge.

Bloom, S. L. (2011). Trauma-organized systems and parallel process. In N. Tehrani (Ed.), *Managing trauma in the workplace: Supporting workers and organizations*. Routledge.

Bloom, S. L. (2012). Trauma-organized systems. In C. R. Figley (Ed.), *Encyclopedia of trauma: An interdisciplinary guide* (pp. 741–743). Sage Reference Publications.

Bloom, S. L. (2021). *Creating presence: A trauma-informed online organizational approach for creating trauma -responsive organizations*. www.creatingpresence.net.

Bloom, S. L. (2023). A biocratic paradigm: Exploring the complexity of trauma-informed leadership and *creating presence*™. *Behavioral sciences (Basel, Switzerland)*, 13(5), 355. https://doi.org/10.3390/bs13050355

Bloom, S. L. & Farragher, B. (2010). *Destroying sanctuary: The crisis in human service delivery systems*. Oxford University Press.

Bloom, S. L., & Reichert, M. (1998). *Bearing witness: Violence and collective responsibility* (1st ed.). Routledge. https://doi.org/10.4324/9781315809687

Brewin, C. R. (2011). The nature and significance of memory disturbance in post-traumatic stress disorder. *Annual Review of Clinical Psychology*, 7(1), 203–227.

Butler, R. K., & Finn, D. P. (2009). Stress-induced analgesia. *Progress in Neurobiology*, 88(3), 184–202. https://doi.org/10.1016/j.pneurobio.2009.04.003

Campbell, R., Greeson, M. R., Bybee, D., & Raja, S. (2008). The co-occurrence of childhood sexual abuse, adult sexual assault, intimate partner violence, and sexual harassment: A mediational model of posttraumatic stress disorder and physical health outcomes. *Journal of Consulting and Clinical Psychology*, 76(2), 194–207. https://doi.org/10.1037/0022–006X.76.2.194

Casey, L. S., Reisner, S. L., Findling, M. G., Blendon, R. J., Benson, J. M., Sayde, J. M., & Miller, C. (2019). Discrimination in the United States: Experiences of lesbian, gay, bisexual, transgender, and queer Americans. *Health Services Research*, 54(Suppl 2), 1454–1466. https://doi.org/10.1111/1475–6773.13229

Centers for Disease Control and Prevention. (2010). Adverse childhood experiences reported by adults—five states. *Mortality and Morbidity Review*, 59(49), 1609–1613.

Christopher, M. (2004). A broader view of trauma: A biopsychosocial-evolutionary view of the role of the traumatic stress response in the emergence of pathology and/or growth. *Clinical Psychology Review*, 24(1), 75–98. https://doi.org/10.1016/j.cpr.2003.12.003

Coates, D., Wortman, C. B., & Abbey, A. (1979). Reactions to victims. In I. H. Frieze, D. Bar-Tal & J. S. Carrol (Eds.), *New approaches to social problems* (pp. 21–52). Jossey-Bass.

Cortina, L. M., & Areguin, M. A. (2021). Putting people down and pushing them out: Sexual harassment in the workplace. *Annual Review of Organizational Psychology and Organizational Behavior*, 8(1), 285–309.

Dewulf, A., Gray, B., Putnam, L., Lewicki, R., Aarts, N., Bouwen, R., & van Woerkum, C. (2009). Disentangling approaches to framing in conflict and negotiation research: A meta-paradigmatic perspective. *Human Relations*, 62(2), 155–193.

Epstein, S. (1994). The integration of the cognitive and psychodynamic unconscious. *American Psychologist*, 49, 709–723.

Erikson, K. (1994). *A new species of trouble: The human experience of modern disasters*. W.W. Norton and Company.

Felitti, V. J., Anda, R. F., Nordenberg, D., Williamson, D. F., Spitz, A. M., Edwards, V., Koss, M. P., & Marks, J. S. (1998). Relationship of childhood abuse and household dysfunction to many of the leading causes of death in adults. The Adverse Childhood Experiences (ACE) study. *American Journal of Preventive Medicine*, 14(4), 245–258. https://doi.org/10.1016/s0749–3797(98)00017–8

Fitzgerald, L. (2020). Unseen: The sexual harassment of low-income women in America. *Equality, Diversity and Inclusion*, 39(1), 5–16. https://doi.org/10.1108/EDI-08-2019-0232

Fitzgerald, L. F., Swan, S., & Magley, V. J. (1997). But was it really sexual harassment? Legal, behavioral, and psychological definitions of the workplace victimization of women. In W. O'Donohue (Ed.), *Sexual harassment: Theory, research, and treatment* (pp. 5–28). Allyn & Bacon.

Freud, S. (1930). *Civilization and its discontents*. Hogarth.

Freyd, J. J. (1996). *Betrayal trauma: The logic of forgetting childhood abuse*. Harvard University Press.

Freyd, J. J. & Birrell, P. (2013). *Blind to betrayal: Why we fool ourselves we aren't being fooled*. Wiley.

Gettman, H. J., & Gelfand, M. J. (2007). When the customer shouldn't be king: Antecedents and consequences of sexual harassment by clients and customers. *Journal of Applied Psychology, 92*(3), 757–770. https://doi.org/10.1037/0021–9010.92.3.757

Glick, P., & Fiske, S. T. (1996). The Ambivalent Sexism Inventory: Differentiating hostile and benevolent sexism. *Journal of Personality and Social Psychology, 70*(3), 491–512. https://doi.org/10.1037/0022–3514.70.3.491

Glomb, T. M., Richman, W. L., Hulin, C. L., Drasgow, F., Schneider, K. T., & Fitzgerald, L. F. (1997). Ambient sexual harassment: An integrated model of antecedents and consequences. *Organizational Behavior and Human Decision Processes, 71*(3), 309–328.

Graham, D. (1994). Graham's Stockholm syndrome theory: A universal theory of chronic interpersonal abuse. In *Loving to survive: Sexual terror, men's violence, and women's lives* (pp. 30–61). New York University Press. https://doi.org/10.18574/nyu/9780814732601.003.0008

Goleman, D. (1995). *Emotional intelligence: Why it can matter more than IQ.* Bantam Books.

Goldstein, D. S. (2019). How does homeostasis happen? Integrative physiological, systems biological, and evolutionary perspectives. *Regulatory, Integrative, and Comparative Physiology, 316*(4), 301–317.

Grosser, K., & Tyler, M. (2022). Sexual harassment, sexual violence and CSR: Radical feminist theory and a human rights perspective. *Journal of Business Ethics, 177*, 217–232. https://doi.org/10.1007/s10551-020-04724-w

Grossman, D., & Christainsen, L. (2012). *On combat: The psychology and physiology of deadly conflict in war and in peace.* Killology Research Group, LLC.

Harber, K. D., & Pennebaker, J. W. (1992). Overcoming traumatic memories. In S.-Å. Christianson (Ed.), *The handbook of emotion and memory: Research and theory* (pp. 359–387). Lawrence Erlbaum Associates, Inc.

Herman, J. (2015). *Trauma and recovery: The aftermath of violence—from domestic abuse to political terror.* Basic Books.

Hershcovis, M. S., Vranjes, I., Berdahl, J. L., & Cortina, L. M. (2021). See no evil, hear no evil, speak no evil: Theorizing network silence around sexual harassment. *Journal of Applied Psychology, 106*(12), 1834–1847. https://doi.org/10.1037/apl0000861

Hirschberger, G. (2018). Collective trauma and the social construction of meaning. *Frontiers in Psychology, 9*, 1441. https://doi.org/10.3389/fpsyg.2018.01441

Hofstede, G. (1980). Culture and organizations. *International Studies of Management & Organization, 10*(4), 15–41. https://doi.org/10.1080/00208825.1980.11656300

Hulin, C., Fitzgerald, L., & Drasgow, F. (1996). Organizational influences on sexual harassment. In M. S. Stockdale (Ed.), *Women and work: A research and policy series, Volume 5: Sexual harassment in the workplace: Perspectives, frontiers, and response strategies* (pp. 127–150). Sage Publications, Inc. https://doi.org/10.4135/9781483327280.n7

James, B. (1994). *Handbook for treatment of attachment-trauma problems in children.* The Free Press, Macmillan, Maxwell M.

Kaori Gurley, L. (2023, October, 19). Child labor violations soared in fiscal 2023. *The Washington Post.* www.washingtonpost.com/business/2023/10/19/child-labor-violations-2023/

Krystal, H. (1978). Trauma and affects. *The Psychoanalytic Study of the Child, 33*, 81–116. https://doi.org/10.1080/00797308.1978.11822973

Krystal, H., & Krystal, J. H. (1988). *Integration and self-healing: Affect, trauma, alexithymia.* Analytic Press, Inc.

Laurence, C. (1940, December 28). Human body held best "democracy": A society modeled after its organization urged by Dr. Cannon before scientists. **The New York Times.**

Le Bars, S. (2022, October 8). Despite a bumpy road, the #MeToo Movement has changed America. *Le Monde.* www.lemonde.fr/en/united-states/article/2022/10/08/despite-a-bumpy-road-the-metoo-movement-has-changed-america_5999638_133.html

LeDoux, J. E. (1992). Emotion as memory: Anatomical systems underlying indelible neural traces. In S.-Å. Christianson (Ed.), *The handbook of emotion and memory: Research and theory* (pp. 269–288). Lawrence Erlbaum Associates, Inc.

LeDoux, J. E. (1994). Emotion, memory and the brain. *Scientific American, 270*(6), 50–57. https://doi.org/10.1038/scientificamerican0694–50

LeDoux, J. (1996). *The emotional brain: The mysterious underpinnings of emotional life.* Simon and Schuster.

Levine, P. (1997). *Waking the tiger, healing trauma: The innate capacity to transform overwhelming experiences.* North Atlantic Books.

Lumley, M. A., Stettner, L., & Wehmer, F. (1996). How are alexithymia and physical illness linked? A review and critique of pathways. *Journal of Psychosomatic Research, 41*(6), 505–518. https://doi.org/10.1016/s0022–3999(96)00222-x

Maslach, C., & Leiter, M. P. (2016). Burnout. In G. Fink (Ed.), *Stress: Concepts, cognition, emotion, and behavior* (pp. 351–357). Elsevier Academic Press.

McCann, C., Tomaskovic-Devey, D., & Badgett, L. (2018). Employers' responses to sexual harassment. *SSRN Electronic Journal.* https://doi.org/10.2139/ssrn.3407960

McCarty, R. (2016). The fight-or-flight response: A cornerstone of stress research. In G. Fink (Ed.), *Stress: Concepts, cognition, emotion, and behavior* (pp. 33–37). Academic Press.

McEwen, B. S. (2012). Brain on stress: How the social environment gets under the skin. *Proceedings of the National Academy of Sciences of the United States of America, 109*(Suppl 2), 17180–17185. https://doi.org/10.1073/pnas.1121254109

Miron, L. R., & Orcutt, H. K. (2014). Pathways from childhood abuse to prospective revictimization: Depression, sex to reduce negative affect, and forecasted sexual behavior. *Child Abuse & Neglect, 38*(11), 1848–1859. https://doi.org/10.1016/j.chiabu.2014.10.004

Office of the Surgeon General. (2024, May 30). Workplace mental health and well-being. *US Department of Health & Human Services.* www.hhs.gov/surgeongeneral/priorities/workplace-well-being/index.html#framework

Perry, B. D. & Pate, J. E. (1994). Neurodevelopment and the psychobiological roots of post-traumatic stress disorder. In L. Koziol & C. Stout (Eds.), *The neuropsychology of mental disorders: A practical guide* (pp. 81–98). Charles C. Thomas.

Petriglieri, J. L. (2011). Under threat: Response to and the consequences of threats to individuals' identities. *The Academy of Management Review, 36*(4), 641–662.

Pinchevsky, G. M., Magnuson, A. B., Augustyn, M. B., & Rennison, C. M. (2020). Sexual victimization and sexual harassment among college students: A comparative analysis. *Journal of Family Violence, 35*(6), 603–618. doi: 10.1007/s10896-019-00082-y

Rawski, S., O'Leary-Kelly, A. M., & Breaux-Soignet, D. (2022). It's all fun and games until someone gets hurt: An interactional framing theory of work social sexual behavior. *The Academy of Management Review*, 47(4), 617–636. https://doi.org/10.5465/amr.2019.0316

Roehling, M.V., Wu, D., Choi, M.G., & Dulebohn, J.H. (2022). The effects of sexual harassment training on proximal and transfer training outcomes: A meta-analytic investigation. *Personnel Psychology, 75*(1), 3–31.

Rogers, A. G. (2006). *The unsayable: The hidden language of trauma.* Random House.

Sapolsky, R. M. (1998). *Why zebras don't get ulcers: An updated guide to stress, stress-related disease, and coping.* W. H. Freeman and Company.

Schein, E. H. (1992). *Organizational culture and leadership.* Jossey-Bass.

Schneider, K. T. (1996). *Bystander stress: The effect of organizational tolerance of sexual harassment on victims' coworkers.* Univ. Ill. Press

Schneider, K. T., Swan, S., & Fitzgerald, L. F. (1997). Job-related and psychological effects of sexual harassment in the workplace: Empirical evidence from two organizations. *Journal Applied Psychology, 82*, 3401–3415.

Schore, A. N. (2001). Effects of secure attachment relationship on right brain development, affect regulation, and infant mental health. *Infant Mental Health Journal, 22*, 7–66.

Schore, A. N. (2002). Dysregulation of the right brain: A fundamental mechanism of traumatic attachment and the psychopathogenesis of posttraumatic stress disorder. *Australian and New Zealand Journal of Psychiatry, 36*(1), 9–30.

Schore, A. N. (2009). Relational trauma and the developing right brain: An interface of psychoanalytic self psychology and neuroscience. *Annals of the New York Academy of Sciences, 1159*(1), 189–203.

Shonkoff, J. P., & Garner, A. S. (2012). The lifelong effects of early childhood adversity and toxic stress. *Pediatrics, 129*(1), e232–e246.

Smelser, N. (2004). Psychological trauma and cultural trauma. In J. Alexander, R. Eyerman, B. Giesen, N. Smelser & P. Sztompka (Eds.), *Cultural trauma and collective identity* (pp. 31–59). University of California Press. https://doi.org/10.1525/9780520936768–003

Stanley, B., Sher, L., Wilson, S., Ekman, R., Huang, Y. Y., & Mann, J. J. (2010). Non-suicidal self-injurious behavior, endogenous opioids and monoamine neurotransmitters. *Journal of Affective Disorders, 124*(1–2), 134–140. https://doi.org/10.1016/j.jad.2009.10.028

Strenz, T. (1982). The stockholm syndrome. In F. Ochberg & D. Soskis (Eds.) *Victims of terrorism* (pp. 149–164). Westview.

Tedeschi, R. G., Park, C. L., & Calhoun, L. G. (Eds.). (1998). *Posttraumatic growth: Positive changes in the aftermath of crisis.* Lawrence Erlbaum Associates Publishers.

van der Kolk, B. A. (1989). The compulsion to repeat the trauma. Re-enactment, revictimization, and masochism. *The Psychiatric clinics of North America, 12*(2), 389–411.

van der Kolk, B. A. (1996a). Trauma and memory. In B. A. van der Kolk, A. C. McFarlane & L. Weisaeth (Eds.), *Traumatic stress: The effects of overwhelming experience on mind, body, and society* (pp. 279–302). The Guilford Press. (Reprinted in modified form from *"Journal of Traumatic Stress,"* 8(4), 1995, 505–525.

van der Kolk, B. A. (1996b). The body keeps score: Approaches to the psychobiology of posttraumatic stress disorder. In B. A. van der Kolk, A. C. McFarlane & L. Weisaeth (Eds.), *Traumatic stress: The effects of overwhelming experience on mind, body, and society* (pp. 214–241). The Guilford Press.

van der Kolk, B. A. (2014). *The body keeps the score: Brain, mind, and body in the healing of trauma.* Viking.

van der Kolk, B. A., & Ducey, C. P. (1989). The psychological processing of traumatic experience: Rorschach patterns in PTSD. *Journal of Traumatic Stress, 2*(3), 259–274. https://doi.org/10.1002/jts.2490020303

van der Kolk, B., Greenberg, M., Boyd, H., & Krystal, J. (1985). Inescapable shock, neurotransmitters, and addiction to trauma: Toward a psychobiology of post traumatic stress. *Biological Psychiatry, 20*(3), 314–325. https://doi.org/10.1016/0006–3223(85)90061–7

van der Kolk, B. A., Van er Hart, O., & Marmar, C. (1996). Dissociation and information processing in posttraumatic stress disorder. In B. A. van der Kolk, A. McFarlane & L. Weisaeth (Eds.), *Traumatic stress: The effects of overwhelming experience on mind, body, and society* (pp. 303–330). Guilford Press.

Walker, P. (2013). *Complex PTSD: From surviving to thriving: A guide and map for recovering from childhood trauma.* Azure Coyote.

Weber, L. (2024, May 16). The surge in young workers has a dark side: Sexual harassment of teens on the job. *The Wall Street Journal.* www.wsj.com/business/teen-sexual-harassment-workplace-43d71242

Williams, J. H., Fitzgerald, L. F., & Dragsow, F. (1999). The effects of organizational practices on sexual harassment and individual outcomes in the military. *Military Psychology, 11*(3), 303–328.

Willness, C. R., Steel, P., & Lee, K. (2007). A meta-analysis of the antecedents and consequences of workplace sexual harassment. *Personnel Psychology, 60*(1), 127–162. https://doi.org/10.1111/j.1744–6570.2007.00067.x

Workman-Stark, A. (2017). *Inclusive policing from the inside out.* Springer Publishing International.

8

THE URGENCY OF ADOPTING AN INTERSECTIONAL LENS TO SEXUAL HARASSMENT RESEARCH AND PRACTICE

Barnini Bhattacharyya and Lucy DeSouza

> *#MeToo was started for black and brown women and girls. They're still being ignored. . . . We are socialized to respond to the vulnerability of white women, and it's a truth that is hard for some people to look in the face. . . . The women of color, trans women, queer people—our stories get pushed aside and our pain is never prioritized. We don't talk about indigenous women. Their stories go untold. Sexual violence knows no race, class or gender, but the response to it does.*
>
> Tarana Burke, Founder of MeToo

Making Visible the Invisible Majority

In 2006, Tarana Burke, a Black American activist and social worker, coined the phrase "Me Too" and founded the MeToo movement to draw attention to the pervasiveness of sexual violence, with a focus on young Black girls' experiences. However, more than 10 years later, the term set forth a global movement for survivors of sexual violence in 2017 when the hashtag #MeToo was used by White actress Alyssa Milano to demonstrate solidarity with Harvey Weinstein's victims and encourage other survivors to come forward. Although there were millions of affirming tweets under the hashtag, there were also critiques from women of color who noted that most attention had been given to the experiences of straight, cisgender, White women, with the voices of marginalized women going unheard. Some highlighted how a White woman was receiving support for MeToo in a manner that Burke had never received 10 years prior. Many did not even know about Burke's work until the hashtag went viral.

DOI: 10.4324/9781003300953-10

Burke noted that she feared that the relaunched #MeToo movement would erase her work and the people she was trying to support with the original movement, and would instead center White women in Hollywood (The New York Times, 2021). She said, "I felt defeated . . . Black women had been screaming about . . . R. Kelly . . . to no avail. Anita Hill, thanklessly, put herself and her career on the line more than 25 years ago" (Burke, 2017).

Burke's concerns are defensible. The resurgence of the MeToo movement laid bare the marginalization that women of color have experienced and continue to experience within the feminist movement in North America, where they are often relegated to sidelines (Onwuachi-Willig, 2018). This is mirrored in research and scholarship on sexual harassment (SH) at work, where the experiences of women who hold additional marginalized identities (e.g., women of color, queer women) remain understudied and overlooked (Berdahl & Bhattacharyya, 2021). Even when SH against women who belong to marginalized groups is acknowledged, their experiences tend to be minimized or discredited (Goh et al., 2021; Klein et al., 2021; Sambaraju, 2020). This is despite the fact that multiply marginalized women are most vulnerable to SH and violence (e.g., ethnic minority women, Berdahl & Moore, 2006; LGBQ women, Rabelo & Cortina, 2014; Silverschanz et al., 2008, low-income women, Fitzgerald, 2021). Women who are part of this invisible majority also often have overlapping identities (e.g., Black and Latina women are overrepresented in low-income jobs), which reinforces their susceptibility to sexual mistreatment. This is especially problematic given the unique and exacerbated ways in which women of color experience SH (e.g., racialized SH, Buchanan, 2005; exoticization, Bhattacharyya & Berdahl, 2023), and the cultural and legal barriers they encounter in seeking recourse (Williams, 2021).

The erasure of Burke's lifelong work as well as women of color's experiences of sexual mistreatment in workplace research fits the pattern of intersectional invisibility—"the failure to recognize, acknowledge, or accurately see non-prototypical members of social groups, such as women of color, who hold intersecting marginalized identities of race and gender" (Bhattacharyya & Berdahl, 2023; Purdie-Vaughns & Eibach, 2008)—that women of color are subject to in research and in workplaces (Buchanan & Settles, 2019; Purdie-Vaughns & Eibach, 2008; Sesko & Biernat, 2010; Smith et al., 2019). Intersectional invisibility is theorized and understood through the lens of intersectionality theory, which posits that people's locations at the margins of social identities and structures of power inform their experiences (Crenshaw, 1989; Collins, 2000; McCall, 2005), and that structures of power and oppression influence whose experiences are perceived as more salient and whose are rendered invisible.

Thus, in this chapter we argue that the lack of attention and credibility accorded to the invisible majority in workplace SH research underscores the need to adopt an intersectional lens to study and understand SH going forward. We further posit that failing to address intersectional issues in workplace SH reinforces the invisibility of women of color's experiences. When scholarship fails to take intersectional issues into account but nonetheless informs policy, it engenders further structural marginalization for those who lie at the intersections of identities. We also note that women of color have variable and complex experiences of sexual mistreatment and are not a homogenous and monolithic category, but experience power and oppression differently. This underscores the need to attend to how systems of power operate differently among different racial groups of women of color, even if they share some similarities. Anita Hill herself, in a conversation with Kimberle Crenshaw, highlights the urgency of understanding SH from an intersectional lens (Heck, 2020), noting that the absence of an intersectional perspective in the MeToo movement has had the harmful consequence of erasing the complex experiences and voices of women of color.

In the next sections, we provide a brief overview of intersectionality theory, review prior scholarship on SH to illustrate the need for integrating intersectionality theory into future SH scholarship, and propose intersectional frameworks and methodologies with which to approach future SH research. We hope that this helps scholars to expand the scope and impact of this body of research.

Theoretical Background

Intersectionality Theory

Intersectionality theory posits that systems of power and oppression create complex forms of systemic harm that profoundly impacts people's lived experiences based on their location in these systems, particularly for those who hold multiple marginalized identities and are located at the intersections of identity and intersecting axes of power (Collins, 2000; Crenshaw, 1989; McCall, 2005). It notes that identities are not independent of each other and unidimensional, but multidimensional, and constitutive. Intersectionality theory is thus an important analytic tool for examining complex inequalities and experiences at the nexus of multiple axes of power and oppression (Collins & Bilge, 2020; Grzanka, 2014; Grzanka et al., 2020). It provides scholars with a multiple-axis framework with which to study social phenomena, instead of a single-axis framework which is a more traditional approach to studying experiences among social groups (e.g., studying White women to generalize to all women in SH research).

For researchers, this implies that, to truly understand the experiences of those who are multiply marginalized, one must examine these intersections of identity and systems of power in conjunction, and how people's identities in these systems affect their experiences. Thus, adopting an intersectional lens to research is inextricably linked to an analysis of power. Due to this, intersectionality theory has gained momentum in recent years as a framework for psychology and management scholars to study the experiences of multiple marginalized subjects in organizational contexts (e.g., Bhattacharyya & Berdahl, 2023; Bowleg, 2013; Collins, 2000; Hurtado, 1989; McCluney & Rabelo, 2019; Purdie-Vaughns & Eibach, 2008; Rosette et al., 2016; Settles et al., 2019; Shields, 2008; Smith et al., 2019). Intersectional perspectives have illustrated that women of color experience unique forms of oppression in workplaces based on their unique histories and stereotypes (Hurtado, 1989).

Scholars have called for expanding the use of intersectionality theory to study various social phenomena, particularly those examining issues of discrimination and justice (Buchanan & Wiklund, 2020; Collins, 2015; Settles & Buchanan, 2014; Settles et al., 2020). Yet, for the most part, this call has been missing within SH scholarship, particularly in workplace contexts. We therefore posit that an intersectional perspective needs to be brought into the workplace context. Despite the overwhelming evidence documenting the frequency, unique nature, and disproportionality of SH experienced by women of color, little research has been centered women of color's experiences of sexual mistreatment, especially adopting an explicit intersectional lens (for exceptions, see Brassel et al., 2020; Woods et al., 2009).

In addition, intersectionality, by definition and origin, compels us to focus on praxis and action in our research (Cho et al., 2013). The term intersectionality originated from Crenshaw's focus on bringing legal justice to Black women, who fell through the cracks of the American justice system due to their experiences of discrimination not falling under race-based discrimination or gender-based discrimination (Crenshaw, 1989). The theoretical framework was in existence before this, however, and emerged from advocacy and activism undertaken by Black feminists such as Frances Beal (1970), bell hooks (1984), Audre Lorde (1984), and Sojourner Truth (1851), a formerly enslaved Black American abolitionist, who famously stated, "Ain't I a woman?" as she advocated for Black women to have equal rights to Black men and White women. Asian women were also addressing these intersectional ideas in their own experiences of oppression in the 1980s (e.g., Asian Women United of California, 1989;

Lim et al., 1989; Yamada, 1981). In 1981, Mitsuye Yamada, a Japanese American activist and feminist, raised important issues of Asian women fighting for their place in American society and the feminist movement, noting that women of color's experiences in the feminist movement were silenced as she worked toward changing these spaces. She said, "In this age, when women are making themselves visible on all fronts, I, an Asian American woman . . . am invisible. One of the most insidious ways of keeping us powerless is to . . . not listen with serious intent" (Yamada, 1981).

Thus, intersectionality, while often only thought of as a theory, an abstract one at that, and perhaps an analytic tool, is much more. This implies that intersectionality offers researchers a means to challenge systems of power and oppression and participate in building more equal and just systems through action-oriented research. This could range from critical scholarship that challenges hierarchies of knowledge and power in academia, to advocacy, social mobilization, and best practices around sexual mistreatment rooted in evidence-based research that influences policies, procedures, and systems. Importantly, it also obliges researchers to look toward the communities and social groups that we are studying to inform knowledge and theory.

Sexual Harassment and the Invisibility Majority

SH is motivated by a desire to reinforce one's social status or put perceived gender-norm violators in their place (Berdahl, 2007a, 2007b; Cortina & Berdahl, 2008; Fitzgerald et al., 1997), rather than sexual desire. Thus, a fundamental aspect of SH is power, wherein the harasser typically holds greater power than the target of harassment (Fiske & Berdahl, 2007), and exercises that power to further enhance their status through SH or violence. Although members of any social identity group can be subjected to SH, members of oppressed groups in current systems of power such as patriarchy especially susceptible to sexual violence, such as women. This is due to power dynamics and hegemony of systems of power being reflected and reinforced in individual experiences. Therefore, women have been the primary focus of research and discourse on SH (Cortina & Berdahl, 2008; Berdahl, 2007). The MeToo movement has further shone light on the pervasiveness of SH of women in workplaces (O'Neil et al., 2018; National Academies of Sciences, Engineering, and Medicine, 2018).

However, the experiences of women with additional marginalized identities have been left out. Specifically, extant research on SH at work has limited engagement with intersectional theory, especially in ways that explicitly take power into consideration and go beyond additive models (e.g., Berdahl & Moore, 2006), and consequentially paid little attention to the intersectional aspects of this phenomenon, such as the unique experiences of women who are located the intersections of gender and race (Brassel et al., 2020; Rosette et al., 2018). This has contributed to a dearth of scholarly examination and theory-building of SH that women with multiple marginalized identities are subject to.

We argue that such single axis thinking within SH research has occurred due to the complexities of structures of power and privilege that exist within social groups that are marginalized on a single axis, such as "women," which is the focal social category of interest in SH research. As intersectional scholars (Crenshaw, 1989; McCall, 2005) have noted, structures of power create hierarchies even within marginalized groups along other axes of marginalization and oppression, which influences which individuals and experiences are made visible and which are not (Brassel et al., 2019; McCormick-Huhn et al., 2019). Such systems also determine who is considered "prototypical" within a social group—the societally agreed upon salience of certain attributes and identities as standard within a social category or group (Purdie-Vaughns & Eibach, 2008; Tajfel & Turner, 1978). Because these prototypes emerge from existing cultures and societal representations, they take on the attributes of hierarchies in society, such that dominant group members are typically perceived as the prototypes of the social groups or categories they belong to (e.g., Black men as the prototypes of the social group Black people, White men as the prototypes of the social group White people). People with multiple marginalized identities typically do not fit the prototypes of the social groups they belong to.

These within-group hierarchies and set prototypes make certain group members "non-prototypical," making them particularly vulnerable to mistreatment (e.g., Black women perceived as not feminine enough and therefore norm-violators, Rosette et al., 2016; queer women punished for deviating from gender roles, Brassel et al., 2019; Konik & Cortina, 2008; masculine women punished through SH for deviating from gender roles, Berdahl, 2007b). Gender is a fundamental social category along which society is organized, and there exists a clear prototype of the social group "women"—White women (Brewer, 1988; Fiske, 2017; Smith et al., 2019). Women of color, due to being non-prototypical women, are rendered intersectionally invisible (Purdie-Vaughns & Eibach, 2008) as well as penalized for their non-prototypicality (Rudman & Glick, 2001) by being subjected to disproportionate and acute sexual mistreatment. Yet their experiences go unseen or are dismissed (Goh et al., 2021).

Sexual Harassment Experiences of Women of Color

The first (and one of the few) empirical examination and documentation of women of color's susceptibility to harassment at work compared to other social groups was conducted by Berdahl and Moore (2006), where they tested the double jeopardy effect (Beal, 1970) for ethnic minority women. Through a survey study of employees in a university, they found that women of color experienced most racial harassment as well as most SH at work compared to White men, White women, and women of color, and therefore experienced more overall workplace harassment as a compounded effect.

This finding is mirrored in national data gathered on SH. The US Equal Employment Opportunity Commission (EEOC) has found that women of color, especially Black women experience disproportionate levels of SH in the United States (Cassino & Besen-Cassino, 2019). Black women have a long history of being subject to sexual violence in America (Crenshaw, 1991), yet continue to be discounted and undermined (e.g., Anita Hill, American Rhetoric, 1991; R. Kelly's victims, BBC, 2022). Black women experience SH at work at three times the rate of White women (EEOC, 2018; Rossie et al., 2018). SH claims filed by White women have declined by 30% since 2000, but claimed filed by Black women have not changed (Cassino, 2018).

Research from intersectional perspectives in psychology and sociology has found that perceptions of Asian women have been historically rooted in racialized sexism and racial sexist stereotypes (e.g., exotic geishas, sex workers, mail order brides; Buchanan et al., 2018), leading to increased risk for sexual objectification and harassment (Buchanan & West, 2009; Cho, 1997; Patel, 2008; Shimizu, 2007), and consequential increased psychological and physiological distress (Ho et al., 2012). Asian women are disproportionately cast as victims of sexual violence in pornography (Park, 2012), which fuels violence against Asian women. Asian women also face overwhelming sexual violence from strangers, mostly non-Asian men, suggesting a fetishization of Asian women's racial identity (Park, 2012).

Indigenous women have experience sexual violence since the founding of America, and continue to the highest rate of sexual assault in both the United States and Canada. According to the US Department of Justice, Native American people are 2.5 times more likely to experience sexual assault compared to all other races, and one in three Native American women have reported being subject to rape in their lifetimes. In Canada, four out of ten indigenous women have experienced sexual assault in their lifetime, almost triple that of non-indigenous people (GSS, 2019). There are over 1,700 missing or murdered indigenous women or girls in Canada, with over a thousand murdered between 1980 and 2012 (RCMP, 2015). As per the Department of Justice, the homicide rate for indigenous women is 6 times higher than non-indigenous women. Yet indigenous women rarely, if ever, feature in national conversations about sexual violence.

Finally, undocumented women and women employed in low-wage jobs (circumstances which also overlap), who are primarily constituted of Latina, Asian, and Black immigrants, face especially high rates of sexual violence and harassment at work (Fitzgerald, 2021), and experience acute vulnerability due to their language and cultural barriers (Malone, 2017). These women, since they are immigrants, often Undocumented, engaged in low-paid work, as well as racialized, are located at the very bottom of social hierarchies of power and privilege. This nexus of race, immigrant status, and class interact to give rise to acute and disproportionate SH, highlighting the invisibility of class as a salient factor and identity in this conversation (see Chapter 10 on socioeconomic status (SES) and intersectionality for more detail).

Researchers outside of management have begun to adopt intersectional approaches and are uncovering the ways in which non-prototypical women's experiences are delegitimized, finding that non-prototypical women are less likely to be seen as targets of SH, SH targeting non-prototypical women is less likely to be recognized, SH claims of non-prototypical women are perceived as less credible and legitimate, and discounted as less harmful (Goh et al., 2021). This further erases the experiences of women of color since credibility and sufficient harm caused to the victim are necessary for women to receive safety and justice (Epstein & Goodman, 2018; Tuerkheimer, 2017; van Doorn & Koster, 2019). For Black women, these challenges are compounded, since they are stereotyped as hypersexual and promiscuous (Harris-Perry, 2011; Lewis et al., 2016), and therefore less likely to be believed or seen as legitimate victims of sexual violence (Tillman et al., 2010). Thus, despite alarming evidence of women of color being acutely subject to sexual mistreatment, not only are their experiences often rendered invisible, they are discredited.

Further, women of color's experiences of sexual mistreatment are uniquely different, and intertwined with their racial identities. Calafell (2014) notes, "For women of color, SH is rarely, if ever, about sex or sexism alone; it is also about race." Her assessment is astute; a small group of intersectional scholars, primarily in psychology, have uncovered unique ways in which women of color experience SH, which have not emerged in prior research studying White women. Black women experience a unique form of SH—racialized SH—that cannot be captured through a single-axis gender framework (Buchanan, 2005; Richardson & Taylor, 2009), since it consists of harassment behaviors that reflect specific stereotypes about Black women (e.g., "sexy Black ass"; Buchanan & Ormerod, 2002). Black women are stereotyped as highly sexual, promiscuous, and sexually deviant (Cho, 1997; Reynolds-Dobbs et al., 2008; Townsend et al., 2010). On the other hand, Asian women are stereotyped as delicate and virginal

(Kim & Chung, 2005; Shrake, 2006) or exotic and seductive (Buchanan et al., 2018). Yet, both Asian and Black women are subject to hypersexualization and fetishism that affect how they experience harassment as well as how others view their harassment (Onwuachi-Willig, 2018). Such harassment cannot be cleanly defined as race-based or gender-based, but is a complex combination of both.

Management research has begun to examine intersectional experiences of sexual mistreatment, finding theoretically compelling evidence for intersectional effects. Bhattacharyya and Berdahl (2023) identified a unique form of racialized SH that women of color face in the workplace called "exoticization," a form of race and gender based sexual objectification, which draws on specific sexual stereotypes associated with different racial groups of women of color. Latina women experienced being called "spicy" at work, indigenous women received sexualized comments about "Pocahontas," East-Asian women were called "chinadoll" and experienced comments about "yellow fever," and in general, women reported being hypersexualized, called "exotic," and receiving sexualized comments about their accents, skin color, and hair.

What this suggests is that women of color experience SH against the complex backdrop of racism and race-based stereotypes and that ignoring the impact of race on women of color's lived experiences erases salient nuances in women of color's SH, further underpinning the necessity of integrating intersectionality theory in research. These findings also highlight that even within groups of women of color, they experience SH and racial sexualization in different forms.

Therefore, studying sexual mistreatment at work only through the lens of gender prevents us from gaining insight into the prevalence and complexity of women of color's experiences (Bhattacharyya & Berdahl, 2023; Nash, 2008; McCall, 2005), who, as noted earlier, are disproportionately subject to SH and also experience sexual mistreatment differently. It also prevents us from identifying ways to challenge the systems and processes that subject women of color to elevated rates of SH. Finally, by not taking an intersectional approach, existing evidence may be perceived as incidental and not related to race at all. On the contrary, they reveal important dynamics based on intersecting systems of power and oppression that are worthy to be explored within SH research, highlighting the need for adopting an intersectional lens to future scholarship on SH at work.

Way Forward for Sexual Harassment Research

The previous sections highlight the importance of adopting an intersectional lens in understanding and examining SH at work. In this section, we briefly discuss the ways in which SH research is currently conducted, and then propose how SH research can be conducted from an intersectional perspective, thus offering novel methodological perspectives and approaches for future research.

Positivist Perspectives to Study Sexual Harassment

Currently, the majority of SH research, including those studying multiple identities, takes a positivist approach, which is based on the assumption that one single tangible reality exists (Comte, 1880; Park et al., 2020), and involves utilizing additive models and approaches to combine identities through quantitative techniques and methods (see Table 8.1). A positivist approach allows us to operationalize different types of SH and identify differences in frequency and prevalence of SH between different social groups. The double jeopardy model is one such perspective that helps draw comparisons across different groups, and it provided the first piece of empirical evidence that women of color experienced the most workplace harassment (e.g., Beal, 1970; Berdahl & Moore, 2006).

However, a significant challenge with the positivist approach is that of suitably integrating the mutually constitutive approach to studying multiple identities as per intersectionality into quantitative study design, which can engender issues of measurement and statistical power. For most studies, sample sizes are too small to compare groups and examine intersectional differences along multiple axes of identities (Burn, 2019). For example, research has found that queer people typically experience significantly higher rates of SH compared to cisgender, straight people (Grant et al., 2011; Hill & Silva, 2005; Kearl, 2014). Yet, we know little about differences in experience and prevalence within the queer community, and how the experiences of, for example, cisgender gay men differ from that of trans women.

Such methods also prevent us from identifying unique forms of marginalization that are only experienced by those located at the intersections of their multiple identities. It only allows us to capture what we already know, or think we know, since previous research and scales are ethnocentric. This engenders issues of operationalization through reliance on existing scale measures and research which leave out the voices and experiences of women of color whose experiences are not adequately or fully captured.

Unfortunately, the biggest and most insurmountable challenge with a positivist approach is that it fundamentally differs from an intersectional philosophy by treating identities as separate and additive. Intersectionality considers identities and experiences as simultaneous and mutually constitutive (Collins, 2019), and not divisible into separate categories. This

TABLE 8.1 Description of theoretical perspectives for studying sexual harassment (SH) and the need for an intersectional lens

Theoretical perspective	Underlying logics	Extent of alignment with intersectionality theory	Approaches	Methods	Contribution
Positivist approach	Based on the assumption that a single tangible reality exists outside of individual perception. Begins with existing literature and theory to build testable hypotheses, conduct empirical studies to test hypotheses, and inform theory through findings.	Allows us to operationalize different types of SH and identify differences in frequency and prevalence of SH and violence between different social groups. Inability to examine qualitative experiences and complexity of experience. Prevents us from identifying or shedding light on unique forms of marginalization that are previously understudied. Differs from an intersectional philosophy by considering identities as additive and separate, not whole and mutually constitutive.	Identify area of research and study sample and context to test hypotheses based on prior SH research and theory. Test additive models such as double jeopardy to study multiple identities.	Quantitative methods such as laboratory or field experiments, surveys, archival data analysis.	Allows researchers to operationalize different types of SH and identify differences in frequency and prevalence of SH between different social groups and among those with multiple identities.

(Continued)

TABLE 8.1 (Continued)

Theoretical perspective	Underlying logics	Extent of alignment with intersectionality theory	Approaches	Methods	Contribution
Critical intersectional approach	Based on the assumption that reality is subjective and determined by perceptions and experiences of individuals which are affected by power structures such as culture, race, gender, class, etc. Begins with an awareness that all systems of knowledge reflect particular worldviews, and focuses on what is nonobvious, left out, and generally forgotten.	Allows us to adopt intersectionality as critical inquiry to shed light on understudied aspects of SH and examine how it can be experienced differently by different people and the reasons for the same. Thus, requires considering SH's relation to power. Helps understand how critical analysis and social action can inform one another. Addresses need to distinguish between research that additively examines multiple identities versus those that are explicitly grounded in invisible majority's experiences.	Identify area of research and study sample and context based on understudied issues and groups and explicitly considering locations in systems of power. Focus on understanding the impact of multiple identities as indivisible instead of additive categories. For example, develop area of research to focus on queer women of color's experiences of SH in low-income occupations.	Mainstream inductive qualitative methods such as interviews, ethnographies, and case studies. Novel inductive techniques such as personal narratives and autoethnographies. Community-based participatory research.	Allows researchers to fully utilize the scope of intersectionality theory through its ability to examine the complexities and nuances of how structures of power and privilege work together and how one's locations within these structures affect experiences.

(*Continued*)

TABLE 8.1 (Continued)

Theoretical perspective	Underlying logics	Extent of alignment with intersectionality theory	Approaches	Methods	Contribution
		Includes fundamental tenets of reflexivity, critical qualitative inequiry, being community-focused, and being cognizant of context and systems, which are consistent with critical intersectional perspectives.			
Critical intersectional quantitative approach	Based on the assumption that certain groups of identities are interconnected within intersecting structures of power and that traditional quantitative methods are insufficient to study this interconnectedness.	Fundamental aspects of research, such as identifying area of inquiry and selecting study sample, are determined through a critical intersectional lens.	Identify area of research and study sample and context based on understudied areas and groups and explicitly considering systems of power.	Quantitative techniques that accommodate intersectional lenses such as case studies, studies focused on variance within intersectional groups, and mixed methods.	Allows researchers to conduct quantitative research with foundations in intersectionality theory as well as test inductive intersectional findings through quantitative techniques.

(Continued)

TABLE 8.1 (Continued)

Theoretical perspective	Underlying logics	Extent of alignment with intersectionality theory	Approaches	Methods	Contribution
	Begins with grounding fundamental aspects of research in uncovering intersecting systems of power, and then employing methodological techniques accordingly. Integrates a critical intersectional lens and corresponding methods with quantitative techniques.	Allows for integrating an intracategorical approach, which focuses on differences and similarities within intersectional groups, to SH research. Develops ways to utilize quantitative techniques from a critical intersectional lens by being reflexive and focusing on intersectional groups such as studying intracategorical complexities within them.	Examine social categories as whole (instead of a 2 × 2 model), examining variance within intersecting groups, or developing quantitative studies based on experiences and findings regarding the invisible majority. For example, studying experiences of racialized sexualization of Black women and testing findings on other samples such as White women.		

requires examining multiple identities in conjunction and taking a bottom-up approach to generating knowledge. Typical quantitative approaches, even those termed intersectional, adopt additive models, which "split" identities up into two-factor models, violating a fundamental tenet of intersectionality.

As such, positivist SH research is not in the spirit of the critical and context-emphasizing nature of intersectionality theory. Thus, it becomes necessary for researchers to adopt alternative methodologies that are more consistent with intersectionality. For this, we recommend a critical perspective for future SH research that integrates intersectionality theory. We also propose ways to integrate an intersectional lens into current quantitative methods to better align SH research techniques with intersectionality.

Critical Intersectional Perspectives to Study Sexual Harassment

We build on prior intersectional scholars (e.g., racialized sexualization Buchanan, 2005; Woods et al., 2009) and argue that intersectionality theory, through its focus on intersecting identities and multiple axes of power and privilege, and in direct contrast to single-axis thinking on SH, is the most suitable theoretical framework to study women of color's experiences of SH at work. It allows us to gain deep understanding of women of color's unique experiences and drives us to develop research on how to mitigate these experiences and obtain justice for women of color through intervention and action. As such, it compels us to center women of color, typically perceived as passive and invisible subjects of both mistreatment and social movements, as repositories of knowledge for and active participants in our research and theory building.

Specifically, we recommend adopting the lens of intersectionality as critical inquiry—considering an issue or phenomenon's relation to power (Cho et al., 2013; Collins, 2019; Collins, 2020)—to future SH research. Critical perspectives in research are based on the assumption that reality is subjective and is influenced by people's worldviews and lived experiences in existing systems of power (Bronner, 2017; Steffy & Grimes, 1986). Thus, critical perspectives and inquiry are consistent with intersectionality theory since they explicitly account for how power affect individuals' experiences. Intersectionality as critical inquiry offers a framework with which to study SH in the context of systems of inequality and power, which allows researchers to shed light on erstwhile blind spots in research due to intersecting systems of power, such as the experiences of the invisibility majority. A critical intersectional paradigm helps us to recognize when traditional frameworks and approaches are insufficient and existing theories do not fully explain social realities, as in workplace SH research currently.

Below, we outline how to integrate a critical intersectional lens to all stages of workplace SH research.

Development of Research Question/Area of Inquiry

We recommend that SH scholars pay explicit attention to the systems of power that SH is embedded in, and identify their research questions accordingly. Integrating an intersectional lens into developing one's area of inquiry allows researchers to be more thoughtful about whose stories get told when designing studies.

An integral aspect of such integration is *reflexivity*, which requires the researcher to 'constantly assesses the relationship between "knowledge" and "ways of doing knowledge"' (Calás & Smircich, 1992, p. 240). It requires the researcher to turn inward and reflect on one's own interpretations of and experiences with the social phenomena being studied as well as one's own position in relation to the individuals and groups being studied (Alvesson et al., 2008; Mead, 1934; Salzman, 2002). As per reflexivity, our positionalities, structural as well as experiential, influences how we understand and build knowledge (Rosaldo, 2004; Yuval-Davis, 2015).

Atewologun and Mahalingam (2018) integrate reflexivity with intersectionality to put forth the concept of *intersectional reflexivity* as a tool to use intersectionality as a methodological framework, defining it as an interrogation of one's own social location and gradients of disadvantages and privileges vis-à-vis the research participants and the research topic. They specify three steps to cultivate intersectional reflexivity—identifying and articulating one's own salient intersectional identities, being sensitive to "sites of intersectional identity salience in collecting and analyzing data" (Atewologun, 2014; Atewologun & Mahalingam, 2018), and managing the implication of one's own intersectional location.

In keeping with this, we recommend that the researcher must reflect on their own identities, social location in systems of power, and lived experiences, to determine what research questions to study, and why those questions are important for the advancement of SH research. For example, a question that may emerge from this line of inquiry would be: how do queer women of color experience SH at work in ways that are different from what existing research and my own experience tells us? Such research questions will consequently entail actively considering how intersections of identity and experience are present in various steps of research such as who we choose to include in our study, where we are conducting the study, study design, data analysis and interpretation, and finally implications of our findings for the groups being studied and if these implications challenge the structures leading to SH in any way. We explicate on each of these steps below.

Selecting Study Sample and Context/Site of Study

A critical intersectional perspective to studying SH calls for paying particular attention to people's lived experiences (McCauley et al., 2019). As such, being attuned to systems of power is important in identifying whom to study, and in what context or location. Due to the paucity of research on the invisible majority's experiences of workplace SH, we encourage researchers to consciously and deliberately attempt to study these groups (women of color, women with other intersectional identities such as low SES) to build more nuanced knowledge.

Brassel et al. (2020) recommend the following structure to doing so: determine what systems of power are present to identify context, followed by determining what identities are present and how these identities interact with the context identified, and finally, determine how the context and systems of power may render certain identities invisible. This structure guides researchers into considering the multiple axes of power and oppression that exist in a particular context in conjunction with the intersections of identity of the individuals or groups being studied, thus meeting the fundamental tenets of an intersectional framework (Collins, 2015).

Methods and Techniques

We recommend that SH scholars adopt and integrate qualitative methods and techniques to their research, which lend themselves well to critical intersectionality due to their subjective and context-driven nature. Qualitative research—defined as the study of the nature of phenomena—is suitable for building new theory, understanding understudied issues, and adding nuance to existing research. Critical qualitative research, in particular, uses qualitative techniques to focus on challenging traditional perceptions of what counts as valid and legitimate research (Denzin, 2017), shedding light on and critiquing inequality, as well as changing unjust systems (Charmaz, 2017; Denzin, 2015), thus aligning with intersectionality theory's fundamental tenet and making it especially suitable for studying SH. Such research has the goal of centering the voices of the marginalized and creating sites for social change (Denzin, 2017). The open-ended nature of critical qualitative research also creates resistance against positivist, mono-categorical approaches to research. We discuss specific qualitative techniques to conduct critical SH research below.

Mainstream Inductive Qualitative Methods

Mainstream qualitative techniques such as interviews and ethnographies (Patton, 2005) are well suited to integrating critical intersectional perspectives into SH research. These techniques typically do not have issues of measurement associated with quantitative research and allow data and theory to emerge from participants, lending them well to identifying novel insights into the phenomenon of interest, centering the voices of participants, and building nuanced knowledge. Such techniques, because they build theory and gain insight based on participants' perspectives and lived experiences, allow researchers to expand our understanding of SH to include the invisible majority. Examples of SH research employing qualitative methods include studies on intersectional invisibility (e.g., Bhattacharyya & Berdahl, 2023), racialized sexualization (e.g., Buchanan & Ormerod, 2002), and contextual effects on SH (e.g., Handy, 2006).

Autoethnography

Extending the idea of centering the voices of the invisible majority, personal narratives and autoethnographies becomes powerful in understanding SH experiences of women of color and other invisibilized groups, particularly through its resistance to and disruption of dominant narratives (Calafell, 2014; Alexander, 2020). Autoethnography refers to "a form of self-narrative that places the self within a social context" (Reed-Danahay, 2009) and is used as a methodological tool that centers reflexivity by systematically reflecting on and analyzing personal experiences to understand social phenomena (Ellis et al., 2011). Chapter 2, through its study of SH in social media, provides an example on how to conduct auto-ethnographies on sensitive topics.

Community-Based Participatory Research

SH research, to further intersectional goals, must be community-focused and occur in partnership with members of the invisible majority. McCauley et al. (2019) argue that intersectional research occurs "in genuine connection with community, and particularly with communities often left out of academic discourse" as opposed to traditional research that occurs in isolation from the communities of interest, reinforces existing power structures, and produces research lacking in context and nuance (; Nnawulezi et al., 2018). One specific method that has been developed for community-engaged research is community-based participatory research (CBPR) (McCauley et al., 2019), which acknowledges the harm caused by traditional research to marginalized communities and actively works toward mitigating power differences between these communities and researchers (Wallerstein & Duran, 2006). In CBPR, researchers and community members hold shared ownership over all stages of the study and utilize shared decision-making to "ensure that the findings and knowledge produced truly benefit survivor communities" (Israel et al., 1998). For instance, community members in CBPR collaborate with researchers and take on an active role in identifying research questions of interest, developing research studies, as well as running the actual studies (Wallerstein & Duran, 2006). Thus, community-focused research engenders mutual learning, dismantling of traditional power differences between researchers and communities, and centering the voices of community members, making it an especially salient aspect of integrating intersectionality with SH research.

Critical Intersectional Quantitative Methods for Sexual Harassment Research

Next, we also propose ways to address issues with traditional quantitative SH research, by integrating a critical intersectional framework with quantitative methodological approaches (Lee, 1991). This entails viewing certain groups of identities as interconnected within intersecting structures of power, to allow for broader thinking regarding SH within the methodological constraints of quantitative techniques. In particular, intersectionality can be used as a heuristic or cognitive tool in quantitative studies to consider invisible experiences and social groups when designing and conducting quantitative examinations of SH. Intersectionality as a heuristic allows us to critique and expand on scholarship that has adopted mono-categorical perspectives. An intersectional paradigm also allows us to recognize when traditional frameworks and approaches are insufficient and existing theories do not fully explain social realities, as in current SH research. This may mean considering the challenges with traditional quantitative perspectives and methods and developing strategies to mitigate them, such as through studying understudied groups or situating research in understudied contexts. It may also demand that the researcher consider how systems of power are embedded in our research methods, particularly how we collect data, and regarding whom. Finally, to most effectively mitigate the limitations of quantitative approaches, we recommend that researchers practice reflexivity at every step of the research process and interrogate their research choices and decisions through such a reflexive lens. Thus, one may still use methods that are traditionally aligned with a positivist lens but still take a critical perspective to what is being studied and how to make sense of findings.

Development of Research Question/Area of Inquiry

To integrate an intersectional lens with quantitative methods, researchers must begin to apply this lens at the development of research question stage.

This would entail asking, who is included in my research, and what role do intersecting systems of power play in my research question. This is especially pertinent to phenomenological topics of research such as SH, which has explicit and implicit relationships with inequality systems. Ideally, this should lead researchers to new research questions that focus on understudied populations or hidden complexities in SH. Some scholars have tried to integrate an intersectional lens into their focus on inquiry to be more thoughtful about whose stories get told when developing and designing studies (e.g., Scheim & Bauer, 2019). A few have focused on Black women's unique experiences of cross-racial and intra-racial SH as their area of inquiry, although using traditional survey methods (Woods et al., 2009). Finally, some scholars have attempted to be intersectional in their approach by specifically focusing on issues of measurement and developing intersectional scale measures and psychometric tools that directly capture intersectional experiences (e.g., Lewis & Neville, 2015). Overall, an intersectional approach to identifying areas of inquiry is likely to highlight limitations in existing knowledge on SH and ways to shed light on them, as well as the need for developing new measures and operationalizations for SH experiences, such as racialized SH for example.

Selecting Study Sample and Context/Site of Study

Similar to purely critical intersectional perspectives, we recommend shifting the context and samples of SH research to understudied populations such as women of color and other underrepresented women. We also recommend that research samples and contexts be community focused, such that the voices and needs of those who have been historically been left out of research and praxis on SH are centered. Overall, researchers must be concrete about their sampling approach and underlying assumptions, the kind of SH they are studying based on whether their selected sample is likely to experience it, and contextualize their focus as much as possible.

Methods and Techniques

To conduct quantitative SH research through an intersectional perspective, we recommend examining complexities and differences within multiple marginalized social groups as opposed to comparing such groups with dominant groups (e.g., double jeopardy models which compare White women with women of color). This requires that researchers pay attention to "intracategorical complexity" (McCall, 2005, Nash, 2008), the heterogeneity and complexity that exist within social groups typically treated as homogenous, such as women of color, and uncovering the different ways in which they are located in systems of power. Adopting an intracategorical intersectional lens entails focusing on differences among and within individuals whose identities cross the "boundaries of traditionally constructed groups" (Dill, 2002, p. 5) in order to shed light on the "complexity of lived experience" (Mccall, 2005) within these groups. An intracategorical approach to SH research would require beginning one's research with a single unified social group (e.g., women of color) and working one's way out by examining each additional social category within women of color (e.g., race, class, immigrant status, etc.) and how experiences vary due to these aspects one by one. Thus, we need to consider how systems of oppression operate differently for different racialized women (even if they might share some similar experiences). Below we include practical ways to do so.

Case Studies

We recommend conducting multigroup studies that analyze intersections of all dimensions of social categories and identities within social groups that have been essentialized, adopting a case-based approach to the research, and treating each additional category as a separate case. This would allow for the invisible majority to be studied in a variance and complexity-focused way.

Within-Intersectional Group Variance Focused Studies

Most quantitative methods studying SH across categories have been intercategorical (Bauer et al., 2021), describing inequalities across intersections, which violate intersectionality's core premise that multiple identities are experienced simultaneously. Researchers have proposed ways to circumvent these issues through more complex quantitative models that integrate multiple social identities simultaneously. These range from cross-tabulation analyses that stratify measures by intersectional groups (Spierings, 2012), regression models with interactions between two or more social positions to allow effects to vary across intersections (Bowleg & Bauer, 2016; Jackson, 2016; Spierings, 2012), and multilevel modelling to incorporate systemic variables such as organizational policies or geographical-level class and race, which affect SH of women (Bauer, 2014; Bowleg & Bauer, 2016; Scott & Siltanen, 2017; Spierings, 2012).

Another approach to focusing on intersectional variance is one that has been proposed by Boyd (2021) to capture the multidimensionality in intersecting social identities and expand the scope of the MeToo movement. Boyd recommends beginning one's research with a focus on Black women and their experiences, and then examining other social identities located at the margins from this standpoint. This would entail starting with Black women's experiences as the standard in experimental or survey research, such as by using measures of racialized SH, or by ensuring that a significant number of participants are Black women. This focus would allow the researcher to engage with the complexity in aspects of SH being studied, as well as decenter whiteness and critique existing systems of power.

Multi-Method Approaches

Mixed methods as an approach to conduct intersectionality-informed research has gained much traction in other research areas, particularly gender studies (e.g., Fehrenbacher & Patel, 2020; Grace, 2014). Mixed-methods research involves combining qualitative and quantitative techniques to best answer a research question (Onwuegbuzie et al., 2009). We suggest that as long as one's research inquiry has been developed through critical intersectional perspectives, integrating qualitative techniques such as interviews with quantitative studies such an experiments, can yield greater insight than just adopting one. Typically, this would entail conducting qualitative research first to draw insight about understudied and invisible groups, and then testing these insights through quantitative techniques. By doing so, findings are grounded in and centered around the experience of women of color, a fundamental tenet of intersectionality. This may involve working with researchers across methodological differences, which can further engender greater insight.

Novel Techniques

Novel methods and techniques to conduct quantitative research from intersectional perspectives are also developing in the past few years. Coles and Pasek (2020) developed a new tool for intersectional quantitative research in their paper on intersectional invisibility, where they analyzed data from a stereotypical attribute awareness task study using nonmetric multidimensional scaling techniques which imitated intersectional complexities in their study. Similar techniques could be used to disentangle intersectional effects in SH, particularly in terms of developing new measures for SH constructs.

Discussion

> There's really no such thing as the "voiceless." There are only the deliberately silenced, or the preferably unheard.
>
> —Arundhati Roy, 2004

In this chapter, we outline an issue that was "shadowed" by #MeToo, whereby sexual mistreatment experienced by multiple marginalized groups, particularly women of color, was rendered invisible. This is mirrored in current scholarship on SH, such that much remains unstudied about this invisible majority's experiences of SH.

To bridge this gap, we suggest integrating an intersectional lens to examine SH, and shed light on the "shadowed" aspects of the MeToo movement. We also discuss the importance of changing the SH legal landscape in order to truly achieve the intersectional endeavor of justice.

The suggestions made earlier require that researchers approach SH research through reflexivity and in partnership with the invisible majority. This may require treating women of color as expert sources of valid knowledge. This knowledge is likely to differ from established research, and will therefore entail developing new theory rooted in this expert knowledge. This also implies identifying strategies and best practices in challenging structures of power, which render these groups invisible (Madison, 2005). If not, we again risk silencing the voices of those who have been silenced thus far and reinforcing structures of power and privilege that cause this silencing.

Importantly, in keeping with what intersectionality theory stands for, we recommend that future SH research focus on social justice concerns and prioritize research implications that shed light on strategies and interventions to prevent and challenge sex-based harassment and violence, particularly for the invisible majority. Identifying substantive solutions to sexual violence will remain out of reach as long as we conceptualize, recognize, and study this violence through mono-categorical and non-justice oriented lenses (Collins, 2019).

Further, legal experts have argued that the persistent racial bias in the MeToo movement is a sign that SH laws need to change to account for intersectional and multidimensional experiences of victims and survivors of harassment (Onwuachi-Willig, 2018). Currently, both US and Canadian law do not consider the complexities of racial and gender marginalization, and how that can influence an individual's susceptibility to and experience of SH, as well as others' perceptions of the validity of such experiences (Onwuachi-Willig, 2018). Legal systemics dichotomously separate racial discrimination and SH into two distinct categories of discrimination, and therefore cannot adequately respond to intersectional ways in which SH occurs such as racialized SH. (Cho et al., 2013). Due to this, women of color become much less likely to be availed recourse and receive justice when they experience SH, creating unique legal disadvantages, with research finding that women of color are half as likely as White women to win discrimination litigations (Best et al., 2011).

We conclude our paper with a quote from McCauley and colleagues (2019) that reinforces the need to reimagine SH scholarship and research to make it truly inclusive—"Every survivor matters. Every story matters. Yet our work over the last 25 years has often centered the lives and stories of those who benefit from power and privilege. This has resulted in the further marginalization and erasure of survivors with marginalized identities."

References

Alexander, B. K. (2020). "I thought I knew you" a performative reflection on knowing the other in autoethnography. *Journal of Autoethnography*, 1(2), 190–197.

Alvesson, M., Hardy, C., & Harley, B. (2008). Reflecting on reflexivity: Reflexive textual practices in organization and management theory. *Journal of Management Studies*, 45(3), 480–501.

Anita Hill—Opening Statement. (1991, October 11). American *Rhetoric*. https://www.americanrhetoric.com/speeches/anitahillsenatejudiciarystatement.htm

Asian Women United of California (Ed.). (1989). *Making waves: An anthology of writings by and about Asian American women* (vol. 807). Beacon Press.

Atewologun, D. (2014). Sites of intersectional identity salience. *Gender in Management: An International Journal*, 29(5), 277–290.

Atewologun, D., & Mahalingam, R. (2018). Intersectionality as a methodological tool in qualitative equality, diversity and inclusion research. In *Handbook of research methods in diversity management, equality and inclusion at work* (pp. 149–170). Edward Elgar Publishing.

Bauer, G. R. (2014). Incorporating intersectionality theory into population health research methodology: Challenges and the potential to advance health equity. *Social Science & Medicine*, 110, 10–17.

Bauer, G. R., Churchill, S. M., Mahendran, M., Walwyn, C., Lizotte, D., & Villa-Rueda, A. A. (2021). Intersectionality in quantitative research: A systematic review of its emergence and applications of theory and methods. *SSM-Population Health*, 14, 100798.

BBC. (September, 2022). R. Kelly: Disgraced R&B star guilty of child abuse. *BBC*. https://www.bbc.com/news/world-us-canada-62909703

Beal, F. M. (1970). Double jeopardy: To be Black and female. *Meridians*, 8(2), 166–176.

Berdahl, J., & Bhattacharyya, B. (2021). Four ways forward in studying sex-based harassment. *Equality, Diversity and Inclusion: An International Journal*, 40(4), 477–492.

Berdahl, J. L. (2007a). Harassment based on sex: Protecting social status in the context of gender hierarchy. *Academy of Management Review*, 32(2), 641–658.

Berdahl, J. L. (2007b). The sexual harassment of uppity women. *Journal of Applied Psychology*, 92(2), 425.

Berdahl, J. L., & Moore, C. (2006). Workplace harassment: Double jeopardy for minority women, *Journal of Applied Psychology*, 91(2), 426–436.

Best, R. K., Edelman, L. B., Krieger, L. H., & Eliason, S. R. (2011). Multiple disadvantages: An empirical test of intersectionality theory in EEO litigation. *Law & Society Review*, 45(4), 991–1025.

Bhattacharyya, B., & Berdahl, J. L. (2023). Do you see me? An inductive examination of differences between women of color's experiences of and responses to invisibility at work. *Journal of Applied Psychology*, 108(7), 1073.

Bowleg, L. (2013). "Once you've blended the cake, you can't take the parts back to the main ingredients": Black gay and bisexual men's descriptions and experiences of intersectionality. *Sex Roles, 68*, 754–767.

Bowleg, L., & Bauer, G. (2016). Invited reflection: Quantifying intersectionality. *Psychology of Women Quarterly, 40*(3), 337–341.

Boyd, A. E. (2021). Intersectionality and reflexivity—decolonizing methodologies for the data science process. *Patterns, 2*(12), 100386.

Brassel, S. T., Davis, T. M., Jones, M. K., Miller-Tejada, S., Thorne, K. M., & Areguin, M. A. (2020). The importance of intersectionality for research on the sexual harassment of Black queer women at work. *Translational Issues in Psychological Science, 6*(4), 383.

Brassel, S. T., Settles, I. H., & Buchanan, N. T. (2019). Lay (mis) perceptions of sexual harassment toward transgender, lesbian, and gay employees. *Sex Roles, 80*(1), 76–90.

Brewer, M. B. (1988). A dual process model of impression formation. In T. K. Srull & R. S. Wyer, Jr. (Eds.), *A dual process model of impression formation* (pp. 1–36). Lawrence Erlbaum Associates, Inc.

Bronner, S. E. (2017). *Critical theory: A very short introduction* (Vol. 263). Oxford University Press.

Brockes, E. (2018, January 15). #MeToo founder Tarana Burke: 'You have to use your privilege to serve other people'. *The Guardian.* https://www.theguardian.com/world/2018/jan/15/me-too-founder-tarana-burke-women-sexual-assault

Buchanan, N. T. (2005). The nexus of race and gender domination: The racialized sexual harassment of African American women. In P. Morgan & J. Gruber (Eds.), *In the company of men: Re-discovering the links between sexual harassment and male domination* (pp. 294–320). Northeastern University Press.

Buchanan, N. T., & Settles, I. H. (2019). Managing (in) visibility and hypervisibility in the workplace. *Journal of Vocational Behavior, 113*, 1–5.

Buchanan, N. T., & Wiklund, L. O. (2021). Intersectionality research in psychological science: Resisting the tendency to disconnect, dilute, and depoliticize. *Research on Child and Adolescent Psychopathology, 49*(1), 25–31.

Buchanan, N. T., & West, C. M. (2009). Sexual harassment in the lives of women of color. In H. Landrine, & N. F. Russo (Eds.), *Handbook of diversity in feminist psychology: Theory, research, and practice* (pp. 449–476). Springer Publishing Company.

Buchanan, N. T., & Ormerod, A. J. (2002). Racialized sexual harassment in the lives of African American women. *Women & Therapy, 25*(3–4), 107–124.

Burke, T. (2017, November). #MeToo was started for Black and Brown women and girls. They're still being ignored. *The Washington Post.* www.washingtonpost.com/news/post-nation/wp/2017/11/09/the-waitress-who-works-in-the-diner-needs-to-know-that-the-issue-of-sexual-harassment-is-about-her-too/?noredirect=o

Burn, S. M. (2019). The psychology of sexual harassment. *Teaching of Psychology, 46*(1), 96–103.

Calafell, B. M. (2014). "Did it happen because of your race or sex?": University sexual harassment policies and the move against intersectionality. *Frontiers: A Journal of Women Studies, 35*(3), 75–95.

Calás, M. B., Smircich, L. (1992). 'Re-Writing Gender Into Organizational Theorizing: Directions From Feminist Perspectives', in Reed M., Hughes M. (Eds.), *Rethinking Organization: New Directions in Organization Theory and Analysis,* pp. 227–253. London: Sage.

Cassino, D. (2018). Sexual harassment claims have fallen among young white women, but not older women or black women. *Harvard Business Review.* https://hbr.org/2018/02/sexual-harassment-claims-have-fallen-among-young-white-women-but-not-older-women-or-black-women

Cassino, D., & Besen-Cassino, Y. (2019). Race, threat and workplace sexual harassment: The dynamics of harassment in the United States, 1997–2016. *Gender, Work & Organization, 26*(9), 1221–1240.

Charmaz, K. (2017). The power of constructivist grounded theory for critical inquiry. *Qualitative Inquiry, 23*(1), 34–45.

Cho, S. K. (1997). Converging stereotypes in racialized sexual harassment: Where the model minority meets Suzie Wong. *The Journal of Gender, Race, and Justice, 1*, 177–211.

Cho, S., Crenshaw, K. W., & McCall, L. (2013). Toward a field of intersectionality studies: Theory, applications, and praxis. *Signs: Journal of Women in Culture and Society, 38*(4), 785–810.

Coles, S. M., & Pasek, J. (2020). Intersectional invisibility revisited: How group prototypes lead to the erasure and exclusion of Black women. *Translational Issues in Psychological Science, 6*(4), 314.

Collins, P. H. (2000). Gender, Black feminism, and Black political economy. *The Annals of the American Academy of Political and Social Science, 568*(1), 41–53.

Collins, P. H. (2015). Intersectionality's definitional dilemmas. *Annual Review of Sociology, 41*(1), 1–20.

Collins, P. H. (2019). *Intersectionality as critical social theory.* Duke University Press.

Collins, P. H. (2020). Intersectionality as critical inquiry. *Companion to Feminist Studies*, 105–128.

Collins, P. H., & Bilge, S. (2020). *Intersectionality.* John Wiley & Sons.

Comte, A. (1880). *A general view of positivism.* Reeves & Turner.

Cortina, L. M., & Berdahl, J. L. (2008). Sexual harassment in organizations: A decade of research in review. *Handbook of Organizational Behavior, 1*, 469–497.

Crenshaw, K. (1989). Demarginalizing the intersection of race and sex: A Black feminist critique of antidiscrimination doctrine, feminist theory, and antiracist politics. *University of Chicago Legal Forum, 1989*, 139–167.

Crenshaw, K. (1991). Stanford Law Review Mapping the Margins: Intersectionality, Identity Politics, and Violence against Women of Source: *Stanford Law Review, 43*(6).

Denzin, N. K. (2015). Postmodernism and deconstructionism. In *Postmodernism and social inquiry* (pp. 182–202). Routledge.

Denzin, N. K. (2017). Critical qualitative inquiry. *Qualitative Inquiry, 23*(1), 8–16.

Dill, B. T. (2002). Work at the intersections of race, gender, ethnicity, and other dimensions of difference in higher education. *Connections: Newsletter of the Consortium on Race, Gender, and Ethnicity (Fall)*: 5–7.

Ellis, C., Adams, T. E., & Bochner, A. P. (2011). Autoethnography: An overview. *Historical Social Research/Historische sozialforschung*, 273–290.

Epstein, D., & Goodman, L. A. (2018). Discounting women: Doubting domestic violence survivors' credibility and dismissing their experiences. *University of Pennsylvania Law Review, 167*, 399.

Equal Employment Opportunity Commission (EEOC). (2018). Sexual harassment in our nation's workplaces. https://www.eeoc.gov/data/sexual-harassment-our-nations-workplaces#:~:text=In%20FY%202018%2C%20the%20EEOC,began%20increasing%20in%20FY%202018

Fehrenbacher, A. E., & Patel, D. (2020). Translating the theory of intersectionality into quantitative and mixed methods for empirical gender transformative research on health. *Culture, Health & Sexuality, 22*(sup1), 145–160.

Fiske, S. T., & Berdahl, J. (2007). Social power. *Social Psychology: Handbook of Basic Principles, 2*, 678–692.

Fiske, S. T. (2017). Prejudices in cultural contexts: Shared stereotypes (gender, age) versus variable stereotypes (race, ethnicity, religion). *Perspectives on Psychological Science, 12*(5), 791–799. https://doi.org/10.1177/1745691617708204

Fitzgerald, L. F., Swan, S., & Magley, V. J. (1997). But was it really sexual harassment? Legal, behavioral, and psychological definitions of the workplace victimization of women. In W. O'Donohue (Ed.), *Sexual harassment: Theory, research, and treatment* (pp. 5–28). Allyn & Bacon.

Fitzgerald, L. (2021). Unseen: The sexual harassment of low-income women in America. *Equality, Diversity and Inclusion: An International Journal, 39*(1), 5–16.

Goh, J. X., Bandt-Law, B., Cheek, N. N., Sinclair, S., & Kaiser, C. R. (2021). Narrow prototypes and neglected victims: Understanding perceptions of sexual harassment. *Journal of Personality and Social Psychology, 122*(5), 873–893.

Grace, D. (2014). Intersectionality-informed mixed methods research: A primer. *Health Sociology Review, 19*(4), 478–490.

Grant, J. M., Mottet, L. A., Tanis, J. J., & Min, D. (2011). Transgender discrimination survey. *National Center for Transgender Equality and National Gay and Lesbian Task Force*. Washington, DC, USA, *1*(1), 2–7.

Grzanka, P. R. (2014). *Intersectionality: A foundations and frontiers reader.* Routledge.

Grzanka, P. R., Flores, M. J., VanDaalen, R. A., & Velez, G. (2020). Intersectionality in psychology: Translational science for social justice. *Translational Issues in Psychological Science, 6*(4), 304–313.

GSS. (2019). *General social survey: An overview.* Statistics Canada. https://www 150.statcan.gc.ca/n1/pub/89f0115x/89f0115x2019001-eng.htm

Handy, J. (2006). Sexual harassment in small-town New Zealand: A qualitative study of three contrasting organizations. *Gender, Work & Organization, 13*(1), 1–24.

Harris-Perry, M. V. (2011). *Sister citizen: Shame, stereotypes, and Black women in America.* Yale University Press.

Heck, S. E. (2020). From Anita Hill to christine blasey ford: A reflection on lessons learned. *Equality, Diversity and Inclusion: An International Journal, 39*(1), 101–108.

Hill, C., & Silva, E. (2005). Drawing the line: sexual harassment on campus. *American Association of University Women Educational Foundation*, 1111 Sixteenth St. NW, Washington, DC 20036.

Ho, I. K., Dinh, K. T., Bellefontaine, S. A., & Irving, A. L. (2012). Sexual harassment and posttraumatic stress symptoms among Asian and White women. *Journal of Aggression, Maltreatment & Trauma, 21*(1), 95–113.

hooks, bell. (1984). *From margin to centre.* South End Press.

Hurtado, A. (1989). Relating to privilege: Seduction and rejection in the subordination of white women and women of color. *Signs: Journal of Women in Culture and Society, 14*(4), 833–855.

Israel, B. A., Schulz, A. J., Parker, E. A., & Becker, A. B. (1998). Review of community-based research: Assessing partnership approaches to improve public health. *Annual Review of Public Health, 19*(1), 173–202.

Jackson, S. J. (2016). (Re) imagining intersectional democracy from Black feminism to hashtag activism. *Women's Studies in Communication, 39*(4), 375–379.

Kearl, H. (2014). Unsafe and harassed in public spaces: A national street harassment report. *Stop Street Harassment.* http://www.stopstreetharassment.org/wp-content/uploads/2012/08/National-Street-Harassment-Report-November-29-20151.pdf

Kim, M., & Chung, A. Y. (2005). Consuming orientalism: Images of Asian/American women in multicultural advertising. *Qualitative Sociology, 28*, 67–91.

Klein, O., Arnal, C., Eagan, S., Bernard, P., & Gervais, S. J. (2021). Does tipping facilitate sexual objectification? The effect of tips on sexual harassment of bar and restaurant servers. *Equality, Diversity and Inclusion: An International Journal, 40*(4), 448–460.

Konik, J., & Cortina, L. M. (2008). Policing gender at work: Intersections of harassment based on sex and sexuality. *Social Justice Research*, *21*(3), 313–337.

Lee, A. S. (1991). Integrating positivist and interpretive approaches to organizational research. *Organization Science*, *2*(4), 342–365.

Lewis, J. A., & Neville, H. A. (2015). Construction and initial validation of the Gendered Racial Microaggressions Scale for Black women. *Journal of Counseling Psychology*, *62*(2), 289–302. https://doi.org/10.1037/cou0000062

Lewis, J. A., Mendenhall, R., Harwood, S. A., & Browne Huntt, M. (2016). "Ain't I a woman?" Perceived gendered racial microaggressions experienced by Black women. *The Counseling Psychologist*, *44*(5), 758–780.

Lim, S., Tsutakawa, M., & Donnelly, M. (Eds.). (1989). *The forbidden stitch: An Asian American women's anthology*. Calyx Books.

Lorde, A. (2012). *Sister outsider: Essays and speeches*. Crossing Press.

Madison, D. S. (2005). *Critical ethnography: Methods, ethics, and performance*. Sage

Malone, C. (2017). Will women in low-wage jobs get their #MeToo moment? *FiveThirtyEight*. https://fivethirtyeight.com/features/the-metoo-moment-hasnt-reached-women-in-low-wage-jobs-will-it/

McCall, L. (2005). The complexity of intersectionality. *Signs: Journal of Women in Culture and Society*, *30*(3), 1771–1800.

McCauley, H. L., Campbell, R., Buchanan, N. T., & Moylan, C. A. (2019). Advancing theory, methods, and dissemination in sexual violence research to build a more equitable future: An intersectional, community-engaged approach. *Violence Against Women*, *25*(16), 1906–1931.

McCluney, C. L., & Rabelo, V. C. (2019). Conditions of visibility: An intersectional examination of Black women's belongingness and distinctiveness at work. *Journal of Vocational Behavior*, *113*, 143–152.

McCormick-Huhn, K., Warner, L. R., Settles, I. H., & Shields, S. A. (2019). What if psychology took intersectionality seriously? Changing how psychologists think about participants. *Psychology of Women Quarterly*, *43*(4), 445–456.

Mead, G. H. (1934). Mind, self. *Society*.

Nash, J. C. (2008). Re-thinking intersectionality. *Feminist Review*, *89*(1), 1–15.

National Academies of Sciences, Engineering, and Medicine. (2018). Sexual harassment of women: Climate, culture, and consequences in academic sciences, engineering, and medicine-FAQ.

The New York Times. (2021, September). The surprising origins of #MeToo. https://www.nytimes.com/2021/09/10/books/tarana-burke-unbound-metoo.html

Nnawulezi, N., Lippy, C., Serrata, J., & Rodriguez, R. (2018). Doing equitable work in inequitable conditions: An introduction to a special issue on transformative research methods in gender-based violence. *Journal of Family Violence*, *33*(8), 507–513.

O'Neil, A., Sojo, V., Fileborn, B., Scovelle, A. J., & Milner, A. (2018). The# MeToo movement: An opportunity in public health? *The Lancet*, *391*(10140), 2587–2589.

Onwuachi-Willig, A. (2018). What about# UsToo?: The invisibility of race in the# MeToo movement. *Yale LJF*, *128*, 105.

Onwuegbuzie, A. J., Johnson, R. B., & Collins, K. M. (2009). Call for mixed analysis: A philosophical framework for combining qualitative and quantitative approaches *International Journal of Multiple Research Approaches*, *3*(2), 114–139.

Park, Y. S., Konge, L., & Artino, A. R. (2020). The positivism paradigm of research. *Academic Medicine*, *95*(5), 690–694.

Park, H. (2012). Interracial violence, western racialized masculinities, and the geopolitics of violence against women. *Social & Legal Studies*, *21*(4), 491–509.

Patel, N. (2008). Racialized sexism in the lives of Asian American women. In C. Raghavan, A. E. Edwards, & K. M. Vaz (Eds.), *Benefiting by design: Women of color in feminist psychological research* (pp. 116–128). Cambridge Scholars Publishing.

Patton, M. Q. (2005). *Qualitative research*. Encyclopedia of statistics in behavioral science.

Purdie-Vaughns, V., & Eibach, R. P. (2008). Intersectional invisibility: The distinctive advantages and disadvantages of multiple subordinate-group identities. *Sex Roles, 59*(5), 377–391.

Rabelo, V. C., & Cortina, L. M. (2014). Two sides of the same coin: Gender harassment and heterosexist harassment in LGBQ work lives. *Law and Human Behavior, 38*(4), 378–391.

RCMP. (2015). *Missing and murdered aboriginal women: 2015 update to the national operational overview*. Royal Canadian Mounted Police. https://www.rcmp-grc.gc.ca/en/missing-and-murdered-aboriginal-women-2015-update-national-operational-overview

Reed-Danahay, D. (2009). Anthropologists, education, and autoethnography. *Reviews in Anthropology, 38*(1), 28–47.

Reynolds-Dobbs, W., Thomas, K. M., & Harrison, M. S. (2008). From mammy to superwoman: Images that hinder Black women's career development. *Journal of Career Development, 35*(2), 129–150.

Richardson, B. K., & Taylor, J. (2009). Sexual harassment at the intersection of race and gender: A theoretical model of the sexual harassment experiences of women of color. *Western Journal of Communication, 73*(3), 248–272.

Rosaldo, R. (2004). Grief and a Headhunter's Rage. *Death, Mourning, and Burial: A Cross-Cultural Reader*, 167–178.

Rosette, A. S., de Leon, R. P., Koval, C. Z., & Harrison, D. A. (2018). Intersectionality: Connecting experiences of gender with race at work. *Research in Organizational Behavior, 38*, 1–22.

Rosette, A. S., Koval, C. Z., Ma, A., & Livingston, R. (2016). Race matters for women leaders: Intersectional effects on agentic deficiencies and penalties. *The Leadership Quarterly, 27*(3), 429–445.

Rossie, A., Tucker, J., & Patrick, K. (2018). Out of the shadows: An analysis of sexual harassment charges filed by working women. *National Women's Law Center*. Retrieved December, 22, 2019.

Rudman, L. A., & Glick, P. (2001). Prescriptive gender stereotypes and backlash toward agentic women. *Journal of Social Issues, 57*(4), 743–762.

Salzman, P. C. (2002). On reflexivity. *American Anthropologist, 104*(3), 805–811.

Sambaraju, R. (2020). "I would have taken this to my grave, like most women": Reporting sexual harassment during the# MeToo movement in India. *Journal of Social Issues, 76*(3), 603–631.

Scheim, A. I., & Bauer, G. R. (2019). The intersectional discrimination index: Development and validation of measures of self-reported enacted and anticipated discrimination for intercategorical analysis. *Social Science & Medicine, 226*, 225–235.

Scott, N. A., & Siltanen, J. (2017). Intersectionality and quantitative methods: Assessing regression from a feminist perspective. *International Journal of Social Research Methodology, 20*(4), 373–385.

Settles, I. H., & Buchanan, N. T. (2014). Multiple groups, multiple identities, and intersectionality. *The Oxford Handbook of Multicultural Identity, 1*, 160–180.

Settles, I. H., Buchanan, N. T., & Dotson, K. (2019). Scrutinized but not recognized: (In) visibility and hypervisibility experiences of faculty of color. *Journal of Vocational Behavior, 113*, 62–74.

Settles, I. H., Warner, L. R., Buchanan, N. T., & Jones, M. K. (2020). Understanding psychology's resistance to intersectionality theory using a framework of epistemic exclusion and invisibility. *Journal of Social Issues, 76*(4), 796–813.

Sesko, A. K., & Biernat, M. (2010). Prototypes of race and gender: The invisibility of Black women. *Journal of Experimental Social Psychology, 46*(2), 356–360.

Shields, S. A. (2008). Gender: An intersectionality perspective. *Sex Roles, 59*, 301–311.

Shimizu, C. P. (2007). The hypersexuality of race: Performing Asian/American. In *Women on screen and scene*. Duke University Press.

Shrake, E. (2006). Unmasking the self: Struggling with the model minority stereotype and lotus blossom image. In G. Li, & G. Beckett, *"Strangers" in the academy: Asian women scholars in higher education* (pp. 178–194). Stylus.

Silverschanz, P., Cortina, L. M., Konik, J., & Magley, V. J. (2008). Slurs, snubs, and queer jokes: Incidence and impact of heterosexist harassment in academia. *Sex Roles, 58*(3), 179–191.

Smith, A. N., Watkins, M. B., Ladge, J. J., & Carlton, P. (2019). Making the invisible visible: Paradoxical effects of intersectional invisibility on the career experiences of executive Black women. *Academy of Management Journal, 62*(6), 1705–1734.

Spierings, N. (2012). The inclusion of quantitative techniques and diversity in the mainstream of feminist research. *European Journal of Women's Studies, 19*(3), 331–347.

Steffy, B. D., & Grimes, A. J. (1986). A critical theory of organization science. *Academy of Management Review, 11*(2), 322–336.

Tajfel, H., & Turner, J. C. (1978). Intergroup behavior. *Introducing Social Psychology, 401*(466), 149–178.

Tillman, S., Bryant-Davis, T., Smith, K., & Marks, A. (2010). Shattering silence: Exploring barriers to disclosure for African American sexual assault survivors. *Trauma, Violence, & Abuse, 11*(2), 59–70.

Townsend, T. G., Neilands, T. B., Thomas, A. J., & Jackson, T. R. (2010). I'm no Jezebel; I am young, gifted, and Black: Identity, sexuality, and Black girls. *Psychology of Women Quarterly, 34*(3), 273–285.

Truth, S. (1851). Ain't I a woman? Retrieved from https://www.nps. gov/wori/learn/historyculture/sojourner-truth.htm

Tuerkheimer, D. (2017). Incredible women: Sexual violence and the credibility discount. *University of Pennsylvania Law Review, 166*, 1.

van Doorn, J., & Koster, N. N. (2019). Emotional victims and the impact on credibility: A systematic review. *Aggression and Violent Behavior, 47*, 74–89.

Wallerstein, N. B., & Duran, B. (2006). Using community-based participatory research to address health disparities. *Health Promotion Practice, 7*(3), 312–323.

Williams, J. (2021). Maximizing #MeToo: Intersectionality & the movement. *Boston College Law* Review, 62(6), 1797–1864.

Woods, K. C., Buchanan, N. T., & Settles, I. H. (2009). Sexual harassment across the color line: Experiences and outcomes of cross-versus intraracial sexual harassment among Black women. *Cultural Diversity and Ethnic Minority Psychology, 15*(1), 67.

Yamada, M. (1981). Invisibility is an unnatural disaster. In Moraga, C., & Anzaldúa, G. (Eds.), *This Bridge Called My Back: Writings by Radical Women of Color*. State University of New York Press. (pp. 35–40). https://doi.org/10.2307/jj.18252715

Yuval-Davis, N. (2015). Situated intersectionality: A reflection on Ange-Marie Hancock's forthcoming book: Intersectionality—an intellectual history. *New Political Science, 37*(4), 637–642.

9

MASCULINITY AND THE CYCLE OF SEXUAL HARASSMENT AGAINST MEN

Natalya M. Alonso, Nicky Cheung,
Darius M. Washington, and Margaret S. Stockdale

Are Men Different?

The most widely publicized #MeToo cases spotlighted severe and disturbing behavior by men against women. Film producer Harvey Weinstein sexually harassed and assaulted dozens of women over his career (Farrow, 2017). Bill O'Reilly was forced to resign from *Fox News* after multiple harassment settlements involving women at the network came to light (Steel & Schmidt, 2017). Similarly, Matt Lauer was fired from NBC due to allegations that he sexually harassed numerous female employees (Setoodeh & Wagmeister, 2017). Although these cases highlight a deeply important issue worthy of attention, they center on women as targets, obscuring the ways in which men may also be targeted by sexual harassment (SH). However, research demonstrates many men suffer SH, though reported prevalence rates vary by context (e.g., from 8.7%, 42%, and 82.6% of men in the federal workforce, US military, and policing respectively; Cortina & Areguin, 2021). More broadly, recognizing SH against men has the potential to challenge popular assumptions about harassment, revealing new insights into the dynamics underlying the harassment of people of all genders.

In this review, we highlight the ways in which SH against men is similar to and unique from harassment against women.[1] We argue that masculinity lies at the core of many of these differences, informing target, perpetrator, and bystander perspectives on the behavior. Masculinity refers to dominant beliefs about what it means to be a man, including prescriptions about how men should behave and the traits they should possess (Prentice & Carranza, 2002). By focusing on masculinity in differentiating the experience

DOI: 10.4324/9781003300953-11

of male targets of harassment, we reveal the potentially cyclical nature of SH against men and suggest new opportunities for furthering research that considers a wider range of targets.

To facilitate this, our review is organized into four sections including the perspectives of (1) targets, (2) perpetrators, and (3) bystanders, and (4) practical implications. In the first section, we discuss why certain men are more likely to be harassed, the differences in both frequency and type of SH experienced by men and women, and how male and female targets differ in experiencing and responding to SH. Troublingly, we highlight that SH can be experienced as a masculinity threat to men; that is, it can be taken as a threat to their standing as a man. In the second section, we focus on perpetrators of SH against men including their motives and characteristics and how these perpetrators are similar and different from those targeting women. In this section, we draw on past research demonstrating that harassment can be a way of reasserting threatened masculinity. This points to a potential cycle, where men who are harassed experience a masculinity threat, which may cause them to engage in similar behaviors trying to reassert their masculinity. The third section explores how masculinity may inform bystanders' perceptions of and responses to witnessing harassment against men. We argue that masculinity may weaken bystander support for corrective actions, thus enabling the potential cycle of harassment against men to persist. The review closes with a discussion of the need for both scholars and the public more broadly to acknowledge SH against men as a legitimate issue and the practical implications that follow.

Male Targets of Harassment

Sexual Harassment Types and Prevalence

Although research consistently finds women are subject to harassment at greater rates than men,[2] men do suffer harassment and negative outcomes from social-sexual behavior at work (Cortina & Areguin, 2021). Various classifications of harassment have been delineated and applied to male targets. Chief among these is the tripartite model composed of gender harassment, unwanted sexual attention, and sexual coercion (Fitzgerald et al., 1988; Gelfand et al., 1995). Under this framework, gender harassment refers to verbal or nonverbal actions that convey insulting, demeaning, or degrading attitudes about men and women at work, such as sexist joking, displaying pornographic content, or making obscene gestures. Unwanted sexual attention pertains to expressions of sexual interest that are unwelcome and unrequited, including repeated requests for dates, nonconsensual touching, or sexual assault. Lastly, sexual coercion refers to the promise of rewards or the threat of punishment in exchange for sexual favors at work, such as threatening demotion unless sexual acts are performed. These three dimensions are typically studied using the Sexual Experiences Questionnaire (SEQ; Fitzgerald et al., 1995), a scale developed to measure women's experiences of harassment but that has sometimes been adapted to capture the experience of male targets.

Research on male targets documents that, similar to women, men tend to experience gender harassment most frequently of the three types of harassment (U.S. Merit Systems Protection Board Office of Policy and Evaluation, 2016). However, gender harassment against men often takes a different form than that against women, highlighting the role of masculinity as central to men's experiences of harassment. Specifically, Waldo et al. (1998) extended the SEQ framework to develop the Sexual Harassment of Men (SHOM) scale drawing on insights about what men may find uniquely threatening discovered in an earlier study (Berdahl et al., 1996). In addition to rewording some of the SEQ items, these authors added items pertaining to what Berdahl and Moore (2006) later termed "not man enough harassment," including "ridiculing men for acting too 'feminine' and pressuring them to engage in stereotypical forms of 'masculine' behavior" (p. 61). Thus, gender harassment—the most prevalent form of SH against men—often centers on punishing men who fail to meet masculine standards and pressuring them to conform to these ideals (Stockdale et al., 1999). In short, harassment against men is often a tool for policing male gender norms.

Waldo et al. (1998) also found that men were at least as likely to suffer harassment from other men as they were from women, particularly for certain types of harassment. Specifically, men were more likely to experience lewd comments (a form of gender harassment) and not man enough harassment from other men, whereas they experienced sexual advance type harassment (sexual coercion and unwanted sexual attention) from women and men. Thus, unlike women who mostly suffer harassment from men (other-sex SH), men suffer harassment from men (same-sex SH) at least as much, if not more, than they do from women (Clarke et al., 2016; Dubois et al., 1998; Kabat-Farr & Cortina, 2014; Magley et al., 1999; Stockdale, 1998; Stockdale et al., 1999; Waldo et al., 1998). This means that same-sex SH is of particular concern in examining male targets. The prevalence of same-sex SH against men supports theorizing that SH, against both men and women, is a technology of sexism used mostly by men to maintain the gender order and their position within it (Berdahl, 2007; Franke, 1996). This understanding is further reflected in the documented antecedents of SH against men.

Predictors of Sexual Harassment Against Men

Limited research has examined the individual and contextual antecedents of SH against men, but much of what is known aligns with the above theorizing that the behavior is a tool for reinforcing the gender hierarchy privileging men and masculinity. This research finds that men who do not conform to traditional gender roles are particularly likely to be targeted by SH, particularly by other men (Berdahl et al., 1996; Berdahl, 2007; Franke, 1996; Waldo et al., 1998). For example, Fitzgerald, Drasgow et al. (1999) found that both men and women in gender atypical military jobs were subject to greater harassment. Similarly, Holland et al. (2016) showed that men who engaged in feminist activism were at increased risk of SH. Uggen and Blackstone (2004) further found that financially vulnerable men were disproportionately targeted for harassment relative to those with more financial means, as were those in more egalitarian marriages.

Other research has explored whether race and/or ethnicity affect men's risk of being targeted by harassment, mostly finding that members of marginalized ethnic and racial groups are disproportionately targeted for harassment. For example, Fitzgerald, Magley et al. (1999) found that Indigenous and Black military men may be at greater risk for SH relative to White men. Berdahl and Moore (2006) found that identifying as an ethnic minority (defined as "Asians, Caribbeans, Africans, Latin Americans, Aboriginals, Arabs, and Pacific Islanders"; p. 430) was marginally significantly related to men and women experiencing greater SH and significantly related to experiencing more "not man enough" harassment specifically. Indeed, a recent survey of over 100,000 US undergraduate students found slightly higher rates of harassment among American Indian or Alaska Native (42.3%) and Black (41.3%) men compared to White men (36.8%), who suffered more harassment than Asian men (29.4%; Association of American Universities, 2020). Taking a contextual lens, Berdahl and Moore (2006) further found that being racially or ethnically dissimilar from their workgroup was related to experiencing more SH. This finding aligns with other research arguing racially dissimilar men and women are categorized as outgroup members and disproportionately targeted for harassment (Bergman & Henning, 2008).

These past findings on race and ethnicity suggest there may be further interesting dynamics to explore by considering specific forms of SH and how those differ depending on men's multiple identities (see also Chapters 8 and 10 on intersectionality). For example, Berdahl and Moore (2006) collapsed across ethnicities to create the "minority" category, but racial and ethnic categories are associated with specific stereotypes that may influence these relationships. For instance, Black men tend to be stereotyped as hypermasculine and can be perceived more favorably when they seem less, not more, masculine (Livingston & Pearce, 2009). This suggests that they may be less beholden to masculine prescriptions and consequently less subject to "not man enough" harassment. On the other hand, these stereotypes may elevate expectations of masculinity, eliciting greater backlash when these expectations are violated. Similarly, it is unclear how these different dimensions may inform the impact of and responses to SH against men, the topic we turn to next.

Impact and Responses

Past research has been fairly consistent in reporting that men, on average, tend to find the same sexually harassing behaviors less bothersome than women and are less likely to label these behaviors harassment (Berdahl et al., 1996; Gutek et al., 1990; Kath et al., 2009; Konrad & Gutek, 1986; Waldo et al., 1998). Indeed, an earlier meta-analysis of 62 studies found that women label a broader range of social-sexual behaviors harassing compared to men (Rotundo et al., 2001), a finding that subsequent studies continue to support (Blackstone et al., 2009; Shechory Bitton & Ben Shaul, 2013; Strom et al., 2022).

Berdahl et al. (1996) proposed a power-based theory to explain this difference in labeling between men and women. These authors argued that behavior is seen as harassing to the degree that it threatens the target's power and social standing. Thus, different behaviors tend to be experienced as threatening by men and women. For women, behavior that associates femininity with subordination is proposed to be threatening, whereas for men, it is actions that challenge male dominance. Since sexual relations tend to reinforce male dominance by positioning women as subordinate, this theorizing explains why heterosexual social-sexual behavior tends to be more threatening to women. In support of this argument, scholars have found that certain types of harassment are more upsetting to men. For example, Stockdale et al. (1999) found that men found harassment from other men more bothersome than that from women, possibly because this type of harassment poses more of a threat to their masculine standing.

Scholars have also explored contextual moderators impacting these processes. Konrad and Gutek (1986) found that men are especially unlikely to label behavior from women harassment when they worked in male-dominated environments compared to gender integrated or female-dominated workplaces. However, since Konrad and Gutek only measured sexually harassing behaviors toward men from women, it is unclear how same-sex harassment would be experienced in these different job–gender contexts. Taken together, more research is needed to understand the contextual moderators impacting men's evaluations of potentially sexually harassing behaviors, and whether these differ from those of women or by perpetrator sex.

Regardless of differences in labeling harassment, Magley et al. (1999) found that for a given level of harassment, men and women suffered similar negative psychological, health, and job-related outcomes. This is consistent with more recent research showing that sex did not moderate the relationship between experiencing SH and negative outcomes (De Haas, 2009). Similarly, Berdahl and Aquino (2009) demonstrated that men were more likely to report enjoying social-sexual behavior at work than women, especially when it was initiated by women. Nonetheless, experiencing social-sexual behavior at work was negatively associated with psychological and work-related well-being. These authors suggest that this could be because, regardless of enjoyment, social-sexual behavior may be implicitly tied to "negative concepts and feelings, such as shame and vulnerability, dominance and subordination, or objectification and derogation" that facilitate these poor outcomes (p. 44). These studies imply that men may be more blind to the harms of social-sexual behavior despite negative consequences for them.

Given that they tend to be less sensitive to the harms of social-sexual behavior at work, male targets may be less willing and able to take steps to address behaviors that constitute harassment. However, engaging in feminist activism can buffer the negative effects of SH on men's psychological well-being (Holland et al., 2016). These authors propose this may be because activist men are more aware of the problematic gender dynamics driving harassment and thus are less likely to blame themselves for being targeted. This suggests there may be greater opportunities for men and women to ally together to prevent harassment and mitigate its negative effects. Future research might fruitfully explore how individuals and organizations can encourage coalition building between men and women to counter SH. For example, it would be interesting to explore whether over time, men engaging in feminist activism at work can shift organizational norms, reducing harassment against both men and women.

Other research has found differences between men and women in terms of how they respond to SH. Interestingly, Blackstone et al. (2009) found that men and women were equally likely to report harassment to their supervisors, but that reporting to a coworker was much more predictive of also reporting to a supervisor for men than women. This suggests that, unlike women, men tend not to discuss harassment with their coworkers unless they plan to also report the harassment formally. This research highlights that there may be greater barriers to men discussing harassment with their coworkers, perhaps because it runs counter to masculine norms to admit to being upset by harassment. In line with this explanation, Stockdale (1998) found that women and men suffer different consequences for using confrontive strategies, such as reporting the harassment, and passive strategies, like avoiding the perpetrator. For men, the use of confrontive strategies tended to exacerbate, not attenuate, the negative work-related outcomes (e.g., getting fired, denied promotion) associated with SH frequency. The authors propose a "wimpy male" (p. 532) effect to explain this latter finding. That is, men who confront may be seen as insufficiently masculine, eliciting retaliation and worse work-related outcomes.

In summary, those men who are already marginalized because they are not stereotypically masculine, are financially vulnerable, or are racially dissimilar from their peers are at higher risk for harassment. This suggests that men with the least resources to cope with harassment may be especially targeted. Further, although men are more likely to view social-sexual behavior at work positively, they experience similar negative outcomes from these behaviors. Troublingly, some research suggests men are less forthcoming about harassment and suffer penalties when they confront the behavior, likely because being a victim of harassment runs counter to masculine prescriptions of dominance and hypersexuality. Taken together, these findings point to the centrality of masculinity in shaping the experiences and responses of male targets of harassment. Masculinity is similarly central for perpetrators of harassment against men, the topic we turn to in the next section.

Perpetrators Targeting Men

Individual Perpetrator Characteristics

Due to the comparative lack of research focusing on male targets of harassment as opposed to female targets, we know relatively little about those who harass men and their motivations. Nonetheless, theoretical discussions of SH against men offer insights into *why* men are sexually harassed and potentially by whom. Motives for harassment fall generally into two categories—approach (come-on) and rejection (put-down; Fitzgerald et al., 1995; Stockdale, 2005). Approach harassment implies a desire to obtain sexual access to the target and usually takes the form of unwanted sexual attention or sexual coercion. Rejection-based harassment implies an intent to ridicule, demean, and belittle the target and often takes the form of gender harassment. Both these types of harassment motives are linked to theorizing on power in that they can be seen as attempts to exercise and maintain power. Approach harassment implies an abuse of power, one that can serve to maintain male dominance by objectifying the target (Berdahl, 2007; Scarduzio et al., 2018). Rejection harassment also concerns power in that threats to the masculine hierarchy, to male power and privilege, and to heteronormative masculine ideals motivate harassment of men to police those systems of power.

In support of the power-SH link, research has shown that powerful people, even those primed to feel momentarily powerful, feel unconstrained in their pursuit of self-relevant goals and automatically associate feeling powerful with feelings of sexiness (Bargh et al., 1995; Galinsky et al., 2003; Keltner et al., 2003; Kunstman & Maner, 2011; Stockdale et al., 2020). Sexy-powerful feelings increase intentions to engage in SH against both men and women (Stockdale et al., 2020). Stockdale and her colleagues primed men and women to feel powerful and then had them complete measures of SH intentions. Female, heterosexual participants rated the likelihood of harassing male targets, and male, heterosexual participants rated the likelihood of harassing female targets. The effects of power priming on harassment intentions, mediated by sexy-powerful feelings, were not moderated by participant sex, suggesting that the effects of power on harassment intentions are ubiquitous. In a follow-up study with a sample of participants who identified as lesbian, gay, bisexual, or queer (73 identified as women and 30 as men), Dinh and Stockdale (2022) found similar effects: Power priming increased sexy-powerful feelings, which in turn increased intentions to harass same-gender targets. The effects were not moderated by participant gender.

Threats to one's standing in the gender hierarchy are another demonstrated driver of SH, especially by men (Alonso, 2018; Berdahl, 2007; Maass et al., 2003). For example, having one's masculinity called into question can trigger men to harass other men (Alonso, 2018). This finding is particularly concerning given that being targeted by gender harassment can be experienced as a masculinity threat, evoking compensatory masculine behavior (Funk & Werhun, 2011). This suggests that male targets may experience a masculinity threat and engage in harassment themselves to reassert their threatened masculinity. Little research so far has examined the potentially cyclical nature of male-male harassment.

Other research examining the individual differences predicting a proclivity to harass have identified commonalities between those inclined to harass both men and women. Preliminary research on a new measure of SH perpetration, the Sex-Based Harassment Inventory (SBHI; Grabowski et al., 2022), showed that such masculinity threats increased men's inclination to engage in both gender harassment and unwanted sexual attention. The preliminary version of the SBHI included two scenarios in which men were the targets, and the final measure included one such scenario.

One of us (Peggy Stockdale) averaged ratings for both types of harassment across the two scenarios involving male targets and examined correlations between intentions to harass these male targets and various individual difference measures. Statistically significant correlations were found with male gender identity, benevolent sexism, and hostile sexism. The strongest predictor, however, was Pryor's (1987) Likelihood to Sexually Harass scale, which measures the propensity to harass female targets, suggesting that men's propensity to harass other men is driven by the same constellation of traits and attitudes that shape proclivities to harass women. This again suggests possible opportunities for greater allyship between men and women in combatting SH, a topic ripe for future research. This individually based theorizing is complemented by contextual perspectives specifying the conditions under which perpetrators are most likely to harass men.

Contextual Risk Factors for Perpetration

Similar to harassment targeting women, working in an organizational climate tolerant of SH is a strong predictor of SH targeting men (Bergman et al., 2002; Holland et al., 2016), although this effect can be attenuated by a high organizational justice climate (Rubino et al., 2018). Likewise, in a sample of men and women, Glick et al. (2018) found that masculinity contest culture—the extent to which the workplace valorizes stereotypically hypermasculine ideals—was significantly related to greater SH. This is in line with theorizing that contexts that make traditional gender roles salient encourage SH against both men and women (Berdahl et al., 2018; McDonald, 2012; Stockdale et al., 1999). This suggests that male-typed occupations, those in which work requirements align with stereotypical notions of masculinity, such as construction, high technology, and the military, may be particularly rife with harassment against men.

In line with the theorized link between SH and environments that make salient traditional gender roles, much research has focused on the role of organizational gender demography in predicting harassment. Unlike SH against women, which has been consistently linked with male-dominated workplaces (Cortina & Areguin, 2021), the results for male targets of harassment have been more mixed. Recently, Rubino et al. (2018) found that sex dissimilarity from peers positively related to SH experiences for both men and women, especially when the climate of the workgroup did not support collective justice. This is consistent with early SH research showing that greater contact between men and women was associated with increased incidence of harassment (Gutek et al., 1990).

However, these findings are qualified by other work suggesting these effects depend on perpetrator sex (Stockdale et al., 1999). Perhaps unsurprisingly, Stockdale et al. (1999) found that men experiencing other-sex harassment were more likely to work in less male-dominated work-places relative to those suffering same-sex harassment or no harassment. However, those men experiencing same-sex harassment were more likely to work in a male-dominated context relative to the other two groups. This suggests that whereas sex dissimilarity may predict SH for women, the relationships for men depend on perpetrator sex, an important consideration given that same-sex harassment against men is prevalent (Kabat-Farr & Cortina, 2014; Magley et al., 1999; Stockdale, 1998; Stockdale et al., 1999; Waldo et al., 1998).

To summarize, perpetrators of harassment against men are much like the perpetrators targeting women. There are both power and gender hierarchy explanations for harassment of men. Power may unleash sexy-powerful feelings in women and men, encouraging them to impose their sexualized will upon other men and women. Masculinity threats and threats to the gender hierarchy motivate harassment against men as well as women. Contexts that make masculinity salient are associated with more SH against both men and women. Taken together, these findings suggest that although some forms of harassment against men may differ from that of harassment of women, there may be an underlying unifying theory of SH perpetration centered on masculinity threats and power. Masculinity also informs how bystanders may perceive harassment against men, the topic we turn to next.

Bystanders to Sexual Harassment Targeting Men

Bystander Perceptions

Target sex significantly impacts bystanders' perceptions of harassment. For example, compared to scenarios where women are targeted by men, scenarios where men are targeted by women are seen as less harassing and are less likely to be labeled as harassment (Baird et al., 1995; Gilbert, 2005; Runtz & O'Donnell, 2003). This bias against recognizing harassment toward men has even been found in lawyers presented with identical case descriptions only differing in perpetrator-target sex (Shechory-Bitton & Zvi, 2020). Further, male targets who report SH are less liked, less likely to be believed, and subject to greater backlash than female targets who report their harassment (Madera et al., 2007). Compared to male targets, the SH of female targets is also seen as less acceptable when motivated by prejudice (Brassel et al., 2019). This may be because Studzinska and Hilton (2017) found that male targets of sexual coercion are perceived to suffer less than female targets. These authors also found that perpetrators who target women are evaluated more negatively.

Thus, perhaps because of the incongruence between masculinity and being the victim of harassment, bystanders are less willing to label a scenario harassment and respond less favorably to male targets of harassment. In line with this explanation, DeSouza and Solberg (2004) found that harassment targeting homosexual males, who tend to be stereotyped as less masculine, was rated as more harassing and in need of further investigation than that involving heterosexual male targets. This suggests that masculinity may explain lukewarm reactions to harassment against heterosexual men. Other research found that observers who held negative attitudes toward homosexuality were more likely to perceive harassment in same-sex scenarios (Castillo et al., 2011). This implies an assumption that sexual desire drives harassment. Thus, it may be interesting to explore the mental models observers hold about harassment and how this impacts their perceptions of harassing scenarios involving male and female targets in future research.

Importantly, bystander experiences can further influence their willingness to label scenarios as harassment. The availability and recall of female SH targets—even from media representation (as in the case of #MeToo)—increased the likelihood that bystanders labeled scenarios depicting social-sexual workplace conduct harassment (Wiener et al., 2005). Although Wiener et al. (2005) did not use male targets in their study, these findings suggest that researchers may want to examine these processes for male targets. Indeed, such findings may be particularly important considering the potentially self-perpetuating effect that not recognizing men as targets of SH (e.g., in the media) may have on recall availability—an issue especially pertinent considering the #MeToo movement's relative focus on female targets.

Perceptions of sexually harassing scenarios can also differ depending on the gender of the bystander themselves with likely implications for the targets of harassment. For example, women perceive and identify inappropriate male-on-male behaviors as SH more than men (DeSouza & Solberg, 2004; Shechory Bitton & Ben Shaul, 2013). Men are also less likely to view possibly harassing interactions between a female perpetrator and male target as SH (Runtz & O'Donnell, 2003). This may be because male bystanders are invested in masculine norms that suggest such attention is welcome. In a study by Smirles (2004), male bystanders attributed more responsibility to the target and less to the perpetrator compared to female bystanders, regardless of perpetrator or target gender. Male observers also assign significantly less blame to the organization than female observers (Plater & Thomas, 1998), suggesting that they may be less willing to support systematic change targeting the organization.

Since men are more likely to form social ties with other men than women (McPherson et al., 2001), these bystander sex effects have troubling implications for the social support men may receive when they confide in others about harassment. Specifically, this suggests that the friends and confidants of male targets may be less likely to take allegations of harassment seriously and label scenarios as harassment. This implies that male targets may have fewer opportunities for social support and may be perceived as more responsible for their own harassment by those closest to them. To this end, future research might explore social network effects in terms of who men seek support from and how different sources of support may help or hinder them.

Other research has found environmental factors can influence bystander perceptions as well. For instance, workplace gender demography can alter judgments about male-to-male SH complaints, such that men—but not women—in a male-dominated (90% men) setting perceived less evidence of harassment than those who observed the same misconduct in a more gender-balanced (55% men) workplace (Wiener et al., 2012). More broadly, Strom et al. (2022) found that both men and women who worked in an industry rife with SH were less likely to label behaviors as harassment, as were those who had previously worked in an industry with a high prevalence of SH. However, this effect was reduced for those who believed their organization had implemented policies against harassment (Strom et al., 2022). Unfortunately, Strom et al.'s (2022) findings were not differentiated between male and female bystanders or targets, leaving little insight as to whether such environmental factors influence labeling for men and women differently. This is unfortunate since bystander perceptions are important, especially because of the links to observers' subsequent responses.

Bystander Responses

Punishment

Unsurprisingly, gender differences are again implicated in determining punishment. For example, female perpetrators who harassed male targets were more severely punished compared to those who harassed other women (Gilbert, 2005). These authors suggest this effect is due to gender role norms about sexuality that suggest women should not be the pursuer in heterosexual encounters. Similar findings were uncovered using a sample of mock jurors who were exposed to a hostile work environment case involving SH—women harassing men were more likely to be found guilty compared to men who harassed women, regardless of bystander gender (Wayne et al., 2001). Taken together, these findings suggest that gender role norms, both masculinity and femininity, are at play in bystander reactions to harassment. Although harassment claims by male targets may be less likely to be believed, taken seriously, and acted upon, women may be disproportionately penalized for harassing men since this violates feminine sexual prescriptions. Gender roles, and specifically masculinity, are further implicated in bystanders' willingness to intervene.

Intervention

Bystander intentions to intervene, for example, by reporting SH, remains an emerging area of interest among researchers (see also Chapter 3 on bystanders). Brassel et al. (2019) found an association between perceived harassment acceptability and bystander recommendations to report, such that the less acceptable the scenario the more likely it is that the target is suggested to report the harassment. Unfortunately for male targets, there is a tendency to view SH toward female targets as more motivated by prejudice and consequently less acceptable, leaving the SH of men at risk of being minimized (Brassel et al., 2019). Thus, when the target is male, bystanders may be less willing to suggest and support reporting the harassment (Brassel et al., 2019).

In summary, harassment against men is often minimized by bystanders. The same behavior tends to be seen as less harassing and more acceptable when it targets men compared to women, perhaps in part because men are perceived to suffer less from harassment. Men who allege harassment are also less likely to be believed than women targets are. Since men tend to be closest to other men and male bystanders are especially unlikely to take seriously harassment, male targets may be further disadvantaged in their ability to receive support compared to women. Masculinity is at the core of many of these dynamics, impacting why harassment against men is not labeled as such, male bystander responses, and perceptions of male targets.

The Cycle of Harassment Against Men

Our review highlights the central role of masculinity in informing SH against men from the perspective of targets, perpetrators, and bystanders. Accounting for the role of masculinity explicates how SH against men is both different from and similar to harassment against women. Like harassment targeting women, men who do not conform to traditional gender norms and are seen as insufficiently masculine tend to be targeted by harassment. Being targeted by harassment in turn can be experienced as a masculinity threat. Research on perpetrators suggests masculinity threats can lead some men to engage in defensive efforts to restore their masculinity, including engaging in SH against men. Because masculinity is at odds with stereotypes about targets, and men are presumed to enjoy sexual behavior, bystanders may be less willing to support and intervene on behalf of male targets, enabling ongoing harassment. Finally, witnessing harassment against men, particularly those seen as insufficiently masculine, may heighten the pressure to be seen as masculine at work (Berdahl et al., 2018), perpetuating the cycle. This review offers a number of future directions for research exploring the potential opportunities of recognizing SH against men and disrupting the cycle (see Table 9.1 for key areas of opportunity).

TABLE 9.1 Key opportunities for future research

Key research opportunities	
Uncover opportunities for men and women to collaborate against harassment	By recognizing that sexual harassment is not just a "women's issue," explore opportunities to foster solidarity between men and women and whether knowledge of harassment against men shifts harmful beliefs about harassment generally
Examine intersectional effects in terms of how multiple identities may impact male harassment experiences	By accounting for men's multiplex identities, assess how masculinity may interact with the target's other identities based in race, ethnicity, sexual orientation, gender identity, etc. to inform experiences of and responses to harassment
Explore interventions to disrupt stereotypes and promote bystander intervention	By accounting for men as targets of harassment, investigate possible interventions to change gendered assumptions about who is targeted by harassment and increase willingness to intervene on behalf of male victims
Examine sources of support for men and women targeted by harassment and how this affects them	By recognizing men as targets of harassment, consider how and from whom they seek social support and how this might be different from the experiences of women targeted by harassment
Investigate the potentially cyclical nature of harassment against men	By clarifying the role of masculinity in harassment, examine the potential cycle of harassment against men and whether de-emphasizing or redefining masculinity at work is an effective tool for disrupting the cycle

Practical Implications

From a practical perspective, this review highlights the necessity for organizational members to recognize and take seriously harassment against men. Directly discussing harassment against men in trainings and using examples involving male targets may help normalize the idea that men can also be targeted by harassment. However, as with any SH training, how the training is delivered matters greatly (see Cortina & Areguin, 2021, for best practices). Specific to addressing SH against men, Bovill et al. (2020) found that open discussion in a group may be a particularly effective method for combating stereotypes and misconceptions that prevent individuals from seeing men as victims. Since these stereotypes prevent decision-makers from labeling and taking seriously harassment against men, scholars and practitioners may explore the possibility of making SH cases "gender blind" so the perpetrator-target gender composition is not known while assessing the evidence.

Expanding the idea of who is targeted for harassment and by whom, for example highlighting cases of heterosexual male-on-male harassment, may also help to dispel SH myths suggesting harassment is driven by sexual desire. Further, given the highlighted role of masculinity in driving harassment against women but also the potential cycle of harassment against men, practitioners may explore opportunities to address both forms of harassment by de-emphasizing masculinity at work. Efforts to align rewarded behaviors with bona fide performance criteria, rather than adherence to gender norms (Berdahl et al., 2018; Ely & Meyerson, 2010), may prove useful in reducing harassment against men and women. At the same time, more theoretical work is needed to explain why men are sometimes harassed in female-dominated industries (Chang & Jeong, 2021) in which masculinity may be less salient.

Finally, organizations should consider whether there are opportunities to build coalitions between men and women in preventing and responding to harassment, for example, by pointing to their common interests in ending this behavior. Such an approach may be particularly helpful if SH against men is characterized by pluralistic ignorance (Miller & McFarland, 1987). That is, since men are less forthcoming about their harassment experiences than women, men and women alike may be under the false impression that men do not find such behavior bothersome, hindering alliances between them. In sum, recognizing SH against men, a topic that has been largely missed by the #MeToo movement in its focus on women, has the potential to make the workplace a safer place, not just for men, but also women.

Notes

1 In line with prior sexual harassment research that has mostly measured gender as a binary, we refer to "women" and "men" in this article. However, we recognize that a diversity of gender identities is possible (Lindqvist et al., 2021) and look forward to further research accounting for this through more nuanced measurement.
2 Estimates vary and depend on the categorization of sexually harassing acts and the setting. For example, a recent analysis by Kabat-Farr and Cortina (2014) categorized sexual harassment into sexual advance (encompassing sexual coercion and unwanted sexual attention) versus gender harassment and found that men and women suffered both forms at similar rates.

References

Alonso, N. (2018). Playing to win: Male–male sex-based harassment and the masculinity contest. *Journal of Social Issues, 74*(3), 477–499. https://doi.org/10.1111/josi.12283

Association of American Universities. (2020). *Report on the AAU campus climate survey on sexual assault and misconduct*. www.aau.edu/sites/default/files/AAU-Files/Key-Issues/Campus-Safety/Revised%20Aggregate%20report%20%20and%20appendices%201-7_(01-16-2020_FINAL).pdf

Baird, C. L., Bensko, N. L., Bell, P. A., Viney, W., & Woody, W. D. (1995). Gender influence on perceptions of hostile environment sexual harassment. *Psychological Reports, 77*(1), 79–82. https://doi.org/10.2466/pr0.1995.77.1.79

Bargh, J. A., Raymond, P., Pryor, J. B., & Strack, F. (1995). Attractiveness of the underling: An automatic power → sex association and its consequences for sexual harassment and aggression. *Journal of Personality and Social Psychology, 68*(5), 768–781. https://doi.org/10.1037/0022-3514.68.5.768

Berdahl, J. L. (2007). Harassment based on sex: Protecting social status in the context of gender hierarchy. *Academy of Management Review, 32*(2), 641–658. https://doi.org/10.5465/amr.2007.24351879

Berdahl, J. L., & Aquino, K. (2009). Sexual behavior at work: Fun or folly? *Journal of Applied Psychology, 94*(1), 34–47. https://doi.org/10.1037/a0012981

Berdahl, J. L., Cooper, M., Glick, P., Livingston, R. W., & Williams, J. C. (2018). Work as a masculinity contest. *Journal of Social Issues, 74*(3), 422–448. https://doi.org/10.1111/josi.12289

Berdahl, J. L., Magley, V. J., & Waldo, C. R. (1996). The sexual harassment of men?: Exploring the concept with theory and data. *Psychology of Women Quarterly, 20*(4), 527–547. https://doi.org/10.1111/j.1471-6402.1996.tb00320.x

Berdahl, J. L., & Moore, C. (2006). Workplace harassment: Double jeopardy for minority women. *Journal of Applied Psychology, 91*(2), 426–436. https://doi.org/10.1037/0021-9010.91.2.426

Bergman, M. E., & Henning, J. B. (2008). Sex and ethnicity as moderators in the sexual harassment phenomenon: A revision and test of Fitzgerald et al. (1994). *Journal of Occupational Health Psychology, 13*(2), 152–167. https://doi.org/10.1037/1076-8998.13.2.152

Bergman, M. E., Langhout, R. D., Palmieri, P. A., Cortina, L. M., & Fitzgerald, L. F. (2002). The (un)reasonableness of reporting: Antecedents and consequences of reporting sexual harassment. *Journal of Applied Psychology, 87*(2), 230–242. https://doi.org/10.1037/0021-9010.87.2.230

Blackstone, A., Uggen, C., & McLaughlin, H. (2009). Legal consciousness and responses to sexual harassment. *Law & Society Review*, *43*(3), 631–668. https://doi.org/10.1111/j.1540–5893.2009.00384.x

Bovill, H., Waller, R., & McCartan, K. (2020). Discussing atypical sexual harassment as a controversial issue in bystander programmes: One UK campus study. *Sexuality & Culture*, *24*(5), 1252–1270. https://doi.org/10.1007/s12119-019-09682-8

Brassel, S. T., Settles, I. H., & Buchanan, N. T. (2019). Lay (mis)perceptions of sexual harassment toward transgender, lesbian, and gay employees. *Sex Roles*, *80*(1), 76–90. https://doi.org/10.1007/s11199-018-0914-8

Castillo, Y., Muscarella, F., & Szuchman, L. T. (2011). Gender differences in college students' perceptions of same-sex sexual harassment: The influence of physical attractiveness and attitudes toward lesbians and gay men. *Journal of College Student Development*, *52*(5), 511–522. https://doi.org/10.1353/csd.2011.0070

Chang, H. E., & Jeong, S. (2021). Male nurses' experiences of workplace gender discrimination and sexual harassment in South Korea: A qualitative study. *Asian Nursing Research*, *15*(5), 303–309. https://doi.org/10.1016/j.anr.2021.09.002

Cortina, L. M., & Areguin, M. A. (2021). Putting people down and pushing them out: Sexual harassment in the workplace. *Annual Review of Organizational Psychology and Organizational Behavior*, *8*(1), 285–309. https://doi.org/10.1146/annurev-orgpsych-012420–055606

Clarke, H. M., Ford, D. P., & Sulsky, L. M. (2016). Moderating effects of harasser status and target gender on the relationship between unwanted sexual attention and overall job satisfaction. *Journal of Applied Social Psychology*, *46*(12), 701–717. https://doi.org/10.1111/jasp.12408

De Haas, S., Timmerman, G., & Höing, M. (2009). Sexual harassment and health among male and female police officers. *Journal of Occupational Health Psychology*, *14*(4), 390–401. https://doi.org/10.1037/a0017046

DeSouza, E., & Solberg, J. (2004). Women's and men's reactions to man-to-man sexual harassment: Does the sexual orientation of the victim matter? *Sex Roles*, *50*(9/10), 623–639. https://doi.org/10.1023/B:SERS.0000027566.79507.96

Dinh, T. K., & Stockdale, M. S. (2022). *Power and sex-based harassment among LGBQs* [Unpublished manuscript]. IUPUI Scholarworks. https://hdl.handle.net/1805/30053

Dubois, C. L., Knapp, D. E., Faley, R. H., & Kustis, G. A. (1998). An empirical examination of same-and other-gender sexual harassment in the workplace. *Sex Roles*, *39*(9/10), 731–749. https://doi.org/10.1023/A:1018860101629

Ely, R. J., & Meyerson, D. E. (2010). An organizational approach to undoing gender: The unlikely case of offshore oil platforms. *Research in Organizational Behavior*, *30*(2010), 3–34. https://doi.org/10.1016/j.riob.2010.09.002

Farrow, R. (2017, November 21). Harvey Weinstein's secret settlements. *The New Yorker*. www.newyorker.com/news/news-desk/harvey-weinsteins-secret-settlements

Fitzgerald, L. F., Drasgow, F., & Magley, V. J. (1999). Sexual harassment in the armed forces: A test of an integrated model. *Military Psychology*, *11*(3), 329–343. https://doi.org/10.1207/s15327876mp1103_7

Fitzgerald, L. F., Gelfand, M. J., & Drasgow, F. (1995). Measuring sexual harassment: Theoretical and psychometric advances. *Basic and Applied Social Psychology*, *17*(4), 425–445. https://doi.org/10.1207/s15324834basp1704_2

Fitzgerald, L. F., Magley, V. J., Drasgow, F., & Waldo, C. R. (1999). Measuring sexual harassment in the military: The Sexual Experiences Questionnaire (SEQ—DoD). *Military Psychology*, *11*, 243–263. https://doi.org/10.1207/s15327876mp1103_3

Fitzgerald, L. F., Shullman, S. L., Bailey, N., Richards, M., Swecker, J., Gold, Y., Ormerod, M., & Weitzman, L. (1988). The incidence and dimensions of sexual harassment in academia and the workplace. *Journal of Vocational Behavior*, 32(2), 152–175. https://doi.org/10.1016/0001-8791(88)90012-7

Franke, K. M. (1996). What's wrong with sexual harassment. *Stanford Law Review*, 49, 691–772.

Funk, L. C., & Werhun, C. D. (2011). "You're such a girl!" The psychological drain of the gender-role harassment of men. *Sex Roles*, 65(1), 13–22. https://doi.org/10.1007/s11199-011-9948-x

Galinsky, A. D., Gruenfeld, D. H., & Magee, J. C. (2003). From power to action. *Journal of Personality and Social Psychology*, 85(3), 453–466. https://doi.org/10.1037/0022-3514.85.3.453

Gelfand, M. J., Fitzgerald, L. F., & Drasgow, F. (1995). The structure of sexual harassment: A confirmatory analysis across cultures and settings. *Journal of Vocational Behavior*, 47(2), 164–177. https://doi.org/10.1006/jvbe.1995.1033

Gilbert, J. A. (2005). Sexual harassment and demographic diversity: Implications for organizational punishment. *Public Personnel Management*, 34(2), 161–174. https://doi.org/10.1177/009102600503400203

Glick, P., Berdahl, J. L., & Alonso, N. M. (2018). Development and validation of the masculinity contest culture scale. *Journal of Social Issues*, 74(3), 449–476. https://doi.org/10.1111/josi.12280

Grabowski, M., Dinh, T. K., Wu, W., & Stockdale, M. S. (2022). The sex-based harassment inventory: A gender status threat measure of sex-based harassment intentions. *Sex Roles*, 86(11/12), 648–666. https://doi.org/10.1007/s11199-022-01294-1

Gutek, B. A., Cohen, A. G., & Konrad, A. M. (1990). Predicting social-sexual behavior at work: A contact hypothesis. *Academy of Management Journal*, 33(3), 560–577. https://doi.org/10.2307/256581

Holland, K. H., Caridad Rabelo, V., Gustafson, A. M., Seabrook, R. C., & Cortina, L. M. (2016). Sexual harassment against men: Examining the roles of feminist activism, sexuality, and organizational context. *Psychology of Men & Masculinity*, 17(1), 17–29. http://doi.org/10.1037/a0039151

Kabat-Farr, D., & Cortina, L. M. (2014). Sex-based harassment in employment: New insights into gender and context. *Law and Human Behavior*, 38(1), 58. https://doi.org/10.1037/lhb0000045

Kath, L. M., Swody, C. A., Magley, V. J., Bunk, J. A., & Gallus, J. A. (2009). Cross-level, three-way interactions among work-group climate, gender, and frequency of harassment on morale and withdrawal outcomes of sexual harassment. *Journal of Occupational and Organizational Psychology*, 82(1), 159–182. https://doi.org/10.1348/096317908X299764

Keltner, D., Gruenfeld, D. H., & Anderson, C. (2003). Power, approach, and inhibition. *Psychological Review*, 110(2), 265–284. https://doi.org/10.1037/0033-295X.110.2.265

Konrad, A. M., & Gutek, B. A. (1986). Impact of work experiences on attitudes toward sexual harassment. *Administrative Science Quarterly*, 31(3), 422–438. https://doi.org/10.2307/2392831

Kunstman, J. W., & Maner, J. K. (2011). Sexual overperception: Power, mating motives, and biases in social judgment. *Journal of Personality and Social Psychology*, 100(2), 282–294. https://doi.org/10.1037/a0021135

Lindqvist, A., Sendén, M. G., & Renström, E. A. (2021). What is gender, anyway: A review of the options for operationalising gender. *Psychology & Sexuality*, 12(4), 332–344. https://doi.org/10.1080/19419899.2020.1729844

Livingston, R. W., & Pearce, N. A. (2009). The teddy-bear effect: Does having a baby face benefit Black chief executive officers? *Psychological Science*, 20(10), 1229–1236. https://doi.org/10.1111/j.1467–9280.2009.02431.x

Maass, A., Cadinu, M., Guarnieri, G., & Grasselli, A. (2003). Sexual harassment under social identity threat: The computer harassment paradigm. *Journal of Personality and Social Psychology*, 85(5), 853–870. https://doi.org/10.1037/0022–3514.85.5.853

Madera, J. M., Podratz, K. E., King, E. B., & Hebl, M. R. (2007). Schematic responses to sexual harassment complainants: The influence of gender and physical attractiveness *Sex Roles*, 56(3), 223–230. https://doi.org/10.1007/s11199-006-9165-1

Magley, V. J., Waldo, C. R., Drasgow, F., & Fitzgerald, L. F. (1999). The impact of sexual harassment on military personnel: Is it the same for men and women? *Military Psychology*, 11(3), 283–302. https://doi.org/10.1207/s15327876mp1103_5

McDonald, P. (2012). Workplace sexual harassment 30 years on: A review of the literature. *International Journal of Management Reviews*, 14(1), 1–17. https://doi.org/10.1111/j.1468–2370.2011.00300.x

McPherson, M., Smith-Lovin, L., & Cook, J. M. (2001). Birds of a feather: Homophily in social networks. *Annual Review of Sociology*, 27(2001), 415–444. https://doi.org/10.1146/annurev.soc.27.1.415

Miller, D. T., & McFarland, C. (1987). Pluralistic ignorance: When similarity is interpreted as dissimilarity. *Journal of Personality and Social Psychology*, 53(2), 298–305. https://doi.org/10.1037/0022–3514.53.2.298

Plater, M. A., & Thomas, R. E. (1998). The impact of job performance, gender, and ethnicity on the managerial review of sexual harassment allegations. *Journal of Applied Social Psychology*, 28(1), 52–70. https://doi.org/10.1111/j.1559–1816.1998.tb01653.x

Prentice, D. A., & Carranza, E. (2002). What women and men should be, shouldn't be, are allowed to be, and don't have to be: The contents of prescriptive gender stereotypes. *Psychology of Women Quarterly*, 26(4), 269–281. https://doi.org/10.1111/1471-6402.t01-1-00066

Pryor, J. B. (1987). Sexual harassment proclivities in men. *Sex Roles*, 17(5/6), 269–290. https://doi.org/10.1007/BF00288453

Rotundo, M., Nguyen, D. H., & Sackett, P. R. (2001). A meta-analytic review of gender differences in perceptions of sexual harassment. *Journal of Applied Psychology*, 86(5), 914–922. https://doi.org/10.1037/0021–9010.86.5.914

Rubino, C., Avery, D. R., McKay, P. F., Moore, B. L., Wilson, D. C., Van Driel, M. S., Witt, L. A., & McDonald, D. P. (2018). And justice for all: How organizational justice climate deters sexual harassment. *Personnel Psychology*, 71(4), 519–544. https://doi.org/10.1111/peps.12274

Runtz, M. G., & O'Donnell, C. W. (2003). Students' perceptions of sexual harassment: Is it harassment only if the offender is a man and the victim is a woman? *Journal of Applied Social Psychology*, 33(5), 963–982. https://doi.org/10.1111/j.1559–1816.2003.tb01934.x

Scarduzio, J. A., Wehlage, S. J., & Lueken, S. (2018). "It's like taking your man card away": Male victims' narratives of male-to-male sexual harassment. *Communication Quarterly*, 66(5), 481–500. https://doi.org/10.1080/01463373.2018.1447978

Setoodeh, R., & Wagmeister, E. (2017, November 29). Matt Lauer accused of sexual harassment by multiple women. *Variety*. Retrieved April 15, 2019, from https://variety.com/2017/biz/news/matt-lauer-accused-sexual-harassment-multiple-women-1202625959/

Shechory-Bitton, M., & Ben Shaul, D. (2013). Perceptions and attitudes to sexual harassment: An examination of sex differences and the sex composition of the harasser-target dyad. *Journal of Applied Social Psychology, 43*(10), 2136–2145. https://doi.org/10.1111/jasp.12166

Shechory-Bitton, M., & Zvi, L. (2020). Is it harassment? Perceptions of sexual harassment among lawyers and undergraduate students. *Frontiers in Psychology, 11*(2020), Article 1793. www.frontiersin.org/articles/10.3389/fpsyg.2020.01793

Smirles, K. E. (2004). Attributions of responsibility in cases of sexual harassment: The person and the situation. *Journal of Applied Social Psychology, 34*(2), 342–365. https://doi.org/10.1111/j.1559–1816.2004.tb02551.x

Steel, E., & Schmidt, M. S. (2017, October 21). *Bill O'Reilly settled new harassment claim, then Fox renewed his contract.* New York Times. www.nytimes.com/2017/10/21/business/media/bill-oreilly-sexual-harassment.html

Stockdale, M. S. (1998). The direct and moderating influences of sexual-harassment pervasiveness, coping strategies, and gender on work-related outcomes. *Psychology of Women Quarterly, 22*(4), 521–535. https://doi.org/10.1111/j.1471–6402.1998.tb00175.x

Stockdale, M. S. (2005). The sexual harassment of men: Articulating the approach-rejection theory of sexual harassment. In J. Gruber & P. Morgan (Eds.), *In the company of men: Male dominance and sexual harassment* (pp. 117–142). Northeastern University Press. http://hdl.handle.net/2047/D20211574

Stockdale, M. S., Gilmer, D. O., & Dinh, T. K. (2020). Dual effects of self-focused and other-focused power on sexual harassment intentions. *Equality, Diversity and Inclusion: An International Journal, 39*(1), 17–37. https://doi.org/10.1108/EDI-09-2018-0160

Stockdale, M. S., Visio, M., & Batra, L. (1999). The sexual harassment of men: Evidence for a broader theory of sexual harassment and sex discrimination. *Psychology, Public Policy, and Law, 5*(3), 630–664. https://doi.org/10.1037/1076–8971.5.3.630

Strom, P., Collins, C. J., Avgar, A. C., & Ryan, K. (2022). Drawing the line: How the workplace shapes the naming of sexual harassment. *Personnel Psychology, 76*(1), 113–139. https://doi.org/10.1111/peps.12496

Studzinska, A. M., & Hilton, D. (2017). Minimization of male suffering: Social perception of victims and perpetrators of opposite-sex sexual coercion. *Sexuality Research and Social Policy, 14*(1), 87–99. https://doi.org/10.1007/s13178-016-0226-0

U.S. Merit Systems Protection Board Office of Policy and Evaluation. (2016). *Update on sexual harassment in the federal workplace.* www.mspb.gov/studies/researchbriefs/Update_on_Sexual_Harassment_in_the_Federal_Workplace_1500639.pdf

Uggen, C., & Blackstone, A. (2004). Sexual harassment as a gendered expression of power. *American Sociological Review, 69*(1), 64–92. https://doi.org/10.1177/000312240406900105

Waldo, C. R., Berdahl, J. L., & Fitzgerald, L. F. (1998). Are men sexually harassed? If so, by whom? *Law and Human Behavior, 22*(1), 59–79. https://doi.org/10.1023/A:1025776705629

Wayne, J. H., Riordan, C. M., & Thomas, K. M. (2001). Is all sexual harassment viewed the same? Mock juror decisions in same- and cross-gender cases. *Journal of Applied Psychology, 86*(2), 179–187. https://doi.org/10.1037/0021–9010.86.2.179

Wiener, R. L., Bennett, S., Cheloha, C., & Nicholson, N. (2012). Gender policing: Harassment judgments when men target other men. *Psychology, Public Policy, and Law, 18*(2), 245–267. https://doi.org/10.1037/a0025904

Wiener, R. L., Voss, A. M., Winter, R. J., & Arnot, L. (2005). The more you see it, the more you know it: Memory accessibility and sexual harassment judgments. *Sex Roles, 53*(11/12), 807–820. https://doi.org/10.1007/s11199-005-8294-2

10

THE HIDDEN EXPERIENCE OF WOMEN IN THE LOWER SOCIAL CLASSES

Marilla G. Hayman, Jennifer Kish-Gephart, and Kristie J.N. Moergen

Left Behind by the #MeToo Movement

In October 2017, Alyssa Milano used #MeToo to call on survivors of sexual assault to share their stories. Within 24 hours, millions of people on social media responded to that call. This one moment became a lightning rod for raising awareness of and holding perpetrators accountable for sexual harassment (SH). Yet, for all the Movement's many merits and accomplishments, it also revealed an uncomfortable truth about whose voices are most likely to be heard and amplified. The #MeToo movement was propelled largely by "wealthy, White Hollywood actresses" (North, 2018) and focused on the stories of those with "economic power" (Berg, 2020, p. 261). Far from its origins a decade earlier, when Tarana Burke had coined "MeToo" in the hopes of assisting young Black girls and members of other marginalized communities, this modern #MeToo movement privileged women with the resources and standing of the middle and upper classes of US society, and left women who occupy the lower social classes—those working in farms, restaurants, hotels, fast-food chains, factory floors, and private homes, to name a few—in the shadows.

The idea that social class, or "a person's perceived place in an economic hierarchy" (Liu et al., 2004, p. 9), matters in the experiences of women at work is not novel. In one example of early twentieth-century women doctors (representing the upper social classes), harassment primarily took the form of verbal insults and exclusion. As one-woman doctor-in-training described, she had to endure the "taunts or gibes or outrageous insults" of her male student counterparts, but she also understood that "if ever . . .

DOI: 10.4324/9781003300953-12

they should as much lay a finger on me physically, there would be an immediate reckoning." In contrast, women who worked in menial jobs endured (and expected) more severe forms of sexual violence in their workplace (Bularzik, 1978).

This example helps to illustrate that discussions of a "universal woman" or "everywoman" experience with SH fail to capture the unique situation faced by women of different social class backgrounds (Richie, 2000). Even the common stereotypes for White middle-class women (e.g., stereotyped as respectable on average) and working-class women (e.g., stereotyped as oversexualized and promiscuous) point to an unequal starting point for members of different social class backgrounds (Kiebler & Stewart, 2022). Despite this, White middle- and upper-class women's experiences are often considered "normative and universal," and this has been reflected in the lack of extant research on the so-called non-normative women of the lower social classes (Fitzgerald, 2020; Kiebler & Stewart, 2022; Waugh, 2006).

In this chapter, we aim to highlight the experiences of women whose stories often do not last long in mainstream discussions, if they make it there at all—that is, women who occupy the lower economic rungs of society. Prior work has distinguished members of the lower social classes from the middle and upper social classes based on attaining a four-year college education (Kish-Gephart et al., 2023). In addition, unlike their counterparts, members of the lower social classes endure resource scarcity, marginalization, and stigmatization (Gray & Kish-Gephart, 2013). Members of the lower social classes include the working poor, such as low-skill, low-wage, and precarious workers (e.g., maids, janitors, home health care workers, and fast-food workers; Benach et al., 2014; Byrd et al., 2024; Clari et al., 2020), as well as members of the working class, such as low ranking blue-collar positions (e.g., unskilled construction or factory workers; Lucas & Buzzanell, 2004).[1]

To write this chapter, we conducted a wide-ranging review of extant research on SH and social class. Early on, it became clear that little scholarly work exists on this topic, and even less work falls within the domain of organization studies. Thus, our literature review focused on research that not only addressed organization-related issues but also could help inform and inspire future scholarship. Based on our results, our chapter is organized into two broad sections—understanding the individual and organizational factors that contribute to heightened vulnerability to instances of SH and recognizing the unique repercussions, including bounded coping opportunities, faced by women in the lower social classes. We end with a discussion of possible future research opportunities.

Before Sexual Harassment: Individual and Organizational Factors

SH occurs at all levels of wealth, status, and class. Yet, for women in lower social class positions, research suggests the severity and incidence of SH may be higher. For example, women in "precarious work"—or jobs in which workers experience low wages, limited workplace rights and the inability to exercise such rights, job insecurity, and unequal and often individualized power dynamics with their employer (Benach et al., 2014)—are especially vulnerable to harassment, with the US EEOC reporting that nearly half of all SH claims occurred in industries where there are a large number of low-paying jobs (Frye, 2017; Morgan, 1999). Similarly, women in blue-collar occupations, who find themselves in more secure, well-paying jobs, also experience SH at an increased rate and in more severe forms, including unwanted physical touching (i.e., unwelcome expressions of interest including behaviors such as sex talk, forcible touching, pressure for sexual gestures, and sexual assault) and sexual coercion (i.e., willingness to comply with sexual demands is made a condition of one's employment) (McCabe & Hardman, 2005).

In this section, we consider some of the individual- and organization-level factors that contribute to this increased risk for women from the lower social classes.[2]

Individual-Level Factors

At the individual level, women in lower social class positions may be at increased risk of SH due to economic insecurity and fear of job loss, consequences to family ties, and fear of deportation, which contribute to their vulnerability and silence. Starting with economic insecurity, women employed in blue-collar occupations often occupy jobs with low skill and education requirements, making them more easily replaceable (Fitzgerald, 2020). In such situations, women may endure SH without reporting the behavior, as losing their jobs is a risk they cannot afford (Kim et al., 2016; Villegas, 2019).

Another issue faced by many women in lower social class positions is concern about family and friends' economic security. In one of the few social-scientific studies of Mexican immigrant farmworkers (see Fitzgerald, 2020), the author reported that "sixty-seven percent of participants reported that they acquired their current jobs through family members and friends . . ."; they also commuted with coworkers and shared vehicles, which together "complicated how women responded to SH, creating a 'double-edged sword' . . . that women confronted daily" (Waugh, 2010, p. 246). Indeed, in many precarious blue-collar jobs, such as farm work, domestic work, and janitorial work, it is not uncommon for family members to have the same employer or for one's coworkers to be neighbors or close friends (Fitzgerald, 2020). Individuals in these positions often understand that their sexual harasser recognizes "the precariousness of their financial situation" and will use it as leverage against them (Waugh, 2010, p. 246). Family ties create a complex web of dependencies and risks for harassed women. Women in precarious positions may fear that speaking up could cause other family members to lose jobs or face retaliation. They may also worry about being ostracized or pressured by family members to endure the harassment silently to avoid such employment risks. This power dynamic contributes to women enduring severe forms of harassment to avoid further exacerbating their financial insecurity and that of those around them (Murphy et al., 2015; Stambaugh, 1997).

Compounding the risk of personal and familial job loss for women in the lower social classes is Undocumented work status. An estimated 50% of the agricultural workforce is Undocumented, with other sectors such as domestic, janitorial, and service work reporting similar numbers (Fitzgerald, 2020; Center for American Progress, 2020; Wolfe et al., 2020). Women working in these sectors are often paid "under the table" and depend heavily on their employers to remain in the country. Reporting or even complaining about their harassment could mean not only job loss but also deportation for themselves and their families (Chen et al., 2016; Cortina & Areguin, 2021; Yeung, 2018).

While the aforementioned factors may contribute to making blue-collar and precariously employed women prime targets for harassment and prevent them from speaking up in the aftermath, another crucial, if perhaps more impactful, set of factors occurs at the organizational level (Cortina & Areguin, 2021; Pryor et al., 1993)—a topic we turn to next.

Organizational-Level Factors

In this section, we discuss five characteristics of the organizational environment that contribute to women's work experiences: organizational climates (e.g., climates characterized by male dominance or climates of sexualized ambiance), individualized power dynamics between worker and supervisor, physical isolation and hours of work, lack of employee protections and reporting options, and lack of social support from other workers.

Organizational Climate

Rates of reported SH tend to be higher in organizations where men are dominant, whether in number, positions held, or stereotyped expectations

(Cortina & Areguin, 2021; McLaughlin et al., 2012; Berdahl, 2007). For instance, women constitute only 4.9% of construction laborers, 6.8% of machinists, and 12.7% of police officers (U.S. Bureau of Labor Statistics, 2022). Extant scholarship suggests that when women are in the minority, particularly in physically demanding environments (Willness et al., 2007) or performing traditionally male-oriented tasks (Fitzgerald et al., 1997), they are more susceptible to SH.

Another potential contributing factor is male-domination of managerial roles in organizations where women work in blue-collar or low-wage jobs. For example, in the service sector, women are significantly outnumbered by men in managerial positions, though they dominate in numbers in both hospitality and restaurant work (Cregut-Aston & Darioly, 2019; National Restaurant Association, 2022). Similarly, in domestic work, women fill over 90% of positions, yet harassment often comes at the hands of their male employers (Wolfe et al., 2020; Yeung, 2018). Women in the agricultural and janitorial sectors experience a double disadvantage—they are both outnumbered by men in regular positions *and* make up the minority in supervisory and oversight positions (U.S. Department of Agriculture, 2019; U.S. Bureau of Labor Statistics, 2022).

Women working in "stereotypically male" organizations are also at an elevated risk of experiencing SH (Gruber, 1998; Ragins & Scandura, 1995). Across a vast array of stereotypically masculine jobs, women report being subject to harassment from both supervisors and coworkers. Examples from one qualitative study include an electrician who had a bucket of water dumped on her by coworkers who wanted to see her wet t-shirt, and a machinist who opened her tool cabinet door one day to find a nude centerfold (Schroedel, 1985; Segrave, 1994).

Men in these stereotypically masculine organizations may view women as a threat, particularly if women earn similar wages and have similar job responsibilities. As women become more integrated into traditionally male-dominated occupations, the absence of traditional means of exerting power, such as withholding job information or training, may lead some male coworkers to resort to SH to assert dominance and maintain perceived status differences (Sullivan, 1998).

In addition to male-dominated industries, an organization's climate can also contribute to women's experiences of SH. "Sexualized ambiance," or a climate in which "employees talk and joke frequently about sex and sexual behavior" (Icenogle et al., 2002, p. 605), may be particularly problematic for women in lower social class positions. As described in one editorial, women in blue-collar roles felt compelled to accept a "boys will be boys" climate and demonstrate they could withstand crude and oftentimes sexual comments to survive (Chira, 2017). Akin to climates of sexualized ambiance, masculinity contest cultures are organizational environments where masculinity is celebrated and femininity is scorned. Within these cultures, men face expectations to demonstrate masculinity by displaying traits like strength and resilience, prioritizing work above all else, and treating colleagues as rivals (Berdahl et al., 2018). Workplaces with this type of culture exhibit elevated incidences of SH and bullying.

One of the ways in which these toxic workplace environments affect women is by discouraging reporting of SH (e.g., by not taking claims of SH seriously, avoiding punishing offenders, targeting the victim with poor work assignments or derogatory slurs; Bowes-Sperry & Powell, 1999). When employers do not take claims of SH seriously, a climate of tolerance is created, further perpetuating the cycle of inappropriate behavior (Pryor et al., 1993). Research indicates that organizational tolerance for SH is a significant predictor of individuals' experiences of such misconduct (Fitzgerald et al., 1997). Supporting this correlation, a survey involving 615 men revealed that respondents admitted to engaging in more harassing behavior when other harassers went unpunished and when the organization's protocols and procedures for reporting harassment appeared weak or inadequate (Patel et al., 2017).

It is also important to note that toxic workplace environments can be similarly detrimental to women as being a *direct target* of SH. A study by Glomb and colleagues (1997) found that ambient SH, or indirect exposure to harassment in one's work environment, had negative effects on women's job satisfaction, psychological conditions such as anxiety and depression, and health outcomes such as severe headaches and difficulty sleeping, pointing to the importance of rooting out toxic workplace environments.

Unbalanced Manager-Employee Power Dynamic

Members of the lower social classes often occupy jobs characterized by a lack of autonomy and power (Sennett & Cobb, 1977), which can manifest in unbalanced power dynamics between employer and employee, including supervisors who have the sole power to hire, promote, discipline, or fire employees and/or represent the only point of contact for employees. For example, for agricultural workers and coal miners, the foreman serves as the main or only link between the worker and the employer (e.g., Segrave, 1994); the foreman also assists immigrant workers with finding housing and transportation and acclimating to the United States (Human Rights Watch, 2012). In the domestic work profession, women often work alone in their employer's home and have no other point of contact than their "supervisor" (i.e., the family that hired them; Wolfe et al., 2020).

The manager's power in these situations cannot be overstated. Whereas white-collar environments often have an elaborate set of reporting outlets, including anonymous hotlines, Human Resource departments, and Ethics Offices (SHRM, 2018), the supervisors with undue power as described earlier often serve as the point person for SH claims, placing women from the lower social classes in an even more precarious position (Morgan, 2001). Both personal stories and scientific studies suggest that sexual coercion from their managers (in which it is made explicit that their employment terms depend on their willingness to comply with sexual demands) is not uncommon. In a 2005 study of white-collar and blue-collar workers, nearly 15% of blue-collar workers reported experiencing sexual coercion at least once over the past 12 months compared to 2% of white-collar workers (McCabe & Hardman). Further, in a study of low-wage Hispanic women, Marín and colleagues (2021) reported that the women who refused, resisted, or reported their harassment were retaliated against both indirectly and directly. The consequences of this noncompliance can include managerial actions such as reducing work hours, cutting off overtime, giving employees more difficult work tasks, moving them to more isolated areas, or ultimately firing them.

Isolated Work

Physical isolation is another potential issue for women workers—from domestic employees and home healthcare workers to janitorial staff to farmworkers to gig workers. Starting with domestic workers, by the nature of being employed in private residences, they tend to work alone, often during late night or early morning hours, with some living full-time in their employer's residence (Yeung, 2018). In one extreme case, a couple in Texas was found guilty of trafficking a domestic worker from Nigeria and abusing her for almost a decade (United States Court of Appeals, 2011). The couple isolated the worker so much that she was practically invisible to the outside world. Similarly, home healthcare workers face unique vulnerabilities due to the uncontrolled environment of clients' homes, which heightens the risk of SH from both patients and their relatives (Fitzwater & Gates, 2000). Unlike in hospital settings, home healthcare workers lack the presence of co-workers or security guards for protection (Clari et al., 2020). Moreover, if the home healthcare workers are not associated with an organization, they face risks similar to those of domestic employees with little recourse to immediate assistance or support.

Physical isolation is also an issue for women who do janitorial work and enter empty buildings during odd hours. Because much of their work is completed alone, their manager can exert high levels of control and, in the case of

SH, ensure opportunities where no one is around to witness the harassment or intervene to help (Fitzgerald, 2020; Chen et al., 2016). Similarly, women farmworkers are isolated from their coworkers in remote areas (even during daytime hours), including working in areas far from where their vehicles are parked or in areas concealed by bushes or trees. Additionally, the nature of their work often requires farmworkers to assume exposing and vulnerable physical positions, such as bending over to harvest crops and eliciting stares, comments, and unwanted touching (Waugh, 2010).

Finally, the growth of "gig work," such as ride-hailing (e.g., Uber), food delivery (e.g., DoorDash), and home services (e.g., TaskRabbit), further disadvantages women with severe physical isolation. Women comprise approximately half of all gig workers in North America (Ziegler, 2020). Barriers to entry and flexible scheduling make it an appealing nontraditional employment opportunity, including for women from the lower social classes who piece together several gigs or who need to juggle childcare while earning an income. Yet, as Ma and colleagues noted (2022), measures are rarely taken within gig platforms to ensure women's safety, and the measures that are taken offer limited help to the gig employee, as illustrated by panic buttons in drivers' cars that turned out to be of little use in crises and functioned mostly as a reporting option. When women drivers experienced harassment, a common response was to try and de-escalate the situation (e.g., by brushing off the harassment or playing along until the customer leaves). The isolation, coupled with the customer rating work assignment system that inadvertently penalizes women who report customer harassment and receive poor ratings by the harassing customer, makes brushing off or playing along the preferred choices (though not necessarily the safest). Women who work in food delivery and home services are similarly isolated, subject to a customer rating system, and vulnerable to SH (Maffie & Elias, 2019).

Access to Reporting Options and Legal Protections

As mentioned earlier, access to reporting options and legal protections can become an issue, especially when supervisors (often the harasser) are the main, if not the only, point of contact with the employer. Even in cases where workers have access to employees beyond their supervisor, employees in these lower-level positions are often unaware of both their rights as a worker and the organization's practices in dealing with complaints (Marín et al., 2021). As Fitzgerald (2020) noted, "Governmental labor law enforcement depends on the assumption that workers know their rights, but because agencies do virtually no outreach, this is often not the case with those who are primed for abuse" (p. 10).

Besides a lack of knowledge, women in certain blue-collar and precarious jobs are simply not protected by the same legal protections that are commonplace in white-collar environments. Domestic care workers, for example, have been explicitly excluded from several Federal labor laws, including the National Labor Relations Act (NLRA; which gives employees the right to form labor unions and organize to improve working conditions), the Occupational Safety and Health Act, and many Federal anti-discrimination laws (Wolfe et al., 2020). Title VII of the Civil Rights Act of 1964, which outlaws workplace SH, applies only to employers with more than 15 employees, a rarity in domestic work (Yeung, 2018). While workers can still file criminal charges, the gaps in workplace civil rights laws make their options for legal recourse unclear.

The case is similar for farm workers. They are excluded from the NLRA and are often not covered by Title VII of the Civil Rights Act (National Farm Worker Ministry, 2022). Because Title VII coverage applies only to employers with 15 or more employees for each working day in at least 20 total weeks in a year, most small to mid-size farms are excluded. Even more, with an estimated 50% of the agricultural workforce being Undocumented, women farm workers have almost no legal protections from the US government and risk deportation if they become involved with the legal system (Fitzgerald, 2020).

Gig workers—described as "the ideal typical member of the precariat, with few or even none of the traditional rights or entitlements associated with employment" (Griesbach et al., 2019, p. 1)—also have fewer legal protections. While their "independent contractor" status grants gig workers flexibility, it also denies them such legal protections as minimum wage, overtime, and workers' compensation, as well as the right to form unions that may help fight for safer working conditions (Hussain, 2022). In response to grass-roots movements for gig workers, many parent companies have spent millions of dollars attempting to prevent the passing of laws that extend federal and state protections to these individuals.

Lack of Social Support

When a woman encounters SH, social support can be a critical factor in managing the situation. However, as discussed earlier, women in lower social class positions endure several circumstances, such as physical isolation and male dominated workplaces, that can limit the social support they can count on. For example, in one study of women who experienced harassment in blue-collar jobs, none of the female participants reported receiving support from their male coworkers, and the coworkers who were aware of the harassment either did not react to it or ended up supporting the harasser

(Schroedel, 1990). According to attribution theory, people are motivated to make causal attributions about both their own outcomes and the outcomes experienced by those around them to feel a sense of control over their environments (Wong & Weiner, 1981). People are motivated to search for the characteristics and actions of someone that could explain why that person is experiencing a certain outcome. In the case of women working in blue-collar and masculine jobs, the harassment they receive is often attributed to their decision to put themselves in that environment, thus blaming victims for the actions of their harassers (Rye et al., 2006). Judgments of controllability precede judgments of responsibility and blame; therefore, women who willingly choose to work in blue-collar and masculine environments are seen as partly, if not entirely, responsible for the outcomes they receive.

These types of victim-blaming attributions, and thus lack of social support, may be further compounded because of the stereotypes women in the lower social classes endure (e.g., sexualized, promiscuous; Bettie, 2003). Female farmworkers, for instance, are often blamed for provoking their male harasser. Even when women wear heavy clothes and scarves to protect themselves from harassment, they are still labeled as "promiscuous" (Waugh, 2010; Kim et al., 2016). Women in the service industry who dress "provocatively" are also criticized and blamed (by both women and men alike)—even when it is a required part of their job or official uniform (Brunner & Dever, 2014). For those in male-dominated industries, such as coal mining, a belief that "a woman would have to be a certain breed of woman to go down there in the first place, not a lady" (as stated by a manager) further blames the victim and rationalizes SH (Segrave, 1994, p. 98).

After Sexual Harassment: Costs and Coping

In addition to the factors that facilitate disadvantage as described earlier, social class may also heighten the price paid and the path taken *after* SH has occurred. While extant research sheds some light on the repercussions of SH and victims' coping responses (Fitzgerald & Cortina, 2018), less is known about the unique ways that *social class* shapes those repercussions and coping behaviors. In this section, we consider how social class shapes the psychological, physiological, and professional outcomes for victims of SH; the role of social class when determining coping strategies; and how the consequences for perpetrators of SH vary across social class.

Repercussions of Sexual Harassment for Victims

SH carries a range of negative repercussions for victims (Chan et al., 2008). Harassment may cause severe emotional and psychological consequences, including increased depression and anxiety (Ho et al., 2012), increased levels of distress and decreased psychological well-being (Chan et al., 2008), and an increased likelihood of post-traumatic stress disorder (PTSD) (Fitzgerald et al., 2013). Harassment also leads to a decline in physical health and an increase in a variety of physiological symptoms (Chan et al., 2008), including increased cardiovascular reactivity (Schneider et al., 2001) and headaches, stomach issues, and sleep loss (Barling et al., 1996).

The psychological and physiological repercussions of harassment may be amplified for victims from a lower social class as this population already suffers elevated levels of stress, increased chronic health conditions, and higher levels of mental illness (AAFP, 2022). As one example of the potential compounding impact of harassment, individuals from lower incomes (i.e., those earning less than $25,000 a year) were twice as likely to develop PTSD as a response to a traumatic event (Lenart et al., 2021). Further potentially exasperating the consequences is a lack of access to affordable and high-quality healthcare facilities (Lazar & Davenport, 2018).

SH also has repercussions professionally, including negative implications for job satisfaction, commitment, withdrawal, workplace stress, productivity, and performance (Chan et al., 2008; Fitzgerald & Cortina, 2018). Insofar as women from a lower social class fill lower-status roles and perpetrators hold higher-status roles, the impact of SH on professional outcomes may be amplified. In such instances, research suggests that the victim's productivity is more likely to suffer and that she will develop negative attitudes toward the organization (Pryor et al., 1993). Moreover, leaving an organization may be more difficult for women from the lower social classes as job loss disproportionally impacts working-class women (Damaske, 2020), who have less access to resources (and to other people with resources who could help) and suffer more significant earnings loss than their white-collar counterparts when reentering the workforce (Podgursky & Swaim, 1987). Seen together, the SH of women who fill lower-status occupational roles (often, women from the lower social classes) can be understood as an attempt to reify workplace hierarchies, as the consequences of harassment disproportionately impact those already at the bottom of the hierarchy (Good & Cooper, 2016).

Coping for Victims of Sexual Harassment

Research suggests that the process of coping, including which coping strategies—the "cognitive and behavioral efforts to manage specific external and internal demands that are appraised as taxing or exceeding the resources of the person"; Malamut and Offermann (2001, p. 1153)—are implemented, is impacted by a victim's social class background (Wasti &

Cortina, 2002). For example, in a sample of working-class women, the frequency of SH was associated with increased avoidance (i.e., avoid the perpetrator if possible) and negotiation (i.e., addressing the harasser through direct or indirect communication) strategies. The higher the perpetrator's status, the more working-class women implemented these two strategies (Wasti & Cortina, 2002). In a sample of professional women, seeking advocacy through reporting, complaining, or speaking with management following SH was also uncommon, but this set of women did turn toward social coping (i.e., relying on colleagues, family, or friends) when SH was more frequent.

A second study used cluster analysis of working-class and professional women to create distinct coping profiles (Cortina & Wasti, 2005). In the sample of working-class women, the largest group fell into an avoidant-negotiating profile, which attempted to avoid the stressor mentally and behaviorally. The second largest group fell into a support-seeking profile, which mobilized social and organizational support in addition to avoiding and negotiating. The final and smallest group demonstrated a relative absence of coping strategies. The profiles found in the sample of professional women (i.e., those working in white-collar or pink-collar occupations) largely mirrored those in the sample of working-class women (Cortina & Wasti, 2005). In other research, however, women working in blue-collar positions reported more SH than women working in white-collar positions but adopted less assertive coping strategies than their counterparts; they were more likely to ignore the harassment, while women in white-collar positions more actively responded (Ragins & Scandura, 1995; see also Tilton et al., 2024). The mixed findings underscore a need to understand better class-based coping mechanisms and their boundary conditions.

Additional Factors That Affect Coping Responses

Sensemaking

As victims make sense of SH, it is critical to remember that "even if organizational members experience similar forms of SH, or even share the same perpetrator, each individual may assign different meaning to the sexual harassment" (Ford & Ivancic, 2020, p. 188). Similar to coping, sensemaking around SH is an ongoing process. Because of varying experiences related to an individual's social class—among other unique backgrounds, experiences, and identities—how SH impacts an individual's understanding of oneself and others is idiosyncratic (Ford & Ivancic, 2020). For example, theory suggests that group social dynamics—such as social class group membership or related intergroup dynamics—can incentivize or trap individuals into accepting harassing conduct (Rawski et al., 2022). Future research may adopt a qualitative approach to understand how social class, alongside other sources of meaning, shapes the sensemaking following SH.

Social Class Cultures

Research underscores the idea that coping is impacted by several cultural factors (Cervantes & Castro, 1985; Lazarus & Folkman, 1984), and while no direct line has been drawn between social class cultures specifically and coping strategies to our knowledge, there is likely a connection. Life in lower social class contexts facilitates a more interdependent sense of self (Stephens et al., 2014) and contextualist social cognitive tendencies that generate a more communal self-concept (Kraus et al., 2012). SH researchers have theorized that social coping, or dependence on social support from friends, family, or work colleagues, is more common in collectivistic, interdependent cultures (Wasti & Cortina, 2002). It is reasonable to expect those from the lower social classes may also engage in more social coping. For example, in a study of service industry workers, SH from customers was often dealt with through informal action wherein workers turned to colleagues for support (Good & Cooper, 2016). This may be partly due to members of the lower social class' understanding of authority figures as more distant or less approachable (Calarco, 2014; Stephens et al., 2014); this group may forego formal routes that involve interacting with authority figures for more informal or peer-based coping strategies.

Social Power

SH research ties low social power to the use of less direct coping strategies, suggesting that "powerless standing can breed powerless behavior" (Cortina & Wasti, 2005, p. 183). Because those from a lower social class have relatively less power than their higher class counterparts (Resnick & Wolff, 2003), they may adopt less confrontational and advocacy-seeking coping strategies. They may sense a greater risk of retaliation or have fewer physical or emotional resources with which to cope. Research also suggests that a lack of power can lead to victim silence, which is especially prevalent in climates where speaking up would put the individual in a position of danger (e.g., physical attacks or job loss) or when saying something is not worth the effort, as might be the case for members of the lower social classes in toxic environments as described earlier. From this viewpoint, "power organizes sexual harassment and mediates silence" (Ford et al., 2021, p. 516). Another potential explanation for silence is that the lower social class's cultural focus on the collective good over individual preferences may increase silence as "individuals in [collectivistic cultures] typically prefer to minimize negative behaviors and/or keep silent when dissatisfied with another's actions" (Wasti & Cortina, 2002, p. 396).

Occupational Status

A related but distinct concept is organizational status or "the target's level of job skills and position in the organizational hierarchy" (Malamut & Offermann, 2001, p. 1153). Social power is derived from membership in certain high-ranking social groups that have control or influence over others (e.g., White, male, or upper class). Organizational status also confers power, but, in this case, it is derived from one's organizational role. While those from the lower social class may occupy a high-level occupational role, they most often fill low-level occupational roles or those traditionally considered "blue-collar" (Kish-Gephart et al., 2023). Extant research reports mixed findings regarding the role of occupational status and coping. On the one hand, some work suggests that women in lower-status occupational roles are less likely to employ assertive coping strategies (Gruber & Bjorn, 1986; Ragins & Scandura, 1995), perhaps because SH is seen as "part of the job" (Brunner & Dever, 2014). On the other hand, other work suggests that those in lower-status occupational roles use more assertive coping strategies (e.g., confrontation) than their counterparts, perhaps because targets in higher-status roles feel as if they have "more to lose professionally" (Malamut & Offermann, 2001, p. 1163).

Research also suggests that service sector work (e.g., retail or hospitality) requires particularly aesthetic and sexualized labor, making it challenging for workers to distinguish between what comprises unwanted sexual attention from customers versus what is expected because of their work role (Good & Cooper, 2016). In a qualitative study, respondents reported being unsurprised when they received unwanted sexual attention from high-status customers; they believed the customers saw them as lower status, and the respondents often responded with deference to the customers. Still, the respondents tried to maintain a sense of dignity, often leading to emotional labor when interacting with the customers or informal coping with co-workers (e.g., joking with colleagues afterward or asking a colleague to intervene) (Good & Cooper, 2016). Quantitative evidence shows a similar pattern: in one study, when interacting with someone of higher status (and whom the victim was familiar with), victims were less than half as likely to confront sexist behavior (Ayres et al., 2009).

Social Capital

Victims' access to social capital outside work is also likely a factor. Because women from lower social classes lack social capital relative to their higher-class counterparts, they may find it more difficult to access helpful resources in the wake of SH. Women from higher social classes, for example, likely have (or can borrow from their families) the personal connections to have an informal conversation with someone with legal training or to formally consult with a lawyer. Moreover, in contrast to their counterparts, women from lower social classes may be less likely to connect with a therapist due to increased demands on their time or resources. Within an organization, a similar pattern of tapping social capital resources may hold. One study conducted by a professional services firm found that only 54% of women had access to more senior leaders when looking for mentors (Warrell, 2017), a number ostensibly lower for women from the working class, especially in male-dominated fields.

Consequences for Perpetrators

In this section, we turn our focus from victims to perpetrators and consider how social class is involved in perceptions of responsibility based on the social class of the perpetrator and the victim; the relationship between stereotypes of social class correlates with notions of who is a sexual perpetrator; and, finally, the impact of social class on sentencing.

Responsibility for Sexual Harassment

Research provides evidence that both perpetrators and victims from a lower social class (in comparison to their counterparts from middle and upper social class) are considered more responsible for SH. In one study, for example, participants read a vignette where the perpetrator of sexual assault was either a bus driver (representing lower social class status) or a doctor (representing higher social class status). When asked who was to blame for the assault, male participants assigned more blame to the perpetrator from a lower social class (i.e., the bus driver) than an upper social class (i.e., the doctor) (Black & Gold, 2008). Similar research demonstrates that when participants (both men and women) read a scenario describing a woman being sexually assaulted, they assign more blame and display more negative attitudes (e.g., less sympathy or credibility) when the woman is from a lower social class than a higher social class (Spencer, 2016). Upward mobility may also complicate who is considered responsible for SH. In the case of Anita Hill and Judge Clarence Thomas, for example, Jordan (1992) argued that the Thomas legal strategy "exploited a complicated irony of women's upward mobility—the undercurrent of competition between women in jobs traditionally reserved for women, such as secretaries and administrative assistants, and women who aspire to break the glass ceiling by joining the executive ranks" (p. 9). The storyline framed Hill as responsible because, if she had plenty of resources, she could have left her job (Jordan, 1992).

Perceptions of a Sexual Perpetrator

Who does society imagine to be a sexual perpetrator? The stereotypes of a sexual perpetrator are often conflated with class identities and cultures—a connotation that has downstream effects in the courtroom (Small, 2015). For example, in a qualitative study of prosecutors and defense attorneys, an informant described a game that he and his colleagues played, in which they matched defendants to their crimes based on stereotypes. In the game, "the sex offender [was] classed as a 'hillbilly,' which invokes rural, poor, White cultures . . . [before] the attorney's knowledge of the alleged criminal behavior"; in this way, "the potential for sexual criminality is written figuratively on the bodies of lower class men" (Small, 2015, p. 132). In contrast, men from the upper social classes are granted class privilege—markers of their lifestyle make it more difficult for others (including lawyers and jurors) to see them as sexual perpetrators, possibly undermining legal evidence.[3] Indeed, in a study examining three cases of SH, participants who held strong power distance beliefs (i.e., accepting an unequal distribution of power) viewed perpetrators as less culpable (Jain & Lee, 2022). Scholars have suggested that SH myths serve to help deny wrongdoing or, when denial is not an option, absolve harassers by helping explain why perpetrators are not responsible (Hershcovis et al., 2021).

Punishment Across Classes

Such stereotypes likely spill over and confer a class advantage for those from a higher social class when it comes to the distribution of punishment. A meta-analysis of research on mock juror judgments found that being from a higher socioeconomic status pays off when it comes to sentencing, with individuals from a lower socioeconomic status receiving longer sentences than their higher class counterparts (Vaughan, 2001). In a second study, individuals characterized by stronger beliefs in a just world assigned more degrees of guilt and longer sentences to low socioeconomic defendants in comparison to defendants from high socioeconomic backgrounds or for whom no socioeconomic information was provided (Freeman, 2006). To the extent that these biases carry over into workplace settings and influence organizational decision-makers, these examples further underscore the need to better understand workplace disciplinary processes around SH.

Future Research Opportunities

Broader Understanding of the Role of Stereotypes

Limited research exists on the factors that explain why women in lower social class circumstances may be more of a target or more vulnerable in the eyes of perpetrators. One avenue for future research is to consider the role of stereotypes, given that women in the lower social classes exist at the intersection of class and gender—both of which are associated with unique negative stereotypes.[4] Members of the lower social class are stereotyped as lazy, uncouth, and undeserving (Kish-Gephart et al., 2023); women are stereotyped as compliant and willing to accept subpar arrangements (i.e., the "ideal worker"; Acker, 2006); and women in the lower social classes are stereotyped as promiscuous and oversexualized (Kiebler & Stewart, 2022; Spencer, 2016). Indeed, even upward mobility comes with its own potential stereotypes. As noted by Jordan (1992), Anita Hill's ambition and upward mobility were portrayed as a vice, rendering her working-class identity invisible. Future research might consider women's experience with upward mobility and how stereotypes, expectations, and treatment change with that trajectory.

The Paradox of Power

Another promising avenue involves exploring the paradox surrounding SH and power in the context of women's workplace experiences. Existing literature has shown that women in positions of authority, despite holding greater organizational power, are frequently the targets of SH (McLaughlin et al., 2012). This contradiction challenges prevailing theories of vulnerability as it contradicts the vulnerable-victim hypothesis that posits the most precarious workers face the highest risk. Instead, support has grown for the power-threat model, suggesting that women who challenge traditional gender roles or threaten male dominance may be more susceptible to harassment (Chamberlain et al., 2008). This phenomenon can be further understood through the lens of masculine overcompensation, where men may react to perceived threats by engaging in aggressive behaviors (Willer et al., 2013). The complexity of this issue calls for a nuanced investigation into the underlying dynamics of harassment, which may vary by levels of workplace authority and the unique power struggles in different organizational contexts.

Social Class and the Perpetrator

Another important area of future research is to consider how perpetrators' social class is related to organizational discipline choices and third-party reactions to harassment. As described earlier, current evidence outside of management literature finds that those from a lower social class are held more responsible for SH (Black & Gold, 2008) and are given harsher punishments (Vaughan, 2001). If the same is true in organizations, then it is critical to understand what underlies these judgments and what effective interventions may be. It may also be that observers' responses to SH (i.e., being silent, silencing, or not hearing) (Herschcovis et al., 2021) depend on the perpetrators' social class. For example, is it that observers enact silencing behaviors (e.g., advising against filing a complaint) when a perpetrator is from a higher social class, or do they simply not recognize the harassment (e.g., dismissing or trivializing harassment)?

The tie between a perpetrator's social class and others' evaluations may also vary depending on the type of SH (e.g., come-ons like sexual assault or unwanted sex talk versus put-downs like obscene gestures or negative remarks about working mothers) (Cortina & Areguin, 2021). Are men from a higher social class held less responsible for sexual coercion (i.e., making the conditions of employment contingent on sexual cooperation) because of the stereotypes mentioned earlier or because it conforms with society's expectations for appropriate behavior in white-collar workplaces?

Another consideration is to examine the systems that facilitate perpetrators' ability to engage in SH. In recent high-profile cases of sexual assault, multiple stakeholders and/or observers needed to be complicit for the misconduct to occur unchecked. In the case of Harvey Weinstein, for example, employees were responsible for setting up private meetings between actresses and Weinstein in Weinstein's hotel room; observers had concerns about misconduct but did not report them; and the Board of Directors ignored women's allegations and chose not to investigate reports, to name a few (Kantor & Twohey, 2017). While understanding the perpetrator's motivations and actions is important, future work should also take a holistic view of how multiple stakeholders and systemic factors (such as common stereotypes about women) play a role in allowing, enabling, and dismissing sexual misconduct.

Conclusion

Women in the lower social classes have been left out of conversations and scholarship around SH. This chapter is aimed at encouraging a change from that status quo. In providing a select review of work done in this area, we hope to bring awareness to the unique circumstances and challenges women in the lower social classes face. We also endeavor to encourage future research that gives more voice to women's stories and, in doing so, speaks to how individual and systemic issues can be addressed by organizational decision makers.

Notes

1 We recognize that the distinctions between social classes are fuzzy rather than clear lines, such as in the case of a blue-collar employee (e.g., electrician, plumber) who makes a salary on par with members of the middle social classes. In this chapter, we focus primarily on the working poor and precarious workers to illustrate the extreme nature of their situation and to highlight groups that have been largely overlooked in extant research. We point interested readers to more detailed discussions of the distinctions between social classes (see, e.g., Gray & Kish-Gephart, 2013; Kish-Gephart et al., 2023).
2 We use the term "Individual level Factors" to describe circumstances that occur at the individual level (rather than within organizations) that can increase women's vulnerability to sexual harassment. We do not use this term to suggest that these are inherent factors or that women should be blamed for them.
3 Professor Jamie L. Small argued that this was evidenced in the Ford-Kavanagh case. Dr. Blasey Ford offered testimony during Judge Kavanaugh's Supreme Court confirmation process, alleging that Judge Kavanaugh sexually assaulted her during a party in high school. In an examination of the testimonies, Small concluded that "cultural ideas about class and status shape our informal determinations of which men have the propensity to commit sexual assault in the first place," and in the Ford-Kavanaugh case specifically, markers of Kavanaugh's upper social class status (e.g., educational attainment, wealth) were used to defuse the idea that he could be a sexual predator (Small, 2018).
4 Given space restrictions, we are unable to address the intersection of race. However, we point interested readers to Chapter 8.

References

Acker, J. (2006). Inequality regimes: Gender, class, and race in organizations. *Gender & Society*, 20(4), 441–464.

American Association of Family Physicians (AAFP). (2022). Poverty and health: The family medicine perspective (Position Paper).

Ayres, M. M., Friedman, C. K., & Leaper, C. (2009). Individual and situational factors related to young women's likelihood of confronting sexism in their everyday lives. *Sex Roles*, 61(7), 449–460.

Barling, J., Dekker, I., Loughlin, C. A., Kevin Kelloway, E., Fullagar, C., & Johnson, D. (1996). Prediction and replication of the organizational and personal consequences of workplace sexual harassment. *Journal of Managerial Psychology*, 11(5), 4–25.

Benach, J., Vives, A., Amable, M., Vanroelen, C., Tarafa, G., & Muntaner, C. (2014). Precarious employment: Understanding an emerging social determinant of health. *Annual Review of Public Health*, 35, 229–253.

Berdahl, J. L. (2007). The sexual harassment of uppity women. *Journal of Applied Psychology*, 92(2), 425–437.

Berdahl, J. L., Cooper, M., Glick, P., Livingston, R. W., & Williams, J. C. (2018). Work as a masculinity contest. *Journal of Social Issues*, 74(3), 422–448.

Berg, H. (2020). Left of# MeToo. *Feminist Studies*, 46(2), 259–286.

Bettie, J. (2003). *Women without class: Girls, race, and identity*. University of California Press.

Black, K. A., & Gold, D. J. (2008). Gender differences and socioeconomic status biases in judgments about blame in date rape scenarios. *Violence and Victims*, 23(1), 115–128.

Bowes-Sperry, L., & Powell, G. N. (1999). Observers' reactions to social-sexual behavior at work: An ethical decision making perspective. *Journal of Management*, 25(6), 779–802.

Brunner, L. K., & Dever, M. (2014). Work, bodies and boundaries: Talking sexual harassment in the new economy. *Gender, Work and Organization*, 21(5), 459–471.

Bularzik, M. (1978). Sexual harassment at the workplace: Historical notes. *Radical America*, 12, 25–43.

Byrd, M. Y., Martinez, J., & Scott, C. L. (2024). 152 Social class and diversity in the workforce. In *Diversity in the workforce: Current issues and emerging trends* (pp. 152–169). Routledge.

Calarco, J. M. (2014). The inconsistent curriculum: Cultural tool kits and student interpretations of ambiguous expectations. *Social Psychology Quarterly*, 77, 185–209.

Center for American Progress. (2020). *Millions of undocumented immigrants are essential to America's recovery, new report shows*. Retrieved December 20, 2022, from www.americanprogress.org/press/release-millions-undocumented-immigrants-essential-americas-recovery-new-report-shows/

Cervantes, R. C., & Castro, F. G. (1985). Stress, coping, and Mexican American mental health: A systematic review. *Hispanic Journal of Behavioral Sciences*, 7(1), 1–73.

Chamberlain, L. J., Crowley, M., Tope, D., & Hodson, R. (2008). Sexual harassment in organizational context. *Work and Occupations*, 35(3), 262–295.

Chan, D. K., Chow, S. Y., Lam, C. B., & Cheung, S. F. (2008). Examining the job-related, psychological, and physical outcomes of workplace sexual harassment: A meta-analytic review. *Psychology of Women Quarterly*, 32(4), 362–376.

Chen, H., Domenzain, A., & Andrews, K. (2016). *The perfect storm: How supervisors get away with sexually harassing workers who work alone at night*. The Labor Occupational Health Program: Center for Occupational and Environmental Health, University of California.

Chira, S. (2017). We asked women in blue-collar workplaces about harassment. Here are their stories. *The New York Times*. Retrieved January 28, 2023, from www.nytimes.com/2017/12/29/us/blue-collar-women-harassment.html?auth=login-google1tap&login=google1tap

Clari, M., Conti, A., Scacchi, A., Scattaglia, M., Dimonte, V., & Gianino, M. M. (2020). Prevalence of workplace sexual violence against healthcare workers providing home care: A systematic review and meta-analysis. *International Journal of Environmental Research and Public Health*, 17(23), 8807.

Cortina, L. M., & Areguin, M. A. (2021). Putting people down and pushing them out: Sexual harassment in the workplace. *Annual Review of Organizational Psychology and Organizational Behavior*, 8, 285–309.

Cortina, L. M., & Wasti, S. A. (2005). Profiles in coping: Responses to sexual harassment across persons, organizations, and cultures. *Journal of Applied Psychology*, 90(1), 182.

Cregut-Aston, H. & Darioly, A. (2019). Why the hospitality industry needs women in managerial positions: The positive influence of female leadership on employee motivation. Retrieved December 20, 2022, from https://insights.ehotelier.com/insights/2019/09/24/why-the-hospitality-industry-needs-women-in-managerial-positions-the-positive-influence-of-female-leadership-on-employee-motivation/

Damaske, S. (2020). Job loss and attempts to return to work: Complicating inequalities across gender and class. *Gender & Society, 34*, 7–30.

Fitzgerald, L. F. (2020). Unseen: The sexual harassment of low-income women in America. *Equality, Diversity and Inclusion: An International Journal, 39*(1), 5–16.

Fitzgerald, L. F., Collinsworth, L. L., & Lawson, A. K. (2013). Sexual harassment, PTSD, and Criterion A: If it walks like a duck. . . . *Psychological Injury and Law, 6*, 81–91. http://doi.org/10.1007/s12207-013-9149-8

Fitzgerald, L. F., & Cortina, L. M. (2018). *Sexual harassment in work organizations: A view from the 21st century.* In C. B Travis, J. W. White, A. Rutherford, W. S. Williams, S. L. Cook, & K. F. Wyche (Eds.), *APA handbook of the psychology of women: Perspectives on women's private and public lives* (pp. 215–234). American Psychological Association.

Fitzgerald, L. F., Drasgow, F., Hulin, C. L., Gelfand, M. J., & Magley, V. J. (1997). Antecedents and consequences of sexual harassment in organizations: A test of an integrated model. *Journal of Applied Psychology, 82*(4), 578–589.

Fitzwater, E., & Gates, D. (2000). Violence and home care: A focus group study. *Home Healthcare Nurse: The Journal for The Home Care and Hospice Professional, 18*(9), 596–605.

Ford, J. L., Ivancic, S., & Scarduzio, J. (2021). Silence, voice, and resilience: An examination of workplace sexual harassment. *Communication Studies, 72*(4), 513–530.

Ford, J. L., & Ivancic, S. R. (2020). Surviving organizational tolerance of sexual harassment: An exploration of resilience, vulnerability, and harassment fatigue. *Journal of Applied Communication Research, 48*(2), 186–206.

Freeman, N. J. (2006). Socioeconomic status and belief in a just world: Sentencing of criminal defendants 1. *Journal of Applied Social Psychology, 36*(10), 2379–2394.

Frye, J. (2017). Not just the rich and famous. The pervasiveness of sexual harassment across industries affects all workers. *Center for American Progress.* Retrieved December 20, 2022, from www.americanprogress.org/issues/women/news/2017/11/20/443139/not-just-rich-famous/

Glomb, T. M., Richman, W. L., Hulin, C. L., Drasgow, F., Schneider, K. T., & Fitzgerald, L. F. (1997). Ambient sexual harassment: An integrated model of antecedents and consequences. *Organizational Behavior and Human Decision Processes, 71*(3), 309–328.

Good, L., & Cooper, R. (2016). 'But it's your job to be friendly': Employees coping with and contesting sexual harassment from customers in the service sector. *Gender, Work & Organization, 23*(5), 447–469.

Gray, B., & Kish-Gephart, J. J. (2013). Encountering social class differences at work: How "class work" perpetuates inequality. *Academy of Management Review, 38*(4), 670–699.

Griesbach, K., Reich, A., Elliott-Negri, L., & Milkman, R. (2019). Algorithmic control in platform food delivery work. *Socius: Sociological Research for a Dynamic World, 5*, 1–15.

Gruber, J. E. (1998). The impact of male work environments and organizational policies on women's experiences of sexual harassment. *Gender & Society, 12*(3), 301–319.

Gruber, J. E., & Bjorn, L. (1986). Women's responses to sexual harassment: An analysis of sociocultural, organizational, and personal resource models. *Social Science Quarterly*, 67(4), 814–826.

Hershcovis, M. S., Vranjes, I., Berdahl, J. L., & Cortina, L. M. (2021). See no evil, hear no evil, speak no evil: Theorizing network silence around sexual harassment. *Journal of Applied Psychology*, 106(12), 1834–1847.

Ho, I. K., Dinh, K. T., Bellefontaine, S. A., & Irving, A. L. (2012). Sexual harassment and post-traumatic stress disorder symptoms among Asian and White women. *Journal of Aggression, Maltreatment, and Trauma*, 21, 95–113.

Human Rights Watch. (2012). *Cultivating fear: The vulnerability of immigrant farmworkers in the US to sexual violence and sexual harassment*. Retrieved December 20, 2022, from www.hrw.org/report/2012/05/15/cultivating-fear/vulnerability-immigrant-farmworkers-us-sexual-violence-and

Hussain, S. (2022). Prop. 22: California gig companies, workers get their day in appeals court. *Los Angeles Times*. Retrieved January 28, 2023, from www.latimes.com/business/story/2022-12-13/california-prop-22-appeals-court-hearing-weighs-gig-workers-fate

Icenogle, M. L., Eagle, B. W., Ahmad, S., & Hanks, L. A. (2002). Assessing perceptions of sexual harassment behaviors in a manufacturing environment. *Journal of Business & Psychology*, 16, 601–616.

Jain, S. S., & Lee, J. S. (2022). Allegations of sexual misconduct: A view from the observation deck of power distance belief. *Journal of Business Ethics*, 175, 391–410.

Jordan, E. (1992). Race, gender, and social class in the Thomas sexual harassment hearings: The hidden fault lines in political discourse. *Harvard Women's Law Journal*, 15, 1–24.

Kantor, J., & Twohey, M. (2017). Harvey Weinstein paid off sexual harassment accusers for decades. *The New York Times*, 5(10).

Kiebler, J. M., & Stewart, A. J. (2022). Stereotypes in attributions about women's gender-based mistreatment. *Violence Against Women*, 28(3–4), 740–760.

Kim, N. J-E., Vásquez, V. B., Torres, E., Bud Nicola, R. M., & Karr, C. (2016). Breaking the silence: Sexual harassment of Mexican women farmworkers. *Journal of Agromedicine*, 21(2), 154–162.

Kish-Gephart, J., Moergen, K., Tilton, J., & Gray, B. (2023). Social class and work: A review and organizing framework. *Journal of Management*, 49(1), 509–565.

Kraus, M. W., Piff, P. K., Mendoza-Denton, R., Rheinschmidt, M. L., & Keltner, D. (2012). Social class, solipsism, and contextualism: How the rich are different from the poor. *Psychological Review*, 119, 546–572.

Lazar, M., & Davenport, L. (2018). Barriers to health care access for low income families: A review of literature. *Journal of Community Health Nursing*, 35(1), 28–37.

Lazarus, R. S., & Folkman, S. (1984). *Stress, appraisal, and coping*. Springer Publishing Company.

Lenart, E. K., Bee, T. K., Seger, C. P., Lewis, Jr, R. H., Filiberto, D. M., Huang, D.-D., Fischer, P. E., Croce, M. A., Fabian, T. C., & Magnotti, L. J. (2021). Youth, poverty, and interpersonal violence: A recipe for PTSD. *Trauma Surgery & Acute Care Open*, 6(1), e000710.

Liu, W. M., Ali, S. R., Soleck, G., Hopps, J., & Pickett, T. (2004). Using social class in counseling psychology research. *Journal of Counseling Psychology*, 51, 3–18

Lucas, K., & Buzzanell, P. M. (2004). Blue-collar work, career, and success: Occupational narratives of Sisu. *Journal of Applied Communication Research*, 32(4), 273–292.

Ma, N. F., Rivera, V. A., Yao, Z., & Yoon, D. (2022). *"Brush it off": How women workers manage and cope with bias and harassment in gender-agnostic gig platforms.* In Proceedings of the 2022 CHI Conference on Human Factors in Computing Systems (CHI '22). Association for Computing Machinery, New York, NY, Article 397, 1–13.

Maffie, M., & Elias, A. (2019). Platform design as a managerial act: Analyzing sexual harassment in the gig economy. *LERA for Libraries, 23*(2).

Malamut, A. B., & Offermann, L. R. (2001). Coping with sexual harassment: Personal, environmental, and cognitive determinants. *Journal of Applied Psychology, 86*(6), 1152.

Marín, L. S., Barreto, M., Montano, M., Sugerman-Brozan, J., Goldstein-Gelb, M., & Punnett, L. (2021). Workplace sexual harassment and vulnerabilities among low-wage Hispanic women. *Occupational Health Science, 5*, 391–414.

McCabe, M. P., & Hardman, L. (2005). Attitudes and perceptions of workers to sexual harassment. *Journal of Social Psychology, 145*, 719–740.

McLaughlin, H., Uggen, C., & Blackstone, A. (2012). Sexual harassment, workplace authority, and the paradox of power. *American Sociological Review, 77*(4), 625–647.

Morgan, P. (1999). Risking relationships: Understanding the litigation choices of sexually harassed women. *Law and Society Review, 33*, 67–92.

Morgan, P. (2001). Sexual harassment: Violence against women at work. In C. M. Renzetti, J. L. Edleson & R. K. Bergen (Eds.), *Sourcebook on violence against women* (pp. 209–222). Sage Publications.

Murphy, J., Samples, J., Morales, M., & Shadbeh, N. (2015). "They talk like that, but we keep working": Sexual harassment and sexual assault experiences among Mexican indigenous farmworker women in Oregon. *Journal of Immigrant Minority Health, 17*(6), 1834–1839.

National Farm Worker Ministry. (2022). *U.S. labor law for farm workers.* Retrieved December 20, 2022, from https://nfwm.org/farm-workers/farm-worker-issues/laborlaws/#:~:text=Farm%20workers%20were%2C%20and%20remain,or%20supporting%20a%20labor%20union.

National Restaurant Association. (2022). *DEI survey report.* Retrieved December 20, 2022, from https://restaurant.org/research-and-media/research/research-reports/DEI?utm_source=press&utm_medium=press&utm_campaign=elevate&utm_content=assoc

North, A. (2018). The #MeToo movement and its evolution, explained. *Vox.com.* Retrieved October 11, 2018, from www.vox.com/identities/2018/10/9/17933746/me-too-movement-metoo-brett-kavanaugh-weinstein

Patel, J. K., Griggs, T., & Miller, C. C. (2017). We asked 615 men about how they conduct themselves at work. *The New York Times.* Retrieved December 20, 2022, from www.nytimes.com/interactive/2017/12/28/upshot/sexual-harassment-survey-600-men.html

Podgursky, M., & Swaim, P. (1987). Job displacement and earnings loss: Evidence from the displaced worker survey. *Industrial and Labor Relations Review, 41*, 17–29.

Pryor, J. B., LaVite, C. M., & Stoller, L. M. (1993). A social psychological analysis of sexual harassment: The person/situation interaction. *Journal of Vocational Behavior, 42*, 68–83.

Ragins, B. R., & Scandura, T. A. (1995). Antecedents and work-related correlates of reported sexual harassment: An empirical investigation of competing hypotheses. *Sex Roles, 32*, 429–455.

Rawski, S. L., O'Leary-Kelly, A. M., & Breaux-Soignet, D. (2022). It's all fun and games until someone gets hurt: An interactional framing theory of work social sexual behavior. *Academy of Management Review, 47*(4), 617–636.

Resnick, S., & Wolff, R. (2003). The diversity of class analysis: A critique of Erik Olin Wright and beyond. *Critical Sociology, 29*, 7–28.

Richie, B. (2000). A Black feminist reflection on the antiviolence movement. *Signs, 25*(4), 1133–1137.

Rye, B. J., Greartrix, S. A., & Enright, C. S. (2006). The case of the guilty victim: The effects of gender of victim and gender of perpetrator on attributions of blame and responsibility. *Sex Roles, 54*, 639–649.

Schneider, K. T., Tomaka, J., & Palacios, R. (2001). Women's cognitive, affective, and physiological reactions to a male coworker's sexist behavior. *Journal of Applied Social Psychology, 31*, 1995–2018.

Schroedel, J. R. (1985). *Alone in a crowd*. Temple University Press.

Schroedel, J. R. (1990). Blue-collar women: Paying the price at home and on the job. In H. Y. Grossman & N. L. Chester (Eds.), *The experience and meaning of work in women's lives* (pp. 241–260). Erlbaum.

Segrave, K. (1994). *The sexual harassment of women in the workplace, 1600 to 1993*. McFarland and Co. Inc.

Sennett, R., & Cobb, R. (1977). *The hidden injuries of class*. Cambridge University Press.

SHRM. (2018). *Harassment-free workplace series: A focus on sexual harassment*. Retrieved March 20, 2023, from www.shrm.org/hr-today/trends-and-forecasting/research-and-surveys/pages/a-focus-on-sexual-harassment.aspx

Small, J. L. (2015). Classing sex offenders: How prosecutors and defense attorneys differentiate men accused of sexual assault. *Law & Society Review, 49*(1), 109–141.

Small, J. L. (2018, October 4). *Does a man's social class have anything to do with the likelihood he'll commit sexual assault?* The Conversation. https://theconversation.com/does-a-mans-social-class-have-anything-to-do-with-the-likelihood-hell-commit-sexual-assault-104207

Spencer, B. (2016). The impact of class and sexuality-based stereotyping on rape blame. *Sexualization, Media, & Society, 2*(2), 2374623816643282.

Stambaugh, P. M. (1997). The power of law and the sexual harassment complaints of women. *National Women's Studies Association Journal, 9*(2), 23–42.

Stephens, N. M., Markus, H. R., & Phillips, L. T. (2014). Social class culture cycles: How three gateway contexts shape selves and fuel inequality. *Annual Review of Psychology, 65*, 611–634.

Sullivan, M. A. (1998). A qualitative inquiry of women's experiences in a male-dominated vocational technical college. *Dissertation Abstracts International, 60*(01), 45A.

Tilton, J., Lucas, K., Kish-Gephart, J. J., & Kent, J. K. (2024). Enduring, strategizing, and rising above: Workplace dignity threats and responses across job levels. *Journal of Business Ethics*, 1–22.

United States, Court of Appeals for the Fifth Circuit. (2011, July 6). *United States of America v. Ngozi Nnaji*. Docket no. 10–10598. United States Court of Appeals for the Fifth Circuit. www.justice.gov/sites/default/files/crt/legacy/2011/07/12/nnajibrief.pdf

U.S. Bureau of Labor Statistics. (2022). *Labor force statistics from the current population survey*. Retrieved January 28, 2023, from www.bls.gov/cps/cpsaat11.htm

U.S. Department of Agriculture. (2019). *2017 census of agriculture.* Retrieved December 20, 2022, from www.nass.usda.gov/Publications/AgCensus/2017/Full_Report/Volume _1,_Chapter_1_US/usv1.pdf

Vaughan, A. (2001). The association between offender socioeconomic status and victim-offender relationship in rape offences. *Psychology, Evolution and Gender, 3*(2), 121–136.

Villegas, P. E. (2019). "I made myself small like a cat and ran away": Workplace sexual harassment, precarious immigration status and legal violence. *Journal of Gender Studies, 28*(6), 674–686.

Warrell, M. (2017, June 26). Mentoring matters: How more women can get the right people in their corner. *Forbes.* Retrieved March 6, 2023, from www.forbes.com/sites/margiewarrell/2017/06/24/women-mentoring/?sh=53954a8722db

Wasti, S. A., & Cortina, L. M. (2002). Coping in context: Sociocultural determinants of responses to sexual harassment. *Journal of Personality and Social Psychology, 83*(2), 394.

Waugh, I. M. (2006). *Latinas negotiating "traffic": Examining the sexual harassment experiences of Mexican immigrant farm working women.* University of California.

Waugh, I. M. (2010). Examining the sexual harassment experiences of Mexican immigrant farmworking women. *Violence Against Women, 16*(3), 237–261.

Willer, R., Rogalin, C. L., Conlon, B., & Wojnowicz, M. T. (2013). Overdoing gender: A test of the masculine overcompensation thesis. *American Journal of Sociology, 118*(4), 980–1022.

Willness, C. R., Steel, P., & Lee, K. (2007). A meta-analysis of the antecedents and consequences of workplace sexual harassment. *Personnel Psychology, 60*(1), 127–162.

Wolfe, J., Kandra, J., Engdahl, L., & Shierholz, H. (2020). Domestic workers chartbook: A comprehensive look at the demographics, wages, benefits, and poverty rates of the professionals who care for our family members and clean our homes. *Economic Policy Institute.* Retrieved December 20, 2022, from www.epi.org/publication/domestic-workers-chartbook-a-comprehensive-look-at-the-demographics-wages-benefits-and-poverty-rates-of-the-professionals-who-care-for-our-family-members-and-clean-our-homes/

Wong, P., & Weiner, B. (1981). When people ask "why" questions, and the heuristics of attributional search. *Journal of Personality and Social Psychology, 40,* 650–663.

Yeung, B. (2018). *In a day's work: The fight to end sexual violence among America's most vulnerable workers.* New Press.

Ziegler, E. (2020). *Understanding the nature and experience of gig work in Canada.* Retrieved January 28, 2023, from https://fsc-ccf.ca/research/understanding-the-nature-and-experienceof-gig-work-in-canada/

11

UNANSWERED QUESTIONS OF #NOWWHAT

Jaclyn M. Jensen and Carra S. Sims

The Role of Resolution in Sexual Harassment

It is evident that the mechanisms that maintain organizational structures, processes, policies, and interactions that facilitate sexual harassment (SH) are persistent and pernicious. Several decades of consideration of the issue of SH has outlined important insights about its nature, who experiences it, and information about organizational causes. A plethora of best practices for mitigation have accumulated . . . but still, women experience SH at work, and in society more generally, at stubbornly high rates. What comes after #MeToo? Aptly coined #NowWhat, many questions remain about what companies can productively to do prevent and end SH (Durana et al., 2018; *#MeToo, Now What?*, 2018).

To understand this issue more fully, this chapter examines the role of resolution in SH. We first turn to the sociological literature to explore its findings on what social and societal aspects might sustain the persistence of SH, as successful mitigation and organizational change can only benefit from taking context into account (Quick & McFadyen, 2017). We then provide an overview of the laws affecting SH in the United States, as the legal landscape has historically affected how individuals, organizations, and societies approach this issue. These literatures provide ample evidence that entrenched workplace sexism, combined with legal structures that often do little to repair the professional and personal trauma experienced by victims, creates challenges for victims and organizations seeking productive forms of resolution. To overcome these roadblocks and offer insights into both preventative and productive recovery strategies, we turn

DOI: 10.4324/9781003300953-13

to the industrial-organizational psychology and organizational behavior (IO/OB) literatures to offer future directions for research.

A Brief Sociological Perspective on Gender and Sexual Harassment

The sociology literature reveals that across and within cultures, women are persistently devalued (Acker, 1990, 2006; Epstein, 2007; Risman, 2004). Acker (1990, 2006) notes the ideal worker is a White male, devoted to work and without outside responsibilities (Kalev & Deutsch, 2018). Ideal worker characteristics are also typically coded as male (Dobbin & Kalev, 2021; Kalev & Deutsch, 2018). This embodiment of the ideal worker has real consequences for women. Their work contributions and work experiences are systematically devalued and deprioritized in the sometimes unconscious replication of the status quo, and sometimes even through processes of bureaucratic systematization put in place with the intention to achieve *more equitable* ends. For example, Acker (2006) described a study of job categorization for comparable worth purposes that revealed that [male] managers were often credited for work done by their [female] administrative assistants, but head-to-head comparison of managerial and secretarial jobs was explicitly restricted.

Moreover, when women advance into organizations or jobs coded as male, they may face penalties for transgressing the boundaries of the "male" role (Berdahl, 2007; Epstein, 2007; Saguy & Rees, 2021), including SH (Berdahl, 2007; Saguy & Rees, 2021; Schultz, 2018). As stated succinctly by Saguy and Rees (2021): "Our review of the sociological literature on harassment suggests that workplace sex-based harassment is best understood as a strategy that some people use to undermine marginalized workers' integration into the workplace and ability to perform their jobs" (p. 430).

The sociological literature further illuminates the importance of approaching the problem on multiple levels. Researchers argue that multiple levels provide richness and necessary explanatory power in examining how inequalities such as those rooted in gender persist: they suggest examining individual participation (however unconscious and automatic), the level of interactions, and the more macro level—which can include organizations as well as society (Ridgeway & Correll, 2004; Risman, 2004).

A multilevel perspective reveals the power dynamics that are often at play in situations of SH, as well as the structures that maintain power imbalances to the detriment of lower power or lower status victims. For example, DiTomaso et al. (2007) describe mechanisms that maintain ine-quality such as social closure whereby such constituencies (at all levels) work to close out lower-power individuals from experiencing access to and benefits of power. This can be done in an institutionalized fashion, for example, by setting requirements for job entry that systematically exclude some groups more than others—purposefully, or less consciously. For example, requirements for a set nine-to-five schedule, although generally regarded as acceptable, may systematically tend to exclude women with childcare responsibilities. As another example, licensure requirements can provide barriers to entry for various jobs and serve to maintain the job security of incumbents. This complements the sociological perspective pro-vided by Acker (1990, 2006) and others (e.g., Saguy & Rees, 2021) that emphasizes dynamics that serve to elevate men at the expense of women. A final example is employer contracting practices, which typically afford top-level employees greater job security and contractual protections than rank-and-file employees, whose behavior may be regulated more aggres-sively as at-will employees (Arnow-Richman, 2018). This can result in a double standard for behavior that is considered inappropriate—but toler-ated—at higher levels, and disproportionately punished at lower levels.

A Brief Legal Overview of the Law and Sexual Harassment

A primer on the legal remedies available to targets of harassment requires a basic understanding of the law that underscores much of the research on the identification of, remedies for, and prevention of SH (see Wiener and Gutek's (1999) review for more detail). Recognizing that different legal systems affect perceptions and what remedies may be considered (e.g., Saguy & Rees, 2021), for the purposes of this chapter, we bound our anal-ysis to that of US law and focus primarily on Title VII of the Civil Rights Act (CRA) of 1964 which prohibits workplace harassment, including quid pro quo and hostile work environment harassment, on the basis of sex. Readers interested in learning more about SH laws in other countries and cultures are encouraged to review Heymann et al. (2023) and Raub et al. (2021).

Social science definitions of SH in the United States quite often adhere to some aspects of the legal framework. One of the most commonly used measures is the Sexual Experiences Questionnaire or SEQ (Willness et al., 2007). This features items that describe the behavioral instantiations of a harassment experience. Some items tap sexual coercion, or *quid pro quo*, in which sexual behavior is subject to some form of exchange for job ben-efit (or absence of punishment). Some items tap unwanted sexual atten-tion, which describes various attempts to establish sexual relations, but job benefit or punishment is not on the line. The third general item type is gender harassment, which ultimately breaks into two types of *hostile environment* experiences—ones in which a target experiences behaviors that are oriented around *sexual* crudity (such as jokes) and ones in which a target experiences behaviors designed to convey *sexist* hostility based on gender (Stark et al., 2002). Examples include being told that one's job is not suitable for one's gender. Also reflecting the influence of the legal context, items are phrased to make clear that the experiences are *unwanted* or *unwelcome*—a key first step in the legal criteria for harassment.[1]

Gender-harassment type experiences rooted in sexual or sexist hostility are much more common than are experiences representing sexual assault or quid pro quo (Cortina & Areguin, 2020). Definitions matter; as noted by Roehling and Huang (2018), it is important that organizations align definitions conveyed through training with implemented organizational incentives: if an organization puts forth an expansive view of harassment that entails behaviors that do not rise to meet a legal bar, they should be prepared to use that more expansive view in practice and not limit punishment and intervention only to cases that rise to meet legal requirements. That said, Saguy and Rees (2021) argue the #MeToo movement itself has served to focus on the generally *sexual* types of offenses (the sexual assaults of Harvey Weinstein, for example) rather than the quotidian *sexism* (including Weinstein's own more generally abusive and toxic gender-based behavior; see Schultz, 2018). On the other hand, they note that #MeToo raised the profile of women's varied experiences and may have led to more types of behaviors being included under the umbrella of the lay meaning of the term "harassment." For example, the experiences of Susan Fowler at Uber (which included women being denied leather jackets provided to men) and Ellen Pao at Silicon Valley venture capital firm Kleiner Perkins (including exclusion from networking and other work-related events to which men were routinely invited) have been highlighted along with discussions of sexual behaviors (Schultz, 2018). This is important, as sexist, gender-based harassment is often far more frequent (Cortina & Areguin, 2020; Farris et al., 2020; Leskinen et al., 2011; Sims et al., 2022)[2] and causes comparable distress to victims as more infrequent sexual coercion (Langhout et al., 2005). Broadening the definitional scope more fully incorporates current thinking that harassment can constitute a range of behaviors from unwelcome conduct to more extreme behaviors and can be experienced by male and female targets alike (see also Chapter 9). The conduct becomes unlawful when it creates a situation where enduring it is a condition of employment, and it is severe or pervasive enough such that a reasonable person would consider it to be intimidating, abusive, or hostile (*Harassment*, n.d.).

When an individual has been sexually harassed and is seeking resolution, filing a complaint with the organization is typically the prescribed first step. Complainants must recognize that the behavior they have experienced is illegal (or at minimum wrong) and be willing to come forward. After a complaint has been filed, by law, organizations must initiate investigations in a timely fashion and may use an external third-party investigator. In some cases, employees' options are bound by the terms of their employment contract, which can include aspects like Nondisclosure Agreements or NDAs or require the use of arbitration. Individuals alleging harassment also have the option of filing a complaint with the Equal Employment Opportunity Commission (EEOC) or a state or local agency (known as Fair Employment Practice Agencies, or FEPAs) with authority for enforcing local employment laws, which have also seen tremendous reform, including the passage of more than 70 workplace harassment bills in 22 states and the District of Columbia, since the #MeToo movement (Johnson et al., 2022). As when an individual files a complaint with their employer, the EEOC and/or FEPAs should also initiate an investigation. Depending on the outcome, a negotiation may ensue between the complainant and their employer to bring the matter to resolution. Claims of harassment may also be resolved via alternative dispute resolution mechanisms, including the practice of mediation and arbitration (Foote & Goodman-Delahunty, 2021).

Beyond attempts to resolve complaints of harassment through either traditional or alternative dispute resolution mechanisms, in the United States, *enforcement* of legislation such as the CRA, including case law that expanded its reach, led to a push by organizations for compliance activities that would serve as an affirmative defense. Given the initial uncertainty regarding what compliance actions would be acceptable, many companies benchmarked anti-harassment policies and practices used by prominent firms, including ways for victims to report and lodge complaints. A potentially unintended consequence was a favoring of "ceremonial compliance practices that do not change career systems" (Dobbin & Kalev, 2021, p. 285). For example, calls for zero tolerance policies against harassment have been longstanding (Ward, 2018) but often ring hollow when accountability mechanisms underlying said policies are weak or non-existent (Stockdale et al., 2004).

Subsequent case law in the United States has enshrined such "best practices" that in some cases also work against diversity, such as grievance procedures and personnel practices that, through paperwork, may serve to add legitimacy to the status quo (Dobbin & Kalev, 2021). For example, before #MeToo, the use of NDAs had long served to silence survivors and hide ongoing harassment in organizations. In the post-MeToo era, however, a growing number of states have passed laws preventing employers from using NDAs to silence victims (Johnson et al., 2022). Beyond this issue, though, lies the challenge that the legal treatment of harassment in the United States offers few if any incentives to ensure that initiatives *work*. Systematic examination of such practices is actively in opposition to organizational priorities: should it be shown that organizations know that the policies and practices instituted are failures, organizations would in fact lose the potential to claim these same policies and practices as an affirmative defense in a judicial court.

Resolution Through Sociological and Legal Lenses

Obviously, one level through which to tackle women's devalued status is societal, through laws and policies intended to remediate harassment and discrimination. However, paperwork and an *appearance* of impartial, unbiased evaluation can serve as a shield against challenging the status quo in the sense that people within the organization itself—including those subject to discrimination and harassment—are more likely to infer legitimacy when a clear process can be pointed to (Dobbin & Kalev, 2021). The comfort of bureaucracy can literally paper over perceptions of bias while not disturbing its underlying operation (see Scott and Martin's (2006) overview of tactics through which perpetrators (and organizations) manage outrage related to harassment, which includes use of official channels and processes to support claims that procedural justice has been served). Indeed, power and hierarchy in organizations can be, and are in some senses designed to be, self-perpetuating (DiTomaso et al., 2007).

Epstein (2007) notes that gender schemas can be activated in almost any interaction. A challenge inheres in the cognitive tendency of women and men in a given culture not to question the cultural schemas around division of labor and boundaries, which facilitate those boundaries' persistence. Thus, beliefs around the ideal (and promotable) worker being present in person at all times may seem appropriate—and both women and men may be inclined not to question the base assumption. Risman (2004) describes how challenging it may be to contravene such schemas: it requires a deliberate effort, and in some cases luck. And this effort must be undertaken simultaneously at multiple levels to work—individual, interactional, and organizational. To achieve success, as Epstein (2007) notes, it is also important to acknowledge the times when these schemas *are* fun and playful at the individual level such that they signal social acceptance and a sense of belonging (see also Aquino et al. (2014)). Organizational or even societal solutions alone do not suffice when this is the case. Social accountability in the form of openly talking about managerial decision making (such as creating task forces comprised of senior managers to discuss, brainstorm, and support the implementation of reforms) has shown promise as a mechanism for promoting equality (Dobbin & Kalev, 2021). The implications of a multiple-level perspective that incorporates individual choice in a way that moves beyond the supply/demand perspective that focuses on self-segregation into dead end jobs and careers might consider social accountability in a broader sense, although it would remain to be seen if this would be successful and how best to implement such a framework.

When considering intervention at the level of society and organization, the balkanized system of legislation and judiciary in the United States does proffer one potential advantage; there are many targets of opportunity. For example, court cases may be brought in multiple jurisdictions. Case law may be set up to perpetuate now-outdated perspectives on what is considered "reasonable" in SH cases; however, alternative rulings with a more modern perspective may also be found to contravene such (Williams et al., 2019). Legislation passed at different levels may also be leveraged to provide protections. For example, prior to the Supreme Court decision in *Bostock v. Clayton County* which found that sexual orientation discrimination was covered by gender discrimination under the CRA and set the standard for the entire United States, individual cities such as Alexandria, VA, outlawed discrimination on the basis of sexual orientation.

Resolution Through Industrial/Organizational Psychology—Organizational Behavior Lenses

The sociological literature offers an important lens through which to appraise harassment in organizations: at multiple levels (individual, interaction, organization, and society), with an eye to how established processes may serve to disenfranchise responses to #MeToo as well as how different types of inequalities may coincide. The legal perspective speaks to how the law in the United States both frames the problem and organizational responses to it and highlights both mechanisms for the persistence of ineffective remedies as well as legal mechanisms that may redirect organizations down a more productive course. The IO/OB literature highlights mechanisms at the level of the individual, interaction, and organization in terms of how processes unfold but can draw from these other literatures broader contextual information that heretofore was imperfectly integrated.

For example, several antecedents of SH are relatively well established in the psychological literature and offer potential levers for intervention. One such is job-gender context, which describes the numerical dominance of women in a given job, and also encapsulates the gender of those who tend to hold positions of power in an organization and occupation. In a related vein, Cortina and Areguin (2020; see also Berdahl et al. (2018)) summarize how some jobs can be characterized by masculinity contest culture. This entails a constellation of several values that center the primacy of traditional (toxic) masculinity—putting work ahead of everything else, emphasis on strength and stamina (including working extreme hours), avoiding shows of weakness, and emphasizing ruthless competition (Berdahl et al., 2018). Although Cortina and Areguin (2020) describe this culture as an antecedent distinct from job-gender context, it is easy to envision these two factors being related—both reflecting the prototypical "ideal" worker that serves to limit women's enfranchisement as organizational participants (see also Chapter 4). With this perspective we can see that organizations taking a more expansive view of the ideal worker may wish to revise practices (such as penalizing employees who take a break or leave in support of family obligations) in which these assumptions fester.

Another influential organizational antecedent to harassment is organizational *tolerance* for SH, which encompasses the incentives surrounding harassment. These incentives occur at multiple levels, including the levels of peer interaction and supervisor intervention. Key elements include whether or not accessing organizational remedies such as the complaint process is perceived as risky for complainants; whether a complainant would be taken seriously; and whether anything would be done in response (Hulin et al., 1996). As noted by Patel et al. (2017), men who indicated that they perceived little chance of punishment for harassing, or who said their supervisors were tolerant of such behavior, were more likely to say that they had engaged in such behavior in the past year. This echoes work by Pryor et al. (1995) that highlighted that men with a propensity to harass are more likely to do so in an environment where it is considered acceptable. Further, Dekker and Barling (1998) found that enforcement of organizational policies predicted SH behavior; that is, when anti-harassment policies were enforced, harassment was less frequent. Because organizations tolerant of SH are organizations in which it thrives (Willness et al., 2007), firms should implement complaint policies and disciplinary procedures that align with a no-tolerance framework.

Research on organizational climate and culture notes that leaders play a critical role in establishing and maintaining climate (Ehrhart et al., 2014). Certainly, organizational-level leadership has a role in setting appropriate organizational policies in which incentives align against tolerance of harassment. However, the actual enforcement of these policies is key (see, e.g., Hulin et al., 1996; Naylor et al., 1980; Zohar, 2002; Zohar & Hofmann, 2012) and can take place at multiple levels. In fact, employees' experience of the enforcement of incentives set by policy is most often at the level of interaction with supervisors (Zohar & Hofmann, 2012). In their review of

SH training effectiveness, Roehling and Huang (2018) also describe how the legal context for harassment reflects the essentiality of supervisors—not just higher-level organizational leadership. Organizations should ensure that supervisors are well trained on how to handle reports of SH, as supervisors play a primary role in not only shaping the climate but also the ability of the organization to avoid punitive damages should supervisors fail to enforce their own antidiscrimination policy (Roehling & Huang, 2018).

Buchanan et al. (2014) point out that a growing body of work suggests bystanders can also contribute to the prevalence of SH in the workplace and associated climate; although bystanders rarely intervene, when they do so they can be a powerful force for good (see also Chapter 3). Bowes-Sperry and O'Leary-Kelly (2005) proposed a typology of the various ways in which bystanders might intervene to positive effect. Certainly, bystander intervention could contribute to climate for SH in the sense that the action (or inaction) of bystanders and others at the peer level can influence perceived contingencies with regard to SH (see, for an example, McLaughlin et al. (2012)). In one theoretical model of harassment (Fitzgerald et al., 1997; see also Lytell, 2010) bystander experiences and norms are aspects of the workgroup context that are relevant for harassment climate. Cortina and Areguin (2020) further posit that recruiting bystanders into allyship with harassment targets through training is one way to reduce harassment and sidestep some training emphasis on wrongdoing that can foster defensiveness and backlash.

It should also be recognized that a sole focus on SH generally (or even particularly on the more popularized focus on sexual rather than sexist hostility) is not the only climate dimension worthy of consideration. Indeed, the extreme examples of SH found in the press rarely happen in a vacuum but rather most often occur in a context in which other forms of workplace mistreatment thrive (Cortina & Areguin, 2020). For example, the #MeToo movement highlighted that the experiences of women of color and lower wage workers are frequently left out of the narrative (Johnson et al., 2022). Moreover, the sociological perspectives reviewed highlight that gender is only one lens through which organizational interactions should be viewed—others include race, class, and sexuality and an intersectional perspective can provide clarity on the potential dynamics underlying such negative events (e.g., Risman, 2004; see also Chapters 8 and 10). Although not their focus, Hershcovis and Barling (2010) also highlight how negative workplace treatment is interrelated. Farris et al. (2020), in a large empirical study of the civilian workforce, also describe how tolerance for sexual mistreatment, racial mistreatment, and incivility are related.

As noted by Ford and Ivancic (2020), policies, while necessary, are not sufficient. Stockdale et al. (2004) note that policies may suffer a loss of credibility depending on how well they are enforced and perceptions of that enforcement. Buchanan et al. (2014) note that the way in which a complaint was handled, both formally and informally, was key to how satisfactory that process was. While complaint and reporting processes are relevant for a tolerant climate for SH, the contrast with the sociological and legal perspectives highlights the key nature of daily interactions that are *easily observable* by participants at all levels. Such quotidian experiences and observations by employees generate shared perceptions of organizational climate. That is, a feedback loop emerges such that climate affects experience of harassment, which in turn affects climate, which then likely reflects organizational reality (Sims, 2005). To address this issue, supervisors should be well trained in how to handle inappropriate behaviors that do not meet a legal bar or generate claims of harassment and also be supported by upper-level leadership and human resources when they raise concerns (Lawrence, 2020).

Training is another organizational intervention that may affect climate perceptions and serve as an antecedent or a response to harassment. In a theoretical model of training effectiveness, Kath and Magley (2014) noted organizations that appear to be using training not to promote a civil workplace but rather to shield themselves from liability may find training ineffective, with employees experiencing harassment at the same rates and becoming more cynical with regard to how harassment is treated. Goldberg et al. (2019) examined training specifically for HR managers—key vehicles of policy enforcement within organizations—and noted that organizational tolerance for harassment affects whether or not HR managers transfer any knowledge and practice modifications to their day-to-day work after training. In a tolerant organization, they are less likely to bother.

Roehling and Huang (2018) reviewed the literature and argued that the legal context makes clear that the use of training as a shield against liability is not a mere paper defense, but instead effective use of the strategy requires that organizations implement *effective* training, and they cite case law in support of this contention. However, they note that the available evidence base for what comprises successful harassment training is relatively limited. They noted key themes in the available evidence to date: training that promotes empathy toward harassment targets may be beneficial, and more extensive exposure to training may be beneficial. With regard to the latter, this entails not only additional time but also multiple modalities including role-playing exercises. An hour of PowerPoint training annually is unlikely to provoke actual behavior change; organizations that are serious about changing climate must provide their employees with a more thorough understanding of, and experience with, acceptable norms for behavior. Dobbin and Kalev (2019) and Lee et al. (2019) take this one step further and argue that giving employees tools to recognize and address harassment through practice recognizing harassment in an ambiguous situation, intervening when harassment has been witnessed, and feedback on the intervention itself aligns well with decades of research on training transfer and effectiveness. Greater investment in these types of tools can also help bystanders with exercises where they work through the costs and benefits of intervening, which can often be a barrier for witnesses to act (Lee et al., 2019).

Rawski et al. (2022) describe in depth one way in which harassment behaviors may be framed in organizations that facilitates perpetuation and exacerbation—a play frame. Though at times these behaviors may be considered fun or engaging, Rawski et al. describe how there may be times where organizations can take advantage of the sensemaking process engaged in by employees to shift the frame on harassment and set a new playing field—one in which norms for civility and respect are emphasized over gendered behaviors that may not be equally fun for all.

Future Directions on Productive Resolution

As we look to future research on productive forms of resolution, we are reminded of the history that got us here. The #MeToo movement put a spotlight on what can happen when you apply a legal lens of when organizations must intervene to stop or address harassment: a context in which organizations are required to act in remediation only when they have discovered a legal violation has taken place. Thus, a large body of the research on strategies for addressing an incident focuses on principles of reporting, accountability, risk mitigation, and formal grievance procedures (Quick & McFadyen, 2017). The challenge is that the efficacy of many of these strategies is highly debatable, with a lack of empirical evidence and a scholarly debate over what appears to be superficial behavior that satisfies the court as evidence of preventive action, but which does very little to actually reduce SH (Arnow-Richman, 2018). #MeToo also brought many of calls for termination, often in reaction to very extreme forms of behavior by individual employees (Boyle & Cucchiara, 2018). However, even when a violation has been discovered, many organizations remain reluctant to take disciplinary action for fear of losing star performers or clients, or because an individual's employment contract failed to specify SH as a punishable offense (Arnow-Richman, 2018). The question remains how to address the less extreme forms of harassment that happen more often (Cortina & Areguin, 2020; see also Chapter 6). Moreover, if the focus is only on legally required solutions that address only the more sexual forms of SH, anything that does not fall into that very prescribed box will not be part of the solution (see Schultz, 2018). These strategies tend to over-anchor on more severe incidents of harassment (i.e., the gross sexual misconduct often reported from high profile offenders) and largely are oriented toward treating the disease of harassment, rather than preventing it.

A mindset that emphasizes disease and risk prevention, along the lines of what is discussed in the public health and risk mitigation literatures (Picture of America Fact Sheet, 2017; Quick & McFadyen, 2017), would suggest that strategies aimed at stopping harassment before it starts may diminish overall risk and prevalence. Promoting a climate of respect and civility, training to raise awareness about SH, and increasing the representation of women in leadership and positions of power (Schultz, 2018) are all highly aligned with this mindset. These perspectives also align with the socio-logical literature, which underscores that harassment occurs in situations where harassers are in positions of power and, when unchecked, use their power to display mastery and superiority over women and denigrate men who are not considered "real men" (Schultz, 2018). These strategies need to address norms in organizations so that they can inoculate against SH in the same way that administering vaccines and altering risky behavior seek to improve public health outcomes (Picture of America Fact Sheet, 2017). Strategies aimed at improving the representation of women and modify-ing organizational culture and climate to be interpersonally safe for all employees presumably also afford organizations the opportunity to achieve more intersectional outcomes, as improving a climate of civility in organi-zations should diminish related forms of hostility, including other forms of harassment and discrimination (Cortina, 2008; Cortina et al., 2013), as well as other forms of gender inequality that flourish alongside SH (see Arnow-Richman, 2018). With respect to SH prevention specifically, these outcomes have been alluded to in the literature, but more empirical work is needed.

Yet, as no prevention strategy is foolproof, SH will still occur and those affected by harassment need additional tools to address the behavior and its consequences. One promising avenue may exist through research on training, particularly for supervisors. Because training is already highly uti-lized by organizations in addressing SH, improving its effectiveness should be welcomed (Roehling & Huang, 2018). Research on new approaches to increase its effectiveness affords significant room to grow. Supervisors play a pivotal role in managing conflict and relationships in the workplace; increasing their skill and facility in managing issues of wrongdoing in the workplace is needed. An emerging area of research on restorative justice offers possible insight.

Restorative justice is a concept focused on healing damaged relationships. It goes beyond traditional justice perspectives on fairness, which typically focus on either helping the victim or punishing the offender. Coined by Goodstein and Aquino (2010), restorative justice comes from the criminal justice literature where there is an attempt to redress wrongdoing, which is typically a violation of the law but also a fundamental violation of a relationship. From this lens, offenders can make amends, victims can (but do not necessarily need to) extend forgiveness, and organizations can foster reintegration of perpetrators (Herman, 2023). Applying a restorative justice frame to situations of SH offers several avenues for research—that are also applicable in a more intersectional context as described earlier, in particular where psychological contract breach may be relevant (e.g., Chrobot-Mason et al., 2013). One of the first areas to distinguish is which behaviors that fall under the umbrella of SH lend themselves to a restorative process. Reporting harassment can be aversive for those who do (Bergman et al., 2002; Cortina & Wasti, 2005) and a restorative framework should avoid re-traumatizing targets. This makes it clear that not all experiences are appropriate for this approach. Rawski et al.'s (2022) research on work-related social sexual behavior (SSB), and the sensemaking process that allows workgroups to set, test, and break frames on SSB appears relevant here. Their theoretical model of how work groups negotiate frames to distinguish between non-harassing SSB (i.e., playful physical contact between "work spouses") and SH describes a process that is fluid and changing, including setting play frames and testing the limits of the frame. The model further describes how behaviors that were once considered playful can be reset as harassing once the play frame breaks (i.e., someone who is not the "work spouse" playfully but inappropriately caresses the "work wife" and causes visible distress) and the conduct is seen through a different lens. While Goodstein and Aquino (2010) note that major transgressions of wrongdoing may not fit a restorative frame due to seriousness of the offense, might it be that behaviors that were once considered playful and negotiated as such by the work group, but no longer fit a play frame, lend themselves to a restorative process?

A second area of research on the viability of a restorative approach to resolving incidents of SH rests with the individuals involved in the interaction, and their fundamental needs. As noted by Neale et al. (2020), for restorative practices to work, victims must have a strong need for justice and offenders must need to restore their image, dignity, or integrity. Coworkers or observers also have needs, including a need for an apology, to see that offenders are met with appropriate consequences for their behavior, to support the victim, and to see social norms upheld. Key question that emerges from this line of thinking, particularly in response to SH, is "what motivates offenders in organizations to acknowledge responsibility for wrongdoing and take steps to make amends?" (Goodstein & Aquino,

2010, p. 627). Often offenders go to great lengths to have their misdeeds concealed, or at minimum, to maintain confidentiality such that their identities never become known beyond the parties most immediately affected. Are there certain offenders who are primed to take responsibility, and why? A second question to be asked is "what motivates victims to forgive offenders and participate in a process of restoration to heal damaged relationships?" (Goodstein & Aquino, 2010, p. 627). In many organizations, those who bring complaints of harassment never learn what happened—it is as if the complaint was never filed. How can organizations square the fact that an investigation took place if there is no receipt of follow up or follow through to even give the victim the opportunity to move on? Targets unaware of substantive responses to their complaints are unlikely to willingly participate in a process that involves forgiveness of the perpetrator. Can reintegration be achieved without greater transparency? Lastly, within the context of a given workgroup and organization, a final question to consider is the extent to which the unit's values and the broader context is likely to support a restorative process of repairing harm and restoring broken relationships (Goodstein & Aquino, 2010). Elements of the environment to consider could include the strength of the play frame around SSB (Rawski et al., 2022), organizational tolerance for SH (Goldberg et al., 2019), and the willingness of the work unit to challenge social network norms (Hershcovis et al., 2021).

A final area of research is how to best train and support managers with the tools to effectively lead their teams through a restorative approach. The limited work on managerial use of restorative practices in managing SH suggests that a punitive approach is still most prevalent (Neale et al., 2020). Notwithstanding, Neale et al.'s (2020) model offers a number of directions for future research that have yet to be answered in the context of SH, including the potential for managerial training to raise basic awareness about restorative techniques, constraints present in the environment that might preclude the use of restorative practices (even when the manager is aware of such practices), and when and how to involve human resources. Our prior recommendations regarding the need for training to adopt behavioral techniques, including opportunities for practice and feedback, are applicable here as well.

Conclusion

The #MeToo movement has put a significant spotlight on women's experiences of SH by revealing the severity and pervasiveness of this issue, as well as the need for organizations to support more expansive and productive paths toward resolution. Organizations have sought to reduce SH through a variety of approaches, including preventive mechanisms such as reporting policies, grievance procedures, and accountability mechanisms, as well as strategies to change workplace culture, enhance training programs, and engage bystanders to reduce ambient effects. Yet, as we argue in this chapter, incremental opportunities remain for organizations to take additional steps toward productive resolution and recovery. We see a potential pathway forward through a restorative justice framework and call for research on strategies that are designed to heal damaged relationships.

Notes

1 A critique of the SEQ is that it does not align perfectly with the legal definition in its imposition of legal requirements. Morral et al. (2014) describe the development of a measure both behaviorally and legal-based measure for the DoD.
2 Williams et al. (2019) present an overview of some of the consequences of this sexualized perspective, along with a consideration of the appropriate definition of "reasonable" in the context of sexual harassment law post #MeToo.

References

Acker, J. (1990). Hierarchies, jobs, bodies: A theory of gendered organizations. *Gender & Society*, 4(2), 139–158. https://doi.org/10.1177/089124390004002002
Acker, J. (2006). Inequality regimes: Gender, class, and race in organizations. *Gender & Society*, 20(4), 441–464. https://doi.org/10.1177/0891243206289499
Aquino, K., Sheppard, L., Watkins, M. B., O'Reilly, J., & Smith, A. (2014). Social sexual behavior at work. *Research in Organizational Behavior*, 34, 217–236. https://doi.org/10.1016/j.riob.2014.02.001
Arnow-Richman, R. S. (2018). Of power and process: Handling harassers in an at-will world. *SSRN Electronic Journal*. https://doi.org/10.2139/ssrn.3190505
Berdahl, J. L. (2007). The sexual harassment of uppity women. *Journal of Applied Psychology*, 92(2), 425–437. https://doi.org/10.1037/0021–9010.92.2.425
Berdahl, J. L., Glick, P., & Cooper, M. (2018, November 2). How masculinity contests undermine organizations, and what to do about it. *Harvard Business Review Online*. https://hbr.org/2018/11/how-masculinity-contests-undermine-organizations-and-what-to-do-about-it
Bergman, M. E., Langhout, R. D., Palmieri, P. A., Cortina, L. M., & Fitzgerald, L. F. (2002). The (un)reasonableness of reporting: Antecedents and consequences of reporting sexual harassment. *Journal of Applied Psychology*, 87(2), 230–242. https://doi.org/10.1037/0021–9010.87.2.230
Bowes-Sperry, L., & O'Leary-Kelly, A. M. (2005). To act or not to act: The dilemma faced by sexual harassment observers. *Academy of Management Review*, 30(2), 288–306.
Boyle, D., & Cucchiara, A. (2018). *Social movements and HR: The impact of #MeToo*. www.shrm.org/executive/resources/research/PublishingImages/Pages/research-by-topic/Social%20Movements%20and%20HR%20-%20The%20Impact%20of%20MeToo.pdf
Buchanan, N. T., Settles, I. H., Hall, A. T., & O'Connor, R. C. (2014). A review of organizational strategies for reducing sexual harassment: Insights from the U.S. military: Confronting sexual harassment. *Journal of Social Issues*, 70(4), 687–702. https://doi.org/10.1111/josi.12086

Chrobot-Mason, D., Ragins, B. R., & Linnehan, F. (2013). Second hand smoke: Ambient racial harassment at work. *Journal of Managerial Psychology, 28*(5), 470–491. https://doi.org/10.1108/JMP-02-2012-0064

Cortina, L. M. (2008). Unseen injustice: Incivility as modern discrimination in organizations. *Academy of Management Review, 33*(1), 55–75. https://doi.org/10.5465/amr.2008.27745097

Cortina, L. M., & Areguin, M. A. (2020). Putting people down and pushing them out: Sexual harassment in the workplace. *Annual Review of Organizational Psychology and Organizational Behavior, 8*, 1–25.

Cortina, L. M., Kabat-Farr, D., Leskinen, E. A., Huerta, M., & Magley, V. J. (2013). Selective incivility as modern discrimination in organizations: Evidence and impact. *Journal of Management, 39*(6), 1579–1605. https://doi.org/10.1177/0149206311418835

Cortina, L. M., & Wasti, S. A. (2005). Profiles in coping: Responses to sexual harassment across persons, organizations, and cultures. *Journal of Applied Psychology, 90*(1), 182–192. https://doi.org/10.1037/0021-9010.90.1.182

Dekker, I., & Barling, J. (1998). Personal and organizational predictors of workplace sexual harassment of women by men. *Journal of Occupational Health Psychology, 3*(1), 7–18.

DiTomaso, N., Post, C., & Parks-Yancy, R. (2007). Workforce diversity and inequality: Power, status, and numbers. *Annual Review of Sociology, 33*, 473–501.

Dobbin, F., & Kalev, A. (2019). The promise and peril of sexual harassment programs. *PNAS Proceedings of the National Academy of Sciences of the United States of America, 116*(25), 12255–12260. https://doi.org/10.1073/pnas.1818477116

Dobbin, F., & Kalev, A. (2021). The civil rights revolution at work: What went wrong. *Annual Review of Sociology, 47*(1), 281–303. https://doi.org/10.1146/annurev-soc-090820-023615

Durana, A., Lenhart, A., Miller, R., Schulte, B., & Weingarten, E. (2018). *#NowWhat: The sexual harassment solutions toolkit.* http://newamerica.org/better-life-lab/reports/nowwhat-sexual-harassment-solutions-toolkit/

Ehrhart, M. G., Schneider, B., & Macey, W. H. (2014). *Organizational climate and culture: An introduction to theory, research, and practice.* Routledge.

Epstein, C. F. (2007). Great divides: The cultural, cognitive, and social bases of the global subordination of women. *American Sociological Review, 72*, 1–22.

Farris, C., Sims, C., Schell, T., Matthews, M., Smucker, S., Cohen, S., & Hall, O. (2020). *Harassment and discrimination on the basis of gender and race/Ethnicity in the FEMA workforce.* RAND Corporation. https://doi.org/10.7249/RRA383-1

Fitzgerald, L. F., Swan, S., & Magley, V. J. (1997). But was it really sexual harassment?: Legal, behavioral, and psychological definitions of the workplace victimization of women. In W. O'Donohue (Ed.), *Sexual harassment: Theory, research, and treatment* (pp. 5–28). Allyn & Bacon.

Foote, W. E., & Goodman-Delahunty, J. (2021). Alternate dispute resolution of sexual harassment claims: Neutral fact-finding, mediation, and arbitration. In *Understanding sexual harassment: Evidence-based forensic practice* (2nd ed., 2021-41323-008, pp. 237–261). American Psychological Association. https://doi.org/10.1037/0000239-008

Ford, J. L., & Ivancic, S. R. (2020). Surviving organizational tolerance of sexual harassment: An exploration of resilience, vulnerability, and harassment fatigue. *Journal of Applied Communication Research, 48*(2), 186–206. https://doi.org/10.1080/00909882.2020.1739317

Goldberg, C. B., Rawski, S. L., & Perry, E. L. (2019). The direct and indirect effects of organizational tolerance for sexual harassment on the effectiveness of sexual harassment investigation training for HR managers. *Human Resource Development Quarterly, 30*(1), 81–100. https://doi.org/10.1002/hrdq.21329

Goodstein, J., & Aquino, K. (2010). And restorative justice for all: Redemption, forgiveness, and reintegration in organizations. *Journal of Organizational Behavior, 31*(4), 624–628. https://doi.org/10.1002/job.632

Harassment. (n.d.). US EEOC. Retrieved May 8, 2023, from www.eeoc.gov/harassment

Herman, J. L. (2023). *Truth and repair: How trauma survivors envision justice.* Basic Books. www.hachettebookgroup.com/titles/judith-lewis-herman-md/truth-and-repair/9781541600546/?lens=basic-books

Hershcovis, M. S., & Barling, J. (2010). Towards a multi-foci approach to workplace aggression: A meta-analytic review of outcomes from different perpetrators. *Journal of Organizational Behavior, 31*(1), 24–44. https://doi.org/10.1002/job.621

Hershcovis, M. S., Vranjes, I., Berdahl, J. L., & Cortina, L. M. (2021). See no evil, hear no evil, speak no evil: Theorizing network silence around sexual harassment. *Journal of Applied Psychology, 106*(12), 1834–1847. https://doi.org/10.1037/apl0000861

Heymann, J., Moreno, G., Raub, A., & Sprague, A. (2023). Progress towards ending sexual harassment at work? A comparison of sexual harassment policy in 192 countries. *Journal of Comparative Policy Analysis: Research and Practice, 25*(2), 172–193. https://doi.org/10.1080/13876988.2022.2100698

Hulin, C. L., Fitzgerald, L. F., & Drasgow, F. (1996). Organizational influences on sexual harassment. In M. S. Stockdale (Ed.), *Sexual harassment in the workplace: Perspectives, frontiers, and response strategies* (1996-97671-007, pp. 127–150). Sage Publications, Inc. https://doi.org/10.4135/9781483327280.n7

Johnson, A., Ijoma, S., & Kim, D. H. (2022). *#MeToo five years later: Progress & pitfalls in state workplace anti-harassment laws.* https://nwlc.org/wp-content/uploads/2022/10/final_2022_nwlcMeToo_Report-MM-edit-10.27.22.pdf

Kalev, A., & Deutsch, G. (2018). Gender inequality and workplace organizations: Understanding reproduction and change. In B. J. Risman, C. M. Froyum & W. J. Scarborough (Eds.), *Handbook of the sociology of gender* (pp. 257–269). Springer International Publishing. https://doi.org/10.1007/978-3-319-76333-0_19

Kath, L. M., & Magley, V. J. (2014). Development of a theoretically grounded model of sexual harassment awareness training effectiveness. In P. Y. Chen & C. L. Cooper (Eds.), *Work and wellbeing* (Vol. III., 2014-09726-015, pp. 319–338). Wiley Blackwell. https://doi.org/10.1002/9781118539415.wbwell031

Langhout, R. D., Bergman, M. E., Cortina, L., Fitzgerald, L., Drasgow, F., & Williams, J. H. (2005). Sexual harassment severity: Assessing situational and personal determinants and outcomes. *Journal of Applied Social Psychology, 35*, 975–1007. https://doi.org/10.1111/j.1559–1816.2005.tb02156.x

Lawrence, A. (2020). Empower managers to stop harassment. *Harvard Business Review, 98*(3), 53–56.

Lee, S. Y., Hanson, M. D., & Cheung, H. K. (2019). Incorporating bystander intervention into sexual harassment training. *Industrial and Organizational Psychology: Perspectives on Science and Practice, 12*(1), 52–57. https://doi.org/10.1017/iop.2019.8

Leskinen, E. A., Cortina, L. M., & Kabat, D. B. (2011). Gender harassment: Broadening our understanding of sex-based harassment at work. *Law and Human Behavior, 35*(1), 25–39. https://doi.org/10.1007/s10979-010-9241-5

Lytell, M. C. (2010). *Influences on women's perceptions of climate for sexual harassment* (2010-99140-446; Issues 1-B) [Doctoral dissertation, University of Illinois at Urbana-Champaign]. ProQuest Dissertations & Theses Global.

McLaughlin, H., Uggen, C., & Blackstone, A. (2012). Sexual harassment, workplace authority, and the paradox of power. *American Sociological Review*, 77(4), 625–647. https://doi.org/10.1177/0003122412451728

#MeToo, now what? | PBS. (2018). [Video recording]. www.pbs.org/show/metoo-now-what/

Morral, A., Gore, K., & Schell, T. (2014). *Sexual assault and sexual harassment in the U.S. military: Volume 1. Design of the 2014 RAND Military Workplace Study*. RAND Corporation. https://doi.org/10.7249/RR870.1

Naylor, J. C., Pritchard, R. D., & Ilgen, D. R. (1980). *A theory of behavior in organizations*. Academic Press. https://bac-lac.on.worldcat.org/oclc/299990421

Neale, N. R., Butterfield, K. D., Goodstein, J., & Tripp, T. M. (2020). Managers' restorative versus punitive responses to employee wrongdoing: A qualitative investigation. *Journal of Business Ethics*, 161(3), 603–625. https://doi.org/10.1007/s10551-018-3935-x

Patel, J. K., Griggs, T., & Miller, C. C. (2017, December 28). We asked 615 men about how they conduct themselves at work. *The New York Times*. www.nytimes.com/interactive/2017/12/28/upshot/sexual-harassment-survey-600-men.html

Picture of America Fact Sheet. (2017). Centers for Disease Control and Prevention. www.cdc.gov/pictureofamerica/pdfs/picture_of_america_prevention.pdf

Pryor, J. B., Giedd, J. L., & Williams, K. B. (1995). A social psychological model for predicting sexual harassment. *Journal of Social Issues*, 51(1), 69–84. https://doi.org/10.1111/j.1540–4560.1995.tb01309.x

Quick, J. C., & McFadyen, M. A. (2017). Sexual harassment: Have we made any progress? *Journal of Occupational Health Psychology*, 22(3), 286–298. https://doi.org/10.1037/ocp0000054

Raub, A., Khachadourian, V., Wong, E., Sprague, A., Pournik, M., & Heymann, J. (2021). Ending sexual harassment at work: Creating a baseline on laws in 193 countries. *Human Rights Quarterly*, 43(2), 378–393. https://doi.org/10.1353/hrq.2021.0024

Rawski, S. L., O'Leary-Kelly, A. M., & Breaux-Soignet, D. (2022). It's all fun and games until someone gets hurt: An interactional framing theory of work social sexual behavior. *Academy of Management Review*, 47(4), 617–636. https://doi.org/10.5465/amr.2019.0316

Ridgeway, C. L., & Correll, S. J. (2004). Unpacking the gender system: A theoretical perspective on gender beliefs and social relations. *Gender & Society*, 18(4), 510–531. https://doi.org/10.1177/0891243204265269

Risman, B. J. (2004). Gender as a social structure: Theory wrestling with activism. *Gender & Society*, 18(4), 429–450. https://doi.org/10.1177/0891243204265349

Roehling, M. V., & Huang, J. (2018). Sexual harassment training effectiveness: An interdisciplinary review and call for research. *Journal of Organizational Behavior*, 39(2), 134–150. https://doi.org/10.1002/job.2257

Saguy, A. C., & Rees, M. E. (2021). Gender, power, and harassment: Sociology in the #MeToo era. *Annual Review of Sociology*, 47(1), 417–435. https://doi.org/10.1146/annurev-soc-090320–031147

Schultz, V. (2018). Reconceptualizing sexual harassment, again. *SSRN Electronic Journal*. https://doi.org/10.2139/ssrn.3165561

Scott, G., & Martin, B. (2006). Tactics against sexual harassment: The role of backfire. *Journal of International Women's Studies*, 7(4), 111–125.

Sims, C. S. (2005). Reconceptualizing the role of climate in sexual harassment [Doctoral dissertation, University of Illinois at Urbana-Champaign]. ProQuest Dissertations & Theses Global.

Sims, C. S., Farris, C., Schell, T. L., Matthews, M., Bicksler, B., Hall, O., & Wagner, L. (2022). *Harassment and discrimination on the basis of gender and race/ethnicity in the FEMA workforce: 2021 survey follow-up.* RAND Corporation. www.rand.org/pubs/research_reports/RRA383-2.html

Stark, S., Chernyshenko, O. S., Lancaster, A. R., Drasgow, F., & Fitzgerald, L. F. (2002). Toward standardized measurement of sexual harassment: Shortening the SEQ-DoD using item response theory. *Military Psychology, 14*(1), 49–72. https://doi.org/10.1207/S15327876MP1401_03

Stockdale, M. S., Bisom-Rapp, S., O'Connor, M., & Gutek, B. A. (2004). Coming to terms with zero tolerance sexual harassment policies. *Journal of Forensic Psychology Practice, 4*(1), 65–78. https://doi.org/10.1300/J158v04n01_05

Ward, S. F. (2018). ABA entities offer resources to address sexual harassment. *ABA Journal, 104*(6), 51–51.

Wiener, R. L., & Gutek, B. A. (1999). Advances in sexual harassment research, theory, and policy. *Psychology, Public Policy, and Law, 5*(3), 507–518. https://doi.org/10.1037/1076-8971.5.3.507

Williams, J. C., Short, J., Brooks, M., Hardcastle, H., Ellis, T., & Saron, R. (2019). What's reasonable now? Sexual harassment law after the norm cascade. *Michigan State Law Review, 2019,* 139–224.

Willness, C. R., Steel, P., & Lee, K. (2007). A meta-analysis of the antecedents and consequences of workplace sexual harassment. *Personnel Psychology, 60*(1), 127–162. https://doi.org/10.1111/j.1744-6570.2007.00067.x

Zohar, D. M. (2002). The effects of leadership dimensions, safety climate, and assigned priorities on minor injuries in work groups. *Journal of Organizational Behavior, 23*(1), 75–92. https://doi.org/10.1002/job.130

Zohar, D. M., & Hofmann, D. A. (2012). Organizational culture and climate. In *The Oxford handbook of organizational psychology* (Vol. 1., pp. 643–666). Oxford University Press. https://doi.org/10.1093/oxfordhb/9780199928309.001.0001

INDEX

Page numbers in *italics* indicate figures; page numbers in **bold** indicate tables.

173; sexual harassment **166–167**, 172–175; within-intersectional group variance focused studies 174–175

cultural trauma 134–135

culture: current literature 88–89; definition 86; gender-based violence (GBV) and 86–87; masculinities and GBV in 93–95; organizational sensemaking 73–74; RCMP 65; relationship between silence and 77–78; sexual harassment and 67–68; social class coping 217; societal, and SH at work 89–90; *see also* masculinity contest cultures (MCCs); societal culture

Cyberscan 37n2

Daily Express (newspaper) 10
Daily Mail (newspaper) 10
Daily Mirror (newspaper) 10
dating, online 30–33
DeSouza, Lucy xx, 154
digital dualism 27
digital media 6
Digital Services Act (2022) 36
digital sexual racism, term 30
digital spaces: bystander intervention xv; sexual violence, harassment, and misogyny 24–27
digital technologies: facilitating abuse and misogyny 22–23; fostering social change 22; power of 22–24
discursive activism 31
Donegan, Moira 54

EBSCOhost 88
emotional contagion, phenomenon of 141
emotional dysfunction 138
enactment, sensemaking process 74
endorphin response system, chronic trauma 140
Englishwoman, The (journal) 9, 10
environmental movements 4
Equal Employment Opportunity Commission (EEOC) 48, 160, 207, 234
Ethics Offices 211
ethnic minority, sexual harassment against men 187–188
EU Directive 97

European Union, gender-based violence (GBV) 87
everywoman experience 206
exoticization 162

Facebook 29, 30, 36, 47
Fair Employment Practice Agencies (FEPAs) 234
Fawcett, Millicent 8
fawn response, trauma 141–143
fear-conditioning, trauma 137
Feminist Frequency's Games 34
fight-flight response, trauma 136–138
Fight-Flight responses xix
First Amendment 28
Fisher, Carrie 55
flashbacks 137
Floyd, George 50
Ford, Blasey 223n3
Fortnightly Review (newspaper) 9
4chan/8chan 38n5
Fowler, Susan 233
Fox News 184
Freewoman, The (magazine) 9, 10
freeze-fawn responses: alexithymia 139; immediate shock or dissociation 139; trauma 138–143
Freud, Sigmund 139, 140

Gamergate 34, 35
gaming, video 33–35
gender: binary 199n1; sociological perspective on 231–232
gender-based violence (GBV) 85–86; current literature 88–89; domains of scholarship 97; gender ideologies and 102–103; laws and policies 96; laws and policies on 97–98; media and 96, 100–101; prevalence around the world 87–88; public health and 96, 98–100; societal cultural ideologies and 91–96; societal cultural institutions and 96–97; societal culture and xvi–xviii; specific cultural contexts 93–95; term 87
gender ideologies: cultural script 93; gender-based violence (GBV) and 102–103; hegemonic masculinity and 91; interventions to change 95–96; term 92; unpacking 91–93
Generation Xers 7

Online Harassment Hotline 34
online spaces, comments
    sections 27–28
O'Reilly, Bill 184
organizational climate, women in
    lower social classes 208–210
organizational culture: process
    of sensemaking xv–xvi; sexual
    harassment and 67–68; trauma and
    134–135
organizational intervention,
    training 239
organizational-level factors, women in
    lower social classes 208–210
organizational sensemaking 66;
    culture 73–74
organizational tolerance 67; sexual
    harassment 237; sexual harassment
    and 67

Pankhurst, Emmeline 8
Pao, Ellen 233
parasympathetic nervous system 135,
    138–139
Partee, Christopher 55, 58, 61n20
patriot, ally and 59
perpetrators: consequences for
    219–221; contextual risk
    factors for 192–193; individual
    characteristics of 190–192;
    perceptions of sexual 220;
    punishment across classes 220–221;
    responsibility for sexual harassment
    219–220; social class and 222;
    targeting men 190–192
Pew Hispanic survey 27
physical isolation, potential issue for
    women workers 211–212
pink jobs 69
platforms, game streaming 34
Polanski, Roman 56
political protest xii
positivist approach, sexual harassment
    163, **164**, 168
post-digital, way of thinking 27
post-digital age 24
post-traumatic stress disorder (PTSD)
    131, 133, 143–144; DSM-5
    diagnostic criteria 143; sexual
    harassment victim 215; *see also*
    trauma
power, paradox of 221

power-based theory, labeling between
    men and women 188–189
power dynamic, unbalanced
    manager-employee 210–211
precarious work, women in 207
P.R.E.S.E.N.C.E. model,
    trauma-informed concepts 146
promiscuous 214
PsychInfo 88
public health, gender-based violence
    and 96, 98–100
public sphere: concept xii, xiv;
    definition of 5; Habermas's
    argument 5–6; use of public social
    media 6–7

qualitative research, definition 170

RAF Greenham Common base 13
Ramirez, Monica 67
Rape, Abuse & Incest National
    Network (RAINN) 33
rape culture, online harassment and 27
Raver, Jana L. xvii, 85
Rawski, Shannon L. xix, 131
"real men": masculinity beliefs 69;
    see also masculinity contest cultures
    (MCCs)
Reddit 38n5; Girl Gamers 34
reflexivity 169
regulation, digital media platforms 36
reporting options, women in lower
    social classes 212–213
Representation of the People Act 8
resolution: future directions
    on productive 240–243;
    industrial organization
    psychology-organizational behavior
    lenses 236–240; role in sexual
    harassment 230–231; sociological
    and legal lenses 235–236
restorative approach, sexual
    harassment 242–243
restorative justice 241–242
Restorative Justice Model xxiii
Reuters 27
Roe v. Wade, overturning 14
rotten apple focus, behavior 65, 68–72
Roy, Arundhati 175
Royal Canadian Mounted Police
    (RCMP) xv, xvii, xviii, 65–66;
    exposing dominant norms in 74–79;

For Product Safety Concerns and Information please contact our EU
representative GPSR@taylorandfrancis.com
Taylor & Francis Verlag GmbH, Kaufingerstraße 24, 80331 München, Germany